Smart Homes For Dummies®
2nd Edition

Smart-Home A/V Needs

Video-Distribution Network

Stuff You Need	Quantity You Need
RG-6 coaxial cable with F connectors	For a two-way network, two runs from each viewing room to the central distribution point
Wall outlets	One per remote-viewing room housing two female connectors
Video distribution panel	One, located in the central wiring closet
Modulators	Variable, each video source device that you want to distribute must be modulated to an unused frequency, but some modulators handle multiple video inputs

Audio-Distribution Network (Single Amplifier)

Stuff You Need	Quantity You Need
Single-zone or multizone integrated amplifier or receiver	One (multizone systems contain one stereo amplifier per zone)
Impedance-matching system	One
Speakers	Two per room (can be in-wall or free-standing speakers)
In-wall speaker cable (16 AWG minimum)	One run between the media room and each remote location
RCA audio patch cords	(Usually) one set per audio component
In-wall speaker wire outlets	Two per remote area (if in-wall speakers aren't being used)
IR-control network (with multizone IR-zone distribution block for one multizone system)	One

Copyright © 2003 Wiley Publishing, Inc.
All rights reserved.
Item 2539-5.
For more information about Wiley Publishing,
call 1-800-762-2974.

For Dummies: Bestselling Book Series for Beginners

Smart Homes For Dummies, 2nd Edition

Cheat Sheet

Smart-Home Communication-Network Needs

Remote-Control Network for A/V equipment

Stuff You Need	Quantity You Need
3-conductor IR cabling or CAT-5e	One run from each remote location to the media room
Wall-mounted IR sensors or remote keypads	One sensor or keypad per remote location
IR distribution block (for IR cabling only)	One installed in media room
CAT-5e A/V control system (for CAT-5e only)	One installed in wiring closet or media room
IR emitters	One per audio source device being controlled in media room

Telephone Network

Stuff You Need	Quantity You Need
4-pair CAT-5e UTP cabling	One run from wiring closet to each outlet
Modular wall outlets with female RJ-45 jacks	One per telephone extension
Telephone patch cords with male RJ-45 plugs	One per telephone extension
Telephone patch panel mounted in wiring closet	One
CAT-5e UTP cable to connect patch panel	One run per incoming line to incoming lines from telephone company NID
Key Service Unit (KSU) (optional)	One

Computer LAN

Stuff You Need	Quantity You Need
4-pair CAT-5e UTP cabling	One run from wiring closet to each outlet (put extra runs in the home office and home theater/media room)
Modular wall outlets with female RJ-45 jacks	One jack per computer or networked device and one extra for your broadband modem
CAT-5e UTP patch cords with male RJ-45 plugs	One patch cord per computer or network printer
CAT-5 rated patch panel mounted in wiring closet	One (can be the same one that works with the phone network)
Home router/Ethernet switch	Minimum of one router/switch in your wiring closet (additional hubs can be installed at remote outlets to allow connection of several computers to a single outlet)
Wireless LAN access point (optional)	One
Cable modem or DSL modem (optional)	One

For Dummies: Bestselling Book Series for Beginners

Smart Homes

FOR

DUMMIES®

2ND EDITION

Smart Homes FOR DUMMIES®
2ND EDITION

by Danny Briere and Pat Hurley

Wiley Publishing, Inc.

Smart Homes For Dummies®, 2nd Edition

Published by
Wiley Publishing, Inc.
909 Third Avenue
New York, NY 10022

www.wiley.com

Copyright © 2003 by Wiley Publishing, Inc., Indianapolis, Indiana

Published by Wiley Publishing, Inc., Indianapolis, Indiana

Published simultaneously in Canada

For general information on our other products and services or to obtain technical support, please contact our Customer Care Department within the U.S. at 800-762-2974, outside the U.S. at 317-572-3993, or fax 317-572-4002.

Wiley also publishes its books in a variety of electronic formats. Some content that appears in print may not be available in electronic books.

Library of Congress Control Number: 2002114812

ISBN: 0-7645-2539-5

Manufactured in the United States of America

10 9 8 7 6 5 4 3 2 1

2B/ST/RS/QS/IN

®Wiley Publishing, Inc. is a trademark of Wiley Publishing, Inc.

About the Authors

Danny Briere founded TeleChoice, Inc., a telecommunications consulting company, in 1985 and now serves as C.E.O. of the company. Widely known throughout the telecommunications and networking industry, Danny has written more than 1000 articles on telecommunications topics and has authored or edited seven books, including *Internet Telephony For Dummies*. He is frequently quoted by leading publications on telecommunications and technology topics and can often be seen on major TV networks providing analysis on the latest communications news and breakthroughs. Danny lives in Mansfield Center, Connecticut with his wife and four children.

Pat Hurley is a consultant with TeleChoice, Inc. specializing in emerging telecommunications technologies. Pat currently concentrates on the field of home and wireless networking and is also TeleChoice's DSL industry analyst. Pat is co-author of *Internet Telephony For Dummies* (now in its second edition). He lives in San Diego, California with his wife.

Dedication

I dedicate this book to my wife, Holly, and also publicly and officially confess that she has a better memory and is smarter than I. Plus, she's usually right. I thank her dearly for putting up with me while I put in long hours at the office to finish this book, including the 19 times that I was late for dinner. Okay, so that's a low number. Okay, so Holly also doesn't exaggerate as much as I do. In any case, I hope that she will continue to let me infiltrate the home with smart-home techniques (which she secretly likes but won't say) and will let me buy a rack for the pots and pans; we need that too.

— Danny

I dedicate this book to my wife, Christine, for allowing me to bore her nearly to death with long, breathless discussions of networking toys that no normal person wants to spend more than three minutes talking about, and for letting me scare the living daylights out of the dogs with remote-controlled gizmos. To thank her more completely, I promise to not bring a robot into the home — thus avoiding all those dog psychiatrist bills. Well, maybe just a robotic vacuum cleaner.

— Pat

Authors' Acknowledgments

It takes a lot of effort, by a lot of people, to put a book together. We probably can't give proper acknowledgment to everyone who's given us advice, opinions, and guidance as we've worked on this project, but we'd like to try.

Sandy Daniels of TeleChoice keeps us organized, connected, and sane. She prodded us along, set up interviews, found people we couldn't find ourselves, and generally acted like a bulldog in breaking through corporate mazes to find the right people to interview for the book. If you ever meet her, you'll wonder how such a nice person can be so effective.

Literally dozens of vendors gave us information, tips, and techniques (and a few home networking toys to try out). Special thanks go to Keith Smith at Siemon, David Allred at DirecTV DSL, Jeff Denenholz at X10 Wireless Technologies, Ian Hendler at Leviton, Mike Hernandez at ChannelPlus, Peter Radscliff and Jim Gist at Monster Cable, Doug Hagan at Netgear, Matt Graves and Sean Ryan at Listen.com, Nick Smith and Vanessa Tuell at Request, Tom Reed of the HomePlug Powerline Alliance, Dave Thompson of CopperGate Communication, Brian McLeod at Harmony, Andrew Liu at Intel, Mel Richardson and his team at BellSouth, Lawrence Cheng at XM Radio, Tom Lucke, Fred Bargetzi, and Ray O'Sullivan at Crestron, Paul Cunningham at Cunningham Security in Portland, Maine, and George Snyder at Home Automated Living. There are more of you out there, and as they say at the Oscars, we can't possibly thank everyone individually, but thanks!

Finally, we want to thank the Wiley team who bought into our vision of a smart home, and made sure we crossed our *i*'s and dotted our *t*'s (or something like that). Thanks especially to Susan Pink, our project editor, and Melody Layne, our acquisitions editor.

Publisher's Acknowledgments

We're proud of this book; please send us your comments through our online registration form located at `www.dummies.com/register/`.

Some of the people who helped bring this book to market include the following:

Acquisitions, Editorial, and Media Development

Project Editor: Susan Pink

Acquisitions Editor: Melody Layne

Technical Editor: Allen Wyatt, Discovery Computing Inc.

Editorial Manager: Carol Sheehan

Media Development Supervisor: Richard Graves

Editorial Assistant: Amanda Foxworth

Cartoons: Rich Tennant (`www.the5thwave.com`)

Production

Project Coordinator: Dale White

Layout and Graphics: Tiffany Muth, Jackie Nicolas, Jeremey Unger

Proofreaders: John Bitter, John Tyler Connley, John Greenough, TECHBOOKS Production Services

Indexer: TECHBOOKS Production Services

Special Help
Gabriele McCann

Publishing and Editorial for Technology Dummies

Richard Swadley, Vice President and Executive Group Publisher

Andy Cummings, Vice President and Publisher

Mary C. Corder, Editorial Director

Publishing for Consumer Dummies

Diane Graves Steele, Vice President and Publisher

Joyce Pepple, Acquisitions Director

Composition Services

Gerry Fahey, Vice President of Production Services

Debbie Stailey, Director of Composition Services

Contents at a Glance

Table of Contents

Introduction

● ●

*W*elcome to *Smart Homes For Dummies,* 2nd Edition. This book is the first to specifically tell you how to futureproof your home to take advantage of the present and upcoming gee-whiz things that can make your home a twenty-first-century castle.

Very few things can prepare you for the massive changes that are taking place due to the innovations offered by an interconnected world. The Internet and electronic commerce will change the way we live, the way we work, and the way we play. (We hope there's more of the last one!)

We're so used to going to stores and buying things. To calling toll-free numbers to ask questions and order products. To going to schools to learn. To going to the movies to watch the latest *Star Wars* release. To going to the music store to buy the top-of-the-charts CDs.

Now it can all come to us. We can buy things through our TV sets. We can ask questions and videoconference through our computers. We can attend classes through computer-based training. We can click our remote controls to get video-on-demand. We can download new CDs, live, over the Internet.

It's at our doorstep. The question is, "Can you let it in?" Without a home net-work, all this might stay outside, or in the TV room, or trapped in that attic office of yours. A home network opens the world to your entire household, and now more than ever is the time to plan.

That's what *Smart Homes For Dummies,* 2nd Edition, provides — a plan for your networked future.

About This Book

Within these pages, you'll find a number of technologies and issues relating to developing smart-home technologies. Among the things you can discover are the following:

- ✔ What a home network is, and what it takes to build one
- ✔ The key points to think about before starting to conceptualize a home-network design
- ✔ What the various home-network devices and services do

✔ What's involved in making a home-entertainment center accessible throughout the house

✔ What you need to create a home-security network

✔ Your options for dressing up your home-telephone capabilities

✔ The best way to design a home-data local area network (LAN)

✔ The best way to connect your home to the Internet

✔ What's coming down the road and into your home in the future

Conventions Used in This Book

Some of the networks and issues that we cover in *Smart Homes For Dummies* are in the realm of the do-it-yourselfer, so we present the big-picture stuff for those readers and give high-level instructions. These instructions don't go into stuff such as removing your drywall and running cables through your house. We recommend *Home Improvement For Dummies* by Gene Hamilton, Katie Hamilton, and the editors of HouseNet (published by Wiley Publishing, Inc.) if you need help with that stuff.

On the other hand, if you don't feel comfortable running cables through your house, you shouldn't feel like you have to do everything yourself. Hire a professional!

If you're renovating a home, building a new home, or trying to figure out how to connect anything with anything else in your home, you need *Smart Homes For Dummies*.

What You're Not to Read

Smart Homes For Dummies isn't a novel. You don't have to read page 1 before going to page 2. So that means that you can just flip around through the book and start wherever you like. You won't feel lost.

You can use the Table of Contents at the front of the book to find out where to look for a topic that interests you, whether it's distributing a VCR signal from your home-entertainment center to your bedroom, or making your lights go on and off by themselves. Or, you can search the Index for a particular term that interests you. However you find the information, read it and then put the book back on the shelf. That's how this book is meant to be used.

Foolish Assumptions

This book is for everyone. Few people don't have a TV, radio, or some sort of computing device that would benefit from being networked in the future. Although it's easy to say now that computers are only for families in certain financial brackets, within five years, many TV sets will start shipping with Internet connectivity options on-board. So, if you want to make the most of your home's electronic systems by networking them, you need to read this book or one like it.

You'll get the most out of this book if you're remodeling or building a home, because you're in a position to run wires through your walls. Apartment dwellers can do some of the stuff that we outline in this book (using wireless technologies), and they can get cool ideas for when they do buy their homes.

One big assumption that we (and many folks in the industry) had to get out of our heads over the past few years regards wireless technologies. Some folks have taken the position that today's wireless technologies (and no-new-wires technologies that leverage existing phone and power lines) have eliminated the requirement to put network wiring in your walls. Well, wireless is great — it can be an invaluable complement to a wired network. If you live in an apartment or condo and can't get inside the walls to run new wire, wireless may even be good enough to build your entire network around. But if you live in a typical home, we think you're going to find that a wired network is more capable, more reliable, and more flexible. And a wired infrastructure can be a good investment that pays you back if you sell your home.

How This Book Is Organized

We realize that not everyone is going to want to do everything we discuss in the book. So we broke the book down into six distinct parts, each of which tackles a different aspect of building a smart-home infrastructure. Part I is the high-level, 50,000-foot view — describing why you might want to create a smart home. Parts II through V look in depth at how to design your home and home network to take advantage of all the neat things coming down the road in each of the major zones, and Part VI tells you how to interconnect them all.

Part I: Future-Perfect Homes

Part I describes where we're trying to get to: our future-proofed home. We talk about the different major network zones of your home, which are your entertainment system, your security system, your phone system, and your computer system. We talk about all the other things that you might want to link together and why you'd want to do that. And finally, we talk about how you can start thinking about the various things you could accomplish with a fully networked home — your smart home.

Part II: Making Your Home an Entertainment Center

Part II looks at how to make your home an entertainment center. You find out about creating not merely a home theater, but a true home-wide entertainment complex. How do you listen to your favorite CD from anywhere in the house? How do you share a satellite dish among multiple TVs. How do you watch your napping baby from your living room TV?

We tell you how to sensibly build a media backbone in your home, without breaking your bank account. We help you plan for things such as flat-screen TVs, intercom systems, whole-home audio systems, and satellite systems. We talk about your wiring (and wireless) options for communicating with each part of your home-entertainment complex.

Part III: Now We're Communicating!

Part III delves into the world of telephones. Life used to be simple in this area. If you wanted a new phone, you could go to the local department store or Radio Shack and buy one. Now, you have all sorts of complications in this area. You can choose a multiline phone, a 2.4-GHz phone, a screen phone, a combined phone-fax-printer-scanner, an answering machine, central-office-based voice-mail services, and a whole lot more. We help you craft your home-telephone network so that you can communicate with anyone from anywhere — without all that scratchy static, we hope.

Part IV: Livin' Off the Fat of the LAN

Part IV looks at your computer zone. A smart home has a high-bandwidth back-bone connection running throughout the house, so you can tap into your data autobahn wherever you like. We help you understand how you can play net-worked games, share files between computers, print or fax from any computer in the home, or even get the whole family on the Net, at the same time! We look at the world of, DSL, cable modems, DirecWay dishes, wireless Internet connections, electrical data connections, and more. Wired or wireless, we help you plan and design your own data LAN for your home. We guide you through the maze of wiring options to make sure that if you want to surf the Net while mowing the lawn, you can.

Part V: Keeping the Bad Guys at Bay

Part V takes you through our home-security boot camp and looks at everything you'd want to do to secure and protect your home. We describe not just fire and burglar alarms, but also video doorbells, closed-circuit TV, driveway sensors, and ways to watch out for your kids. We help you plan your way to a more secure and protected home.

Part VI: Putting It All Together — Home Automation and Control

Part VI brings it all together — the ultimate guide to home networking. We walk you through a whole-home approach to network design. We provide home-design and -layout tips, as well as expose you to the various products on the market for centralized home networking.

Want to fire up that coffee pot while you're still asleep? Or how about set the mood with automated lighting? We look at all the latest trends and gadgets governing home automation, including the details about X10 home automation.

Part VII: The Part of Tens

Part VII is the infamous Part of Tens, where we give you ten common pitfalls to avoid when automating your smart home and the top ten toys of the future.

Icons Used in This Book

We use helpful graphical icons to point out items of interest — sort of like Kodak Picture Spots at Disney World. These icons are meant to encourage you to pause and take in what we're saying at that point. Following are some of the icons we use.

This is the fun stuff. This icon highlights neat new technical and other advances that are either just arriving or not too far away. It's like a free pass to the World's Fair and a glimpse at the World of the Future.

This is a helpful reminder to do certain things, which translates to "we've forgotten to do this so often that we put it here just to remind ourselves."

When you see this icon, you may want to wait to make a decision until the industry decides which way it wants to go. Remember the Betamax VCR?

A few people in every crowd raise their hands and ask what's underneath the hood, so every now and then we stop to point out some of the neat stuff that makes this technology work. (We say *neat* because we're nerdy enough to enjoy writing about it.)

A shortcut or timesaving secret that we wished someone had told us before we learned the hard way.

This is never a good icon to see. It means you're working in a part of the Internet or your computer that's dangerous. It's like knowing the Wicked Witch of the West is in your neighborhood and you're wearing the ruby slippers. Be careful.

This icon tells you about a wireless technology that you can use instead of ripping your walls out.

Where to Go from Here

To help you keep up with the latest and greatest in smart-home devices and technologies, we created a companion Web site. Just type www.smarthomes book.com in your favorite Web browser, and you can catch up on the latest smart home news, find bonus material that we just couldn't fit into the book, and read our reviews of the coolest new gadgets.

See something that is not quite right? A typo? Something we should correct in the next edition? Drop us an e-mail at smarthomes@telechoice.com.

Whew! As Willy Wonka says, "So much time, so little to do . . . reverse that." Let's get going!

Part I
Future-Perfect Homes

The 5th Wave   By Rich Tennant

WIRED HOME OF THE FUTURE

"I'm setting preferences—do you want Oriental or Persian carpets in the living room?"

In this part . . .

In the olden days, your home network was comprised of basically electrical wires and phone lines, with a smattering of alarm wiring here and there. Now your home network covers all sorts of wiring and wireless options, to connect any of a number of different devices — including your car and your microwave.

You can connect home-entertainment systems, security systems, computer networks, telephone systems, and appliances together and come up with all sorts of neat applications to help make your home living simpler and more enjoyable.

In this part, we tell you all about the potential of a home network. We discuss the major elements of a whole-home network and describe the advantages of connecting them together. By the end of this part, you'll be more excited than ever about hooking everything together.

Chapter 1

Mi Casa, Cool Casa

• •

• •

*I*f you stop the average person on the street and start talking about home networks, he or she would probably make references to ABC, CBS, NBC, and FOX, or mention the Home Shopping Network or some other cable network show. *Network,* until recently, has meant little else to most people.

But times, they are a changin'. The invasion of telecommunications into all aspects of life is creating a different meaning of the word *network.* Most people have had some contact with a network through their work environment — computer local area networks (LANs) in the office, control networks in factories, telephone networks in many mid-sized or larger businesses . . . heck, the Internet is a huge network.

You can think of networks simply as things that help you do your work. As you concentrate on printing a document, calling up a database, or checking out the price of a product online, the network is invisible. (That is, invisible until it's broken.)

The network concept has begun to move from the workplace to the home, and smart home builders and remodelers (and forward-looking owners of otherwise perfect existing homes) are starting to think in terms of wiring (or *wirelessing*) their homes both to make use of a network today and to future-proof against upcoming requirements.

Before you go any further, do this little exercise (don't worry, we won't grade you): Write down all the things in your house that you think you may want to network. Be as creative as you can. Think about your lifestyle and the way your house is set up. When you finish, put the list aside and read on in this chapter. Toward the end, we'll share our list with you.

Living in Your Smart Home

Your smart home can seep into all aspects of your life. It helps you do those day-to-day tasks that can take up so much time — such as opening the draperies, dimming the lights, and flipping on the Weather Channel to see whether the kids have a snow day. How far you go with your smart home depends on your lifestyle, budget, and tastes.

This section spends a virtual day in a fictitious smart home. Here's the scenario: You, the reader, are part of a family of six, plus the requisite pet (we prefer dogs). You and your spouse both work, and the kids range in age from 8 to 17.

Starting your day

Anyone with kids knows the importance of keeping on a schedule. Your home network helps you do just that, in style.

At first light, you wake to your home-controlled alarm — a stream of pleasant classical music coming over your home audio network into your bedroom. After a preset length of time, the music fades out and the TV kicks on to your favorite local station, where you can get the weather and traffic reports and information about any school closings or delays. Down the hall, the kids awaken to the music of their choice.

In the kitchen, the coffeemaker starts brewing your morning caffeine requirements. Select shades and drapes throughout the house open to let the day's light stream in. It's winter, so the towel warmers and radiant heat in the bathrooms' floors are turned on. The automatic pet door out back opens and lets the dog out for his morning constitutional.

By this time, you're already in the kitchen making school lunches. Being the nice person that you are, you take a cup of coffee to your spouse, who is listening to National Public Radio in the shower. As you finish setting out breakfast for the kids, a glance at the upstairs monitors shows that two of your four kids are still in bed. Your eldest son is videoconferencing with his girlfriend on his computer. You punch the intercom and tell them all to get a move on.

As the children cycle into and out of the bathroom, the home-control system times their showers to make sure that no one hogs the bathroom. The shower's water temperature is just to their liking, but that's hardly a surprise — it's the same setting they use each day this time of year.

As you sit down to breakfast, your spouse comes running through, late for the office. A printout of major headlines and personal stock standings sits waiting in the printer, having been created and downloaded from the Internet overnight.

Your spouse works down the street (we did tell you that you work at home, didn't we?), and your smart home knows that you both like a warm car when you get into a 15-degree garage, so the home controller starts the car 15 minutes before the scheduled departure time. Before your spouse climbs inside the toasty car, the home-control system gives a verbal reminder to put the bottles and cans next to the curb because today is recycling day.

As your spouse leaves the garage, your home-control system talks to your phone system and redirects all of your spouse's home-business line calls to the car phone. Once at work, a simple push of a speed dial button on the office phone dials in and redirects the calls again to your spouse's office.

Back at home, you confirm that the kids caught the bus by using the video monitor in the kitchen, and then you get ready for work. You ask the home controller to put the house in your personal mode — in terms of temperature, music, lighting, drape settings, and anything else you may have set.

Getting down to work

You get a second cup of coffee and decide to work for a little while in the sunroom. You tell the home controller where you are, and the controller transfers all your business calls to the extension near the table. Your laptop is wirelessly connected to your server and to the Internet. You check your e-mail and voice mail and make a few conference calls on the multiline home-telephone system. While you're on one phone call, you access the online ordering page for that posh take-out shop down the street. Twenty minutes later, the delivery person arrives at the front door; you take your wireless two-line headset phone — conference call and all — to the door, where you pay the delivery person and retreat back to the sunroom for lunch.

For a mid-afternoon break, you head for the exercise room to work off some of that lunch. When you enter, you announce yourself to your voice-activated home-automation system, and it automatically sets the music and other environmental settings to your previously defined preferences. You sit down at your rowing machine, which is front-ended with a large monitor that shows real-life settings of popular rowing locales.

Halfway through your workout session, a delivery person shows up at your door. An announcement that someone is at the door interrupts the music, and the nearest video display shows a picture of who it is. You don't want to stop mid-workout, so you reply that you are busy and ask him to leave the package inside the door. You prompt for the control system to unlock the front door, and watch as the front door unlocks itself and the delivery person places the packages in the foyer. He leaves, and you start rowing again along Boston's Charles River.

Internet, intranet, extranet . . . it's all the same stuff

Everyone talks about the Internet, but you'll soon hear more and more about intranets and extranets. For the most part, intranets and extranets ride over the Internet. If you work at home, you may be accessing the Internet, an intranet, and an extranet for various activities.

An *intranet* is merely a secured sublayer of the Internet. Many corporations want to use the Internet to send information to parts of the company in other locations — such as remote offices or telecommuters — but the communi-

cations must be secure and private. So they buy hardware or software to create a *virtual private network (VPN),* giving the corporation its own internet within the Internet: an intranet.

An *extranet* is similar, except it involves parties outside the corporation as well. For instance, a large automobile manufacturer may have an extranet that links its suppliers with its various plants and other key locations. Because the link is with firms outside the corporation, it's called an extranet.

It's your turn for a temperature-controlled shower, where you listen to CNN from the TV set, via moisture-resistant speakers mounted in the bath. Squeaky clean, you go back to work. At 3:00, you have your first videoconference of the day from your office downstairs. While in the basement, you call up your home-control system and start the roast cooking in the oven.

The kids drift home in the afternoon and spread out across the house. While you access your corporation's data network, your kids take advantage of the computers. The youngest kids — twins — play multiplayer games on the home's high-speed Internet connection. Your eldest daughter logs onto the school's educational extranet to do research for the midterm paper due next week. And your son, when home from football practice, logs onto his school's extranet to collaboratively work with three others on a joint presentation for the next day.

The home controller's voice enunciator reminds you that the roast should be done by now, and you head upstairs.

Dinner time

Meanwhile, at work, your spouse glances at the clock and remembers in a panic that the family needs groceries. A quick dial into the home LAN yields the grocery list that's on the computerized message board in the kitchen. On the way home, a phone call into the home controller redirects calls back to the car phone in case someone tries to call.

The magnetic driveway sensor tells the home-control system to announce your spouse's arrival. As your spouse leaves the garage, the home controller again redirects all calls to the home office, completing the day's cycle. As your spouse brings the groceries into the kitchen, you receive a kiss (sorry, not automated).

Ready to eat, you ask the home controller to set dinner mode in the dining room. A microphone in the light switch hears the command and interfaces with the lights in the room, dimming them, and with the fireplace, turning on the gas-driven fireplace. The home-control system selects some family-oriented music from the MP3 server and plays it over the in-wall speakers in the dining room.

After dinner, you start cleaning up as your kids race to their rooms to finish their homework. Later, they watch a TV special in the living room, while you take in an old Spencer Tracy movie in your bedroom. In the meantime, your spouse has a late videoconference in the home office downstairs with clients in Japan. Occasionally, you access the picture-in-picture (PIP) capability on your TV set to check around the house, making sure that no one is getting into any trouble. After the movie, you give a simple command to the home controller and the lights are dimmed, the temperature in select zones is lowered, shades and draperies close, nightlights come on, and the intercom goes into monitor mode for the youngest kids, in case they're sick during the night. (The sound from those monitors plays only in the master bedroom area.)

Peace at last!

With the kids asleep for the night, you decide to take a nice relaxing bath. You instruct your home-control system to prepare the bathroom — dim the lights, open the skylight, run the bath at your favorite temperature, turn off the telephone extensions nearby (route them to voice mail instead), and play your favorite album on the bathroom speakers.

While lounging in bed watching the wide-screen TV, your spouse tells the home-entertainment system's *PVR* (personal video recorder, a hard-drive-based system that can record video digitally) to search the shows it has been archiving every day and play the last *Enterprise!* episode.

Your house is in off-hours mode. The dog is inside, and the doggy door is secure. All phones have muted ringing volumes; some don't ring at all. All drapes are closed. The temperature is lower to save energy when your family is tucked in tight under the covers. All security systems are now alert, looking for movement outside the house.

After your bath, you climb in bed and read for a while. You finish your electronic book and decide you want to read the sequel right away. You surf the Web from your TV set, find the book, buy it, download it to the home LAN and thus to your electronic book via a wireless connection.

Your dishwasher kicks on at midnight when the rates are low (you loaded it at dinnertime and turned it on, but the home controller activates it when rates drop). All night long, your home controller and its various sensors keep an eye on everything for you. You sleep peacefully.

The home-network revolution

What's brought about this progression of intelligent home networks into everyday life? One word: computers. And when we say computers, we don't mean only the PC sitting on a desk in a spare bedroom in 60 percent of American homes (although that's an important part of it). We mean also those little blobs of silicon that reside in so many things in your house, such as phones, televisions, refrigerators, and even the car in the garage.

Most of these systems are islands of computing power plugged into the power outlets of your home. The computer chips have no way of talking to each other or sharing the information that they gather and control.

The network revolution — the home-network revolution — is taking place as these things begin to talk to each other. Imagine a refrigerator that talks to your electrical utility and goes into its power-hungry defrost mode when the electricity rates are lowest. Or suppose after a power outage that all your clocks reset themselves automatically because they're set to "network time."

Home networks aren't as advanced as the Jetsons' home, but they will be soon. And you'll missing the boat if you build a new home or remodel your existing one without taking this kind of future into account. Although you can't know today exactly what will be connected to what (and how) tomorrow, you can a design a wiring system for your home that will enable you to do the most you can today and be ready for tomorrow's needs.

What's in a Smart Home?

A smart home is a harmonious home, a conglomeration of devices and capabilities working according to the Zen of Home Networking. At the beginning of this chapter, we suggested that you make a list of all the things you might want to network. Following is our list. Notice that practically anything in your home can be, and ultimately will be, networked. That's the whole point of whole-house networking:

> ✔ **Household items:** Drapes and shades, gates, garage doors, door locks, doorbells, lights, dishwasher, refrigerator, heaters, alarm clocks, washer, dryer, microwave, coffeemaker, hot water system, air conditioners,

central vacuum system, water controls (shower, sink, and so on), pool cover, fireplaces, toys, lawnmower, cars and other vehicles, piano, weather station, furniture

✔ **Audio/Video:** Receivers, amplifiers, speakers, VCRs, CD players, DVD players, PVR players, TVs, WebTV devices, DSS dish, radios, remote controls, cable TV devices, TV videoconferencing device

✔ **Security:** Baby monitor, video camera, surveillance monitors, motion detectors, smoke detectors, occupancy sensors, pressure sensors, infrared sensors, intercoms, voice enunciators

✔ **Phones:** Corded phones, cordless phones, 900-MHz phones, 2.4-GHz phones, fax machine, answering machine, PDAs, screen phone, video phone, cell phones

✔ **Computers:** PC, Mac, laptop, modem, scanner, printer, home server

The key is getting information to and from each of these devices. That takes a network. As explained throughout this book, your home network is actually a collection of networks — communications in and among the different devices travel over various network layers, such as your home-telephone network, your computing network, your security network, your electrical communications network (yes, you can talk over your electrical lines, believe it or not), and so on. These collectively are what we call your *home network,* and you mix, match, and jump among these network layers as you communicate throughout your household.

History of home wiring

Traditionally, homes have been wired for only two things: power and telephones. Add a few haphazardly run cable-TV outlets and some doorbells, and you have the sum of the wiring in most homes. Some people put in an alarm system or an intercom system, each with its own set of wires. The result is a house with an expensive bunch of wires that don't talk to each other and aren't good for anything else.

Even more important than the quantity of wires is the quality, especially when it comes to home-automation and high-speed data services. Wiring systems that are inadequate for the needs of today's wired citizens occur not only in homes wired 50 years ago but also in many new homes. Low-voltage wires (telephone and cable TV wires, for example) don't have adequate

capacity for high-speed data use or for multiple lines. They don't go to enough places in the house, and they have no flexibility of configuration. When your needs change, you'll probably have to rewire.

Even the electrical power cables may be inadequate (and not just because you don't have enough outlets) for home-automation and control systems to do such tasks as turn on lights and start the coffeemaker. These systems require a power system that is adequately isolated from interference and line noise, which is not the case in many homes.

Luckily, overcoming these problems isn't difficult — or even that expensive. All you need is a little knowledge and a good plan!

Home servers

Traditionally, you buy a lot of boxes for your house, such as VCRs, DVD players, and CD players. As the movement towards digital storage has blossomed, you find VCRs with hard disks and CD jukeboxes that can store hundreds of CDs. We call these boxes *servers* because they mimic the role of computer servers in a corporate environment.

On the horizon is the merging of these servers into two platforms. The first is the PC platform.

The second is the standalone, all-in-one home server that stores CDs, DVDs, games, software, and more and "serves up" its content to devices that want to play that information. So you'll see personal video recorder functionality available on PCs. You'll need to decide whether to get a standalone PVR or network your PC to your entertainment system. We tell you how to do both.

Why Network Your Home?

A network allows you to do a bevy of things. For instance, you can

- ✔ **Access the Internet from anywhere in your house:** A home network lets everyone share in the broadband wealth, so you can stop fighting over the one computer with the high-speed connection. What's more, by having a communications *backbone* (wiring infrastructure) in your house, you can let anything — from your TV set to your car — tap in and make use of that connectivity.

- ✔ **Remotely control your home:** After your home network is connected to your other networks, such as the Internet, you can suddenly do amazing things from almost any interconnected spot. The capability to control a device after it is hooked up to the network is limited only by the openness of the device itself. (In other words, the only limit is the degree of controllability of the device — your home's infrastructure won't hold you back.) Want to turn off the lights downstairs from the bedroom? Click your remote control, and out go the lights. Want to check the babysitter while you're at your neighbor's July 4th bash? Just log on to their machine and check up on things.

- ✔ **Save time:** Think about how much time it takes every day to open the shades, turn on the morning news, let the dog out, and so on. Wouldn't you like to do all that (and more) with one command? By programming these chores into task profiles, you can.

- ✔ **Save money on electronics:** With a true home network, you have to buy fewer devices to outfit your home. Instead of having a VCR hooked to every TV set, for instance, you can centralize this functionality and distribute the signal around the house through remote control as you need it. The same is true of almost any network-connected device, such as DSS satellite receivers, PVRs, and cable boxes.

✔ **Save money on communications costs:** By centralizing access to certain telecommunications services, you can cut monthly service costs. For instance, with a home-network backbone, both you and your spouse can connect to the Internet on separate computers while sharing one line and one account. What's more, you can share a high-bandwidth option — such as a cable modem, DSL link, or DirecWay-type satellite service — with the entire family.

✔ **Save money on your home expenses:** A wired home can turn back those thermostats when you're away on vacation or cuddled under your blankets at night. It can turn lights off automatically, too. Over time, you may save a surprising amount in heating, cooling, and electricity costs.

✔ **Save money on the future:** At different times in your life, you may find yourself changing the way you use certain rooms — a guest room becomes a nursery or the garage becomes an office, for example. Changes like these can be expensive if you try to bring your network along for the ride. Instead, have a flexible home-network design — one that's futureproofed for all sorts of contingencies — and save money down the road.

✔ **Be more flexible and comfortable with your technological assets:** A home network frees you from being tied to one spot for one activity. For instance, when working late at night, you might want to move the laptop to a comfy recliner instead of a damp basement office. And you can with a distributed means to access the Internet — and therefore your central-ized e-mail, calendar, and contact database.

✔ **Lose more fat:** A smart home won't stop you from eating chocolate cake, but it will spice up the exercise room. You can run Internet access, CNN, or exercise videos over your home network to help you keep pace and pass the time on a treadmill or bicycle. And, with Internet access, you can access many of the neat new software programs that combine with new exercise equipment to provide passing scenery or live competitors as you row, row, row your rowing machine!

What Does It Take to Network Your Home?

Okay, so you have the big picture: A networked home is a happy home. What's it take to get there? Surprisingly little, or surprisingly a lot. (Can you tell we make good consultants?) It depends on whether you go whole hog or do baby steps.

Bill Gates and his totally smart home

No one's as wired as Bill Gates. He started to lay the foundation for his home in 1992 on five acres of land, situated on the shores of Lake Washington near Seattle. When it was completed, its final price tag was around $100 million. Included in the plans for this home, besides the 500-year-old oak timber, are some of the newest technologies. Check out these hot home-networking technologies:

✔ **The electric pin:** Can you say "Gates to Enterprise"? When you arrive at the front door, you get an electronic pin to wear. This pin drives your Gates home experience because the house always knows the location of your pin, whether you are in the main house, the guesthouse, or touring the grounds. If a phone call comes for you, it can be transferred to the extension nearest your current location. As you move throughout Bill's home, the lights turn on just ahead of you and fade just behind you, and room temperatures adjust to make you comfortable. When you enter a room, wall-mounted display screens exhibit art that changes to match your taste. And if you're listening to music, the audio system plays the type of music you like. If two or more pins are in the same room, the computer responds with a mix of styles.

✔ **Home controls:** Augmenting the electric pin are conspicuously placed touch pads that allow you to change the lighting, temperature, and music in various rooms. These controls enable the computer to create a profile of your preferences. The next time you visit, the home-control system adjusts everything as you walk in the door. Or you can use a handheld remote control to communicate with the house and be in control of your overall environment.

✔ **Home theater/business rooms:** You wanna talk about a home-entertainment system? Included in Bill's guest wing is a 20-seat art deco theater. The screen is HDTV capable. That area also has a conference room, a few offices, and a computer room.

✔ **Wires everywhere:** Throughout the home are miles of communication wires — mostly fiber connections but also some copper cabling — connecting the various devices and elements with a group of computer servers running, of course, on Windows NT operating systems.

✔ **Servers everywhere:** You find a smattering of regular PCs throughout the house — home printers and other peripherals connected to high-capacity T1 connections for online access and the phone system. These PCs make exhaustive use of Microsoft software for a wide range of home applications. In addition to Microsoft Office, the software includes Cinemania interactive movie guide, Music Central interactive music, and various reference guides.

✔ **Heat everywhere:** All floors, as well as the driveway, are heated, so you don't have to worry about cold floors in the morning or shoveling his driveway after a snowfall.

More specific details about Bill's home network , particularly the security system, are confidential. If you have the right pin, however, we bet you could get access to anything you want to know in Bill's house. Sounds like a job for *Mission Impossible!*

You can make a home network based on the existing wiring in the walls and the existing air in your house, with wireless options. No cost for infrastructure there. Is it as powerful as an installed system? No, but for many it will do the trick.

Alternatively, you can install a whole system from scratch. The cost varies, just like the cost of building a house: the more you put in, the more it costs.

We've used both approaches. We put investment upfront into our transport layer — the wiring and connectivity in the walls — and less on the things we connect to that layer, to give us more flexibility as things change. For instance, at Danny's house in Maine, rather than design for a big 32" TV, he left the living room unfinished because he knew that the price of flat-screen plasma TVs would plummet in price. He waited patiently for prices to drop. He's still waiting. So is his wife.

Table 1-1 shows you some of the rough costs for getting into a smart home, with reasonable expectations set forth in this book. These are the costs of the components and the installation — you'll have some additional ongoing costs for services such as Internet and cable TV.

Table 1-1	The Cost of It All!			
Expense Area	*Low*	*Midrange*	*High*	*Obscene*
Wired infrastructure	$1000	$2500	$4000	$6000
Wireless infrastructure	$250	$500	$1000	$1800
Entertainment system				
Home theater	$1000	$3000	$25,000	$200,000
Components (six)	$1200	$1800	$6000	$30,000
Phone system	$200	$500	$1500	$4000
Intercom system (standalone)	$500	$1200	$1500	$2000
Data system	$300	$600	$1000	$2500
Security system	$300	$1200	$2000	$20,000
Home automation	$50	$1000	$10,000	$30,000
Totals	**$4300**	**$12,300**	**$52,000**	**$296,300+**

In this book, you'll go through the following process of thinking smartly:

1. Finding out all you can about your options

2. Putting your thoughts on paper

3. Figuring out the costs of your desired options

4. Refining your thoughts based on cost

5. Getting help where needed

6. Installing the systems in a methodical and somewhat structured process

7. Adding all the cool devices that put your smart home to use

8. Sitting back and enjoying yourself. (We'd like to stress this one, but the reality is that you'll enjoy your smart home for a moment and then go back to the first step and start over, because you'll want more.)

We provide detailed steps as well as more budgeting information in Chapter 4.

Chapter 2

Zen and the Art of Whole-Home Networking

As you think about your home network, think in terms of the big picture. Instead of talking about how to link one computer to another, think about a computer network that extends to every room. Instead of trying to extend your cable TV signal from one room to another, think about a video-distribution strategy for the whole house. Instead of discussing your home-entertainment center, map out a media backbone for your entire home.

In this chapter, you look at networks in a broad, whole-home sense. We tell you how all the networks in your home fit together physically and how you can make home networking easier by designing a central location (or two) to house all of your networking equipment. We also discuss some of *structured cabling* solutions, which are packages of bundled cabling and distribution panels that can take care of most of your home-networking infrastructure needs in one easy-to-buy-and-install single-vendor system.

All Together Now!

Your home infrastructure may consist of one or more of the following networks:

  ✔ A phone network

  ✔ A data network (often called a *local area network,* or LAN)

  ✔ An electrical network

 ✔ A security network

 ✔ An intercom network (may be part of your phone network)

 ✔ An entertainment network

 ✔ A home-automation and -management capability that allows your house to do common tasks on its own

 ✔ Access to the Internet and other external programming sources (such as satellite broadcasts, cable, and telephone services)

You may not want or need all these different networks in your home. However, if you're at a point in the construction or remodeling of your home where running cables is easy, consider providing the cables so that you (or someone who owns your home after you) can add these capabilities later.

One of the difficulties when thinking about home networking is that different networks sometimes do the same thing. To simplify, you can think of your home network in three ways:

 ✔ **Physical configuration:** The cables, connections, and specific pieces of equipment that make up the physical aspects of your network. This is where all the detail work comes in.

 ✔ **Logical configuration:** Each network is viewed as a single object (such as a phone network) or as a model. Most of the networks we discuss in this book use a star model, in which all the cables meet at a single junction point, just as the spokes of a wheel meet at the hub.

 ✔ **Applications:** The network's purpose, or application, and connections. Your entertainment network, for example, may represent a combination of different physical components and logical entities aimed at distributing audio and video around your house. A typical system might include audio and video devices such as VCRs and CD players, a broadcast satellite that runs to receivers that require phone line access, and home-management software to control the network's functionality.

Although it's easiest to discuss the building of home networks by talking about the cables and connectors (as we do throughout the book), the beginning phases of conceptualizing a home network start from the opposite end. You usually begin by thinking of what you want to accomplish (the applications), move on to considering each individual network and its layout (the logical configuration), and then get to the nitty-gritty of cables, connectors, and specific hardware components (the physical configuration).

Thinking of networks by application, logically, and physically can reveal ways to save money, time, and headaches. For example, if you think strictly in terms of the phone network and data network being logically different networks, you could overlook that these networks may be able to transmit over the same in-wall cables at different frequencies.

Someday, homeowners will be able to install an integrated, unified network that carries voice, video, data, audio, and home control signals over a single kind of cable. When that day comes, we'll write a really short version of *Smart Homes For Dummies* and spend more time on the golf course or basketball court. Unfortunately (for Pat's jump shot and Danny's swing), that day is still quite a ways off. Today's home network consists of a number of independent networks, each doing its own thing over its own set of wires and cables. That's not to say that there aren't places where today's individual home networks come together and work together. A typical house has a whole bunch of network interconnection points, making these separate networks behave somewhat like a unified, single network.

Networks can physically interconnect in a home in three ways:

- **Networks can share the same media (or cables) to carry different kinds of signals at different frequencies.** For example, telephone wiring might be used to carry both telephone service and data networking using a phone-line networking system.

- **Specific devices can connect to multiple networks.** A DSS satellite receiver, for example, connects to both video and telephone networks. A media server such as a PVR could connect to your video network and your data network.

- **Incoming service provider feeds can carry multiple services and connect to different networks in the home.** For example, a cable company might provide television, Internet access, and telephone service over three different home networks.

Moving Your Network into the Closet

When integrating a home network in your home design or remodeling plans, the following two points are key:

- Designate an appropriate location for all your network's central distribution equipment.

- Make sure that you have an adequate quality and quantity of network cabling running to each potential network outlet in your home.

In this section, we discuss the first of these points — designing a central location for your network components. In the following section, we discuss the pieces and parts — the cables and connectors that make up the physical network.

Talk to your builder or remodeler about designating a space as a *central wiring closet.* (For a remodel, it often makes sense to have multiple locations.) The wiring closet should be out of sight but easily accessible, with plenty of space and adequate power to run a great deal of equipment.

By designating a central wiring closet, you gain the following benefits:

- ✔ **Hidden wires:** The walls of a truly wired home contain lot of cables: wires for a phone network, a video network, an audio network, a computer network, a security network, and a remote-control network. Add the connections to the outside phone lines, cable TV, and satellite feeds, and it can become a bowl of spaghetti pretty quickly. You don't want to have to tuck these wires behind your furniture if you can avoid it. In a wiring closet, these cables are neatly terminated in a series of wiring panels, away from prying eyes.

- ✔ **Hidden hardware:** Much of the hardware that facilitates home networking, such as distribution panels and punchdown blocks (these panels and blocks are special *wiring-termination* devices that connect all the cables running to remote locations in your house), is designed for function rather than form. A central wiring closet puts this hardware out of view.

- ✔ **Single point of connection:** Most networks we describe in this book connect to the outside world at a single, central location. Why not have the wires of all these networks terminate in the same area to make it easier to do things such as connect your Internet line to your computer network?

- ✔ **Easy access:** When you want to change the capabilities of your networks or troubleshoot a problem, having everything neatly arranged and easily accessible can eliminate a source of frustration.

The contents of your wiring closet

Most of the cabling and infrastructure components of a home's networks should be installed in the area of your home designated as your wiring closet. A few items — mainly parts of your home-entertainment network — are better located elsewhere (we get to the concept of a *media center* later in this chapter). In addition, a few systems in a home network are inherently decentralized, such as X10 components, security systems, and wireless phone or data network systems. These devices don't necessarily have central control units, or they have control units that should be out in the open and readily accessible, not hidden away in a wiring closet.

The devices that *should* go in a wiring closet include

- ✔ The coaxial video-distribution panel (see Chapter 6)
- ✔ Patch panels for CAT-5e phone and data wiring (see Chapter 10)
- ✔ Central controllers for KSU telephone systems (see Chapter 10)
- ✔ Cable and DSL modems and routers (see Chapter 13)
- ✔ Ethernet hubs or switches (see Chapter 14)
- ✔ Stand-alone home-automation control units (see Chapter 19)

You can also put home servers and some of your central media equipment in the wiring closet if you don't need to get to them and need the extra space elsewhere. More on these centralized devices later in the chapter.

Some newer cable and DSL modems utilize a USB instead of an Ethernet interface. This simplifies connecting one of these modems to a single computer, but it makes it just about impossible to directly connect them to a centralized LAN hub. If your service provider leases or sells you one of these modems, it must be installed next to a server computer in your home office or other location. Most providers give you the choice of USB or Ethernet, but the offer may not be advertised. So ask the question upfront, and ask for an Ethernet modem.

The location of your wiring closet

In the best-case scenario, you can create a dedicated room for your networking equipment — a central wiring closet just like those in modern offices and other commercial buildings. If we were starting a home from scratch, we'd design the wiring closet

- ✔ On the main floor of the house.
- ✔ Near an outside wall for easy interconnection to incoming service feeds.
- ✔ Above an accessible part of the basement (if we have a basement).
- ✔ With adequate lighting, ventilation, and climate protection (not in the garage, in other words). Electronic gear generates heat, so if you live south of the Arctic Circle, it's a good idea to have air-conditioning vents in the wiring closet.
- ✔ With adequate AC power-line receptacles to power devices such as video amplifiers, Ethernet hubs, and key phone systems.

Such a closet needn't be too large. An 8-by-8-foot room would be more than adequate to handle the centrally located network equipment for even the largest home. You can get away with half that floor space if you need to.

Of course, the vast majority of home builders or remodelers don't have the luxury of adding this kind of dedicated space for a network wiring closet. In these cases, some other part of the house has to do double duty as your wiring closet. Here are some locations to consider:

- **The utility or laundry room:** The biggest disadvantage of this location is the potential for high humidity, so make sure your clothes dryer is well ventilated to the outdoors.

- **A protected garage:** The potential for dust and extreme temperatures may make this location less than optimal for some homes.

- **The basement:** A basement can be a good location because it's easy to run wires through a drop ceiling, but keep in mind that basements can be both dusty and damp.

- **A weather-protected outdoor closet:** This location is a last resort, but it could be acceptable if you live in a mild climate. However, we don't recommend putting any active electronics, such as Ethernet hubs or phone systems out here.

The natural enemies of electrical and electronic equipment are moisture, dust, and temperature extremes, so locations that may work for someone in Florida or California may not make as much sense for those in Maine or Arizona.

Feeding Audio and Video from the Media Center

Most network systems in your house — specifically, the data wiring, phone wiring, and the coaxial video-distribution wiring — are best located in a wiring closet. The parts of your network that provide the audio and video signals that you send through your house, however, are more appropriately centralized in the room where you use them the most. We call this area the *media center*.

For most people, the media center is also their home theater, the place where the fancy surround-sound audio receiver, the biggest and best TV monitor, and the handcrafted, wood-veneered, titanium-woofer speakers all live.

The contents of your media center

Chances are, you want to be able to quickly access your CD player (unless it's one of those CD jukeboxes that holds 200 CDs or an MP3 home server) and your video source equipment (such as the VCR and DVD player) to change discs or tapes and for local (in-room) listening and viewing. So it makes sense to locate your audio network and the source equipment for your video network in a different place than the rest of your wiring closet. We like to call this location the media center, but if that sounds a bit too much like CNN Central in Atlanta, you can call it the "room with all the fun toys."

What goes into a media center? All your audio and video equipment:

✔ Video source devices such as VCRs, DVDs, and laserdisc players (see Chapter 7)

✔ Audio source devices such as CD players, radio tuners, satellite radio receivers, and turntables (see Chapter 8)

✔ Video modulators (see Chapter 6)

✔ Audio amplifiers and controllers for your whole-home audio system (see Chapter 8)

✔ Impedance-matching panels for audio amplifiers (see Chapter 8)

✔ Connecting blocks and emitters from your IR control network (see Chapter 19)

Your video-distribution panel doesn't go in the media center — just the source equipment and a modulator that can distribute signals back over your two-way coaxial network to the panel in the wiring closet.

In addition to the audio/video equipment that you're distributing across your network, you want to have all the stuff needed to do local listening and viewing in your media center. In other words, a television or video monitor, speakers, and a surround-sound receiver or controller/amplifier system should also be in this room.

Setting up your media center

Locating all this gear and related wiring discreetly in your media center can be a bit problematic. This room, unlike a wiring closet, is a public space in your house, not a place where you can hide unsightly bundles of wire and racks of equipment. So your aesthetic requirements will be a bit higher.

The best solution is to design the room with an enclosed equipment-and-connection area. This is where you would put your *whole-home equipment* — the equipment that you don't need to access to watch a program or listen to something — such as impedance-matching equipment and modulators. Your equipment-and-connection area could be a well-ventilated closet. We've seen sophisticated setups with a false wall behind the TV and equipment racks to allow access to the backs of all of the gear. If you can't find a separate space for your whole-home equipment, you can connect all your outgoing speaker wires and IR cables to wall outlets behind your equipment rack, and then use short cables to connect these outlets to the equipment itself.

If you can't find an aesthetically pleasing way of getting all this stuff in your media center, you might consider putting the audio-amplification and imped-ance-matching equipment in your wiring closet (along with your whole-house speaker-wire connections). Use the shortest run possible of high-quality, shielded audio interconnects to connect these amps to the audio source equipment back in your media center.

You may face one more issue in equipping your media center: integrating source components both into your whole-home audio and video networks and into the TVs, receivers, and amps that you use locally in the media center. For example, you may want to connect your DVD player to both your video-distribution panel (through a modulator) and a multichannel surround-sound receiver and widescreen TV for home theater use. Or you may want to connect your CD player to the same receiver for listening over those fancy speakers in the media center and also to a multi-room audio system. Most of this source equipment has only a single set of outputs, so how do you con-nect it to two separate systems? Following are a few ways:

- For video source devices, choose modulators that have a loop-through connection. You can then run one set of A/V cables from the source to the modulator and another set from the modulator to your surround-sound receiver and TV.

- Many of the newest DVD players include two sets of A/V outputs, so you can send one set to the modulator and another to the surround-sound receiver and TV.

- Audio-only sources, such as CD players, are trickier. If you're using a dis-tribution amplifier to feed the output of the source device to several amplifiers for a multizoned or multiamped whole-house audio network, you can use one of the distribution amplifier's outputs to feed the sur-round-sound receiver. Another solution is to skip the CD player if you have a DVD player because most DVD players can also play audio CDs.

Choosing Cables

After electrical wiring, telephone-type wiring is the most common type of wire in home networks. This category of cabling, usually referred to as *twisted pair*, does more than just carry telephone signals. Twisted-pair cabling is the basis of most computer LANs and can be used to carry other data, such as audio and video signals, in your home network. (The wires are twisted inside a sheath — you can't see the twisting except to note slight bumps at regular intervals in the cabling.)

Fiber-optic faux pas?

Perhaps you've been skipping around the book, reading up on the stuff that goes into all the different networks in a home, and you've been scratching your head and wondering why you can't find any mention about installing fiber-optic cabling in the home.

Well . . . we didn't forget about it. We don't recommend installing fiber in the home, mainly because somewhere around zero applications for fiber are available among all the thousands of consumer electronics devices sold today. The only place that fiber ever comes into play is for some specialized digital audio interconnects, the kind used to connect CD and DVD players to external digital-to-analog converters (such as the ones inside fancy home-theater receivers).

But isn't fiber the future — and isn't this book all about taking a long-term view? The answers to those questions are "Yes" and "Yes, but . . ." Someday, fiber-optic cable may be the most common cabling for connecting home audio, video, data, and phone networks. Today, however, no clear standards govern which of the many various kinds of fiber will be commonly used to connect home devices, and no consensus has been reached on how fiber will be connected and laid out in a home.

We *do* recommend that you give yourself a head start by designing your home in such a way that adding new cable types such as fiber will be easier when the time comes. But for now, we think that running fiber in a home is a waste of time and money.

The wiring in modern phone and LAN systems is twisted for a reason (besides the fact that colored wires woven together look pretty). Through some magical properties of physics, the interweaving of the wires protects against electrical interference. No interference, no *cross talk,* which occurs when, for example, the fax transmission on line one bleeds through to the voice call on line two.

You usually find twisted-pair phone and data wiring in a cable jacket that has no electrical shielding. Those in the know refer to it as *UTP,* or unshielded twisted pair.

Older homes were usually wired with *quad cable,* a flat, untwisted cable that contains two pairs of wires, sufficient for carrying two phone lines. This type of wiring is much more susceptible to interference and cross talk and is ill-suited for modern, high-speed communications and networking. If you currently have quad cable, our advice is to replace it.

Newer homes are generally wired for telephone service with a round cable (usually in a gray jacket) that contains two twisted pairs of wires (four conductors). This cabling is much less prone to interference problems, and most types can carry up to two POTS or ISDN phone lines (described in more detail in Chapter 10). In most cases, these cables are not adequate for high-speed data networks but are perfectly adequate for distributing telephone and low-speed analog data service throughout your house. Although these cables are just fine for telephone service, in most cases the architecture (network design) of existing home-phone networks isn't flexible enough for more sophisticated, multilane phone systems.

Cable categories

UTP cables are rated by their *category,* or measure of the cable's bandwidth capacity, as shown in Table 2-1. Higher-rated cables can handle higher-speed data networks. Rated cables are usually referred to as CAT-*x*, where *x* is the category rating. For example, Category 5e cable is CAT-5e.

Table 2-1	Category Ratings of UTP Cabling
Cable Rating	*Performance Rating*
Category 1	No performance criteria
Category 2	Rated to 1 MHz (used for telephone wiring)
Category 3	Rated to 16 MHz (used for Ethernet 10BaseT)
Category 4	Rated to 20 MHz (used for 10BaseT)
Category 5	Rated to 100 MHz (used for 100BaseT, 10BaseT)
Category 5e	Rated to100 MHz (used for 100BaseT, 10BaseT, and 155-Mbps ATM)

If you're starting from scratch, you can use lower-rated, generic, four-pair twisted phone wire for your telephone network, but we prefer higher-quality wire. Specifically, we recommend that you choose Category 5e (CAT-5e) UTP data-grade wiring. This wire doesn't cost much more than the nonrated variety, and it's better suited to the high-speed technologies that your phone lines may carry in the future, such as *digital subscriber line* (DSL) data connections (see Chapter 13 for more about DSL).CAT-5e, the highest-rated UTP cabling, can carry Fast Ethernet networks (such as 100BaseT) and ATM networks at speeds up to 155 Mbps. CAT-5e cable can also handle anything a lower-rated UTP cable does, such as carrying telephone signals.

Although CAT-5e wiring is overkill for most current phone applications, we strongly recommend that you spend the extra money and go with CAT-5e everywhere, just to be on the safe side for the future. Doing so everywhere gives you the flexibility to switch between data and telephone applications. If you're also building a computer LAN in your home, you're probably buying CAT-5e cabling in bulk anyway, so why bother with two separate crates of wire? You'll probably have a fight with your contractor about this, but show him this book. Smart people use only CAT-5e in their homes.

The NID

When you're talking telephone cabling, you might hear someone mention NID (network interface device), SID (service interface device), or some other similar term.

A network interface device is a small plastic box that serves as the point of demarcation between your home's telephone networks and your service provider's network. Incoming phone lines connect to one side of the NID, terminating within a locked portion of the box (only the phone company's techs are allowed in there). This side of the NID is electrically connected to the consumer side of the NID, where your internal phone wiring begins.

The NID is part of a standard telephone-company line installation. Its demarcation function makes the NID a significant part of a phone network. Everything on the telephone company's side of the NID (all the way back to their central telephone-switching office) is their responsibility to maintain and repair. The consumer side of the NID is your inside wiring, and if something goes awry, you pay for its repair.

Many local telephone companies offer inexpensive inside-wiring-repair policies that they tack onto your phone bill every month. If something goes wrong with your inside wiring, the phone company sends someone out to troubleshoot and repair the problem for free. This service can be a good deal if you have an older house.

If you peruse the brochures and Web sites of cable manufacturers and resellers, you may run across someone who is selling UTP cables that appear to have a higher rating than CAT-5e. CAT-5e is currently the highest category rating, although cable manufacturers are pressing standards organizations to create a higher category.

These higher-rated cables may indeed be capable of carrying even higher-speed networks than CAT-5e, but right now no standard ensures that one company's CAT-6 — or whatever they may call it — will carry the same amount of data as another company's. We've seen references to CAT-7 as well. The good news is that CAT-5e cable is more than capable of handling home-networking needs for the future.

CAT-5e commonly comes in a four-pair configuration. If you don't use CAT-5e, we still recommend that you install *four-pair wire* — the kind that can handle four phone lines on one cable — to give you some leeway as you add lines. You might find that certain applications, such as audio, make use of these other lines to create subnetworks in the home.

A final comment: Although your house has other cables, especially the RG-6 cabling we discuss in Chapters 6 and 7, telephone cabling gets most of the attention because there are so many types and because the trend in home-networking circles is to use CAT-5e for just about everything. Other forms of cabling have different classes and performance characteristics but are more application specific. We discuss them in turn in their respective sections in this book.

Patch me in!

The many cables that run through your house can be a big mess when you get to the point where you want to hook them up with the telephone company, the cable company, or something else. Fortunately, you can use a *patch panel* (also called a terminal block or punchdown block) to neatly patch together telephone and security application lines.

You connect your incoming telephone lines (including DSL service, if you have it) through the patch panel to centrally homed telephone cables running to jacks throughout your home. (*Centrally homed* refers to the star-wired architecture of a phone network, where each jack is individually wired back to the central hub.)

A patch panel is a wall-mounted piece of equipment that serves as a junction point for lines. Consisting of a plastic frame with several evenly spaced wire receptacles, or *lugs,* the patch panel makes future changes to the phone system easier and eliminates having to reroute cables in the walls.

Depending on your installer and how much you want to spend, a patch panel can have the following interfaces:

- ✔ **Pole and nut terminal interface:** You unscrew the nut, put the wire in, and screw the nut back in.

- ✔ **RJ-style interface:** You plug the individual runs of phone wire directly into modular jacks.

- ✔ **Punchdown interface:** You push the wire into the receptacles by using a *punchdown tool.* This tool simultaneously strips the wire of its insulation and connects the wire electrically to the panel.

Figure 2-1 shows a phone patch panel with RJ-11 connectors.

Typical patch panels are based on standard designs (known as 66 or 110 panels), although some home-cabling companies offer proprietary designs. In the simplest terms, centrally homed cables connect to one side of the patch panel and incoming phone lines from the NID connect to the other side. The patch panel is then wired internally to distribute each incoming line to multiple outlets, a process known as *bridging,* or *cross connecting.*

CAT-5e cable can be used for many things (such as phones, computer networks, and audio/video networks). We — and just about everyone else in the home-networking world — recommend that you run at least two CAT-5e cables to every significant room in your house (every place but bathrooms and closets). This setup gives you flexibility because each cable can be reconnected to different networks back at the patch panel. So a cable that today provides extra voice outlets in a bedroom can be reconfigured to connect to your data LAN by simply changing the termination of the cable in your panel from the phone network to the data network.

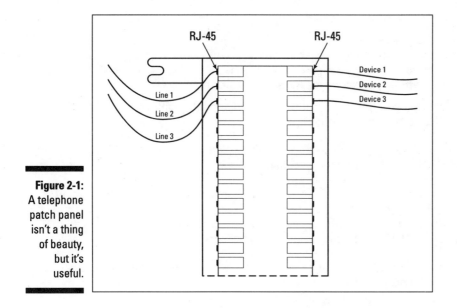

Figure 2-1:
A telephone
patch panel
isn't a thing
of beauty,
but it's
useful.

Unlike the main network UTP cabling, which you buy in bulk and run inside
your walls, *patch cables* are usually purchased in precut lengths (of a few feet)
with the connectors already attached. Patch cables are also constructed differently than main backbone cabling. Specifically, *stranded wire* — dozens of thin-
ner wires wrapped together to make one, creating greater flexibility — make up
each of the eight conductors (four pairs) in a patch cable. The UTP cabling used
for the wire runs from your patch panel to individual rooms is constructed from
solid-core wires (one thicker wire for each of the eight conductors).

For video-cable wiring (typically RG6 coaxial cable), the patch panel is usually called a *distribution hub.* But the principles are the same: lines in and
lines out. We discuss distribution hubs in detail in Chapter 6.

If you use a structured prewiring system, such as those offered by Siemon
(www.siemon.com) or Leviton (www.leviton.com), the patch panels and distribution panels are housed in the central wiring hub. These wiring hubs are
modular, so you can easily add patch panels or distribution panels as you
expand your network. We talk more about these systems shortly.

Jacks and plugs for everyone

For the past 20 years or so, telephone wires have been using standardized
modular connectors — plugs and jacks — to connect equipment to the wiring
infrastructure. These modular connectors come in three physical variants,
which look basically the same but come in different widths to accommodate
more wires (or positions):

- ✔ **Four-position jack and plug:** Connects handsets to telephones.

- ✔ **Six-position jack and plug:** Handles one, two, or three lines, which means that two, four, or six wires, respectively, terminate in the jack. Most of these jacks on our phones have only four wires used in the six positions, but you can see six positions if you look closely.

- ✔ **Eight-position jack and plugs:** Used for data applications such as Ethernet and other computer LANs; not normally used for phones.

Businesses sometime use 25-pair jack and plugs as well, but you're not likely to need or see these in your house.

We recommend that you use eight-position jacks @ not six — throughout your home so that the jacks can be used for voice or data or whatever. Most consumer phone equipment, whether it be one-, two-, or three-line capable, can use RJ-45 outlets for these RJ-11 standard connectors.

Beyond physical size, the communications industry also differentiates jacks by their *configuration* (how many wires are connected to them). You may see documentation referring to jacks and plugs as

- ✔ **RJ-11:** Two wires connected for a single-line connection

- ✔ **RJ-14:** Four wires connected for a two-line connection

- ✔ **RJ-25:** Six wires connected for a three-line connection

- ✔ **RJ-45:** Eight wires connected for data LAN (wider than phone jacks)

Security systems use a special kind of RJ jack called the RJ-31X. We talk about this jack in Part V, which covers home-security systems.

All of this "RJ-this" and "RJ-that" talk quickly gets confusing. Even the experts get confused because an RJ-11 can mean different things, depending on whether you're following an old Bell Telephone standard, a Telecommunications Industry Association (TIA) standard, or something else. We usually refer to six-position phone jacks as RJ-11s, regardless of how many wires are connected, and eight-position jacks as RJ-45s. That's the way most people talk, regardless of what the standards say.

Like all cable connectors, RJ-connectors come in both male and female varieties. We leave the reasons for naming each variety to your own imagination, but we will tell you that you find the male version of the connector on the end of a cable and the female connector on wall outlets or inside equipment such as your PC.

You'll also run into some similar video-cable options — there are cable connectors, but far fewer of them, and we discuss those in Chapter 6.

Accessorize your phone network

A range of small, useful accessories are handy with your home-wiring network, including the following:

- ✔ **1-to-2 splitter jacks:** These jacks take a single RJ-14 or RJ-45 connection (which has two pairs of wire) and split it into two single-pair RJ-11 or RJ-45 connections so that you can connect two devices.

- ✔ **2-jack modular adapter:** These adapters take a single RJ-14 or RJ-45 connection and split it into two RJ-14 or RJ-45 connections, allowing you to have two two-line phones sharing the same wall jack, for instance.

You can readily find three- and five-jack versions as well.

- ✔ **Inline coupler:** This accessory connects two four-wire phone cords together, which is great when you have to run an extra-long-distance across the room. For example, you can use an inline coupler to connect two six-foot telephone cords to get one twelve-foot cord.

These gadgets offer more flexibility when you find that your wired network doesn't quite give you exactly what you want. Grab a handful and keep them in your toolbox — you'll need them.

Modular wall outlets

The *endpoints* of your telephone network are the wall outlets in each room. These wall plates have holes that are populated with modular connections corresponding to what you want to terminate — such as a phone, data, or cable connection.

Although you can find wall plates equipped with RJ-11 modular jacks (and you can plug any of your old telephone equipment into these), RJ-11 jacks are not going to be much good if you want to change the use of the outlets. We recommend that you install RJ-45 outlets everywhere — your standard RJ-11 modular phone connectors will work fine in them.

When you're choosing phone wall outlets for a room, consider what other home-network outlets you'll need in the same location. You can find many modular outlets that take up a double- or triple-gang-sized junction box (a single gang, which we talk about in Chapter 7, is the size of a standard light switch or wall outlet) and allow you to connect data and video networks all in one large outlet.

Investigating All-in-One Wiring Solutions

We believe that most homeowners want to install, at a minimum, a home network that can handle the three main types of network applications (telephones, data, and video). Most major wiring and network infrastructure vendors believe this, too, and offer all-in-one *structured cabling systems*. With these systems, a single vendor supplies (and in many cases, installs) a complete, integrated home-networking infrastructure.

Structured cabling systems

Most structured cabling systems for the home are offshoots of similar (and more complicated) packages of hardware and wiring that networking system vendors have been offering their corporate customers for years. The concept is simple — go to the vendor, tell them your requirements, and get an off-the-shelf, soup-to-nuts system ready for installation.

For the most part, structured cabling systems are made up of the same parts that you'd use if you were building separate home networks by yourself. Specifically, you'll find that most contain the following components:

- **A service center:** Combines phone and data patch panels and a video distribution center in a single unit — making for a neater installation. Service centers are usually modular, wall-mounted components.

- **All-in-one cables:** Cabling that combines telephone and data cabling and coaxial cable for video in a single cable jacket. Some systems even include fiber-optic cables in the same jacket. (See the "Fiber-optic faux pas?" sidebar for our opinion on the matter.)

- **Customized wall outlet plates:** Matched up with the all-in-one cable, these faceplates provide modular connectors for your phone, data, and video outlets.

As you can see, nothing about these systems is different than the pieces you'd install if you were designing your own home networks. They're simply put together in one big kit to facilitate buying, designing, and installing your network infrastructure.

Where all-in-one systems work (and don't work)

If you read the product literature from most manufacturers (we tell you where to find it in just a moment), you get the impression that a structured cabling system can do everything but clean the kitchen sink. However, some of the capabilities and applications listed for these systems are based on forward-looking marketing projections rather than on what you can actually do now.

We mention this not to disparage the structured cabling system, but to warn you that installing one may not take care of all your home-networking needs.

For example, the following applications are usually *not* easily supported by most structured systems:

- ✔ **Alarm systems:** Although some security features, such as security cameras, can fit in a structured cabling system, a full-featured, monitored, hardwired security system requires its own wiring — usually installed by a registered professional installer. Structured wiring systems allow you to interface the alarm to an outgoing telephone system for monitoring.

- ✔ **Whole-home multizone hi-fi audio:** You can add components to your structured wiring system to distribute *single-zone* audio throughout your home (meaning everyone hears the same thing everywhere), but many don't include the speaker wiring and distribution systems to get hi-fi multizone audio around your home (which allows you to send different audio sources to different parts of the house simultaneously).

- ✔ **Remote-control distribution for audio and video systems:** Most systems don't support this functionality. The few that do, provide IR (infrared) signaling over the video coaxial cable or use extra CAT-5e cables to carry IR signaling data.

So, you're probably thinking, what *do* these systems support? Quite a lot, actually. At a bare minimum, a structured cabling system should provide

- ✔ **A flexible telephone network** using high-quality, unshielded twisted-pair (UTP) phone cabling and a modular, configurable termination system at the service center.

- ✔ **A computer network** of CAT-5e UTP cabling for data networking.

- ✔ **A centrally distributed coaxial cable (usually RG6) network** for distributing video signals.

- ✔ **An all-in-one modular termination panel** to neatly terminate all this network wiring in your wiring closet.

You'll find structured systems capable of handling additional applications such as alarms, hi-fi audio, and infrared networking as standards supporting such connections become popular.

Makers of all-in-one systems

Just about every company that specializes in network cabling offers a residential structured cabling system. Those that haven't are sure to begin soon. Keeping in mind the fact that this is a growing marketplace, here's a list of some of the major vendors and their Web pages:

- ✔ Monster Cable Products (MonsterCentral): www.monstercable.com

- Leviton: www.leviton.com
- HomeDirector: www.homedirector.net
- ChannelPlus: www.multiplextechnology.com/channelplus/
- Siemon Home Cabling Systems: www.siemon.com
- OnQ Technologies: www.onqtech.com
- Smart Systems Technologies: www.smartsystemstech.com
- FutureSmart: www.futuresmart.com
- Unicom: www.unicomlink.com
- USTec: www. ustecnet.com

Hints for Designing a Futureproofed Home

Here's a collection of some of our best tips for your home adventure:

- **Anticipate your needs:** You need to think, think, think when planning your home network. A smart home is only as good as your design. And it will cost you a bundle to add something later that you forgot. We know it's hard — you never know where you're going to end up. (Ask Danny, he's got *two* sets of twins.)

- **Read everything:** Different publications and books have different perspectives and goals, and they each add a different aspect to your planning. So, read . . . a lot.

- **Overdo it:** You start working at home and need a home office. So does your spouse. You have more kids. You need more computers. You add a wing to the house. Running the bare minimum of wires only to rooms that you're sure will need them is not always enough. We admit that we overbuilt our houses. There, we said it. We overbuilt. Why? Because we believe in futureproofing our homes. Can you get by with other options? Yes. Can you add later? Yes, at more cost. Is it easier to do it up front? Oh yes! So overdo it. Run that extra wire.

- **Leave room for expansion:** No matter how much you believe that you'll think of everything upfront, you won't. Plan for expansion. If you have a choice of two models, and one is slightly larger, go with the larger one. Will this add cost up front? Absolutely. But it will save you money down the road.

- **Run conduits:** Think about access and flexibility for future growth when you run your wires. You never know when you're going to have to run more cable for some reason or another. Run PVC conduits between floors and in the walls, instead of just running wire, so you can add more cable in the future if you need to. Be cognizant of elbows in these PVC runs — cable, especially thicker cable, does not travel around corners well. Figure 2-2 shows how this might work. Leave pull cords in the conduit — *pull cords* are cords that you use to pull cables through that conduit. Also be careful about what you run in the same conduit — some signals running inside cables can interfere with each other. Never run electrical wiring inside these PVC conduits no matter how much money it saves you.

If you're planning on blowing foam insulation into your house, running conduits is even more critical. Most foam insulation is blown into the wall space after the wiring is completed, so you don't get a lot of second chances if you don't run PVC.

✔ **Don't forget the power:** Ouch. Nothing's worse than buying the latest and greatest telephone, bringing it home, plugging the telephone cable in, and then realizing there's no electrical outlet anywhere nearby. Argh! When you renovate your house or build your new home, you need to talk about the location of electrical outlets with your electrician and cabling contractor. Most electrical outlets are installed every so many feet along the wall (per electrical regulations) and aren't coordinated with your phone lines or other smart devices.

In areas that will have lots of electronic gear, such as the home office or home theater, have your electrician run dedicated circuits. There's nothing worse than finding out — a month after you've finished your network — that plugging the vacuum cleaner into that outlet in the foyer knocks out the circuit breaker in your home office because the electrician put them on the same circuit.

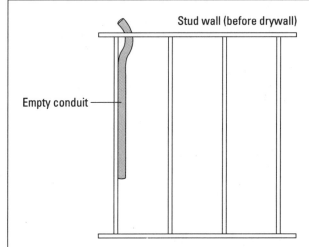

Figure 2-2:
Running
PVC pipe in
the wall.

Stud wall (before drywall)

Empty conduit

✓ **Don't get fooled by all-in-one, all the time:** A big theme in home networking, particularly home automation, is to find a single solution that does everything. True, integration is good and something to look at seriously. But all-in-one solutions are also sometimes the lowest common denominator. Hard-core stereo buffs tend to go with the best-of-breed approach — they buy a tuner from one manufacturer, a CD/DVD player from another, and an amplifier from yet another for a reason: The individual elements have enough to offer on their own to make the hassle of interconnecting them worthwhile. So look at individual options as well as overall solutions in your buying process.

✓ **Be creative:** Planning a smart home is an opportunity to have fun and be creative. The infrastructure you put in place will enable the fun stuff, but it won't create it. Only by hanging neat technologies off the endpoints of that infrastructure will you see the fruits of your efforts. You're creating an investment. When you go to sell your home after all the kids have left for school and they never call you anymore (sigh), the unique attributes of your home will provide value for the buyer.

Chapter 3

Cool Stuff Home Networks Can Do

• •

In This Chapter

▶ Finding a flexible phone network

▶ Entertaining yourself with today's home network

▶ Saving energy the smart-home way

▶ Accessing the Internet all over your house

▶ Exercising remote control

▶ Getting in the swim

▶ Attaining the paragon of smart homes

• •

> *"I am platform neutral — it doesn't matter to me whether people receive telecommunication services by cable, satellite, streaming, wires, wireless cable, or mental telepathy."*
>
> *— Rep. Tom Bliley, Chairman, Senate Commerce Committee regarding 1999 telecommunications network regulation*

*W*e can't help you create a futureproofed plan for mental telepathy, but we certainly can help you with the rest of the telecommunication services that Representative Bliley speaks of. (We'll just assume that mental telepathy falls into the wireless category.) Soon, your home network will enable you to do numerous things that you never thought were possible.

Neat Phone Tricks

When you define a phone in its historical sense — that is, a device with a handset and a base unit — lots of options are available to the home networker. You can

✔ **Go multiline:** Why install a second home-phone line that goes only to one phone? With the proper wiring, you could access that second line from any outlet in the house. Two lines not enough? How about three, four, or more lines?

✔ **Get distinctive:** How about giving all the members of the household their own distinctive ringing tones so that they know whom the call is for when the phone rings? You can use certain phone-company features along with your home-phone network to avoid buying extra phone lines for your household.

✔ **Get conferenced:** Though it may sound really corporate, consumer-grade conferencing systems make sense if the speakerphones of most phones don't do the trick.

✔ **Get transferred:** With a home-phone system, you can transfer calls around the house. Know that your spouse is in the garage? Send the call out there.

✔ **Intercom someone:** A home-phone system is a great way to get a home-wide intercom system. You can access different rooms by entering different extensions. And you can monitor rooms, too. By tying the system to your front door, you can have visitors leave a message on your phone system when you're not home.

✔ **Answer the door:** Use one of the new Doorcom systems to answer the door when you're away. These systems have a doorbell, speakerphone, and microphone, and with a smart home, they can call you where you're vacationing to let you speak with the person at the door through the telephone.

✔ **Get video:** With a videophone, you can see who you're talking to. (Depending on the time of day, that may or may not be a good thing.) Some videophones link up with your TV set for even better viewing but still use regular phone lines.

✔ **Go wireless:** A home phone is only as good as the length of its cord, but cordless phones give you freedom when you need to run all over the house. That's not new. But what is new is the convergence of cordless base stations with cellular or digital mobile phones. These so-called dual-mode phones allow you to talk all you want for free (at least no air-time charges) when you're near your base station, but they switch over to cellular or PCS frequencies when you leave your home. The phone — and your phone number — goes with you wherever you go. And lately, with the emergence of a lot of wireless 802.11b (a wireless computer network system) access nodes around the country and in homes, new multimode phones enable you to make free or low-cost calls over the 802.11b networks when they're in range — including at home.

✔ **Control your home network:** Some of the leading home-automation systems use the telephone as the interface to their system, using voice

recognition and tone input to drive things around your house. Imagine
calling your house and telling it to turn on the fire, turn down the lights,
and let your spouse figure out the rest!

✔ **Get some sleep:** You can program your home-telephone system to automatically route inbound calls to an answering machine without ringing
any of the phones in the house. Or you can selectively ring only certain
phones in certain places.

With the convergence of the computer and telephone realms, telephones
look and act more like computers, and computers work more like phones.
Some phones can send and receive e-mail as well as send faxes. Screen
phones allow you to do everything from home banking to grocery shopping
from the comfort of your nearest phone outlet. You can make phone calls
from your PC through a microphone and a headset, or watch the called party
on your computer screen. A properly designed home network will let you do
whatever you want with any of these devices.

Entertainment Everywhere

Your home-entertainment system can cost a lot of money, but when you go to
your bedroom at night, that stack of electronics equipment in the living room
is pretty much useless. A home network allows you to tap into that media
complex instead of duplicating it in each room. A great home network will
take that showcase of an entertainment center and distribute it around the
house. That makes each room a showcase.

A smart home allows you to

✔ **Roam the house:** Want to watch a movie on the living room VCR in your
bedroom or watch CNN while cooking dinner? By running your home
network to these rooms, you can distribute the audio and video signals
to these locations as easily as you route the signal to your TV set in the
living room.

✔ **Be flexible:** Want to watch the beginning of a movie-on-demand in the
living room but watch the end of the movie in the bedroom? No longer
are you a slave to where the device is located.

✔ **Be creative:** How about using the picture-in-picture capability of your
TV set to monitor the kids in the playroom while you're watching HBO?
By linking your video-monitoring capability with your television sys-
tems, you can have the best of both worlds.

✔ **Stay sane:** Want to listen to holiday music over your intercom system,
instead of blasting the stereo loud enough on the first floor so that you
can hear it in your office on the third floor?

✔ **Focus your investments:** By making the most use of the devices you have, you can focus future investments on only those pieces that enable you to take maximum advantage of your existing equipment. Already have a VCR, DSS receiver, tape deck, CD player, and receiver? Great, put your money into a great display or widescreen TV, and let those other devices drive the new video capabilities over the home network.

The technology has arrived that allows you to hang your high-quality, flat-panel TV set on the wall, perhaps over the fireplace. Moreover, this same TV set will be able to function as your computer screen and video monitor. The components of today's computers tend to be close together (generally sitting right on top of each other or at least taking up a general area of a desk), but in the future, computer components will be able to be separated from each other, communicating through a wireless connection. So you'll be free to sit in a comfortable place with your wireless keyboard.

Because video is such a critical feature of most households, it makes sense to make sure that you can maximize your pleasure through an entertainment network in your home.

Save Energy — and Money Too

When you network devices in your home, you build value. Part of that value is saving money. Following are some tasks that a smart home can perform that will save you money over the long term:

✔ **Motorize window coverings:** Large picture windows can hike the temperature of your house by several degrees, making the air conditioning work more often and harder — thus boosting bills. Motorized window coverings help keep your utility bills under control. Window coverings also save money by blocking out ultraviolet rays, which fade your upholstery and carpeting. You can control your coverings in many ways, including handheld remote controls, manual control from wall switch locations, timer controls, and even weather controls (for example, temperature sensors that close the blinds when it's hot or cold).

✔ **Control thermostats:** You can save up to 18 percent on your heating and cooling bills if you better coordinate your heating and air conditioning systems. You can set up thermostats so that temperature settings change based on the time of day and the day of the week. You can also change settings based on factors such as energy costs, the weather, and occupancy. (Schedule higher thermostat levels when areas are occupied.)

✔ **Control heaters and water pumps:** Hot-water heaters and hot-water circulation pumps are big consumers of power. To save power, turn them on and off according to a schedule.

✔ **Control gas usage:** If you're like Danny, you forget to turn off your gas grill, and it runs all night until the tank runs out of gas sometime during the next few days. Some advanced built-in grills for pools and outdoor terraces have sophisticated controls. If the grill has an electric component, it can be controlled. The same is true for gas fireplaces.

✔ **Manage when you're away:** When you go to work, you can tell your house to go into a user-defined away mode. This can mean closing drapes, lowering (or raising) temperatures, shutting off lights, and more. If you go away on vacation and leave lights on, your smart home can turn these on and off to better simulate someone being home.

Internet Outlets

For years, *getting connected* meant that you were having a phone line installed. Today, it means getting hooked up to the Internet.

The Internet is becoming commonplace all over the globe. No joke. You can watch people climb Mount Everest; the transmissions are coming live, from the mountain itself, compliments of the Internet. British millionaire Richard Branson was connected to the Internet from his balloon floating 25,000 feet high in the sky — allowing him to write blow-by-blow reports of his efforts to be the first to fly around the world in a balloon. The new Mercedes prototypes provide Web surfing through a monitor built into the back of the car seat. The Internet is everywhere.

A smart home turns electrical, telephone, cable, and other wired interfaces into Internet outlets — tunnels through your brick and mortar to the wired world beyond. And smart homes don't use just wireline access. They can be wireless, too.

With a smart home, you can

✔ **Network your computing resources:** Why have a printer at each home workstation when printers are not used that much? Share one printer, one scanner, and Internet access among multiple devices to save money and make your overall data LAN simpler.

✔ **Simultaneously access the Internet:** Work in your office downstairs, accessing the corporate internal network (intranet). Your spouse could be in the living room on the couch ordering groceries from the local grocery store's online Web site. Your 12-year old son could be upstairs in his bedroom playing Everquest on a multiplayer Internet network. And your studious 10-year old daughter might be accessing her school's extranet, working on homework with other kids. All this could happen at the same time, over the same network.

If you think you'll have a lot of people in your household accessing the Internet at the same time, you might want to consider getting a high-speed access option, such as a cable modem or DSL link. We tell you more about that in Chapter 13.

✔ **Make and receive phone calls through the Internet:** With the right end-point equipment, you can send and receive phone calls over the Internet. You make Internet phone calls with your PC, an adapter for your phone, an adapter for your fax machine, a videophone, or a special Internet telephony appliance (that essentially looks like a phone). Any of these things will allow you to communicate over the Internet, for free (or nearly so), with parties conceivably very far away.

The quality of your Internet telephony will vary substantially based on the type of device you use and the distance you're calling. The more hops that your data takes as it traverses the Internet, the more delay that can occur, causing poor quality.

The true benefits of Internet connectivity come later, when all sorts of devices expect Internet connectivity. More on this in Chapter 4.

Remote Control of Almost Everything

Another great thing about a smart home is the control that you have. Depending on the complexity of your home-automation system, you could control everything from the drapes to the heating system. A smart home allows you to add control later by tapping the endpoints, so you can start modestly.

With a home network, you can

✔ **Control your lights:** Simple X10 home-automation systems attach to the electrical system and allow you to control your electrical devices from a common computing platform. You can turn lights on and off and check out the heating levels in different zones.

✔ **Control your remote controls:** We hate to admit it, but one of us (we won't tell who) has *seven* remote controls in one room. Extending that functionality to other rooms in the house would require a lot of remote controls. But with a truly smart home, you can extend control over those devices to other rooms by radio frequency or infrared extension units, so that you maintain the same level of control that you'd have if you were in the same room. We recommend (at least one of us does) that you get a universal remote control for those rooms, however.

✔ **Control your computers:** One of the benefits of having connectivity to your various computers on the same network is that you can do things in a coordinated way. For instance, suppose you wanted to back up the computers on a regular basis. You can create a schedule on one computer and have it access the hard disks of the other computers on the LAN and create a copy of key files. A truly wired user will store these files off site, in case of fire or the theft of the machines. You can also coordinate new software upgrades as well as virus and junk e-mail protection. Being connected makes a lot of functionality possible in the computer realm.

✔ **Control your life:** Some home-management systems have automated enunciators that can tell you things you ought to know, such as today is your mother's birthday or the day to take out the trash. Linked with the Internet, telephone, or intercom systems, these commands can be sent to specific locations — such as catching you as you walk out the door.

"I've Fallen and I Can't Get Up!"

You don't just have to keep a smart home for yourself; you can share it with others. A smart home has something for everyone and can be tailored to the needs of special interests, such as the elderly, families with young children, or family members with specific disabilities. The great thing about having a strong smart-home foundation is that you can make it flex many ways depending on what you want to do. Here are some examples:

✔ **Turn on lights:** We joke about "Clap on, clap off," but we have to give the nod to the Clapper as one of the early moves toward home automation — after all, it's merely an occupancy sensor switch based on sound. The familiar Clapper has gone high-tech over the years and now includes clap indication lights to aid with proper clapping and a sensitivity dial to increase or decrease the Clapper's sensitivity to your unique clap. You can also program it to turn on when it hears any sound at all. This isn't good when you're home, but it's a great theft deterrent when you're at work or on vacation.

GPS: Where the boys are

Global Positioning System (GPS) is a location-finding system that can tell you where you are based on its capability to triangulate signals from three or more satellites that orbit the Earth. It can usually spot you within 10 to 100 meters of your location.

You're going to hear more about GPS. GPS capability is now being built into cars, cell phones, clothing, and more. GPS equipment and chips are used in amusement parks to help keep track of your kids. There are even fun games for kids based on GPS; for information about a treasure hunt game, for example, check out www.geocaching.com.

✔ **Watch your grandkids:** It's never been easier to have a video chat with your kids. No more fancy phone lines, special devices, and expensive software. All you need is a standard broadband connection (you can use dial-up lines, but you won't be satisfied), a $50 to $100 Web camera (we like www.logitech.com), and free software from any of a range of players, including Yahoo (messenger.yahoo.com). With Yahoo's Super Webcam, for instance, you can have great quality pictures.

The video picture frames refresh up to 20 frames a second, and the maximum resolution is 320 x 240. This is not quite TV-picture resolution, but it's getting there.

✔ **Talk to your doctor:** One of the leading manufacturers of implanted medical device, Medtronic, Inc. (www.medtronic.com), has developed a service that allows doctors to monitor patients at home. At the core of this offering is the Medtronic Monitor, a small, easy-to-use device that allows patients to collect information by holding a small "antenna" over their implanted device. The monitor automatically downloads the data and sends it through a standard telephone connection from anywhere in the 50 states directly to the secure Medtronic CareLink Network. Clinicians access their patients' data by logging onto the clinician Web site and make decisions at any time and from anywhere through an Internet-connected computer or laptop. Patients can view information about their devices and conditions on their own personalized Web site, and family members or other caregivers also can view this information if granted access by the patient. The Medtronic CareLink Network is intended to support a wide range of implanted cardiac devices — including Medtronic pacemakers, heart failure devices, and monitoring and diagnostic devices — as they become available following FDA approvals.

✔ **Get help now!** Surely you've seen the "I've fallen and can't get up!" commercials. This cuts to the heart of a major issue for those who are often alone at home: What if something happens and no one is around to help? Various firms (www.seniorsafety.com, for one) have put together a service that links a waterproof wireless transceiver (worn around your neck or wrist) with a central unit plugged into your phone jack and electrical outlet. When the button is pushed on the receiver, it contacts the central unit, which calls a 24-hour monitoring center. In about 40 seconds, they open a voice-to-voice channel to the central unit, which means they can speak back and forth with you from basically wherever you are in your home; you don't even have to touch the phone. (The central unit usually has a very loud speaker and supersensitive microphone).

✔ **See who's outside, and then let them in:** With a simple wireless camera and a link to your TV set, you can see who's knocking at the door, so you don't have to get up. And if you want to let them in without getting up, use your Kwikset Maximum Security Remote Keyless Entry System (http://www.kwikset.com).

"Sit, Ubu. Sit!"

Pets are a big part of any family, and if you ask us, they're just one of the family (although Pat needs to stop taking his dog out for ice cream all the time). A smart home doesn't care what species you are. Here are some neat things you can do for your pets. Some are networked; others are smart on their own:

✔ **Feed your pets when you're away:** From fish to cats to dogs, you can program automatic pet feeders to dispense food up to eight times a day, 7 days a week, 365 days a year. It's perfect for anyone who is not always on time to feed Rover, or who suddenly needs to take a trip.

✔ **Keep your pet wet:** Automatic drinking fountains continuously circulate and filter your pet's water, making it more appealing than standing bowl water. A charcoal filter absorbs tastes and odors. A pitcher-like spout stands five inches above the floor, creating a long waterfall. Other products can keep your pet's outdoor water bowl above freezing — hook the outlet to your temperature monitor and turn it on when it gets cold.

✔ **Let your pet out:** It's one thing to put a pet door into your house, but how do you keep other animals out? Smart pet doors today sense a magnetic key on your pet's collar and unlock to allow your pet to push through the flap.

✔ **Stop your dog from barking:** Is your neighbor's dog driving you crazy? Systems can detect dog barking and issue a humane and effective high-pitched tone that quiets noisy dogs without inflicting harm or pain. The tone doesn't cause pain to animals, but most dogs don't like it and will stop needless barking.

✔ **Stop those scratches on the doors:** Most dog or cat owners have a lot of scratched paint by the door, where Fido or Fifi wanted to be let out. Well why can't they just page you like most normal pets? They can, with a wireless door chime. When your pet steps on the paw-shaped pad, it signals a wireless chime to the speaker unit.

✔ **Keep your pet in the yard:** Some electronic dog fences work off of the principle of a small low-voltage wire that you string under the ground along your yard's perimeter; others are wireless. A sensor on your pet's collar issues a warning tone when he or she starts straying off your property. Soon, you'll have computer chips in your pet's collar that can interface with the Global Positioning System (GPS) so that you can look on your computer and see where your pet is.

✔ **Keep your dog warm (or cold):** Make your doghouse a zone on your HVAC system and keep it automated with the rest of your house. Put a floor warmer in the doghouse, and in cold weather, turn up the heat on that puppy, literally!

✔ **Keep your dog company:** We can't make any promises, but think of pairing your pet with a robotic one, and see if they hit it off. Robotic pets are in vogue now with names such as Tekno and Aibo (whatever happened to Spot and Rover?) We talk more about these in Chapter 22.

You can find smart pet-device sections at Smarthome, Inc. (www.smarthome.com).

Pool, Anyone?

Pools are great to have, a pain to have, and a worry to have. Pools provide fun under the sun, but have to be maintained. And if you have little kids around, a pool is a constant worry. A smart home can maximize your enjoyment and minimize your fears in the following ways:

✔ **Control your watery environment:** While a pool seems simple — it's just a hole in the ground with water — it can get quite complex, particularly if you add spa, waterfall, house and garden lighting, and other such amenities. Vendors such as Jandy (www.jandy.com) offer home-automation kits that can help you control filter pumps, pool and spa heaters, and many more electrically operated features with the push of a button. The system also allows for handheld wireless remote control access, telephone access, and PC access of all features driven by its system. It can also interface with any RS-232 "intelligent" home-automation system. (RS-232 is a communications protocol used by many computers and automation systems. See Chapter 20 for more information.)

✔ **Monitor water levels:** A low water level risks serious damage to your filter system and pump. Overfilling your pool wastes water and greatly reduces filter and skimmer effectiveness. A water level controller maintains water at the preset level. You just attach a garden hose, adjust the float level, and you're ready to go. Check out www.poolkeeper.com for one that's easy to install.

✔ **Use in-pool movement alarms:** A range of devices can alert you if someone falls in the pool. These protect kids and pets alike. (Pets find it difficult to climb out of pools.) Make sure that the alarm solution you select can be used with a solar blanket on the pool. Check out www.poolguard.com for its Pool Guard PGRM-2.

✔ **Use gate alarms:** All pools should be fenced, but the weakest link in a fence is the gate. A gate alarm mounts next to any gate that gives easy access to your swimming pool. The gate alarm has a delay switch that allows an adult to pass through the gate without the alarm sounding.

✔ **Get some turtles:** If you have a child, especially one aged 1 to 4, you need a turtle for your pool: a Safety Turtle that is, from Terrapin Communications (www.safetyturtle.com). Safety Turtle is a watchband-like water-sensitive device that transmits a special signal to its base station when the wearer comes into contact with water for a duration of time. Fencing and gate alarms aren't enough. If you want to talk to a professional installer who links these to your alarm system, e-mail Chuck at Engineered Solutions Corporation (chuck socorp.com) and ask him about his experience with the installation at Cory's house. If that story doesn't convince you to buy one, nothing will.

Safety Turtle is not just for kids. Pet owners buy them for their precious furballs, and spouses buy them for their elderly in-laws (in Florida, more elderly people die in pool accidents than kids).

✔ **Think about automatic pool covers:** Automatic pool covers eliminate water evaporation, seal in heat, and reduce pool equipment use. In fact, a good cover can act as a giant passive solar collector, and in combination with its thermal qualities, can raise the pool water temperature 10 degrees or more in season. This in turn can mean up to a 70-percent reduction in heating costs, chemical bills, pool pump electrical bills, and pool water bills. And you can link your pool-cover-control mechanism to your home-automation system to make sure that your pool is covered when it's not in use. No more Saturday mornings cleaning the pool. Check out www.poolsaver.com.

The great thing about a lot of the pool safety devices is that they can be integrated into your regular alarm and security system, including their monitoring and alert mechanisms. So if you're not at home and someone is in your pool, something can still be done about it. (Sorry, Pat, no more sneaking into the neighbor's pool!) Remember, though, none of these safety products replaces the need for adult supervision of all people in the pool area.

To Infinity and Beyond!

In the previous sections of this chapter, we describe things you can do today, to some degree. In this section, we want you to imagine what you'll be able to do with a home network in the near future.

Connect your kitchen appliances and more

Being interconnected will make it possible to use common consumer devices to do seemingly odd tasks. Here are some examples:

✔ **Check your e-mail on your refrigerator:** New, thin, touch-screen, flat-screen computer monitors will fit nicely into your refrigerator door — which is mostly insulation anyway — without compromising much. Add the appropriate computer chip and LAN access to the innards, and you have a heavy computer that also serves ice. Now you'll have a place to keep your shopping lists, send and receive e-mails, and maintain all your phone numbers.

✔ **Surf the Web on your microwave:** We have no idea why you'd want to use this feature, but trial products are on the market that allow you to surf the Web from your microwave. Waiting three minutes for your lunch to warm up can be a pain, but that's probably not enough time to check a Web site. Still, occupy your lunch-warming time with closing stock quotes, appointment reminders, weather predictions, school closings, and so on. Personally, we'd go with the refrigerator.

✔ **Tie your sprinkler system to** www.weather.com: Never get caught watering your lawn in the rain again! By tying your sprinkler to the Internet, you'll be able to check the weather predictions and let your sprinkler system decide whether to water the lawn as scheduled. During periods of high temperatures, the system may decide to water more frequently. And if you're in a drought area, it can forgo a cycle by monitoring bans on watering lawns.

✔ **Keep your car tuned:** Most new cars have computer chips that track the vehicle's health. Imagine driving into your garage each night and having a remote sensor interrogate your automobile about its day — and interact with remote databases and troubleshooting systems at your car's manufacturing facility. This system will be able to track your oil change needs and automatically schedule an appointment with your dealership. It will also be able to download to your car's hard disk the latest maps for your area, your updated calendar, and revised phone contacts for your car's cell phone.

✔ **Talk to your TV:** New technology coming out of the voice recognition industry will turn your home into *Star Trek*'s USS Enterprise. If your smart home has a microphone in each room, you can say, "Computer, put the incoming message on the screen," just like Captain Picard. (By the way, in case you haven't figured it out yet, our lives revolve around *Star Trek* and Disney World!) For more information on this brave new technology, check out the sidebar titled "A speech odyssey."

✔ **Stay healthy:** Interconnecting your kitchen with computer resources in your home and on the Internet will give you great access to all sorts of nutritional information and online recipe sites. Imagine tracking your diet on a device in your kitchen, and asking for a suggested dinner based on what you ate last week and what you have in the pantry right now. You'll be able to converse with your virtual chef to refine the menu given your preferences for the evening.

A speech odyssey

HAL2000 software, from Home Automated Living Company (www.automatedliving.com), will allow you to operate TVs, VCRs, CD players, tape players, and other household components just by ordering them around. HAL2000 uses its own speech-to-text software to send commands to designated devices. You can turn on lights, announce who's on the phone all over the house, and check your e-mail. If the system doesn't understand you, it prompts you to be more specific, with questions such as, "Did you mean a tape from the VCR or a tape from your audio tape player? . . . Dave? . . . Dave? . . ."

Let your TV show you the Web

Because people without computers are keen on using their familiar television interface to surf the Internet, manufacturers have been scurrying to bring the Web to your TV screen. A smart home allows you to directly access the Web through your TV set. The current technology works almost like a toggle switch — you can either view the TV or surf the Internet, but not necessarily at the same time (except maybe by using picture-in-picture capability). (This is what MSN TV, the new name for WebTV, does.)

What's coming down the pike is a wonderful combination of the two together, and the sky is truly the limit here. Here are some things you'll be able to do:

- ✔ **Click your favorite actor:** Ever watch a movie and say, "I know that actor from somewhere," and then for the rest of the movie try to figure out who the guy is? With these emerging TV/Internet technologies, you simply point to the actor and click his image to access his resume, complete with prior roles. Want to go to that actor's fan site? Click an icon designed for that purpose. Want to send the actor an e-mail? Click another icon. When your TV and the Web are connected, they can intertwine shows and databases to create awesome opportunities.

- ✔ **Click your favorite product:** Imagine watching a 30-second commercial and wanting to find out more about the advertised product. With converged TV/Internet products, you'll be able to click the product and go to a Web site that lists the product's features and characteristics. Click another place and see reviews from leading publications such as *Consumer Reports*. Click an icon and see the lowest prices for that product. Like the new gadget James Bond is using in his film? Find out where to buy one by clicking on it. The appearance of specific products on TV shows will change drastically, going well beyond the crass commercialism in *The Truman Show*.

- ✔ **Click Grandma:** Combine a small video camera and microphone with your TV monitor, and you create an instant videoconferencing opportunity. Using your smart home's data backbone, you'll be able to hop on the Internet and conference with others. Let Grandma share in your Christmas by enabling her to watch her grandchildren open their presents on the screen. Click your siblings, too, and have a family videoconference. What a great way to show everyone the new baby!

Make phone calls on your computer

You may not realize that your phone calls are really data calls. When you speak into your telephone, your local phone company most likely digitizes your call and sends it across its massive telephone network to either another phone locally or another local or long-distance carrier for completion. These telephone networks are carrying data — bits of your phone conversation.

So when people first started talking about carrying voice calls over data networks, many said, "What's new about that? Businesses have been doing that for a while." What is new is consumers having the capability to make calls from their computers.

You can buy most new computers with a multimedia configuration, which includes high-quality speakers, a video camera, and a microphone. Well, a telephone consists of a microphone and a speaker.

When you make a phone call, your words are converted into data bits and sent to your telephone company's network of computers. From there, your phone company may transfer the call from network to network until the signal reaches the person you're calling. New computers with their speakers and microphones work much like telephones; the Internet is a massive network. For the first time, consumers can combine the two technologies to make telephone calls from their home computers.

With the capability to make calls from your computer, you can do the following:

- ✔ **Have a home PBX:** A PBX (private branch exchange) or switch, which most companies use to run their phone networks, is like a mini telephone-company switch that allows can transfer calls from one extension to another, provide voice mail, do call parking, and so on. By running your home phones on your data network instead of your phone network, you can provide each handset with sophisticated features that you may not otherwise be able to afford. Some of the newest services on the market enable firms to extend their PBX functionality to employees' homes through high-speed, local-access connections. You could have one or more extensions at home that look and operate the same as at work, including allowing interextension dialing within the corporation.

- ✔ **Receive faxes on your TV:** Just like phone calls, fax transmissions are beginning to move to the Internet. You can buy equipment or services that translate faxed documents into digital Internet packets and send them over the Net. At the receiving end, you can choose to print the fax on a fax machine or receive the document as an e-mail attachment. When your TV becomes part of your home's Internet connection — and that will happen soon — you'll be able to preview and read your incoming faxes on your TV screen. (Later, you can print them over your home-computer network.)

- ✔ **Shop in Hong Kong:** Envision going to a booth at your local mall, having your body's dimensions scanned, and then using this information to shop anywhere in the world. No more too-short shirts! You'll be able to surf the Internet on your TV, find the outfits you want, choose the color and patterns, and then order a custom-fitted garment. You'll even be able to use your videoconferencing link or Internet telephony capability to talk with the tailors about your suit. In addition, many larger firms in the textile industry cut their garments using computer-driven lasers. Imagine having your scan feed directly into that!

Check on your house over the Net

Although home-automation systems have been around for a long time, they're still in their infancy. Most of the systems are either old technology (the inexpensive X10 systems) or expensive, custom-built systems.

However, we're starting to see home-control systems that integrate more fully into your data and telephone networks, enabling them to be controlled remotely. Right now, a few of the custom systems have a telephone interface that enables you to dial in and use the keypad (or even your voice in some instances) to issue commands to the system controller. The next logical step in this process is to provide a Web interface — and many are launching these services now.

Suppose that one of your home's PCs, using an always-on fast Net connection, also powers your home-control systems. This home-control software functions as a Web server to allow you to access your home-control system from your office desktop, an airport kiosk, or even your Web-enabled hand-held PC. You simply bring up the URL of your home server, log in, and then navigate through the home-control Web page to turn on lights, turn up the heat, or even fire up the hot tub. Pretty cool, huh?

Here are just a few of the tasks that this type of interface will be able to perform:

- **Control your appliances' usage:** More and more, companies will give you incentives to behave in certain ways. For instance, the power company may encourage you to run laundry at certain hours of the day. A smart home-automation system will be able to interact with the power company's pricing system to determine the best time of the day to do certain tasks, and then perform those tasks according to those schedules, if that's what you want. Power companies in some parts of the country already have different rate periods.

- **See-through walls:** Your home-network security system will include a video monitor for the front door, allowing you to see who's there before you open the door. By further interconnecting your security system with Internet access, you can monitor your home remotely, from any Web interface. Suppose that you're at work but think that someone sent an important, overnight package to your home office by accident. With this technology, you'll be able to call up your smart home's Web page and check out the video picture of your front stoop. If your hunch is correct, you can go home and get the package. You'll also be able to monitor your nanny from work, or make sure that the kids aren't throwing wild parties while you're away!

✔ **Turn up the heat:** With a good smart-home design, your telephone system will be interconnected with your heating and cooling systems, which will allow you to monitor and control those systems remotely. Going to go up to your smart vacation home for the weekend? With a remotely controlled home-automation system, you'll be able to call ahead and turn the heat on.

✔ **Check who's home alone:** Or have your system dial out to your own pager number when someone (maybe a burglar) enters the back door. With an interconnected system, almost anything is possible.

Chapter 4

Timelines and Budgets

. . . .

. . . .

*Y*our smart-home adventure starts in two places — in your head and in your wallet. You need to know where you're going and how much you're willing to spend to get there. In addition, you need to figure out how much of this project that you're willing to do yourself. All sorts of consultants, systems integrators, contractors, and others can help ensure smart-home success. This chapter helps you figure out when to use these folks and helps you determine the budgetary and timeline considerations involved.

New or Existing Home?

The most important issue when wiring your home is whether you have a new home or an existing one. We present all possible options in a home that you're wiring from scratch. But we also describe choices that you can pursue if a whole-home wiring solution isn't possible in all parts of your home.

Even if you have an existing home, wired solutions aren't necessarily out of the question. Contractors can snake cables through walls to install alarms, intercoms, phone systems, data networks, and automation systems. You may want to rely more heavily on wireless systems or ones that utilize existing wires. If you instead decide to run new wires, you should search for an experienced telephone or alarm installer who can find some creative ways to run and hide new wires without having to rip open walls.

What Do You Want from Your Home Network?

The first step in planning your home network is determining what you want it to do. Do you want a fully automated home, with lights that turn themselves on, drapes that open and shut on their own, and a remotely controlled HVAC (heating, ventilation, and air conditioning) system? Do you want a high-speed computer network that lets you plug a PC or laptop into a jack anywhere in the house and get Internet access? Do you want a sophisticated communications system, with multiple telephone lines, video monitors at the doors, and intercoms throughout your home?

Going for broke (literally) from the beginning is neither necessary nor wise. However, it is wise to use any wiring or rewiring opportunities (such as a newly constructed home or one that you're ripping apart for remodeling) to get enough wires to enough places to enable your home network to grow with your needs, without the hassle and expense of doing the wiring all over again.

Whatever you decide to do, it's best to install a home network all at once in a well-thought-out fashion. Home networking in a haphazard way results in, well, what most ad hoc do-it-yourselfers' wiring projects look like — a mess.

So before you begin designing a network and wiring plan for your home, think through how you're going to use each room in the home. Do so with an eye toward the future. Suppose that you have a spare bedroom that needs only a phone jack and a cable TV outlet. That room may be your home office some-day, in which case you'd need wiring for an extra phone as well as some com-puter networking capabilities. Or perhaps the room will turn into a nursery, so you'd want an intercom and maybe a video monitor. And when the kids get older, they may need a place to hook up a computer or plug in an entertain-ment system.

As you explore your many home-networking options, aim toward flexibility for the future.

Deciding How Much to Spend

Prewiring your entire home for every contingency may not be as expensive as you think. Several well-respected vendors offer all-in-one kits that put high-speed data communications, telephony, video, home entertainment, and (in some cases) security wiring in place with little or no thinking on your part. Check out Chapter 2 for more information on all-in-one cable solutions.

You can also apply the everything-everywhere solution and run high-speed data cables, coaxial video cables, and speaker cables to several jacks in every room of your home; many homeowners follow this route. (We don't think that fiber is worth the effort today — check out the "Fiber faux pas" sidebar in Chapter 2.)

Even though you'll be making choices about what you can do right now, don't forget about building a robust, futureproof wiring system into your home. In fact, running higher-quality, more capable wiring doesn't cost much more than running old-fashioned telephone and cable TV wires. And while you're at it, install conduits (mentioned in Chapter 2) to make running cables easier in the future.

One of the great things about building a smart home is that many of the network's components — wiring panels, cable runs, keypads, switches, and so on — are already part of the home's structure, which means that you can usually finance this cost as part of your mortgage. This option helps you stretch out the upfront cost of installing these systems.

Going Over the Costs

The cost of a home network varies depending on many factors, such as the costs in your particular area and how fancy you get. We can, however, provide general information about how much you can expect to spend. We base our prices on a typical home: two floors, three bedrooms, two-and-a-half baths, and a partially finished basement. To cover a larger area, you need to add the cost of extra wiring runs and some extra endpoints.

Most of the cost of an audio and video distribution system is in the audio and video equipment itself rather than in the networking infrastructure and components. Audio and video equipment is usually housed in the home-media center. (Part II explains this equipment in detail.) Here are some general costs:

- **Home theater:** A home theater can cost you as little as $1500 if you go with a moderate-sized TV set and a home-theater-in-a-box surround-sound audio system. A really great home theater runs $10,000 to $20,000. Installation costs about 10 percent of your component parts.

- **Coaxial distribution panel:** Expect to spend about $300 to $400 for a coaxial distribution panel for your home network.

- **Modulators:** The modulators that create in-home, video TV channels start off at about $150 for simple single-channel models and go up to about $800 for models that can create several channels of stereo TV for your in-home TV network.

Other networks in your home involve the following costs:

- ✔ **Phone system:** A phone system costs $50 to $100 per outlet or from $500 to $1500 for a centralized whole-home phone system.

- ✔ **Data network:** Data networks are relatively inexpensive — less than $200 to buy and install the necessary central components and about $50 to $100 per cable run, including cable, connectors, face plates, and so on.

- ✔ **Home-security system:** A home-security system averages about $1200 to install. You also pay about $25 a month for monitoring fees.

- ✔ **Home-automation system:** The cost of your home-automation system can vary widely. The cost to turn some lights on and off with a computer-controlled timer is much less than the cost to have androids serve breakfast in bed, for example. The average home-automation project costs around $1000.

Depending on what you need to do, you may be able to get away with paying less than this amount. But we'd rather scare you with big numbers first — while showing you all the ways that you can step down in price and still have a great home network — than throw unrealistically low numbers your way and set the wrong expectations.

Whatever you do, don't start the process by saying, "I don't want to spend a lot of money on this project." Instead, approach the process with an open mind: Think about what features you'd like to have, share that information with some home-networking experts, and see what happens from there.

The Home Team

The people involved in your project vary according to what you're trying to accomplish. If you plan to put a major home theater in your home — complete with theater seats, a popcorn and candy stand, and screen curtains — you'll probably bring a home-theater consultant into the process. Most people don't want or need to go to that level.

The cast of characters for your home-networking project can include the following:

- ✔ **Architect:** This person helps you lay out the initial plans for your home and coordinate with other designers to get their respective visions on paper. Architects create the plans that guide all the activity in the house, but they need the contribution of your individual contractors. Many architects don't have the level of specialty necessary to finalize your wiring plans, but the architect's drawings are key to making sure, for example, that all your speakers are correctly placed in your home-entertainment theater.

- **Audio/video consultant:** Your audio/video (A/V) consultant helps you select and the right mix of components for your sight and sound systems and then integrate all those components. Your A/V consultant makes sure that the appropriate wiring is run to support your installations and then installs the gear in when you're ready. If you're installing a dedicated home theater, expect your A/V consultant to get involved with the architect early on, too, making recommendations for room sizes, building materials, and so on. The A/V consultant may also hand you off to a specialized home-theater consultant if the job is too complex for his or her comfort. (Home-theater consultants get into additional details such as soundproofing, seating, lighting, and the room's shape and construction).

- **Contractor/builder:** The general contractor/builder's role is to direct the other specialty contractors and make sure that they carry out the intent of the designers. Passing correct information from one contractor (such as the home-theater consultant) to the people doing the work (such as the cabinetmaker who builds the home-theater cabinetry) is crucial. The details are what count here, such as cutting out the right size cubbyhole for the kitchen media center.

- **Computer-systems contractor:** If you work at home or have complex computer-networking needs, bringing in a computer-systems contractor to network your computer hardware and interface it to the appropriate systems can be a great timesaver.

- **Electrical contractor:** The electrical contractor is a staple of any new home project. Because your smart home may require additional or different electrical wiring (for example, special configurations in your electrical panel to allow home automation over power lines), hiring an electrical contractor who is experienced with smart homes is a plus.

- **Heating/cooling contractor:** Having a smart home is not just about having a home-control system that turns fans on and off. A smart heating and cooling system has many nuances, such as different zones for maximum control and specialized controls for specific areas (such as that wine cellar you were thinking about). Your heating/cooling contractor can make sure that your system is energy efficient while meeting your requirements.

- **Home-systems integrator:** This person integrates all the different electronic systems in your house but may or may not do the actual installations; specialists for each subsystem may do part of the work. The integrator should be able to provide your architect with recommendations regarding where to put your centralized wiring closet or where to run the wires for specific applications. The home-systems integrator also works with the interior designer to address layout and appearance issues.

- **Interior designer:** This person is responsible for making sure that your home-network technology doesn't stick out like a sore thumb. Installing a state-of-the-art home-entertainment center in the living room is one thing — making it fit with the overall scheme of your home is another. The interior designer works with your consultants to ensure that what is visible is pleasing to the eye.

✔ **Kitchen designer:** This expert helps you figure out not only a sensible layout for your kitchen but also your options for integrating the latest technologies into your smart-home design. This designer should work closely with the home-systems integrator.

✔ **Lighting consultant:** Often an overlooked task on a to-do list, lighting design has an important effect on the ambiance of your home, so consider specialized lighting in key areas. A lighting consultant works early on with the home-systems integrator and the architect to define the lighting control requirements and to select a system. The actual wiring, however, is typically handled by the electrical contractor or home-systems integrator — unless the lighting arrangement is complex, in which case a specialized lighting contractor may be called in.

✔ **Security consultant:** The security consultant and contractor design a system specifically for your home, and then install it. They make sure you have the right coverage to meet your security goals and ensure that the system interfaces with other subsystems, such as with telephone lines for calling out to the central station when a burglar trips a sensor.

Whew! Did we leave anyone out? Depending on the amount of money you want to spend, you may indeed have this many people making your smart home a reality. A more modest project has a more modest number of people stomping around your house. Also, many of the previously mentioned professionals — kitchen designers, for example — include their services when you purchase their equipment.

Make sure that you choose advisors who share your vision of an ideal smart home. The people you choose should have experience with smart, networked homes. Some contractors are conservative and don't want to overbuild. Others are liberal and plan for everything under the sun. Find your wired personality and match it with your contractors, and you'll have a winning combination.

You might have a hard time finding some of these contractors — it's not like the phone book has a section titled "Smart Homes" (at least not yet!). For the more traditional groups of professionals (such as architects), we tend to rely on word-of-mouth, recommendations from in-the-know friends, and a thorough review of the contractor's references. For contractors who will be installing your home's electronics and wiring infrastructure, we do these same things, as well as check their credentials. The Custom Electronics Design & Installation Association, or CEDIA, is one of the best places to start. This group (www.cedia.net) has a rigorous training and qualification program for people who do nothing but build and install smart-home systems for a living.

Starting Down the Smart-Home Path

Your first step in building your whole-home network is to visualize what you want. Then you need to sit down with your designers and consultants to refine your vision into a cost-effective reality. The following list is a rough timeline you can use as you're planning and building your wired home. Your timeline, however, may take half as long or twice as long:

✔ **Month 1:** Meet and interview various key consultants, and then hire your choices; visit demonstration rooms; visit libraries and bookstores for ideas and cappuccino. (By the way, you'll be doing great if you can keep this effort to only one month.)

✔ **Month 2:** If you're part of the 1 percent who can afford a custom-designed home, you're ready to sit down with your architect and start brainstorming the design. Plan to spend at least a month or two in this process. Then the architect or builder creates the plan with your specific needs in mind. Although it's early in the process, you may also want to choose an interior designer.

✔ **Month 3:** You make the final refinements to your plans. Typically, the architect draws up not only floor plans but also electrical wiring plans for key subsystems. Unfortunately, few architects will read this book before designing your system, so they may provide a standard plan. You need to find a home-networking specialist or work closely with the architect to describe the needs of each room and the system as a whole.

✔ **Month 4:** You request bids and select a builder; you finalize the budget and plans; you and the builder approve the detailed drawings of wiring schematics and special construction; the builder applies for and receives permits. These things may take more than a month, but we're optimists.

✔ **Month 5:** The lot is cleared; the foundation is dug; the security team is on hand to survey the site survey and external installations; the pipes and wiring are installed under the foundation; the foundation is poured.

✔ **Months 6-8:** The framing is finished; the windows and roof are installed; key consultants tour the site for revisions and planning; plumbing and heating contractors install their wiring, piping, and conduit. (If your new house is big or the weather is bad, this phase could take longer than two months.)

✔ **Month 9:** Both before and after the electrician does the electrical work, various contractors install data, telephone, security, audio, video, and other special wiring. The insulation goes in.

✔ **Months 10-12:** Sheetrock and plaster are installed; interior wood and finishing work begins, including any special cabinetry; the A/V contractor installs any in-wall speakers and intercom systems; the telephone/data systems team installs the data/telephone systems; the security contractor installs endpoint devices and the control system; the electrical contractor and lighting designer install lighting and controls; the plumber installs fixtures; the home-automation expert coordinates installation of the home-control system.

✔ **Month 13:** Final construction work on the interior of the house; subcontractors finish their installations; testing; system checks. You're probably closer to month 18 by now, and you've probably blown your budget by a bit. But the important part is to make it through alive and with your marriage intact.

Don't forget about the building inspector. The best-laid plans can succumb to a busy building inspector whose approval is often required to go to the next stage of your multistage project.

You do need to coordinate what kind of cables will be installed in any special conduits placed to make running wires easier. For instance, running electrical wiring in the same conduit as your telephone, data, or A/V wiring is a bad move because electrical lines create electromagnetic flux that ruins your data and video throughput, not to mention your phone calls. Installing electrical cables adjacent to other cables is surprisingly common in many new-home construction projects, so look out for it.

After all the rough-in work is complete (and wires are all over the place), the sheetrock and other wall coverings go up. Although some items, such as in-wall speakers, go in before all the finish work is complete, much of it goes in only after everything else is just about finished. You attach all your components to their connection points, and install the control panels.

After the rough-in work and wiring is finished but *before* the sheetrock goes up, use a video or digital camera to document what wires are running where (including where the empty conduits start and stop. Some day you might need to add a cable to a conduit, or fix a wire that a rodent ate through (yes, they do that; and yes, we're talking about rats; and yes, depending on where you live, you can get rats in your house, no matter how often you clean the kitchen and take out the trash).

Testing can be exhaustive, but you can never test too much before accepting a house from your collective of contractors. Make sure to hook equipment to all your outlets and test, test, test.

Part II

Making Your Home an Entertainment Center

The 5th Wave   By Rich Tennant

"Would it ruin the online concert experience if I vacuumed the mosh pit between songs?"

In this part . . .

Face it: The television is a major focus of almost any home, worldwide. In our business, we've traveled all over the globe. We've seen tents in the desert with camels parked out back, dinner cooking over a fire, and a TV set inside. People like and want their video. Those enamored with audio feel just as strongly.

The key is building your home-entertainment system so that you can enjoy it everywhere you want to — not just in the confines of a particular room or a particular space. Your home-entertainment system should be in the whole home, omnipresent to the point of total flexibility.

In this part, we tell you how to create a home-entertainment backbone in your house. We discuss all the major elements of a whole-home audio and video network and the advantages of connecting all multimedia elements together. We talk about the different inputs and outputs required, as well as some tips and tricks for ensuring the success of your home-entertainment system.

Chapter 5

Breaking the Entertainment Bottleneck — Without Breaking the Bank

*M*ost homes contain a plethora of entertainment equipment — televisions, radios, CD players, stereo receivers, and so on. (If you're like us, you also have a turntable sitting prominently on a shelf someplace.) People tend to think of home-entertainment gear as stuff that's used in a particular room — a stereo in the living room, televisions in the family room and bedroom, and maybe a radio in the kitchen.

The best home-entertainment system is a network that leverages your investments in expensive audio and video equipment and lets you enjoy it wherever you are in the home. You put the bulk of the equipment in a common media center (like a home-theater room), and then set up a suitable network infrastructure (wired or wireless or something else) to distribute the audio and video. In this chapter, we discuss the components you need to set up a home-audio and -video network.

TV and Video Systems

This section looks at some of the radical changes that television is undergoing — and we're not talking about programming. Like most other devices before it, the television is beginning to make the leap from the analog to the digital world. Unlike many of those devices, however, TV is making the leap in a series of agonizingly slow steps. We discuss how this transition might affect your choices in the video world. We talk also about the various kinds of TVs you can buy.

The conversion from analog to digital and old-style TV to next-generation TV comes into play in many places:

- ✔ The encoding of the programming signal itself
- ✔ The transmission path that the signal takes in getting to your house
- ✔ The receiver — internal or external — that receives and decodes the signal for display

In the progression of standards and technical development, change is taking place along all three of these paths.

Analog still rules the roost (for now)

The vast majority of television signals coming into homes are still analog. Analog TV signals reach homes through over-the-air broadcast TV, by traditional cable TV systems, and by satellite. (We discuss all the different ways TV signals get into you house later in the chapter.)

In North America, an analog system known as NTSC (National Television Standards Committee) has been in place for decades — in fact, it hasn't been changed or updated since the advent of color television in the 1960s. Although this system is capable of producing a surprisingly good picture under ideal circumstances, its analog nature makes it susceptible to various kinds of interference and signal degradation. Consequently, the picture can be downright awful by the time it actually gets to your television (which is why the TV world is slowly turning digital).

There's not much we need to tell you about analog TV — if you've turned on a television in the past fifty years, you've seen it.

Just as the NTSC standard is common in North America (and Japan), a couple of other standards — known as PAL and SECAM — are common in other parts of the world. Unless you have a special TV designed for the purpose, you can't watch PAL with an NTSC TV, and so on. This is one reason why you can't buy videotapes in many parts of the world and use them at home.

Digital is (part-way) here!

The move from analog to digital is well afoot. Millions of homes have some form of digital TV, but the conversion from analog to digital is still an evolving process. The key concept behind any kind of digital TV is that the audio and video programming is converted from an analog signal into a series of digital bits (a whole lot of ones and zeros that make up a video picture). The primary technology behind any kind of digital TV (at least in the United States and Canada — other countries have their own variant of digital TV) is something called MPEG.

Several video and audio compression and digitization standards are based on *MPEG* (Motion Picture Experts Group). Most are named by adding a number to the end of the word *MPEG*. The MPEG-2 standard is by far the most common in the video world, with MPEG-4 coming on strong.

The digital television that people receive today uses MPEG-2 to carry standard, analog NTSC TV signals digitally. This is an important fact to repeat: Typically, a digital signal is not carried via digital transmission. Digital over digital is our nirvana and is coming soon, as we discuss shortly.

When this digitized signal gets to your house (over a digital cable system or a DBS satellite system), a set-top box converts the signal back to analog NTSC TV, which your TV understands and can display. This digital signal coming into your house isn't inherently different than an analog one, but it usually looks and sounds better because the digital transmission path is cleaner and isn't susceptible to the interference that usually messes up analog signals.

Next-generation digital TV

Today's digital television isn't all it can be. Several years ago, the FCC (the controlling regulatory authority for broadcasters, cable companies, and telephone companies in the United States.) brought together a big bunch of television industry folks and — after a long, painful, and contentious process — came up with a new generation of digital TV. This new system, which goes by the name *ATSC* (Advanced Television Standards Committee), had defined a bunch of new, higher-definition television standards.

Specifically, digital-video signals (not analog ones) are transmitted using digital technologies and played on TVs set up to display these digital signals. It's digital all the way, baby, as sportscaster Dick Vitale would say. (Did we mention we're Duke Blue Devils fans, too!)

These new higher-definition television standards are different than the digital TV discussed in the preceding section. To view them in all their glory (and we've seen enough of high-definition television to tell you that it is indeed glorious), you need to buy the newer, fancier, better, more expensive TV.

ATSC signals can be divided into different groups, depending on the resolution and the scanning method (as we discussed in the "What's different about ATSC?" sidebar). They are further divided into SDTV, or standard-definition television (signals that are about the same or a little bit better than NTSC), and HDTV, or high-definition television (which has truly spectacular, film-like, picture quality). Within the ATSC standard are dozens of SDTV and HDTV variations, but you're most likely to see just three, as shown in Table 5-1.

Table 5-1		Common Digital-TV Variants	
Name	*Lines of Resolution*	*Scanning Method*	*Quality*
480i	480	Interlaced	Standard definition (same as NTSC)
480p	480	Progressive	Standard definition
720p	720	Progressive	High definition
1080i	1080	Interlaced	High definition

To take advantage of all the benefits of digital TV, you'll eventually have to replace your televisions. Today's televisions don't have the internal circuitry to decode digital TV signals, and they generally don't have screens that can display high-definition ATSC pictures in all their glory. (And HDTV is the big deal in this story — we focus our discussion on HDTV rather than SDTV.)

Today's TVs aren't even the right shape; the *aspect ratio* — the ratio of screen width to height — of HDTV signals is wider than that of NTSC signals. NTSC is 4:3; HDTV is 16:9. Figure 5-1 shows the difference in aspect ratios — the HDTV screen has an aspect ratio like the elongated screens in movie theaters. (You may have already been exposed to this aspect ratio because many movie DVDs today allow for this sort of viewing as an option.)

Figure 5-1: An HDTV screen is this much wider than today's NTSC screen.

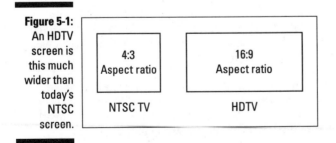

4:3
Aspect ratio

16:9
Aspect ratio

NTSC TV

HDTV

What's different about ATSC?

When we talk about new ATSC-based televisions, we're talking a whole new ballgame (or at least a whole new way to watch a ballgame). It takes only a glance to see the striking difference between older NTSC displays and the new ATSC ones.

In general terms, the clarity and crispness of a television's display is determined by the resolution, the scanning refresh rate, and the scanning method.

You may be familiar with the concept of *resolution* if you own a PC, because PC displays are usually rated in terms of their resolution, or more specifically, the number of *pixels* (individual points of light and color in the display) that you can see. For example, smaller home-PC displays are set to show 800 pixels across by 600 pixels vertically; larger displays are often set to show 1024 across by 768 vertically.

Television manufacturers don't usually mention the number of pixels across the screen, but they do list the vertical number — the *lines of resolution,* or scan lines. Today's analog TV systems usually max out at 480 lines of resolution (and you don't even receive all 480 — a few lines carry other information such as closed captioning). ATSC systems can broadcast at 480, 720,

on up to 1080 lines of resolution. When looking at two screens of the same size and quality, the more lines of resolution, the better the picture.

The other factor in determining the quality of a television or video signal is the *scanning method.* People generally talk about PC monitors and video systems in terms of their screen refresh rates — often using a number such as 75 hertz. This figure means that the picture on your PC's video screen is updated 75 times every second. When talking about televisions, people discuss the scanning method to illustrate the same principle.

TV puts an interesting twist on the scan line refresh rate, however. A TV with a *progressive scan display* refreshes *all* of its lines of resolution (480 or 720 or 1080) during a cycle. (TVs refresh at a rate of 60 cycles per second — for comparison, film movies do so 24 times a second.) Other TVs offer *interlaced scan display,* which means that they refresh half the screen — every other line — each cycle, so each line is refreshed only 30 times per second. Theoretically, a progressive scan system has a better picture than an interlaced one, but because both refresh the picture many of times per second, the difference isn't immense.

HDTV-capable TV sets, which became available at the end of 1998, are more expensive than traditional sets. However, prices have come down significantly. When we wrote the first edition of this book, HDTVs were often more than $6000, but now you can get one for $1500 or less.

Two types of digital HDTVs are available: HDTV-ready TVs and HDTVs. HDTV-ready televisions have only a standard NTSC receiver; they have no built-in digital television receiver. However, you can connect them to an external HDTV receiver and display high-definition programming. The second type, HDTV, has a built-in receiver (or at least comes with an HDTV receiver that you hook up externally), so there's nothing more to buy to receive over-the-air HDTV. Many HDTV receivers can work as DSS receivers (that can receive satellite TV signals) and let you view HDTV programming from providers such as DirecTV (as we discuss in the next section).

We think it's better to buy an HDTV-ready TV — you save a few hundred bucks, and then you can buy a receiver that works best with the system that provides HDTV (that is, an over-the-air antenna, digital cable, or satellite).

TV types

For a long time, televisions have been pretty much identical, except for differences in their internal electronics and the quality of their construction. The advent of technologies from the computer world and the desire of many consumers to build home theaters that use large-screen TVs have dramatically altered this situation.

We've already talked a bit about digital TVs and HDTV. Now we're going to talk about three different forms of TVs (direct-view, projection, and flat screen). None of these TV styles are inherently analog or digital — a specific model within each of these groups can be analog only or HDTV and digital compatible. Having said that, almost all projection and flat-panel TVs on the market today are HDTV-ready.

Tubes for all: Direct-view TVs

The traditional television — or a video display of any kind, for that matter — has always been the direct view, picture-tube type. The screen you see is actually the front of a specially treated glass tube with an electron gun built into the back of the tube. This system works by shooting electrons through electronically controlled devices and onto the back of the picture tube's screen. When the electrons hit the specially treated glass, it lights up in different colors and intensities (depending on how the electrons are aimed) and creates your picture.

Tubes are a mature technology — having been on the market in large quantities for about 50 years — and they work pretty darn well. They do, however, have a few disadvantages:

- They're big (in depth) and heavy (ever try to move a 35-inch television?).

- The technology itself limits screen size (very few direct-view televisions are larger than about 40 inches measured diagonally).

- Large picture tubes with electron guns sophisticated enough to handle HDTV's high resolutions are difficult to build (several makers have such models on the market, but they don't offer the full 720 or 1080 lines of resolution needed for real HDTV).

When will HDTV really be here?

Where are you going to get your HDTV programming? (And yes, we want our HDTV!) As we hinted, the three possibilities are the same places where you get NTSC today: over-the-air broadcasters, cable TV systems, and satellite TV systems.

For broadcast TV, the FCC gave (for free) each broadcast TV station the requisite additional broadcast spectrum for a different channel over which they could broadcast in ATSC digital format. The deal was this: The TV stations had to completely transition to digital by 2006, and then give the FCC their old channel so it could be assigned for other uses. Because HDTV is waaaay behind where everyone thought it would be, it's a fair bet that the date will be extended. In the summer of 2002, the FCC, trying to push this process along, made a ruling that every TV sold in America must have a receiver that can get ATSC broadcasts by 2007. Keep in mind, this doesn't mean that these TVs will be able to display HDTV (for example, they may not have a high enough resolution, or they may not be able to display widescreen content properly), but they will be able to receive it and display it at lower resolutions and at a 4x3 aspect ratio. Eventually, when enough of these TVs are in people's homes, analog TV as we know it will go away, replaced by SDTV and HDTV.

So far, there have been no requirements for cable and satellite companies to offer ATSC signals, but each have begun offering a few channels of HDTV to go along with their existing programming. As the number of HDTV-ready TVs grows, and demand grows along with it, they'll probably offer more. However, most non-movie and non-sports programming will probably end up being SDTV rather than HDTV because HDTV takes up a lot of bandwidth on these companies' networks — and bandwidth is scarce for them.

After the switch to digital TV is complete, you won't have to pitch your old TVs. Digital TV tuners, like those that the FCC is requiring in new TVs, will allow you to watch DTV programming on older TVs. Of course, the picture quality and resolution won't be as high as it would be with a new digital set, and you might not have a widescreen (16x9) aspect ratio.

Although sales of projection and flat-screen TVs will take off in the next few years, we're confident that picture-tube TVs will remain the standard for quite a while.

Projection TVs

After you move beyond pretty large big-screen TVs (35 inches or so) to really huge, oh-my-goodness big-screen TVs, the form of the television changes from direct-view to projection, or *PTV*. Projection TVs come in two main types, as shown in Figure 5-2:

- **Front-projection models:** These high-end models consist of a projector mounted on the ceiling and a separate screen. Like a movie projector, these models project the TV video onto the front of the screen.

- **Rear-projection models:** The screen and projection systems are in the same chassis in these all-in-one units. Like a direct-view TV, these models beam the TV image onto the back of a screen.

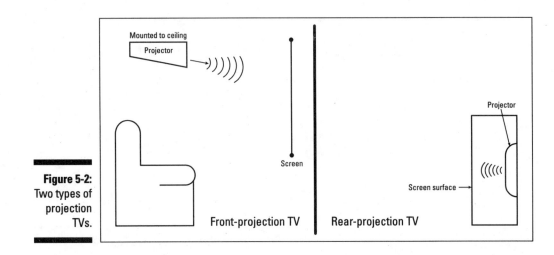

Figure 5-2:
Two types of
projection
TVs.

The cheapest rear-projection models cost between $1000 and $2000. High-quality, front-projection models cost up to $20,000 or $30,000 for the projector alone (not to mention the cost of the screen and professional installation, alignment, and focusing).

One neat trend for projection TVs (used mainly for front-projection models so far) is based on a new technology developed by Texas Instruments called Digital Light Projection *(DLP)*. This system uses a complex computer chip with thousands of tiny mirrors (rather than a moving cathode ray or thousands of LCDs) to reflect and project the picture. If you saw *Star Wars Episode II* in a "digital" theater, you most likely saw the theater-sized version of this chip in action. Video experts say that the quality of home-DLP projectors isn't quite up to that of the finest CRT-based projectors, but it is very good, and the technology has already brought the cost of front-projection models down to the sub-$4000 mark.

We believe that these models will remain popular for home-theater rooms but probably won't be widely used anywhere else in the home. Most folks don't need a television that big in the kitchen or bedroom.

Hang your TV on the wall: Flat-screen TVs

The really hot item in the TV world today is the flat-screen TV. Similar to the screen of a notebook computer stretched to previously unimagined proportions, these new TVs use computer technologies such as LCD (liquid crystal diode) and plasma display systems to provide a large-screen television system that is usually only four or five inches deep. Several models of these TVs are on the market.

You can find flat-screen TVs at big home-electronics stores and warehouse clubs. The first models were super expensive, often costing $12,000 to $15,000. Since several major Asian consumer electronics manufacturers entered the game, prices have come down rapidly. Some smaller (42-inch) models retail for $3500 or less, but this is still about twice as much as a direct-view TV of the same size.

Many consumer electronics companies have taken advantage of the low prices of LCD displays to build inexpensive (about $1000), small, personal LCD-based flat-panels displays. These units are usually less than 20 inches diagonally and are designed to be used in the bedroom, kitchen, den, or motor home. (In other words, they're too small to be the primary TV.) What's neat about these smaller displays (and many of the larger ones as well) is that they can be used not only as televisions but also as large computer screens, so they can do dual duty as TVs and remote display units for your home's networked PCs.

If you're considering buying a flat screen, keep in mind that the same amount of money buys you a bigger and better picture from the best projection TV. However, nothing is cooler than hanging your TV on the wall.

Video source components

Video source components are the magic black boxes that let you record or watch movies, play games, watch the baby, or even surf the Web on your home's televisions. A huge number of video source components are on the market (and probably already in your home), including the following:

- ✔ VCR (videocassette recorders)
- ✔ PVR (personal video recorder), such as ReplayTV and TiVo, which uses a hard drive to record, store, and play back video
- ✔ Laserdisc player (rare, but not quite gone yet)
- ✔ DVD (digital versatile disc or digital video disc) player
- ✔ In-home video devices such as a doorbell camera or a video baby monitor
- ✔ Video game machine
- ✔ Web-enabled TV set-top box (device that lets you use your television to surf the Web)

Most folks tend to view these kinds of video source devices as dedicated, one-room components. If you want to watch a movie on the DVD player, for example, you go to the room that has the DVD player. In a properly net-worked home, however, you can connect your video source devices to your video network and use them from any TV in the house. (We show you how in Chapter 6!)

Serving up media

Over the past few years, the world of PCs and home-video and -audio entertainment components have mixed in an exciting way. You can put a TV-tuner card in your PC and watch cable on it, or you can plug the PC into your TV and use its DVD player, online streaming video player, and MP3 jukebox to play back material on your audio/video network's big screen and good speakers. Perhaps the neatest development of all, however, is the rise of PC technology–based *media servers* that store videos, music, digital pictures and other content on a hard drive, and then connect to both your PCs and audio/video systems. With a media server, you can watch videos, listen to audio, and look at any of your digital pictures on *any* of the display devices or networked audio systems you have in your house.

ReplayTV and TiVo — the PVRs — are a great example of the current generation of media players, as are the multitude of MP3 audio jukebox devices that can store your CD collection on a computer hard drive. This initial generation of media servers sits next to your TV or audio amplifier and plays back media over that local connection — much like a DVD player or CD player does today. Request (www.request.com) uses the TV as the interface to these media servers and allows remote servers to synchronize so that you never have to worry that your favorite song is on the other server. But like stand-alone players, media servers can be incorporated in your home-entertainment network so you can use them anywhere in the house.

Hitting the streets is a new generation of media servers that are network-ready and can store all types of media. Those from Sony and Toshiba let you centralize the storage of video, audio, and photos, and then use your data network — even a wireless data network — to get the media files to TVs, speakers, and PCs around the house.

You can also build your own media server, using a fast PC with a big hard drive, the proper audio and video cards, and some specialized software. We talk about creating these PCs in Chapter 12.

TV Connections from the Outside World

An important part of television is its capability to bring programming into your home from the world beyond. Like televisions themselves, these connections to the outside world are undergoing a series of major changes. New ways of receiving programming are becoming common, and established methods are revamping themselves for a digital world.

Broadcast TV

In spite of the proliferation of cable and satellite television and compact discs, old media such as broadcast television and radio are still alive and kicking. In addition, increasing consumer acceptance of DBS satellite television systems has resulted in a resurgence of demand for run-of-the-mill television antennas. Why? Unless you live in a big city, these systems don't carry programming from the big networks or local stations. If this scenario sounds familiar, you need to keep some level of cable television service or buy an antenna to watch local news or the local weather report.

Luckily, television antennas have improved, so without spending too much money, you can avoid the nightmare of fine-tuning a set of rabbit ears on top of your television. The two general categories of television antenna are

- ✔ **Indoor antennas:** These antennas sit on or near your television.
- ✔ **Outdoor antennas:** These antennas mount on your roof or alongside your DBS satellite dish.

Whether your television antenna is outside or inside, you have to connect it to the TV. Most modern antennas use the same coaxial cable that cable television and DBS satellite systems use. (See Chapter 7 for strategies for wiring antennas into your video network.)

Cable TV

The prevalence of cable service nationwide makes it an important part of any home-networking strategy — both for you and future owners of your home. And with the range of services offered by cable companies, you can get a lot more than television (Internet access and even telephone service, for example).

The operation of a cable system is straightforward. A central office, or *head-end site* (similar to the central equipment office of the telephone company), receives television signals from various sources (mainly from satellite feeds, as well as local over-the-air broadcasts). Cable companies then assign the signals to specific channels and distribute them over a combination of fiber-optic and coaxial cables (which, coincidentally, make up the final portion of the network that enters your home).

The channel system for cable is different than the one for over-the-air broadcast television. Therefore, the frequency of, say, Channel 20 on a cable system is likely different than the frequency of Channel 20 in a broadcast environment. What this difference means to a you as a homeowner is that you can't plug your cable TV feed into the back of any old television and expect it to work. Instead, you have two options:

- ✔ **Cable-ready television set or VCR:** You select a cable mode and then use the internal television tuner to decode and display the television signals. Most TVs made in the last few years are cable-ready, so all you have to do is plug the coaxial cable into the back of the TV and you're set (after you run through the set-up routines to set the time, add the channels, and so forth).

Note: Cable-ready TVs do have a few disadvantages. Most of these sets can receive only a limited number of channels. Second, these sets probably can't take advantage of special services from the cable company, such as digital cable, premium movie channels, and pay-per-view programs.

✔ **Set-top box (or converter):** These devices use a single broadcast channel (usually Channel 3 or 4) to feed the cable television signals to your television. With your television tuned to that single channel, you channel-surf through the set-top box. For digital cable services, which we discuss in a moment, you *must* use a set-top box.

These set-top boxes, which your cable service provider furnishes for a monthly fee, are becoming increasingly sophisticated. Most cable providers now offer a digital service, with two-way communications from the head end to the box and back again. The fancy set-top boxes used with these services have lots of extra built-in features, such as an onscreen program guide, reminder timers, VCR timers, and hard drives to store shows online for later viewing. As an aside, this is an example of competition at work: When we wrote the first edition of this book, only DBS satellite systems offered this kind of neat TV functionality, but the cable companies responded to the threat and now match the DBS providers feature for feature.

Most digital television signals sent over digital cable systems (which aren't even all the channels you get — lower numbered channels are still sent in analog) are *not* ATSC, SDTV, or HDTV signals. They're just NTSC signals transmitted digitally. A few cable companies are sending a few HDTV channels to their customers, but most channels are still old-fashioned NTSC.

Satellite TV

Millions of homeowners are cutting the cord to cable TV and installing satellite TV receivers. Satellite TV, especially the new, small-dish varieties, can provide high-quality video programming — with more channels than all but a handful of cable systems — to homes just about anywhere in the world.

Direct broadcast satellite TV

If you look around your neighborhood, you've no doubt noticed a profusion of small (18 inches to be exact), white or gray satellite dishes popping up on housetops. These are receiving dishes for direct broadcast satellite (DBS) television.

Here's what you get when you choose DBS:

✔ **Channels galore:** Depending on which service and service level you buy, you can get hundreds of channels.

✔ **Digital quality:** DBS systems use MPEG-2 to transmit channels digitally, reducing interference. The majority of these channels are NTSC, not ATSC. Also, as with digital cable, a few of the channels are in HDTV.

✔ **Audio channels:** Plug into your stereo or home theater for audio-only programming.

✔ **Easy-to-use graphical interfaces:** Easy-to-view menus, with telephone-line access to providers for pay-per-view programming.

✔ **Internet access:** With a slightly different dish, you can also have high-speed Internet access, as we discuss in Chapter 13.

As with everything, DBS has some downsides:

✔ **You might not get local programming:** In rural parts of the country, you still need a broadcast antenna or basic cable television service to view local channels and local news as well as the broadcast (FOX, ABC, NBC, and CBS) programs.

✔ **You need a receiver:** The receiver acts like a digital cable converter box, and converts the satellite's digital television signals to signals that your television can understand. If you have more than one television, you may want additional receivers for each TV because, like a cable converter box, the receiver puts out only one channel at a time. (We tell you how to share a single receiver with multiple TVs — but keep in mind that you'll be watching the same thing on each set).

✔ **You need a free telephone line:** The receiver must be plugged into a telephone line to communicate with the DBS provider's headquarters for billing and service provisioning. This can be your normal phone line, because the system typically talks to headquarters in the middle of the night when most of us are asleep. Digital cable, however, talks back to the head end over the cable line, so it doesn't need that extra phone jack.

✔ **You need to be able to "see" the satellite:** You may have a hard time getting a satellite signal if you live in areas far away from the satellites' orbits. If you live in upstate Maine, for instance, you may have more problems getting an EchoStar signal than a DirecTV signal because of the satellite's physical location. (In some cases, the dish has to be aimed so low towards the horizon that mountains and atmospheric clutter can get in the way.)

✔ **You have to install the system:** The system isn't hard to install, but something about getting up on the roof conjures up visions of back surgery. Of course, you can mount the dish on the side of your house or put it in the yard. One company even makes nifty fake rocks that cover the dish and keep your neighbors happy. And a growing number of companies will do the installation for free.

When we wrote the first edition of this book, DBS systems had a huge advantage over cable in terms of features and quality. As we mentioned earlier in this chapter, cable companies have reacted to this competitive threat, and now digital cable systems provide most of the same bells and whistles: digital transmission (of at least some channels), onscreen programming guides, music channels, and so on. We like both systems. Compare prices and features in your town before you decide. One new feature is *video on demand* (VOD), which lets you watch movies (for a fee) like you watch VCR tapes and DVDs — you can pause, rewind, and fast forward. This feature is more prevalent (for technical reasons) with digital cable than with DBS, but DBS providers are experimenting with built-in PVRs to allow a similar service on their networks.

Two competing DBS systems are currently on the market in the U.S. Compare prices and services and choose the one you like best. As we write this, DirecTV and EchoStar have agreed to a merger and are just awaiting regulatory approval. So don't be surprised if there's just one "choice" when you go shopping.

- **DirecTV:** DirecTV (www.directv.com) uses an 18-inch dish and the digital MPEG system to send its audio and video signals. A variety of companies manufacture the widely available DirecTV hardware — and some TV manufacturers incorporate DirecTV receivers into their high-end TVs.

- **EchoStar, or the DISH network:** EchoStar (www.dishnet.com) is similar to DirecTV, using an 18-inch dish and digital MPEG encoding technology to transmit its video and audio. EchoStar sells their own receivers.

If you live in Canada, you're prohibited from getting DirecTV or EchoStar service. These are legal prohibitions, not physical ones, because the satellite signals cover much of Canada. Bell Canada offers a similar system called ExpressVu (www.expressvu.com).

C Band

The grandfather of today's DBS satellite television systems is the C Band satellite system — those huge satellite dishes that used to sprout up like monstrous mushrooms. At about 7 feet across, the average C Band dish is expensive and difficult to place. Zoning restrictions keep C Band dishes out of many suburban areas, so you tend to see them only in rural areas. Still, in the early 1980s, having one of these dishes in your backyard meant that you could pick up all sorts of channels from all over the world. Unfortunately, many of the channels that C Band systems once picked up for free are now encrypted, so you must subscribe to a service to receive them.

The advent of DBS and almost universal access to cable television has severely limited the growth of the consumer C Band marketplace. These days, most C Band users are either satellite hobbyists or businesses, such as hotels. Many television networks and cable systems also use C Band systems to distribute programming.

Satellites and your home

If you decide to go with a satellite dish, you may run into some resistance from homeowner's associations, neighborhood covenants, zoning laws, and the like. Don't take this lying down — the FCC ruled in 2001 that these laws can't be used to prevent you from installing a small dish (not a big C-band seven footer!). The only big exceptions are for safety (for example, you can't be too close to a power line) and for those homes in historic districts. Otherwise, no one can keep you from using a dish if you want to. Know your rights (and look online at `http://www.fcc.gov/mb/facts/otard.html` for the actual, long-winded bureaucratese text of this ruling).

C Band refers to the chunk of frequency spectrum allocated to these services. DBS satellite systems use the Ku band — though only hard-core satellite techie types call them Ku band systems.

Audio Systems

The other piece of the entertainment puzzle is an audio system — components that will play back your own music collection, radio, and the sound from movies, TV, and audio-only channels on cable and satellite systems. Today's audio systems are designed to reproduce audio signals in *high fidelity*. In other words, the equipment should recreate the music so that it sounds like it did in the studio or concert hall where your favorite recordings were made.

A high-fidelity sound system has several components:

- **Source component:** This component can be a CD player (or one of the new SACD or DVD-audio players), a cassette deck, a radio tuner, a satellite tuner (such as an XM radio), an MP3 player or jukebox, or the audio portion of a video source such as a VCR, laser disc, or DVD. The source component produces a low-level audio signal — called a *line-level signal* — that's usually transmitted over an RCA cable.

- **Preamplifier or control amplifier:** This device amplifies (or increases the power of) the line-level signal and also serves as a switching device to allow you to select from different source components. The preamplifier also contains a volume control, which determines how much the signal is amplified. The control amplifier connects through another interconnect cable (or internal wiring if you're using an integrated amplifier) to the next stage in the sound reproduction process.

- **Power amplifier:** This unit adds more power to the audio signal — enough power to make your audio signal audible through the speakers. The preamplifier doesn't have enough power to drive your speakers. (Yes, we know it sounds silly to have two amplifiers, but that's just how it is.)

   Note: An *integrated amplifier* is a preamplifier and a power amplifier integrated into one component. Add a radio tuner to this box, and you have a *receiver.*

- **Loudspeakers:** Connected to the amplifier by speaker cables (what else?), the speakers use electromagnets to move sound drivers — the woofer and tweeter — back and forth. This movement, which corresponds with the audio signal coming from the amplifier, pushes the air in front of the drivers rhythmically, creating the sound waves that you hear. Loudspeakers can range from a full, surround-sound five- or seven-speaker home-entertainment center to remote speakers in your kitchen or dining room to the intercom speakers throughout your house.

As audio systems expand from a single room to multiple rooms, a new breed of components has come onto the marketplace — the *multizone* system. Traditional audio systems have always been *single zone,* meaning that the control portion of the preamplifier — the switches that let you select which audio source you want to listen to — lets you select only one source at a time. This is fine for a stereo system that you're using in only one room (you can't really listen to more than one thing at once, right?), but this solution lacks flexibility for multiple rooms.

Newer, multizone systems have control sections that let you select more than one source component at once. You and your spouse can listen to a Dunne Roman CD in the living room and your kids can bang their heads to Linkin Park in the basement. As we mentioned, if you want to use a multizone system, you need additional amplifiers — one for each independent source that you want to play back at one time.

Intercom Systems

Unlike a stereo system, an intercom system isn't designed with the highest audio quality in mind. Its main function is to get your voice from point A to point B without weakening or incurring interference. Intercoms aren't cheap or unsophisticated; they just have a different mission.

Intercoms fall into two main categories:

- **Wireless systems:** These intercoms use radio *transceivers* (*trans*mitter and re*ceiver*) to carry voice signals from room to room. Just install a simple device on your desk, raise the antenna (and do the same with the other device), and you're ready to communicate. Variations on this theme include fixed wireless intercoms (which you can mount on the wall), portable baby monitors, and many cordless phones that use a speakerphone on the base station to create a simple, point-to-point intercom system.

✔ **Wired systems:** As the name implies, these intercoms are wired together and send your voice as an electrical audio signal between rooms. Wired intercom systems run the gamut from simple voice systems to advanced audio systems that can also carry radio and other audio signals. Figure 5-3 shows a typical wired intercom system. Some telephone systems have intercom systems; these are covered in more detail in Chapter 10.

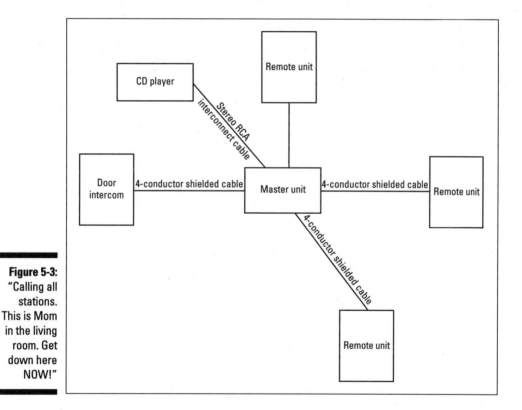

Figure 5-3: "Calling all stations. This is Mom in the living room. Get down here NOW!"

Intercoms can be a useful feature (though phone networks can serve a similar function). Danny finds his intercom useful in his four-story house. The Fisher Price monitor that he and his wife used with the first set of twins has been replaced with a simple press of the Monitor button on the Nursery intercom unit. The babies' cries can now be heard all over the house. (Wait, is that good?)

Most decent intercom systems have an *audio in* source option, too, whereby you can plug your home-entertainment system into your intercom system. By tying the two together, you save yourself money.

As you map your wiring runs, keep in mind that many intercom manufacturers void your warranty if you don't use their proprietary wiring systems. However, using their wiring is more expensive and goes against the idea of a uniform backbone over which all communications travel.

Chapter 6

Getting Video Where You Want It

In This Chapter

▶ Choosing between base or broad

▶ Going the distance

▶ Getting the most with coaxial cable

▶ Doing the modulate thing

*Y*ou can wire gobs of capabilities into a video network — a much greater variety of choices than is possible in most other networks we discuss (such as data networks or phone networks). That's the good news. The bad news is that we have to hold the number of pages in this book to under that of the *Encyclopedia Britannica,* so we can't go into all the possible choices. On second thought, maybe that's good news, too, because rather than confusing you with a laundry list of all the different video possibilities and boring you with technical drivel on this super-video whatsit and that video-switching doodad, we concentrate on showing you how to wire the most common video network features. These features include the following:

✔ Coaxial video outlets in all rooms that may one day contain a television

✔ Return video connections in rooms that may contain video sources, from VCRs to baby-monitor cameras

✔ Inputs for cable television and a broadcast TV antenna

✔ Provisions for adding a DBS satellite system to the network

✔ A central distribution node tying all this good stuff together

These devices, taken together, make up the video backbone in your smart home. The network we lay out for you uses *broadband RF video distribution* (whew!), which means that special devices called *video modulators* send the signals from video sources (such as VCRs or security cameras) through the wires in your walls and broadcast them on TV channels not used by your local or cable TV stations. Just tune into the right channel — like you tune to channel 3 for your VCR — and you can watch these sources anywhere in your house. In this chapter and the next, we take you through the process of wiring such a home-video network backbone.

Distance Counts in Video Signals

You can get video signals from place to place in two basic ways: *baseband distribution* and *broadband distribution*. The difference between these two methods is in the amount of information that the cable can carry. Baseband transmission has enough capacity to carry only a single channel of video, so you generally use baseband cable for the connections between video components, such as your VCR and TV. Generally, baseband cables are short. Broadband cable (such as coaxial cable), on the other hand, has enough capacity to carry many video channels over greater distances.

If you've read Chapter 5, you know that we concentrate on a broadband video-distribution network. However, you can find elements of both methods in just about any video network.

Cabling between components (baseband)

Baseband video is the distribution of a single channel or program over a cable. The *Video Out* port on the back of VCRs, cable converters, satellite receivers, DVD and laserdisc players, and camcorders are baseband video signals, as are the *S video* ports of the same devices (we discuss S video in more detail shortly). In general, baseband video distribution is best suited for connections over a short distance, such as between components in the same room. Baseband video uses video patch cables to connect components in a system and requires audio patch cables to carry the corresponding audio signals — because you need both sets of cables, we refer to this set of cables as *A/V interconnect cables*.

Home systems commonly use three types of baseband video connections (which we list from least sophisticated to most sophisticated):

- **Composite video:** This connection system is on all video source devices. Composite video carries all components of an NTSC video signal over a single wire and connects devices using standard RCA or phono plugs — the same type of plugs used to connect stereo components such as CD players and amplifiers. (For more on NTSC, the standard U.S. television system, see Chapter 5.)

- **S video:** You find S video on more sophisticated VCRs and on DVD players, DBS dishes, digital cable boxes, as well as on many camcorders. This method uses a single cable with multiple conductors to carry the brightness and color parts of a video signal separately, resulting in a better picture.

- **Component video:** The majority of DVD players and most new televisions have component connections, usually in addition to composite and S video connections. (You also find component video connections on some digital TV receivers — it's one of the most common ways of carrying HDTV signals to an HDTV.) Component video breaks down the video signal into three parts, each carried on a separate cable. This breakdown lets you avoid much of the internal circuitry in both your DVD player and your TV, so you get a better picture. At least that's what all of the videophiles we know tell us.

When more than one of these options is available to you, always choose the most sophisticated first. If your source and TV both have component video, use that. Most of these source devices also have an RF (antenna cable) output that works on Channel 3 or 4 of your TV, but consider this choice only as a last resort because the video quality will most likely be lower than one of the baseband connections.

In the digital video — HDTV — world, a bunch of new interconnection standards are in the works as well as a ton of controversy about them. On one side of the standards war are TV and equipment vendors, who want to create a generation of digital interconnects that can replace the rat's nest of wires (up to nine of them) connecting digital TV receivers to HDTV monitors.

On the opposing side are content owners — the TV and movie studios — who want tight control over the *Digital Rights Management* (DRM) aspect of digital entertainment. Because you can make bit-for-bit perfect copies of digital material, they're pushing their own digital interconnect technologies that incorporate strong encryption and authentication techniques. These schemes tend to tie the material to a specific format and device, so they may keep you from using the media in a different way — such as playing it on your computer or recording it to watch in the bedroom or your vacation house.

Several competing efforts are underway to standardize connectors and incorporate a DRM system. Following are the leading candidates in the fight for standardized digital interconnection of video equipment:

- ✔ **DVI, or Digital Video Interconnect:** Content providers favor this system because it prevents users from networking, recording, manipulating, sharing, or doing anything else with a digital TV signal other than watching it as it comes into their TV. According to the consumer electronics manufacturers who have chosen to not use DVI, this interface makes their TVs dumb monitors rather than interactive parts of a home network.

- ✔ **FireWire, or IEEE 1394 (or one of many other brand names):** This is a more open, computer-like system that doesn't prevent you from doing your own, legal things with the signal (such as recording the signal on a PVR or VCR). Many PCs use FireWire to connect peripheral devices such as camcorders, hard drives, and iPods.

If we were in charge of this industry, we'd make sure that FireWire became the standard. *Fair use* — the right to take content that you've paid for and use it however you want on any device — is a long-standing legal concept. You can play video when you want on whatever TV you want, and you can make an MP3 copy of your CD and play it in your car or on your iPod. DRM is important — people should be paid for their work — but schemes such as DVI will take away a customer's ability to use the content in the way he or she wants to. It also will make home networks less effective by making it difficult to use them for entertainment.

Keep an eye on these standards as you shop for an HDTV. A concern in the marketplace is that the imposition of the DVI standard may cut out owners of older HDTVs because they won't have the correct interfaces. People who have spent thousands of dollars on HDTVs in the past few years might not be able to connect them to new copy-protected HDTV receivers.

Cabling the video-distribution network (broadband)

A broadband video-distribution system combines many different video signals — and their corresponding audio signals — onto a single cable by *modulating* the signals onto different radio frequencies, or channels. In simplest terms, this process involves dividing the available bandwidth of a cable into equal parts (channels), and then placing the information representing the video program into one of these channels by varying the electrical signal in some standard way (this is the actual modulation). These frequency divisions correspond to the standard channels on your television, which has an internal tuner that demodulates the signal and displays it on the screen. Figure 6-1 shows how program signals are assigned by broadcasters or cable service providers to different frequencies (channels) and sent over the same cable.

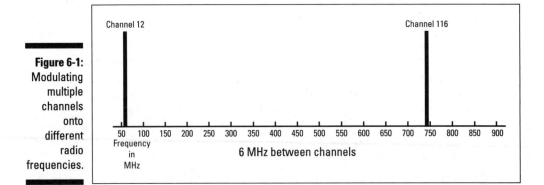

Figure 6-1: Modulating multiple channels onto different radio frequencies.

Broadcast and cable networks modulate multiple channels. (In the case of broadcast, the modulation doesn't use up bandwidth on a cable but rather divides the over-the-air radio frequency spectrum into smaller parts). Just about all video source devices include a broadband output — usually switchable between Channel 3 and Channel 4. An internal modulator converts the baseband video signal into a modulated video signal, and allows you to connect the source to older televisions that don't have baseband video inputs.

Coaxial Video Networks

Although you can create a video network without running cables (as described in Chapter 7), running cables for your network almost always increases performance, flexibility, and capacity. Wireless alternatives are usually more expensive than their cabled partners, and they do less. Bottom line: Anytime you can build a video network by running wires, we recommend that you do so.

The wired version of a video network is one that distributes video signals (separated into different channels) over coaxial cable to each television in your home. If you've had cable TV, you've had a network similar to what we describe, except that traditional cable TV networks have been paltry, one-way video networks in comparison to the two-way video-distribution system that we describe.

Cable-modem broadband services run on coaxial cable. Because they send data in two directions — as do the new digital cable set-top boxes — cable modems affect your coaxial video network design. We discuss the implications of these technologies as we go through building a network in Chapter 7.

Coaxial cable

Coaxial cable — usually called *coax* — is a metallic cable most often used for transmitting radio frequency (RF) signals such as broadband-television video and radio signals. Coaxial cable has two conductors, or *axes*, that carry data. A layer of dielectric insulating material surrounds a single, center conductor. The other conductor is a metal shield that goes around the dielectric (insulating) layer. The outermost layer of coax cable is an insulating jacket.

Coaxial cables are rated by their *impedance,* which is basically the AC version of electrical resistance. Different applications require different impedances. In the home, almost all systems that require coaxial cable use 75-ohm impedance coax, although some computer LAN systems (older ones, not commonly found in the home) use 50-ohm coax. (*Ohm* is the unit of measurement for impedance.) Table 6-1 lists the three main type of coaxial cable found in homes.

Table 6-1		Video Coaxial Cable Grades	
Coaxial Cable Type	*Cost*	*Use*	*Comments*
Unrated 75-ohm coax	Lowest	Older cable TV installations and aerial antenna-to-TV connections	This low grade of coaxial cable suffers from high resistance to the video signal and provides poor picture quality. Not recommended for video networks.
RG-59 coax	Medium	Cable TV and antenna-to-TV connections	This is the standard grade of coaxial cable found in most existing installations, suitable for standard cable TV and broadcast antenna use.
RG6 coax	Highest	Cable TV, DBS, and cable-modem connections	This is the highest grade of of coaxial cable found in the home. It provides the best resistance from interference and the least amount of signal degradation. Required for DBS and cable-modem installations and recommended for all new installations.

You may encounter coaxial cables labeled RG6QS or RG6 Quad Shield, which means that the cable has four layers of additional shielding beneath the cable jacket. These layers provide additional protection from external interference. The difference between RG-59 and RG6 is similar to the difference between CAT-3 and CAT-5e UTP cables, which we discuss in Chapters 11 and 15. They look similar and do similar things, but the higher-rated cable is a bit more capable of carrying your signals cleanly — and for longer distances. The price difference is minimal, and we strongly recommend that you choose RG6 for your coaxial cabling needs; the small extra cost ensures that your wiring can handle the future needs of your network. In fact, applications such as DBS require RG6 and specifically tell you not to use RG-59.

Coax connectors

Like almost all the networking cable we cover, coaxial cables use standardized connectors. Residential applications use only one type of connector — the *F connector,* which is shown in Figure 6-2. If you have cable television, you're already familiar with this screw or push-on connector.

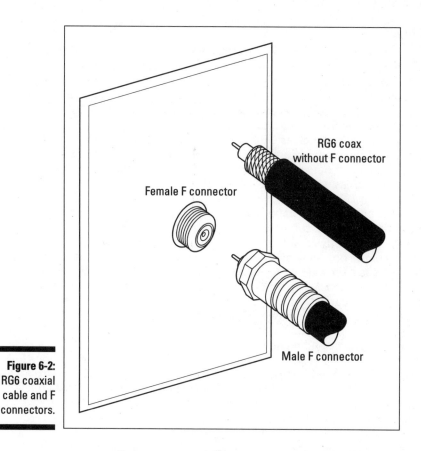

RG6 coax
without F connector

Female F connector

Male F connector

Figure 6-2:
RG6 coaxial
cable and F
connectors.

Like most connectors, F connectors come in male and female versions. In general, female connectors are on video equipment and wall outlets, and male connectors are used to attach the cables to these outlets.

Components

The cable and connectors are the permanent parts of your video-network infrastructure — the parts that you put in your walls and expect to keep there for 20 years or so. The other components that your video network needs, such as distribution panels and modulators, will probably be less permanent members of your household electronic family. Over time, your network needs may change and new technologies such as digital television will become available, precipitating changes in some of your network components. These changes will cost money (the price of progress?), but the main part of your investment — namely the materials and labor used in installing the coaxial cabling in your walls — will remain intact and useful.

Outlets

If you're like us, you don't want coaxial cables and F connectors dangling out of holes in the wall. Luckily, an assortment of coaxial cable in-wall outlets fit into standard electrical junction boxes and use standard faceplates. Dozens of companies manufacture these outlets, which come in many combinations and sizes. If your budget allows, we recommend running two RG6 cables to each room. The first coaxial cable allows you to receive video signals from an external source such as cable TV. The second lets you send out video signals — from devices such as VCRs or baby monitors — to the rest of the home. You might not want to run two cables to every spot in your home, but certain areas will require that you do.

A coaxial outlet for this cabling consists of two female F connectors, one above the other, in a compact, single-gang junction box. Single-gang means that the Dalton boys don't ride with Jesse James. Okay, *gang* simply refers to the size of the box and cover. For reference, a single-gang junction box is the same size as a typical two-receptacle electrical outlet or a single switch-toggle light switch. Many twin coaxial outlets have large faceplate openings and use a standard-sized faceplate called a Leviton Decora. (These are the same faceplates accompanying large light switches in many newer homes.)

As you design your home networks, you may find that you want to put several different kinds of outlets together on a wall — speaker connections for an audio network, a phone line or two, and your coaxial outlets, for example. Consider using a larger double- or triple-gang junction box and installing a multipurpose outlet that can terminate all these cables in one place. Most major outlet manufacturers make all sorts of combination outlets.

Low-voltage signals such as coaxial video networks don't get along with AC power lines. You should keep at least three feet between the two to avoid noise and interference. Never try to connect your coaxial lines and power lines in the same junction box — the result is a mess. If you're building a house, make sure that the electrical and communications cable are not through the same holes in the studs — some contractors to do this, thinking that it's compact and tidier.

Distribution panels

The key component in your video network is the *distribution panel.* This device is the central node for your video network — all coaxial lines to the various rooms of your house begin here. A distribution panel has several functions:

- ✔ It accepts one (or optimally more) coaxial, broadband, video signal inputs.
- ✔ It combines these input signals into a unified broadband output.
- ✔ It splits this output to feed *multiple video endpoints* (in other words, televisions).

✔ It amplifies the outgoing signals to make them stronger (because splitting the signal weakens it).

Figure 6-3 shows a typical video-distribution panel.

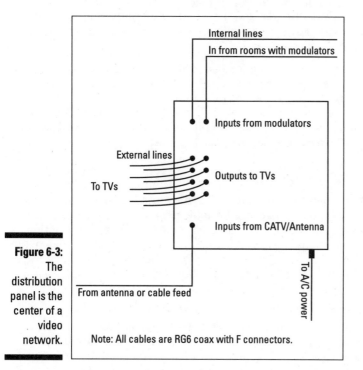

Figure 6-3:
The distribution panel is the center of a video network.

When you're shopping for a video-distribution panel, look for the following:

✔ **Number of inputs:** Choose a unit that has at least two (and preferably more) inputs. Doing so allows you to take a local video source (such as a DVD player) and distribute its signals throughout your home, instead of to the nearest TV.

✔ **Number of outputs:** Each television that you want to connect to your video network needs its own output on the distribution panel. These panels are engineered to maintain the proper signal strength and quality when used in a "one television per outlet" way. If you try to cheat and use a coaxial splitter to connect an extra television to a single output, you're throwing away the design and engineering expertise that went into the panel, and you probably won't be happy with the results. Most panels have from 5 to 12 outputs, so you should be able to satisfy your home's needs without having to install a second panel.

Distribution panels are often described as 3 x 8 or 5 x 12. The first number is the number of inputs, the second is the number of outputs.

✔ **Amplification:** To maintain a signal that's strong enough to produce a good television picture, you need to amplify the signal. Most distribution panels have built-in amplifiers that take care of this for you. Sophisticated models have different levels of amplification so that some outputs are optimally amplified for shorter cable runs, and others are optimized for longer runs.

Why different levels of amplification? Because overamplifying a signal is almost as bad as underamplifying it. Panels that have different tiers of amplification typically have several outputs designated for short distances (0 to 50 feet, for example) and some for longer runs (perhaps for 50 to 150 feet). Models with several outputs (such as the 5-x-12 panel) may even have a middle tier of distance ranges.

If you're using a digital cable service, make sure you chose a bidirectional video-distribution panel. Many older-design distribution panels don't let signals flow back through them onto the cable network. Because digital cable set-top boxes communicate back to the cable network, you need to choose a distribution panel that will let them do this! You can also find distribution panels with a cable-modem bypass that lets you keep your cable modem out of the loop — further reducing the possibility of your distribution panel's amplifier causing interference and slowing down your Web surfing.

More than you ever wanted to know about modulators

After the RG6 cabling and multiple-input distribution panel are in place, you have the makings of a two-way, whole-home video network. Now you just need an easy way to select the source you want to watch. That's where modulators come in. A *modulator* translates a source's baseband video and audio signals into a standard TV RF channel — just like the ones that broadcast and cable companies send you. So that they don't interfere with existing channels, modulators must be *frequency agile.* In other words, instead of transmitting on only a single frequency, modulators must be capable of transmitting over a range of frequencies (or TV channels), so that you can adjust them to an open channel on your system.

Following is a typical scenario for modulator use. Suppose that you have a main VCR in the living room, a baby monitor in the nursery, and a PVR and a DBS satellite receiver in your home-theater room. You want to be able to view any of these signals on any TV in the house. No problem. You just need a modulator that can modulate four inputs onto different channels on your coaxial cable, so that they're available at each jack in the house. Perhaps channel 87 is the baby monitor, channel 89 is the VCR, channel 91 is the PVR, and channel 93 is the satellite receiver. When you want to watch one of these devices somewhere else in the house, you tune to the appropriate TV station. Simple!

You probably have several modulators already: in your VCR, DVD player, laserdisc player, or DSS receiver. However, these modulators give you only two choices — Channel 3 or 4. Their sole purpose is to provide a means of connecting these devices to televisions that lack separate, baseband A/V inputs. In most television networks, Channels 3 and 4 aren't unoccupied, so these modulators make use of an internal switch (the VCR/TV button on your VCR's remote) that disconnects the antenna or cable feed to the TV, preventing interference with existing channels.

Chances are that you won't be able to use these channel 3 and 4 modulators for distributing video throughout the home because your coax will have existing cable or over-the-air channels. (The VCR/TV switch works for a TV connected directly to the device but doesn't work for the whole house.) Even in the unlikely event that you don't have existing channels on channels 3 or 4, building a channel 3/4 modulator into a source device won't do much for a whole-home network because you can add only one source device for the entire house. You can't modulate more than one device onto a single TV channel. And even if channels 3 *and* 4 are unoccupied, modulators shouldn't be used on adjacent channels.

Think about the following when you're choosing a modulator:

- **Digital or analog:** Analog modulators are much cheaper than digital ones, but they usually aren't as flexible in the frequencies you can choose from, so you have to buy a modulator that is factory-set to the channel you have available. Analog models tend to drift off stations just like those old dial radios did, requiring frequent readjustment. Digital models, though more expensive, are more reliable and accurate; you basically set them once and forget them.

- **Single or multichannel:** You can buy modulators that translate a single video source onto a single television channel, or you can buy ones that translate up to four separate input sources onto four different output channels. A multichannel unit may better serve your needs for two reasons:

  - A multichannel unit allows you to distribute the video signals from several collocated video sources (such as in a home-theater room) throughout your whole house.

  - With a multichannel modulator, you eliminate the confusion and complexity of using coaxial splitters to increase the number of internal video inputs on your distribution panel.

- **Mono, stereo, or no audio:** Most modulators transmit the audio output of your source device as *monaural audio* — no stereo separation, no surround sound, just mono (the same thing out of both speakers). Even if they have two inputs (for left and right channel audio), they're probably mono. You can buy modulators that transmit *MTS* (the stereo system that TVs use), but they cost significantly more. If you're installing a modulator that will be carrying the video from a surveillance camera, you can save money by purchasing a modulator that has no sound input.

✔ **Shape and size:** Modulators don't come in a standard shape and size. You can choose from the following options:

- **Black box:** These modulators don't look pretty, but they will fit in with the rest of the stuff on your A/V equipment shelf.

- **Wall outlet size:** Much less obtrusive are modulators that fit in a standard wall outlet gang box. The same size as a light switch (or a coaxial outlet, for that matter), these miracles of miniaturization make sense for places where you don't have a huge rack of video equipment already in place.

- **Distribution panels:** You can get modulators out of the room entirely by purchasing an all-in-one distribution panel that has a modulator or two built right into the same box. This option does limit you because your source devices must be close to the distribution panel — so that VCR on the fourth floor is out of luck!

✔ **Loop-through capability:** Many modulators offer something called an *A/V loop through*. Many source devices — except for some DBS receivers and DVD players — have only one set of baseband video and audio outputs. If you plug these into a modulator, you don't have any way to make a baseband A/V connection to the local TV — you have to use the source's built-in Channel 3/4 modulator instead. The loop through provides an extra set of baseband video and audio outputs on the back of the modulator so that you can connect to the local TV directly using composite or S-video cables, instead of using the modulated signal that is routed back through the distribution panel.

When you're using a modulator system to create your own TV channels in your home, keep the following points in mind:

✔ **Install a signal amplifier between your antenna and the distribution panel or modulators:** When you create your own TV channel, you're doing pretty much the same thing in your house that cable companies and broadcasters do at their head-end offices and stations. If you're using an antenna feed to receive broadcast TV stations, you could end up sending your video out your antenna and over the airwaves (and into your neighbor's TV perhaps). The FCC doesn't like this idea, so it requires you to install a signal amplifier between your antenna and the distribution panel or modulators. Amplifiers are inherently one-way — signals don't pass back through them — and they help pick up those distant stations better. Bidirectional amplifiers let signals go both ways, but the ones going back upstream to the cable company are low-frequency signals that won't interfere with television channels.

✔ **Skip channels between modulated channels:** Most modulator manufacturers recommend that you skip at least one channel between modulated channels to avoid interference.

✔ **Be aware of signal interference:** Channels that your TV can't pick up may still be strong enough to interfere with your internal channels —

this is often the case in the higher UHF band for broadcast TV. The same can apply to cable TV — just because you don't subscribe to a particular channel doesn't mean that its signal isn't taking up bandwidth space on your coax. If this problem occurs, adjust the modulator to a different channel.

✔ **Make sure that you have free channel space:** Channel space isn't too much of a problem if you use an antenna — even the most crowded urban areas have plenty of unused channels. However, cable service providers in many areas are beginning to saturate their available channels with programming. They're also using TV channels for other services, such as cable modems and audio services. So if you're planning on modulating several channels onto your network, do your homework and make sure that you'll be able to find open channels. You can do this by physically looking at channels you think are unused on one of your televisions (making sure there's not a scrambled signal there) and by checking the complete listing of channels provided by your cable service provider.

Chapter 7

Wiring a Video Network

In This Chapter

▶ Cabling and connecting to create a video network

▶ Integrating a satellite system into your whole-home network

▶ Leveraging your CAT-5e network

▶ Plugging into wireless and phoneline alternatives

*I*n Chapters 5 and 6, we spend a fair amount of time talking about all the pieces and parts that fit into a video-distribution network. That's important stuff to know — but it doesn't do you much good if you don't have everything connected properly. So in this chapter, we tell you about the model to use in setting up your network. The technical term for this model is *topology* or *network architecture,* but don't be intimidated. These words just mean a way of thinking about your network so that you know what to connect where.

In this chapter, we tell you how to get the right cables in the walls (and how to buy the right infrastructure devices) to create a futureproof, two-way video network. Maybe you don't plan to install all the equipment that we describe in Chapters 5 and 6 right away. No problem. As long as you get your wires in place, the general network model that we describe in this chapter will serve you well in the future as your needs change and grow.

Don't feel like you have to wire a video network (or any network) yourself. If you're hesitant about drilling holes and running cables through your walls, do yourself a favor and hire a professional.

The discussion of video networks and especially that of modulators is probably the toughest in the book. You might need to reread some sections a few times. That's okay. We get confused here too. Stick with it, because video entertainment is the heart of your smart home.

Connecting Your Video Network

The fundamental building block of your video network is the coaxial cable. We recommend that you build your whole-home video network with two segments of RG6 coaxial cable connected to each video outlet you install in your major rooms — one cable that brings video into the TV and one cable that allows you to distribute video source devices (such as VCRs) through the network. Specifically, you should have at each location:

- ✔ **An *external* video connection:** This connection carries video signals from your distribution panel to your television. Think of *external* as *outbound*.

- ✔ **An *internal* video connection:** This connection carries video signals from any source devices in the room back to the distribution panel, where they can be combined with your external video source (cable or broadcast TV) and sent back out on the outbound lines. Think of *internal* as *inbound*.

Note: We use the words *external* and *internal* in reference to the central hub of the video network, the video distribution panel. *External,* or *outbound,* means away from the video distribution panel, and *internal,* or *inbound,* means toward the video distribution panel.

Consider running four RG6 cables (two double outlets) to your home office and your media room or home-theater room. You might need the extra capacity or you might decide you want to rearrange the furniture. (It sure helps to have an identical set of outlets on the other side of the room when you switch the sofa and the TV to opposite walls.)

Running just one outbound coaxial cable allows you to receive signals in that room and may be sufficient for rooms where you don't intend to send any video sources back through the network. However, it's hard to predict which rooms will fall into that category.

Figure 7-1 shows the layout of a typical, centrally homed, coaxial video network. In the next sections, we walk you through the network, from a single room back to the distribution panel.

If you use digital cable and also want to use modulated sources in your video network, building such a network can get complicated. Digital cable systems do some funky things with their signals *and* they use up a lot more of the frequency spectrum. So you'll have a hard time even finding a free channel to modulate your source devices onto. In the "Dealing with digital cable" sidebar, we talk about some ways to get around this problem.

As we discuss in Chapter 6, digital cable set-top boxes *and* cable modems need to send data back upstream to your cable company. You might wonder if internal RG-6 cables can carry this data — the answer is no. Cable modem and digital cable upstream data goes back up the *external* cable. The key here is to buy a video distribution panel that is labeled bidirectional and that allows data to pass back through the amplifier and onto the cable provider's network. Look for these words on the manual: *a 5 to 42 MHz return path.*

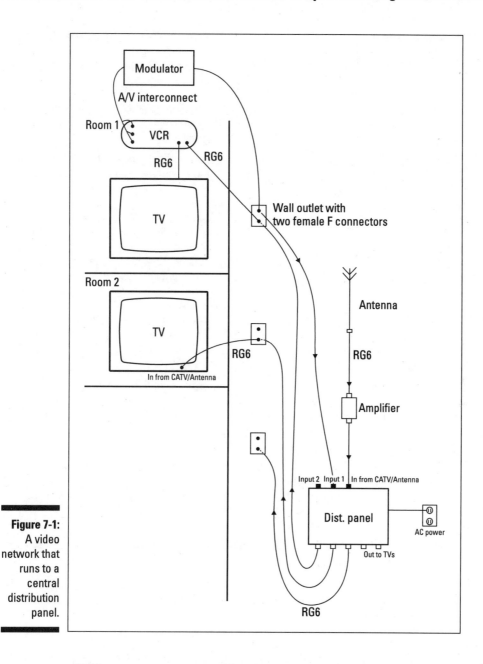

Figure 7-1:
A video network that runs to a central distribution panel.

Filling your walls: Running the cables

When wiring a video-distribution network, the first task is to run two RG6 coaxial cables between the distribution panel and each area of the house where you want video outlets. You'll probably want to hire a professional

Dealing with digital cable

Digital cable is a great service. Tons of channels, a neat on-screen program guide, and more. Unfortunately, the sheer number of channels and the different channel structure used by digitally transmitted channels (typically, the lower channels are still transmitted in analog) make it hard to find empty slots in the bandwidth in which to insert your modulated programming. Even if you find an empty channel, there's no guarantee that it will stay open — cable providers constantly add channels and reshuffle their lineups. To make things more complicated, the channel numbers you see on your digital cable set-top box (for example, 200 for HBO) don't equate to the channel numbers you select on your modulator.

If you have digital cable and want to use a two-way, modulated video network, you can try the following:

✔ **Talk to your cable company:** Ask the installer or call the technical support line — see whether they'll identify some open channels for you.

✔ **Use a notch filter to block out a chunk of channels:** This isn't an elegant solution. *Notch filters* block multiple channels (often five to ten), not just one. So you might lose access to some channels you want. Notch filters start off at around $70 to $80, and the price goes up rapidly as the "width" of the notch (the number of channels being blocked) gets smaller because blocking fewer channels is more difficult.

✔ **Separate the digital cable signals onto a different RG6:** This scenario is similar to how satellite TV signals are incorporated into a video network (discussed in the "Special Needs of Satellite Systems" section later in this chapter). You'd need a third RG6 cable for locations using a digital cable set-top box. Instead of being connected to your distribution panel, these cables would be patched together in a physically separate network (using a splitter from the cable company or another distribution panel). Modulated video from in-house sources would then be distributed over the other two RG6 cables.

✔ **Skip the modulation and use a different network to distribute internal video sources:** We describe these systems at the end of the chapter (video over CAT-5e, wireless, and phone lines).

We think the last two approaches are the best ways to go. And using a good installer — someone who's familiar with your local cable company — can really pay off.

---

cable installer to run this cable for you. For an attractive appearance, the cables should connect to wall-mounted female coaxial connectors, as described in Chapter 6.

To make connection and future system changes easier, label your RG6 cables. At a minimum, you need to know which room the cable is coming from and whether it's the internal or external line. (Nothing inherent about a cable makes it internal or external — it's just the logical use you apply to the cable.) We recommend that you buy RG6 cable in two colors (it usually comes in white or black); use one color for all internal runs and the other for all external runs.

TIP

Where does DTV fit in?

High Definition TV (HDTV). The mere words make us smile. Widescreen TV images with film quality. Is your video network going to be ready for it? Or for any of the new digital television (DTV) variants we discuss in Chapter 6?

In most cases, the answer is yes (aren't you glad?). DTV signals are compatible with the standard RF infrastructure (RG6 cabling) that carries today's NTSC signals. The only thing to keep in mind is that many over-the-air DTV broadcasts use higher frequencies and have larger variations in signal strengths than do regular broadcast and cable TV stations. So to handle HDTV, you must have a high-quality distribution panel and amplifiers. The major vendors of these systems — such as Channel Plus (www.channelplus.com) or Leviton (www.

leviton.com) — offer amplifiers and distribution panels that are HDTV capable, and they often clearly label them so (using an official DTV logo authorized by the ATSC — the group that sets the standards for DTV).

Modulators are a different story. They're designed to work with today's NTSC analog TV standard. As new video source devices (such as digital VCRs or High-Definition DVDs) are developed to record or display HDTV/DTV pictures, your existing modulators won't be able to do anything with those signals. In the long-term, you'll probably need to replace your modulators. By then, there will be modulators specifically designed to deal with HDTV signals. We'll deal with that when the time comes!

Tying it together: Making connections at the distribution panel

If you do everything right when completing the steps in the preceding section, you should have a gob of cables running into a central point, which we call the *central wiring closet* (see Chapter 2 for more info on the wiring closet). Here's how to connect these wires to your distribution panel to complete your network:

1. **Connect each external RG6 coaxial cable to one of the distribution panel's external female connection interfaces.**

   If your distribution panel comes with multiple levels of amplification, take the time now to double-check the amplification levels. Each of your meticulously labeled cables should be connected to outputs with amplification levels that correspond to the distance of each cable run. (Check the manufacturer's recommendations — often each output has a recommended distance label right next to where the cable plugs in.)

2. **Connect each internal RG6 cable into one of the modulator inputs (sometimes labeled "local") on your distribution panel.**

You may find that you have more internal video cables in your wiring closet than you have inputs (remember that most panels have five or fewer inputs). If you don't currently have any video sources connected to a particular cable, you can leave it disconnected — but well labeled — until you need it.

If you *still* don't have enough inputs on your panel, you can use a good quality splitter/combiner to connect two or more internal cables to a single panel input. If you choose this option, don't try to save a few bucks on a cheap splitter/combiner — the 99-cent specials from your local discount store are worth exactly what they cost (next to nothing). Spend $15 or $20 on a high-quality model from a manufacturer such as ChannelPlus or Channel Vision (www.channelvision.com).

3. **Connect the RG6 cable from your antenna or cable TV feed to the Antenna/CATV input on the distribution panel.**

If you're using modulators and an antenna to pull in local broadcast stations, you need to install an amplifier between the antenna and the distribution panel — otherwise you can actually start broadcasting your internal video over your antenna and out to the world. You probably don't want to be doing this (for many reasons), and the FCC wants you doing this even less. Most manufacturers of distribution panels have such signal amplifiers for sale, as well — use the amplifier that they recommend for your specific distribution panel.

You can't simply plug the output of your DSS satellite system into your distribution panel's Antenna/CATV input. Read the "Special Needs of Satellite Systems" section, later in this chapter, for information on this unfortunate phenomenon.

Most distribution panels (except those without built-in signal amplification) need electrical power to do their job. The majority use a small *wall wart* AC/DC power adapter like those used by cordless phones, modems, and tons of other small electrical appliances. Make sure you install a nice quad electrical outlet nearby — we always seem to be adding something in our wiring closets that needs power.

As we mentioned, if all this two-way video sounds like something that you'll never, ever want to get involved with, you *can* build a similar video-distribution network that forgoes the second RG6 cable to each outlet. Just follow the same basic architecture guidelines — all outlets individually wired with a length of RG6 cable running back to your central distribution node — and skip the second cable run. At the risk of being repetitive, we think this type of abbreviated network is a false economy, but it's a perfectly valid way of constructing a home-video network. If you set up your network this way, we strongly recommend that you at least run a second cable to the room containing your home theater or media center. Chances are that's where you'll have all the fun source devices, and having a second cable there gives you the opportunity to share those sources throughout the home later.

Hooking up: Making connections in the TV rooms

With the cables run, it's time to connect the TVs and video source devices in each room to the network. Figure 7-2 shows typical *in-room* video connections.

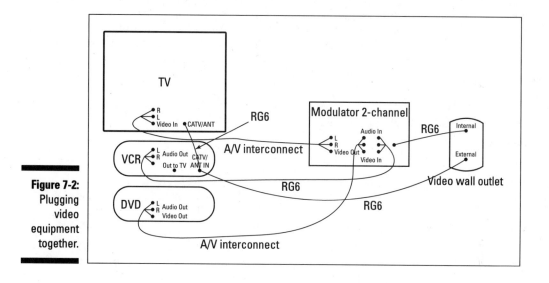

Figure 7-2:
Plugging
video
equipment
together.

Assuming that you've finished making your cable runs between the rooms and the distribution panel, just follow these steps:

1. **Determine the video source devices (such as a VCR, DVD player, video-capable PC, or camcorder) that you want to distribute to other areas of the house, and connect them to a *modulator,* typically using an RCA or S-video cable.**

   Modulators allow you to broadcast a device's video signal around your house over an unused TV channel. We explain modulators as well as RCA and S-video cables in detail in Chapter 6.

   If you have several video source devices in the same room (such as your home-theater room with a PVR and a DVD player), you can use a *multi-channel modulator* to broadcast multiple audio and video signals onto unused channels.

2. **Run a length of RG6 coaxial cable with male connectors on both ends from the output jack of your modulator to the *internal* female coaxial connector jack in the wall.**

   A coaxial wall jack is basically a faceplate with a female connector sticking out both sides. Remember that your point of reference for *internal* is inbound to the distribution panel. So when you're standing in the room with the TV, the internal jack runs *out* of the room toward the distribution panel. If you think about it too long, you'll get a headache.

3. **Connect another length of RG6 cable with male connectors between your TV or cable set-top box and the *external* connector on your coaxial outlet.**

   If you're using a VCR or PVR, it should be connected in-line between the wall outlet and the television or set-top box with an RG6 coaxial cable. Use another RG6 coaxial cable to connect the output of the VCR or PVR to the TV. You can also use RCA or S-video cables from the Audio and Video Out jacks of the VCR or PVR to the Audio and Video In jacks on the TV. Figure 7-3 shows the signal path for watching a VCR in another room.

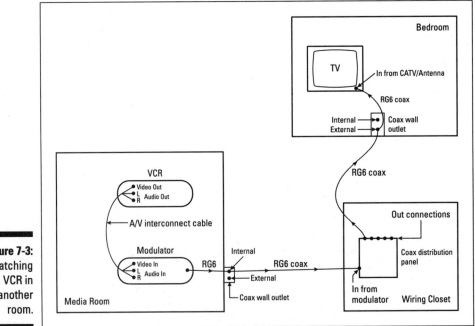

Figure 7-3: Watching a VCR in another room.

If your VCR or PVR is connected to a modulator that has a loop-through connection (see Chapter 6), you can use these outlets and RCA cords to connect your VCR to your TV.

4. **Perform Steps 1 through 3 for each room and pair of coaxial cables in your network. Lather, rinse, and repeat as desired.**

You now have a whole-home video network up and running! However, your work isn't finished. You still need to program each modulator to an unused channel. We're not going to give you step-by-step instructions on this task because each manufacturer's model is different. For the most part, though, digital modulators are easy to tune in — it's just a matter of pressing a program button a few times. Many models even have LCD or LED digital displays so that you can't mess up.

Summing Up

The information in this chapter is a lot to grasp in one big gulp, so we thought we'd step back and give you a quick recap of what goes where in your whole-house video network:

✔ In the wiring closet:

- RG6 coaxial cable feeds from your antenna, or cable company, or both

- A coaxial distribution panel to tie everything together (some vendors call these RF distribution panels)

- An amplifier (may be built into the distribution panel) to boost antenna signals and to keep modulated signals from being broadcast over your antenna (optional for cable TV)

✔ In each room:

- Two RG6 cables connected to the distribution panel (one to the in side of the panel, and one to the out side). Optionally, home offices and media rooms get four RG6 cables for extra flexibility.

- An additional RG6 cable for the satellite receiver (optional).

As long as you've installed a bidirectional distribution panel and amplifier, you should be able to install a cable modem onto any of the external RG6 outlets in your house. An even better approach, however, is to get a distribution panel with a bypass for the cable modem (as we mention in Chapter 6). In this scenario, you just need to connect one of the RG6 cables running to your home office (or wherever the cable modem ends up in your house) to this bypass, instead of to one of the outputs of the distribution panel.

Special Needs of Satellite Systems

DSS (Digital Satellite System) small-dish satellite systems are a great way to receive TV programming, but they're sort of a pain to integrate into your video network. The frequencies that satellite systems use and the way that coaxial cables carry the signal are different than those for standard TV signals. You can't connect your satellite to your video distribution panel's connector and distribute it through your house. To integrate a satellite into your network, you have to be a bit devious. In this section, we tell you how.

We provide two methods of running your DSS satellite signal across your video network. The difference between these methods depends on whether or not you want a two-way network that can bring video back from various rooms.

Running a one-way satellite network

You may be thinking to yourself, "Heck, I've got this dish, so I don't need cable." And we have just the solution. You can build a video network for your DSS system that will carry the outputs from a DSS dish to multiple receivers throughout the home by using a *multiswitch* instead of a distribution panel. The downside to using a multiswitch is that the satellite network is one way. You still have to install a distribution panel if you want to share video sources across the network as we describe in the "Connecting Your Video Network" section, earlier in this chapter. If you want a two-way network with a satellite, check out the following section on a hybrid video network.

To run your satellite picture to different receivers around your home, you need to replace the distribution panel with a special device known as a *multi-switch,* or *voltage switch.* The multiswitch connects to both of the outputs of a dual LNB (low noise block) dish and provides coaxial connections for up to four separate receivers. You simply use RG6 coaxial cable to connect each LNB output to your multiswitch and then run individual lengths of RG6 to each receiver location.

Some DSS dishes include *integrated multiswitches,* so you don't need to buy anything extra. Just run RG6 cables from the back of the dish (where the multiswitch is located) down to the receiver locations.

In some locations, you can't get signals from the major broadcasts networks (such as Fox, NBC, CBS, or ABC) with a satellite. Nor can you get any local independent channels. You have to hook up an aerial antenna or get the basic package from your local cable company.

If you're interested in running an aerial TV antenna to pick up local stations, buy multiswitches that accept the output from a broadcast TV antenna and carry it over the same RG6 cables to your DSS receivers and televisions. These multiswitches include a device called a *diplexer* (check out the sidebar "What if I just want satellite and none of that fancy stuff?"), which lets you integrate both the satellite and local TV signals onto the same RG6 coaxial cable.

Creating a hybrid satellite/video network

The drawback to using a multiswitch as the hub of your video network (as we describe in the preceding section) is that it creates a one-way network — from the satellite dish to the TV. If you want to be able to watch in one room video that's sent from a device in another room (whether from a VCR, a DVD player, or a video camera in your baby's room), you need to use a separate distribution panel for the return signal (or use alternate technologies such as CAT-5e, wireless, or phoneline systems — which we describe later in the chapter).

You have a couple of options if you want to get the best of both worlds in a hybrid two-way satellite/video network:

- **Build a separate video network for your satellite.** Build a video-distribution network for your DSS dish, with independent runs of coaxial RG6 cable from the dish, down through the attic (or from wherever the dish is mounted), and on to each location that will have a satellite receiver. With a multiswitch connected to the outputs of your satellite dish, you can connect up to four separate receivers to a dish. You can then build a video-distribution network using a distribution panel to handle the return signals and any signals you receive from cable or broadcast TV.

  The benefit of this system is that it gives you the ability to watch up to four DSS channels on four TVs simultaneously, while still allowing you the benefit of being able to watch in your bedroom a tape playing in a VCR in the home-theater room. The drawback of this system is the added expense and complexity of building a separate network — more cable to run, more equipment to buy, and more money to spend.

  Although most people mount the multiswitch right at the dish, you might also consider mounting the multiswitch in your wiring closet (vendors such as Leviton and Siemon make rack-mounted versions you can install right next to your video-distribution panel). In this scenario, you'd just run two RG6 cables from the dish to the wiring closet (to connect the two satellite LNBs to the inputs of the multiswitch), and then add another RG6 out to each room that will have a satellite receiver. In fact, if you're not using a modulator in these rooms, you can take the second RG6 from that room (the internal one) and connect it to the multiswitch instead of the distribution panel — so you don't need a third RG6 for satellite in that room.

- **Treat your DSS receivers as source devices — just like VCRs or DVD players.** You still need separate RG6 cabling runs from the dish to the receivers, but you can then use modulators to send the output of these receivers to every television in the house. Just install receivers in your two favorite watching areas and modulate them onto different channels for viewing from other TVs in the house.

This solution has the benefit of adding only moderate cost (you have extra runs only to the receivers) and limited complexity. The drawback is that without using a multiswitch or voltage switch, you can watch only two DSS stations simultaneously (assuming that you have a *dual-LNB satellite* that allows you to run two coaxial lines from your receiver. With a single-LNB receiver, you can watch only one station).

As we mention in Chapter 6, DSS systems can carry high-definition TV signals to your home. To view these signals (assuming you've subscribed to them), you have to jump through a few extra hoops. First, you need to have an HDTV-ready TV and an HDTV satellite receiver (or an HDTV with a built-in HDTV receiver). Second, in most cases you need an antenna with a *third* LNB (because the HDTV signals come in on a different satellite than the normal programming). You might not need to run extra cables from the dish to your receivers, however, because some of these triple LNB dishes include a built-in multiswitch that combines all three LNB outlets onto single runs of coax. If the dish isn't so equipped, you may need to run an extra RG6 cable to the locations that have the HDTV receivers.

Making satellite connections

After running a satellite network, you should have a satellite input coaxial connector in each room. Depending on whether you opted for a hybrid system, you may or may not also have internal and external video jacks for sharing modulated source video devices.

To complete the installation, use a short RG6 patch cable to connect the satellite receiver to the jack on the wall. Doing so brings the satellite signal from the wall to the satellite receiver. After connecting the receiver to your television, you should see crystal-clear satellite television.

Here are a few more tips on DSS systems that are important to remember:

- ✔ **You need a phone line in every room that has a DSS receiver.** The DSS service provider uses this phone line to authenticate your box and provide pay-per-view movies, ACC basketball games, and the like. If your receivers aren't connected to phone lines, you won't be able to get pay-per-view or certain sports programming, and you'll have to pay a full subscription fee for each additional receiver in the house — instead of an extra $5 per receiver.

- ✔ **You can use a so-called *wireless phone jack* to run the phone line across your electrical cables.** They're not really wireless, because they use electrical cabling, but they save you from stringing a phone line across the room like a trip wire. (See Chapter 11 for more on these devices.)

✔ **You should install special *inline amplifiers* if the distance between the dish and a receiver is longer than 100 feet.** These amplifiers boost signal strength for long cable runs and are pretty cheap (between $25 and $100, depending on the level of amplification). They draw their power over the coaxial cable from the receiver, so they're easy to install — just cut the cable and connect the amplifier between them.

✔ **You may want to install coaxial surge protectors on the RG6 runs from your dish.** Doing so prevents lightning strikes on your roof from destroying your DSS receivers. Be careful when you choose a surge protector, though, because the standard cable TV models available in most electronics stores don't pass the entire DSS signal. You need to buy special-purpose surge protectors that specifically support DSS. Some surge protector manufacturers (such as Panamax — www.panamax.com) sell surge protectors that do triple duty — protecting the RG6, the phone line, and the power cord connected to your receiver.

We don't tell you in this chapter how to remotely control all this video equipment from other rooms. We haven't forgotten; we have a long description of how to remotely control video (and audio) network components in Chapters 19 and 20.

What if I just want satellite and none of that fancy stuff?

If you decide that you don't need or want a full-fledged, two-way video network and you're going to use just DSS and local channels in your video network, you need to become familiar with the diplexer. The *diplexer* looks just like the splitter/combiner but combines broadcast or analog cable TV signals with the output of a DSS dish on a single length of RG6 cabling.

You must use diplexers in pairs — one near your DSS dish where the antenna/cable feed is combined with the output of your LNB, and another at the far end of your RG6 cabling, immediately before the cable plugs into your DSS receiver. The first diplexer combines the two cable feeds onto a single RG6 cable. The second splits this signal back into two separate signals — one

connects to your receiver's LNB input, and the other connects to the Antenna/CATV input on the back of the receiver.

If you feed two DSS receivers directly from a dual LNB dish (without using a multiswitch) and you want to add your local channels from cable or antenna, you need four diplexers. If you use a multiswitch to send the output of your dish to more than two receivers, you need to buy a multiswitch with a built-in diplexer and then use an additional diplexer at each receiver.

Even though diplexers and regular splitter/combiners look pretty much the same, they're two different devices. Don't try to save $20 by using any old splitter in your system: It won't work.

And in This Corner, CAT-5e

The backbone of your video network — the primary electrical highway that carries TV and other video programming around your house — should be constructed using RG6 coaxial cable. Bottom line: It's just the best (and easiest, and most compatible) way of doing things. But sometimes you need to get video to and from places where RG6 doesn't go. And sometimes you just can't put any more video on the RG6 cable. A smart home has a great alternative already in the walls — the CAT-5e cabling that's also used for phone networks, data networks, and more.

CAT-5e is great for distributing locally sourced video (from DVD players, PVRs, and the like) around the house, but it's not suited for carrying multichannel incoming video from broadcast antennas, cable TV feeds, or satellite dishes. So don't mistake what we're about to discuss as an alternative to an RG6 network. Instead, it's a complementary network.

The key to using CAT-5e to carry video lies in the electronic devices attached at the ends of the CAT-5e network. These electronics make the CAT-5e unusable for other services, such as telephones or data LANs. You can't just plug a video device into one of your phone jacks and expect it to work. It won't, and neither will the phones until you unplug the video electronics.

But if you read our discussion of a flexible CAT-5e network in Chapter 2, you might have an inkling of what we're getting at. (If you don't, take a break from this discussion and take a quick peek.) To use CAT-5e for video, you need to go into your wiring closet and separate (physically and electrically) the cable runs you want to use for video from your other networks. These cable runs then need to be cross-connected together on your main distribution panel (or on a separate panel set up for your video over CAT-5e network) so that all locations on your CAT-5e video network are wired together. Some manufacturers, such as Leviton, make a special hub for your wiring closet to connect together video over CAT-5e systems.

After your CAT-5e cables are connected together in your wiring panel, all you need to do to enable video over your CAT-5e cables is to install some endpoint devices designed for the task. These devices can take a few forms:

✔ **Stand-alone sender and receiver units:** These are small boxes (smaller than many video components) that can sit on the rack next to the TV. The sender device sits in your media room (or wherever you want to share the video component) and connects to it like a modulator does — using the RCA composite or S-video connections from the back of the shared component. The sender is also connected by a CAT-5e patch cable to the RJ45 jack in the wall that you've dedicated to video. On the far end, you do the reverse — plug the receiver into the video-dedicated RJ45 jack, and plug the composite or S-video outputs into your TV or home-theater receiver. The majority of these CAT-5e video-distribution systems also carry stereo audio signals coming from your source device, so they can do double duty as a music distribution source.

✔ **Senders and receivers integrated into wall outlets:** These devices are functionally the same as the stand-alone units but are shrunk to wall outlets. The connection between the source components and the remote TVs stays the same, but instead of connecting an external box to an RJ45 outlet, you replace your RJ45 outlet with this device.

Note: In some systems, you'll see a bit of a mix-and-match approach, with a stand-alone sender and remote wall outlet receivers.

The stand-alone units are the most common, and typically have better picture quality. Eventually, the outlet-sized units will catch up, but right now they're better for low-fidelity applications such as babycams.

The majority of the video-over-CAT-5e systems we're discussing can carry only one video program at a time — they're basically like extensions of composite or S-video — You can't plug a DVD and a PVR, for example, into one of these devices and carry the signals to different TVs in the house simultaneously. Every TV receives the same signal with these systems, and you can't put two senders on a single CAT-5e. A few high-end, expensive systems, such as those made by Crestron (see Chapter 20), can be used as a multisource video-transmission system.

Ack! Two warnings in one section — you must think that video-over-CAT-5e is bad news. It's not, but we need to tell you one more thing. Some video-over-CAT-5e solutions on the market are *point-to-point* solutions, meaning there can be only one receiver to go along with the sender — you can send video from one spot to another but not to several others. If you want multiple receivers, make sure you buy a system that can handle that demand.

As we write this, video-over-CAT-5e systems are still new and haven't reached their full potential. We think that they'll become a better alternative to distribution of in-home video sources than the more traditional modulator and RG6 approach — mainly because they'll be able to carry higher-quality video signals (such as S-video and even component video) and fully digital audio signals. For example, ChannelPlus's SVC-10 system can carry S-video and Dolby Digital surround sound to a remote location over CAT-5e (try that with a modulator!). As these systems mature and become capable of supporting higher-quality video and audio signals in a truly *multipoint* way (from one location to several others), they may make modulators obsolete.

Cut the Cord: Wireless Alternatives for Video Distribution

Phones and data networks aren't the only things in your home that can benefit from advances in wireless networking. A few products that use wireless technologies work well for your home-entertainment network if all you need to do is add a device (for example, one TV or one set of speakers) rather than take care of your entire whole-home networking needs.

Wireless video-distribution systems accept the video and audio outputs of a video source — such as a VCR, DSS satellite receiver, or DVD player — and send them somewhere else in the home using an RF wireless link. These systems basically consist of two small units, each containing an antenna. The transmitter unit attaches to your video source through standard RCA-type audio and video connectors; the receiver unit usually offers both an RCA and an RF output to connect to the television on the far end. Figure 7-4 shows a wireless video-distribution network.

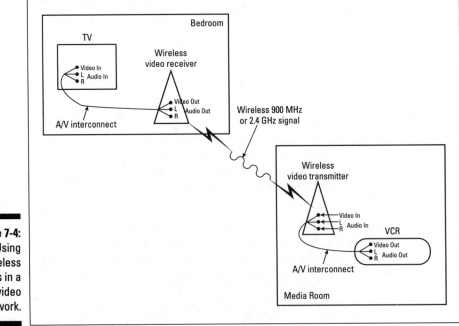

Figure 7-4:
Using wireless systems in a video network.

If you're looking into a wireless video system, here's what you should keep in mind:

✔ **What frequency spectrum does it use?** Some of these systems use the 900-MHz frequency band; others use the higher 2.4-GHz band. In general, 2.4-GHz systems perform better because higher-frequency RF signals run cleaner with less interference from other systems and pass through walls and ceilings better. Additionally, 2.4-GHz systems provide more available bandwidth to carry the video signals.

✔ **Does the system transmit audio in mono or stereo?** If your video source includes high-quality sound, you probably want to spend a bit more to get stereo audio.

✔ **Does the system carry IR (infrared) control signals?** Some do, and it sure is handy to be able to do things such as pause, rewind, or change channels while watching a program in the bedroom without having to walk to the living room. This feature is a must-have to us, unless you already have an IR control network built into your home — but if you have an IR network installed, we're pretty sure that you want to have a coaxial video-distribution network as well, so you won't be needing the wireless system.

If you live in an older historic home, the type with tin ceilings, know that these reflect and block signals. Therefore, RF video transmitters may not give you the quality you'd like.

Use What You Already Have: Phoneline Alternatives for Video Distribution

Most of the action in developing home-networking systems that run on existing phone wires is in the data-networking field, but some companies are looking into ways to use phone lines for home-entertainment systems. Like the phoneline data-networking systems we discuss in Chapter 16, these products utilize digital signal processing to carry entertainment signals on different frequencies than those used by telephone service. This means they can be used simultaneously with telephone equipment connected to the network.

These systems use different frequencies than analog telephone systems use, but there's no guarantee that they use different frequencies than the phoneline data-networking systems use. That means interference could be a major problem if you try to use both systems in your home, so we strongly recommend against it. Single-purpose wiring eliminates these kinds of conflicts, which is why we think it's the best way to go.

Terk Technologies is a major manufacturer of antennas and home-theater accessories. The Leapfrog HomeNetwork by Terk (www.terk.com) consists of a pair of devices that transmit video and audio signals from a source device (such as a satellite receiver or PVR) to a remote location over existing phone lines. The transmitter half of the pair connects to the RF or line-level video and audio outputs of the source unit and plugs into a standard RJ-11 or RJ-45 phone jack. At the remote end, the receiver also plugs into an RJ-11/45 phone jack and connects to the RF or line-level audio and video inputs of the remote television or audio system. Leapfrog also carries infrared control signals over your phone lines, so you can carry your remote with you to the room containing the receiver and do all the pausing, freeze-framing, fast-forwarding, and channel-changing you like, without running back and forth.

Chapter 8

Bringing You Music

. . . .

. . . .

*L*ike the video systems we discuss in the previous two chapters, home-audio systems are increasingly becoming *whole*-home audio systems. Wiring your home to provide music everywhere and anywhere from a central set of source components is convenient and a money saver. What's more, it's probably the only way you can effectively tap into some of the music services and Internet music functionality coming down the road. By focusing and centralizing, you make it easier to interface with anything.

This chapter looks at many of the cabling issues involved in creating a whole-home audio network. In Chapter 9, we tell you about some wireless options.

Zoning Out: Single-Zone versus Multizone Systems

In a *single-zone audio system,* you have only one audio source, which you distribute across the network at any given time. You can turn various sets of speakers on or off, but you don't have the ability to listen to different audio sources in different parts of your house at the same time. A *multizone audio system,* on the other hand, allows one family member to listen to, say, a CD while another person listens to the audio channel of a VCR.

Single-zone systems have a few advantages:

✔ **Inexpensive:** A single zone needs the smallest number of components to get up and running, and the components themselves are the least expensive to purchase.

The trouble with multichannel audio networks

The stereo audio standard, in which sound is separated into two channels (one for the left channel and one for the right), still dominates music production. With the advent of home theater, however, music can now be produced using multiple channels to drive a multitude of speakers. These new audio standards use speakers in front of you, behind you, and possibly alongside you to re-create the spatial dynamics of the concert hall in your home (at least that's how fancy magazines describe it). They can simulate a train passing by on the left, for example, by having sound come from the front speakers, then the left speakers, and finally the rear speakers, with fading at the end.

You can buy an audio system that supports home-theater standards, such as Dolby Digital or DTS, or the new SACD (Super Audio Compact Disc) and DVD-Audio systems, which use a multichannel system to create neat sound effects. Movie soundtracks, multichannel audio discs (still rare, but becoming more common), and a few TV shows come through speakers in front of you, behind you, and beside you. These multichannel systems also sometimes support subwoofers (which give you really deep bass sounds), floor-shaking transducers (devices that mount in the floor and literally shake it), a special-effects channel, and other wild-and-wooly add-ons.

For the average home (read that as a non-millionaire home), we recommend that you don't add multichannel capabilities to your whole-home audio network, at least not right now. The wiring solutions we recommend here will enable you to add multichannel capabilities in the future. Although you can build an audio network that goes beyond the two-channel (stereo) limit today, the network quickly becomes extremely complicated and prohibitively expensive.

By all means, go ahead and set up a special multichannel amplifier, a surround-sound decoder, and surround-sound speakers, but do so in your home-theater or home-entertainment room. When you run your whole-home audio network, stick with good old stereo.

✔ **Easy to set up:** In the simplest case, a single-zone system can consist of a single source — such as a CD player — connected to one amplifier and then, through an *impedance-matching system,* to several sets of speakers. (We discuss impedance matching in the "Matching impedance" section, later in this chapter).

✔ **Upgradeable:** The hardest part about building an audio network is getting the right wires into the walls in the right places. Once you do that, you can easily switch from a single-zone system to a multizone system by simply upgrading a few components and swapping out a few connections.

Multizone systems provide the following benefits:

✔ **Multiple audio sources:** Multizone systems allow different members of your family to listen to different audio sources in different areas at the same time. For example, you can send the output from your CD player to one room and the output from your AM/FM radio tuner to another. This feature tends to increase domestic tranquility, just as our Founding Fathers recommended.

✔ **Video-network integration:** Multizone systems integrate better with your video-distribution system. The video-distribution network that we describe in Chapters 5 and 6 brings audio and video to each television in your house. With a multizoned audio network, however, you can take that one step further to send the stereo audio portion of any video program to a set of speakers near your remote TVs. This feature is appealing for two reasons: Stereo video modulators are pretty darn expensive, and separate speakers usually sound much better than those inside your TV.

Regardless of whether you choose to install a single-zone or multizone system, the basic wiring infrastructure is similar (see Chapter 9). You can start with something simple and make it more sophisticated later.

Audio Connections (in the Short and Long Run)

The wires that connect the various parts of an audio system can be divided into two groups: the wires that run between components such as CD players and amplifiers, and the wires that connect amplifiers to speakers. (A third group of wires — those that connect control devices such as touchpad panels from Crestron (`www.crestron.com`) — is covered in Chapter 20.)

Your audio system generally carries audio signals between components in one of two ways:

✔ **Line-level signals:** These are low-power electrical signals that contain an analog, electrical representation of the musical sound wave but not the electrical power to move your speaker diaphragms and create sound. Line-level signals are used by everything in an audio system up to the power amplifier — the CD player, the tape deck, the audio outputs of a VCR or DVD player, to name just a few. These are usually short-run connections between components.

✔ **Speaker-level signals:** These are higher-powered signals that come out of your amplifier (or receiver, if you don't have separate components) and drive your speakers — that is, they cause the electromagnets in your speakers to move, creating the sound you hear. These are generally the long-haul connections that run through your walls and around your house.

Cool new audio source devices

In the old days — back in 1998 — there weren't many audio-source devices to connect to your whole-home audio network. You had CD players, cassette decks, radio tuners, and the audio coming out of video devices such as VCRs and DVD players. That was about it.

Several new trends have turned the audio world upside down. The biggest of these is the *convergence* of the computer and audio worlds. Computer-based audio files, such as MP3s, have taken the music world by storm — millions of people use MP3 players as their primary means of storing and listening to music. You can take advantage of this in a whole-home audio system in two ways. You can connect your computer — with its stored MP3 files, streaming online music services, and network connection — to play music through your audio system. You can also buy special-purpose devices such as Request's AudioRequest (www.request.com) or Sonic-Blue's RioCentral (www.sonicblue.com). These devices are a kind of *home-media server*, as we discuss in Chapter 5. They use standard audio interconnects (RCA jack) and connect to

your whole-home audio system just like a CD player does.

The other big news in the audio world has been the advent of new optical disc standards to supplement (and in the dreams of their creators, replace) the CD. An SACD or DVD-Audio disc can fit a lot more data than a CD can. This extra capacity lets these new discs carry higher-quality music (because, in the digital world, more data equals better sound) and also enables them to provide multichannel, surround-sound music. We've heard both SACD and DVD-Audio systems, and they sound great — though we think CDs can sound pretty great too. The biggest issue with SACD and DVD-Audio is that they're not compatible — so we've reached another VHS versus Betamax type battle. We think that your best bet is to hold off on buying either one — a few consumer electronics manufacturers are coming out with players that can handle CD, SACD, and DVD-Audio (and video DVDs for that matter) all in one powerful box. These aren't widely available yet, but we expect that they will be.

We'd be remiss if we didn't tell you that you *can* run line-level signal cables between rooms. Doing so, however, exposes you to some problems that you don't face with speaker-level signals, such as loss of audio information over long distances and interference from other wires. Moreover, if you run low-level signal cables through your walls, they must be amplified; every room in which you want to hear your audio network would need an audio amplifier. Some vendors offer systems that can carry line-level signals around your home over CAT-5e cabling. Because these systems use standard CAT-5e UTP cabling (as discussed in Chapter 2), they make your audio network more flexible. For example, you can take an extra CAT-5e cable in your bedroom (perhaps one that's hooked up to the phone system but doesn't have a phone connected to it) and hook it into your audio network instead.

Some digital audio devices — such as CD, SACD, and DVD players — let you carry a digital (rather than analog) signal between the component and the amplification system. To use such a function, you need a digital-to-analog converter built into the amplifier or receiver to convert the digital signal to an analog signal that can drive your speakers. (If your amplifier or receiver supports this function, you should see a Digital In jack on the back.) Several types of cables are used for this kind of connection, including fiber-optic cable and coaxial cable with a standard RCA jack on each end (which one you use depends on what kind of connections your equipment manufacturer installed on its equipment — there's no single standard). At present, digital signal transmission is an uncommon method of distributing audio, but we expect that to change as systems that can use CAT-5e cabling for digital audio become prevalent. (See Chapter 9 for more information on these CAT-5e systems, and how they can form an alternative to speaker wiring in your walls.)

Line level (for the short haul)

Cables called *line-level interconnects* carry *line-level signals,* the unamplified signals that move between audio components. Any cable with this type of jack is generically called an *RCA cable* (because RCA created it). Interconnect cables are usually shielded wires and typically come in *stereo pairs* (two separate wires bound in a left and right channel configuration).

The rise of multichannel audio in home theater has lead many manufacturers to create interconnects with an odd number of cables and connectors — five, for example, to connect the two front, two rear, and single center channels, or single cables to connect subwoofers to the receiver.

The number of choices you'll find in the interconnect marketplace can be bewildering. Go to a stereo store, and you'll find interconnects ranging from freebies thrown in with a stereo system to $1000-a-foot cables wired with precious metals — silver or gold or copper mined by old-world artisans at the purest mine in the world, somewhere in Bolivia (or so the typical advertising pitch goes). Whether or not these super-expensive cables make any difference is a matter of intense debate among audio aficionados — go check out one of the audio newsgroups on the Internet (such as rec.audio.opinion) if you want to see some people really slugging it out on the subject.

You probably get what you pay for with really cheap (or free) cables. You may want to seek out a knowledgeable and trustworthy expert if you haven't made up your mind on what to buy.

Speaker level (for the long haul)

The wires that connect your speakers to your amplifier are beefier than those that carry delicate line-level signals. Like interconnects, a huge range of speaker-cable designs are available, but in general, all cables consist of two conductors (a solid wire or a bunch of smaller wires stranded together) within a common jacket or insulator.

In a whole-home audio system, you can run speaker wire in two places:

- **Through the walls:** You use special in-wall speaker cabling to connect your centrally located amplifier or amplifiers to remote outlets or in-wall speakers throughout your home. (We talk about what to look for when you choose in-wall cabling in just a moment.)

- **From the wall to the speaker (patch cabling):** This speaker wire connects your stand-alone speakers to speaker outlets installed in your walls. You can use the same cable you have in your walls if you'd like, or you can run down to the stereo shop and pick up some shorter lengths of precut and preconnectorized standard speaker cable for this job.

The only reason not to use the same wire that's in your walls is aesthetics, really. The wire in your walls is usually covered with lots of silk-screened writing and labeling that stands out like a sore thumb. You can buy speaker patch cables that are easier to hide than the in-wall stuff, and you can even paint some brands to match your walls.

Cables and Components

Like the other networks in your home, a home-audio network can be as simple or as complicated as you'd like. In this section, you find out about a few components that are common to just about every home-audio network.

Control systems

A *control system* is the switch that allows you to select your audio sources, such as your CD, tuner, or cassette deck. The control system matches the audio source device that you want to listen to with the amplifier that powers your speakers. (We're not talking about the remote-control networks that allow you to switch from, say, your CD to your tuner from another room. For more information about remote-control networks, check out Chapter 20.)

The preamplifier or control amplifier installed in your audio system — or the one built into your integrated amplifier or receiver if you aren't using separate components — performs the source-switching function for a single-zone, single-amplifier system.

Single-zone control systems

If you're creating a single-zone distribution system but want to use multiple amplifiers, you face an obstacle. In general, audio source devices such as CD players have only one set of line-level outputs, so you can't just plug one device into two separate amplifiers. You can choose one of the following strategies to distribute your audio signal. Each uses a different piece of audio equipment:

- **Multiroom integrated amplifier:** This special amplifier accepts the stereo line-level input from a source device and amplifies *the same signal* into several pairs of stereo speaker outputs (these amplifiers usually feed up to four or six pairs of speakers).

Don't confuse a multiroom amplifier with *multichannel amplifiers* in surround-sound systems for home theaters. In a home theater, each speaker (the front, center, surround, and subwoofer) receives a different audio signal — for example, a five-channel amplifier has five separate line-level inputs from your surround-sound decoder. A multiroom integrated amplifier takes a single stereo pair of line-level inputs and internally sends this signal to more than one pair of amplifiers.

- **Signal-distribution amplifier:** This device takes the output of a source device, splits it into multiple outputs, and then amplifies these outputs to ensure that your signal is not degraded (if you split the signal without amplifying it, it would be too weak and would cause distortion that you would hear as a background noise or hiss). You can then connect these outputs to individual stereo amplifiers — one for each pair of speakers.

If you're just splitting the signal from an audio source device to a pair of amplifiers, you can save money by using a Y-splitter audio cable that splits a single pair of stereo audio signals into two pairs — one for each amplifier. You can buy these cables at Radio Shack and similar retailers. If you're trying to send a signal to more than two amplifiers at once, you're much better off with one of the solutions we just mentioned.

Multizone control systems

Multizone systems require special control systems that can take the output of several source devices and route these line-level signals to multiple amplifiers (one for each zone, remember).

Two kinds of components can be the basis of a multizone audio system:

- A high-end preamplifier or receiver with built-in multizone capabilities (most of these systems are limited to two zones).

- Multizone control systems that can feed any of your audio source component's signals to a specific zone's amplifiers (these systems allow up to eight or more zones).

Do not attempt to put in a multizone system unless you have access to an audio geek. The documentation is awful, and the installation requires adept handling of a remote-control device.

Because of the increased costs, you may decide *not* to install a multizone audio system in your home right away. By following some of our guidelines throughout this book, however, we feel that you can indeed get a multizone treatment without breaking your bank account. No matter what decision you make, you should install the proper wiring infrastructure in your house ahead of time (and we tell you how in Chapter 9).

Amplifier and speakers

The basic job of an audio amplifier is to increase the power of an audio signal enough to let the speaker recreate sound. How loud those speakers get depends on two factors:

- ✔ **The power of the amplifier:** How many watts of head-banging power the amplifier pumps out.
- ✔ **The sensitivity of the speakers:** How many decibels of loudness the speaker produces when a given number of watts comes from the amplifier.

Amplifiers are one of the largest issues you confront when putting together a multi-room home-entertainment system, so be sure to put adequate time into researching your options. Don't make the mistake of assuming that you can just run speaker wire all over the house and then use your present amplifier. The salesperson at your local stereo store should be able to help you figure out all your amplifier needs. To get the best help from the stereo-store techie, we recommend that you draw a picture of the interior of your house and note where you want each device and speaker to go, along with accurate distances and likely conduit paths. This way, the salesperson can help you calculate your needs based on the equipment that store carries. Try a few stores, compare differences in approaches and pricing, and make a decision.

Impedance matters

When making the match between an amplifier and speakers, you need to take into account the speakers' impedance. *Impedance* is the force that the current coming from your amplifier pushes against. All you need to know about impedance is that if you don't have enough, you may damage your amplifier! That's because lower-impedance speakers may cause an amplifier to overheat, which is never a good thing for a piece of electrical equipment.

The impedance rating of your speakers and your amplifier must match. Most speakers are rated at 8 ohms impedance, but some are rated at 4 ohms. Lower-impedance loudspeakers are more difficult for amplifiers to power. In fact, many inexpensive amplifiers are incapable of powering 4-ohm speakers and may overheat or just plain not work if you try to combine them.

Wiring more than one speaker to an individual amplifier channel greatly decreases the overall impedance that the speakers present to the amplifier. So even if you have an amp rated for 8-ohm impedance and speakers that are rated at 8 ohms as well, if you wire two speakers to the same output (in different rooms, for example), you effectively halve the impedance — to 4 ohms. Drat. Adding more speakers lowers the impedance even more. Double drat. Pretty soon you're going to damage your amplifier.

Matching impedance

Adding more than two sets of speakers to an amplifier may cause it to malfunction, because you lower its impedance. If you're thinking about installing a multizone system, you can skip this part — multizone systems are designed with individual amplifiers for each set of speakers.

You can avoid this impedance problem in one of the following ways:

- ✔ **Use separate amplifiers for each extra pair of speakers:** If you use a separate amplifier for each set of speakers, you won't need to worry about impedance matching. You can blithely skip this section.

- ✔ **Use an *impedance-matching device:*** This device lets you connect multiple speakers to an individual amplifier channel without causing impedance problems, but it does decrease the amount of power that each speaker receives (and therefore the speaker's maximum loudness).

You may be tempted to hook several speakers up to one central unit, but overall, the more amplifier power you have, the better. If you can afford additional amplifiers — they're relatively inexpensive — go ahead and get them.

If you decide to go with a single amplifier for your home-audio network, you need to get some sort of impedance-matching device into your system. You have a couple of choices:

- ✔ **A central impedance-matching transformer system:** This device is a small box that accepts a single stereo pair of speaker-wire connections and has several sets of speaker outlets. The internal transformer matches the impedance, so even if you have several pairs of speakers simultaneously connected to the amplifier, the amplifier functions correctly. Many of these transformer boxes also double as speaker selector switches — on/off switches for your speakers — so you can control which speakers are playing music and which are blessedly silent.

- ✔ **An impedance-matching transformer built into an in-wall volume control:** These volume controls, which you place in each room with speakers, perform the same function as a central matching transformer, plus they let you adjust the volume without using a remote control. Some of these devices even have built-in on/off switches, so you can disable the speakers in the room — a nice feature to have in a single-zone system when you don't want to be disturbed.

If your audio network will be limited — feeding only two rooms, for example — you can probably get away with not using an impedance-matching system. Just be sure to choose an amplifier or receiver that has two sets of speaker outlets, and make sure that it can handle the impedance load that your speakers put upon it. After you get beyond two sets of speakers, though, we highly recommend that you install an impedance-matching system. Skipping this step is not worth the risk of damaging expensive equipment.

Speaker cable

The backbone of your home-audio network is the speaker cable you install in your walls. You can't just pick up any old speaker cable for this job — you need to use cabling designed for in-wall use. Look for the following when choosing cable:

- ✔ **Gauge:** The thickness of the conductors in your speaker wire is measured in units known as AWG (American Wire Gauge). AWG works on an inverse scale: lower numbers denote thicker cables. Most audio experts recommend that you choose a minimum of 16-gauge in-wall wiring (a recommendation with which we agree). Many people go with 14 or even 12 AWG wires, which is probably overkill; these heavy gauge cables are really thick, making them hard to pull through the walls.

- ✔ **UL listing:** Underwriter's Laboratories (UL) rate in-wall cables for safety and quality. Look for wires that are rated at least class two (UL CL2) or class three (UL CL3). The class rating is usually silk-screened on the wire jacket.

Always check with your electrician or local building inspector to confirm the cable rating that your town requires. Although there is a *national electric code,* which lays out minimum standards for in-wall wiring, many municipalities have more stringent requirements. In fact, there's a bewildering array of such requirements, and not meeting them could result in your local building or electrical inspector making you rip out your wiring and start over.

- ✔ **Extra features:** Some wire manufacturers design their speaker cables with features such as super-slippery cable jackets that slide through your wall more easily, length markers silk-screened on the jacket, and easy-to-remove insulation for terminating the wires — the kind of stuff that makes installers happy.

Audio connectors

Unlike video cables (and most of the other wires and cables we discuss throughout the book), speaker wires have no standard, one-size-fits-all family of connectors. You can terminate speaker wires in many different ways, leaving enough options to make the whole matter confusing.

Following are the ways you can connect the speaker wires:

✔ **Bare wire:** Many people choose not to get too fancy and just strip off the insulation and use the bare wire ends to terminate their speaker wires. We don't like this method because the exposed copper wiring tends to corrode. Also, having exposed wire ends increases your chances of accidentally short-circuiting the wires.

✔ **Pins:** Many manufacturers install (or sell for you to install) gold-plated pins that you can crimp or solder onto the ends of your wires. These pins make hookup much simpler, and they look neater, too (in case your neighbors are snooping around the back of your speakers). Hardcore audiophiles tend not to prefer this method of terminating speaker wires, but we think it's a good, reliable, and flexible choice.

✔ **Banana plugs:** No fruit is harmed in the manufacture of these speaker terminations — they're so named because these cylindrically shaped pins bend outward in the middle and roughly approximate the shape of a portly banana. Banana connectors come in both single and double varieties. In other words, you can have a single banana on both the positive and negative conductors of your speaker wire, or you can connect both wires to a double banana. The double bananas are spaced apart by a standardized distance, so they fit correctly into the banana connectors on your amplifier, speaker, or speaker outlet. We really like banana plugs because they're so easy to plug in and the outward bend in the middle of the plug ensures a nice, tight connection.

✔ **Spades:** Hard-core audiophiles (the people who live and breathe audio equipment and have a stack of dog-eared stereo magazines next to the bed) believe that these connectors offer the most secure, airtight connections. Spade connectors are U-shaped and fit over standard, screw-type binding posts — allowing you to get in there with a wrench or strong pair of fingers and tighten things down. We agree with the audio types — spades are the best connection method if your equipment has binding posts.

Any of the last three speaker-wire terminations is better than using bare wire ends. Which one you choose will probably be driven by the kinds of connections available on your amplifiers and speakers. You find the following connectors on typical amplifiers, speakers, and wall outlets:

✔ **Spring-loaded clips:** These are simple connectors with a spring-loaded clip that you push down to accept a thin, bare wire or pin connector. When you release the spring, it holds the wire or pin in place. You find these on most older audio systems and on less-expensive current models.

✔ **Banana-plug receptacles:** Some speakers and amplifiers accept only banana plugs. Be sure to check that your banana receptacles are designed to accept double bananas before you terminate your speaker wires. (Double bananas do have a standard, but some audio equipment — mainly from Europe — is not built to this standard and requires you to use two single bananas on your speaker wire.)

✔ **Five-way binding posts:** This speaker connector is the most flexible, because it can accept single and double bananas, bare wire, pins, and spades. These connectors consist of a pair of metal posts with a couple of holes — one running parallel to the length of the posts to accept bananas, and one running through the posts at a 90-degree angle to accept bare wires or pins. Spade connectors simply slide over the posts, like a well-thrown horseshoe wrapping around a metal pole. Five-way binding posts also have plastic, screw-down caps on the posts, which you use to tighten the connection on bare wire, pins, or spades.

Speaker outlets

A whole-home audio system uses speaker-wire connections to distribute music — that is to say, you run speaker wires through your walls to each room that's part of your network.

If you don't want speaker wires dangling out of holes in your walls, you'll need finished outlets for ending runs of in-wall speaker cable. Like the video outlets we discuss in Chapter 6, these outlets are designed to fit into standard single-, double-, or triple-gang electrical junction boxes, and they come in all sorts of neat combinations. For example, you can buy a double-gang-sized outlet that contains two RG6 video-cable outlets and a pair of five-way speaker binding posts, which allows you to make your audio and video connections right next to each other. You'll find a host of speaker outlets in any good home-electronics store or catalog.

When you purchase speaker outlets, do yourself a favor and skip any that have those spring-loaded, clip-style connections and go right for the banana or five-way binding post types. The spring-loaded clips won't accept expensive speaker cables with the huge, gold-plated spade connectors. Besides, they're pretty flimsy.

In-wall speakers

When you're considering a whole-home audio system, you need to know about a subcategory of speakers: those that can be flush mounted in your walls or ceiling. (See Chapter 5 for information on woofers and tweeters and that kind of stuff.)

And now for something completely different

Traditional speaker-wire systems are not the only way to get audio around your home, but for most people they're the best and easiest method. As computer networks and audio networks converge in more ways, however, it's possible to skip the traditional speaker-wire network and get your music by alternate means. We describe in detail some other options for audio networks in Chapter 9, but thought we'd mention a few cool options for you right now.

✔ You can use CAT-5e cabling (the same kind used for computer networks) to distribute line-level audio signals around the house. You'll need some special devices on the ends of these cables to make this work (described in Chapter 9), but these new devices are becoming cheaper by the day. Audio over CAT-5e networks is still new and rare, but that will change as more people wire their homes with CAT-5e.

✔ You can converge (or combine) your audio and computer networks and use PCs and computer-based PC peripherals to store and play your music. You still need speakers and amplifiers to play the music, but you can use the CD player inside your PC to play CDs, or you can store your music as MP3 files on the PC (or on a special music server, such as an AudioRequest). Music can then be carried over your home's computer LAN to remote locations for playback. Computer-based audio systems also give you the option of getting your music from online music services offered by many broadband ISPs such as DirecTV DSL and Road Runner.

Some of these computer-like audio systems are sophisticated. For example, Request's ARQ Zone system syncs with your main AudioRequest to provide multizone audio in your home. You can even sync these devices remotely.

In-wall speakers are appealing to many homeowners because they greatly increase the neatness of your installation, and give you that cool, custom look. Just imagine — no outlets, no exposed wires, no ungainly speakers to put on stands or bookshelves. Definitely a great way to go!

In-wall speakers, like conventional models, come in all sizes and shapes, but you should look for a few specifics:

✔ **Check the speaker size:** Make sure that whatever speakers you choose are going to fit in your walls without major modifications. Most of the common, rectangular wall models are designed to fit between standard stud spacings (16 inches), but all the same, go ahead and check your walls ahead of time.

✔ **Check the speaker depth:** You probably don't want your in-wall speakers sticking out a few inches. Again, most in-wall designs take into account the average depth of your wall, but double-check before you start cutting holes.

✔ **Think upward:** The walls aren't the only place to stick a speaker — ceilings are appropriate locations as well, especially in locations where your audio system serves primarily as background music. In those situations, you won't be quite as concerned about having some geometrically perfect speaker arrangement that allows you every nuance of the stereo music experience. If keeping your sound out of sight is a priority, you can even find round, in-ceiling speakers that look just like light fixtures.

✔ **Listen to them:** Unlike standard models, in-wall speakers require a commitment — namely a big hole in your wall. Always listen to your speakers in a reputable stereo store before you take the leap. You'll be glad you did.

✔ **Check out the speaker grill's design:** Many models have paintable grills, so you can make them match the walls around them — or make them stand out if you like that kind of design statement. Most speaker grills are innocuous (some even claim to be invisible when installed), and we won't fault you if looks are just as important as sound quality.

If you really want to hide your speakers, check out the speakers sold by Gekko (www.artgekko.com). These very thin speakers hang on the wall, like a picture. You can even outfit them with digitally printed artwork!

Chapter 9

Running Audio Here, There, and Everywhere

*I*n Chapter 8, we describe the various pieces and parts that fit into a whole-home audio network. In this chapter, our goal is to tell you how to hook all these pieces together. We begin with a description of the simplest whole-home audio network: a single-zone system that provides a single audio source simultaneously to each room. Then we move on to a brief description of more sophisticated, multizone audio systems, which let you listen to different audio programs in different parts of the house. Hot on the heels of this discussion is a description of systems that distribute audio using CAT-5e cabling (the cables used in a computer LAN). We don't stop there — we also discuss wireless alternatives to a home-audio network.

Although you can choose to run line-level cables between different amplifiers located in each room, we prefer to run speaker wires to different sets of speakers to build a home-audio network. Using line-level wiring complicates the network and makes it more susceptible to interference. We're excited about the line level over CAT-5e systems coming onto the market, but most of today's systems are not as flexible as a multizone speaker-wire audio system. That's because most of these systems are only single zone (and many can distribute only a single audio source, so you can't use them to send audio from your CD player and the radio and the music coming out of your MP3 jukebox).

Although most CAT-5e systems don't have multiple inputs for audio source devices, you can get around this limitation. Use your audio receiver as the source device for the distribution system, and then use the receiver to switch between different sources (radio, CD, and so on). To make this work, you need a set of Audio Out RCA jacks on the back of the receiver. You may also be able to use the Tape Out jacks on the back of the receiver, if you have a spare set, because these also send audio out of the receiver.

Reaching for a Star

The speaker-wire audio network that we recommend is similar to the video network (and most of the other networks we talk about): a centrally distributed star configuration. All audio sources, amplification, and control systems are in one place, and speaker cables are distributed in a star fashion, with individual runs going to each speaker location. As is the case with your video network (but not with the other networks we describe), you probably want to use your home-theater room (or media room) as the central distribution point for your audio network. We describe the media room in Chapter 2.

The audio network is different than the other networks in one major way — it's a one-way network. All audio source devices are located at the central distribution point. This type of network doesn't lend itself to a two-way architecture, in which remote source devices can send signals back to the central distribution point.

You can distribute an audio source located in a room other than your media room, but the process is difficult. Connect a long run of line-level component cable (the type of cable that typically connects components such a CD player and a receiver) from the remote audio source to your central amplifier control point. We don't address this option in our basic network architecture, so consult with a knowledgeable installer if you want to do this.

The best way to distribute line-level audio signals over long distances is to use something called a *balanced line-level cable.* The pros use it in recording studios. The problem with trying to set up this kind of audio distribution on a consumer level is that only a small percentage of home-audio equipment is outfitted with these kinds of connectors (only the expensive stuff, for the most part). Many audio manufacturers have decided that these traditional balanced audio systems are not practical for the residential market, but they have found an alternative: using CAT-5e UTP cabling to carry line-level signals around the house. We discuss this in detail in the "Catching up with CAT-5e" section, later in this chapter.

Single-Zone Simplicity

The simplest and most inexpensive way to move into whole-home audio is to build a *single-zone audio network,* which is a network that allows you to send an audio source to speakers in different rooms (although you can't listen to different audio sources in different rooms). We tell you about the functions of the individual components of such a network in Chapter 8; in this section, we tell you how to hook up this network.

Even simple, single-zone audio networks have a ton of variations. Your personal preferences, budget, and existing audio components play a big role in shaping your network. For example, you can choose between an all-in-one receiver and an integrated amp to handle the control and amplification roles, or you can use separate components. You can decide to use a single amplifier with impedance-matching devices, or you can set up separate amplifiers in your media room for each pair of speakers. You can choose in-wall speakers or conventional models.

Regardless of what you decide, the basic network architecture remains the same: pairs of speaker cables run in a star-wiring configuration from a central amplification point to each speaker location in the house.

Installing a single-zone, single-amplifier system

Here's a general layout for a single-zone, single-amplifier system:

1. **Using pairs of line-level audio interconnect cables, connect your source devices to the inputs of your preamplifier, or *control amplifier.***

2. **Use a pair of RCA cables to connect your amplifier to your power amplifier.**

   If you're using a receiver (or an integrated amplifier) instead of separate components, you can skip this step. Instead, connect your audio source components directly to the receiver.

3. **Choose an impedance-matching system and do one of the following:**

   a. **If you're using multiple impedance-matching transformer/volume controls in each room, connect the main speaker outputs from your amplifier or receiver to a *parallel connecting block* with a short length of speaker wire.**

      The parallel connecting block splits a single audio output into multiple audio outputs — like an audio cloning device.

    b. **If you're using a single impedance-matching/speaker-selector device that resides in the media room, connect the impedance-matching device to your amplifier's speaker output with a short length of speaker wire.**

    The impedance-matching/speaker-selector device both matches impedance and acts a central selector for turning speakers on or off.

4. **Connect the speaker outputs of your connecting block (3a) or speaker-selector device (3b) to individual runs of speaker wire for distribution throughout the house.**

5. **Run pairs (left and right speaker) of speaker wire through your walls to the desired locations.**

6. **If you're going with multiple impedance-matching volume control units in each room, connect the speaker wires to the inputs of the wall-mounted, impedance-matching volume control.**

    The impedance-matching volume control units usually fit in a standard, single-gang junction box, which can be mounted just like a light switch in a convenient spot on the wall. (We explain junction-box sizes in Chapter 7.)

    If you're using a central impedance-matching/speaker-selector switch instead, just blithely ignore this step and continue to Step 7.

7. **Terminate your speaker-wire runs (or a shorter run of speaker wire leading from the impedance-matching volume control's outputs, if you went that route) in one of two places:**

    a. **If you decide to use external, stand-alone speakers in this room, connect the ends of your speaker wires to a speaker-connector wall plate.**

    We prefer the kind with banana jacks or five-way binding posts.

    b. **If you're installing in-wall speakers, connect the ends of the speaker wires to each speaker's inputs.**

8. **For each set of speakers in your home, repeat Steps 4 through 7.**

    A wiring layout for a single-zone audio system is shown in Figure 9-1.

Put on your favorite CD, pour your favorite beverage, and sit back for a listening break.

You may decide to start small, with speakers in only a few rooms. That's a fine way of setting up this kind of network, but go ahead and install runs of speaker cabling to other rooms now — while you have the walls open — in case you want to expand your audio network later. You can put a blank cover on the outlet box so that you don't have wires hanging out of your walls.

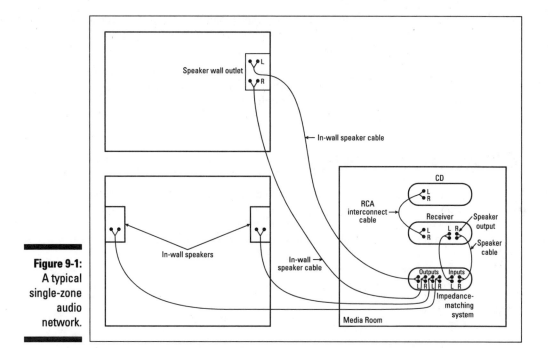

Figure 9-1:
A typical
single-zone
audio
network.

Implementing a single-zone, multi-amplifier system

A single-zone, multi-amplifier system uses separate amplifiers in the media room for each set of speakers in the audio network. This network eliminates the need for an impedance-matching system and provides more power to each set of speakers.

The process for installing a single-zone, multi-amplifier network is similar to the one we delineated in the preceding section. The two main differences are

✔ You don't need the impedance-matching system because each speaker is powered by its own amplifier.

✔ You need to split the audio signals from your source components — a single stereo pair of outputs — to several pairs of amplifier channels. Doing so can be a bit of a sticking point. You have three options:

- If you're installing speakers in only two locations, you can probably use a Y-connector cable, which takes a single pair of line-level outputs and splits the signal into two pairs of connectors.

- You can buy a *distribution amplifier* that accepts the line-level input and provides multiple pairs of outputs (sort of an audio cloning device). This device also amplifies the signal (which gets weaker as it's reproduced) so that each power amplifier has the signal strength it needs.

- You can buy an integrated amplifier specifically designed for a multi-room system. This amp internally splits your source device signals amongst its amplifier channels.

Mega-Multizoning

The basic steps for installing a multizone audio system (which is capable of sending different music sources to different rooms in your house simultaneously) in your home are similar to those needed to install a single-zone system. At least they are in a high-level overview.

As long as you get the right wires in the wall, you can change from a single-zone system to a multizone system later, by changing the components of your audio system and how some wires are connected in your media room.

The devil is in the details when you start setting up one of these systems, especially when you set up the control system. (We talk about how to remotely control audio systems in Chapter 20.) Figuring out the routing of the audio signals isn't too difficult, but equipment variations keep us from giving many details.

Multizone audio systems can become nightmarishly complicated. Not only does the setup depend on marrying components from different manufacturers that may have strange quirks and weird setup routines, but also, when you get to *controlling* the zone audio with your remote control, it gets deadly. The goal is to be able to accomplish certain things regardless of which zone you're in (such as select and play a CD) but to accomplish other things *only* in your current zone (such as turn up the volume or select the VCR audio as the input source). Whether you can do something from all zones or only the current zone depends on how you hook up the wires from the IR network and how you set up the multizone amplifier. Believe us, getting all this stuff to work seamlessly is a major hassle that increases as you add zones.

Many home-audio servers — the devices that store your music on a hard disk drive — are being upgraded to allow multizone audio over a computer network. Because these devices (available now from Request and available soon from Sony and Toshiba) are basically computers, they include built-in Web servers that let you stream music around your house — just like music Web sites do. Eventually, you'll be able to stream different music programs to different parts of your home over your computer network.

Phase matters

When you're working with speaker wires, you need to keep in mind the concept of phase. All speaker-level inputs and outputs are color-coded, usually with a red and black connector. It's important to make sure that you maintain consistency when you connect speaker wires, so that both speakers in a stereo pair have their wires connected to the amplifier in the same way. If you cross a pair of wires (red to red and black to black on one speaker, but red to black and black to red on the other speaker, for example), you won't blow up anything or start a nuclear meltdown at your local power plant. You will, however, have degraded sound, with decreased bass and a totally messed up stereo image.

Most speaker wires are well marked, with different colors of wire in the pair or with markings on one of the conductors. If you really can't tell or remember what's connected to what, use a test CD that puts your system through its paces to make sure you've hooked it up correctly. Pat has one for *Stereophile* magazine (www.stereo phile.com) that features "Ralph the barking dog," who woofs from both speakers in and out of phase so that you can hear the difference.

If you're going to jump right into multizone audio and you're not a gearhead, let a professional installer do the job.

Following is the basic layout of a multizone system:

1. **Use standard RCA cables to connect your source devices to the multizone controller.**

   The multizone controller contains all the electronics to switch each incoming source to different amps and zones.

2. **If the controller doesn't have built-in amplification, use interconnect cables to connect the controller's outputs (one stereo pair per zone) to a multichannel amplifier.**

3. **Connect the amplifier outputs to pairs of speaker wire (one pair per zone).**

4. **Run the speaker wires through your walls to each speaker outlet or in-wall speaker location, as shown in Figure 9-2.**

It sounds simple, doesn't it? And it is, from our 40,000-foot perch here. But getting the pieces together and working in sync can be a bit of a pain. That's why we recommend professional help (otherwise, you may end up seeking professional help of another sort).

How do your audio and video systems work together?

How your audio and video systems complement each other is a confusing subject, no doubt. After all, your video network (by the very nature of the programming it carries) also distributes audio signals around the house. So why have two networks?

The coaxial network that carries TV signals around your home isn't suited to carrying the audio signals from other sources such as CD players, and the audio network is similarly unable to carry video signals. In the future,

when all audio and video signals that run between components are fully digital, you'll probably be able to use a single network to carry both. For now, if you want both audio and video, you need two networks.

If you're using CAT-5e to carry your audio (as we discuss later in the chapter), you may find that the system you choose can carry both the audio *and* video signals over a single cable. This isn't the case with all systems, but some systems will do this for you.

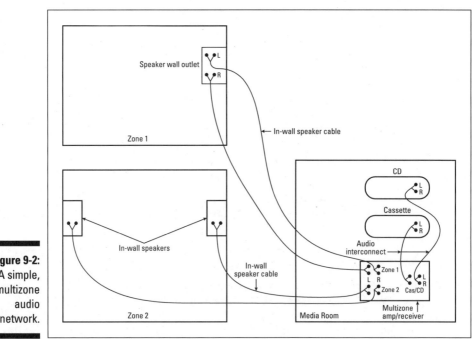

Figure 9-2:
A simple, multizone audio network.

Other Ways to Send Audio

Perhaps building a whole-home audio network is not high on your list of priorities, or you don't have an opportunity to run wires while the walls are unfinished. You can, however, still get sound from your stereo system to some other place in the house using one of a few alternatives to wired audio networks. Like some of the alternative methods of distributing video that we talk about in Chapter 7, many of these systems are more useful for a point-to-point connection — getting audio from one specific room to another — than for connecting every room.

CATching up with CAT-5e systems

As you skip around this book and look at the various networks we describe, you might note a recurring theme: CAT-5e cabling is versatile stuff. CAT-5e not only is the standard cabling for computer LANs and phone networks but can also be used to carry an increasing amount of other data around the house. In Chapter 7, for example, we talk about using CAT-5e cabling to transport video signals around the home, and in Chapter 20, we discuss using this cable for carrying remote control signals (IR signals). There's almost nothing (networking-wise, at least) that you can't do with CAT-5e.

Audio is no exception. Line-level audio signals can be successfully carried over CAT-5e cables in your walls using systems from a variety of manufacturers. These systems range from inexpensive systems that convert the left and right line-level outputs of an audio device into a balanced signal to full-fledged, expensive audio (and video!) distribution systems that provide true multizone audio over CAT-5e.

When you use CAT-5e to carry audio, you can't use those same wires for your computer LAN or phone network. It's an either-or situation, and you need to use a separate network of CAT-5e cables for each leg of the audio network. You *might* be able to use the same CAT-5e cables to carry both audio and video signals — it depends on which CAT-5e audio-system vendor you use.

Yep, two warnings in a row. No, don't go run and hide. CAT-5e audio systems are still new, and many of the companies that sell them use proprietary technologies. So it's best to stick to one brand. Don't try to mix and match, because it just might not work.

A few of the most common ways of sending audio over CAT-5e are discussed in the following sections.

Balun-ce your life

A balun is named for its function in the network — it converts a signal back and forth from *balanced* cable systems (such as CAT-5e cables) and *unbalanced* cable systems (such as audio RCA cables). As we discussed, a balanced line-level signal is capable of going a long distance — up to 1000 feet, in some cases. A balun isn't much to look at. It's not a big fancy box with shiny lights. Instead, it's just a little passive device (meaning it doesn't need any external power) about the size of a deck of cards, with receptacles on both sides (an RJ-45 on one side, and two or more RCA jacks on the other).

Baluns are deployed in pairs, so you're not going to build a whole-home audio network with them. They fit into your network when you just want to get audio from one place to another (what we call a "point-to-point" network).

One balun is associated with the source device (such as a CD player or the Audio Out ports of a receiver), and connects, through an RCA patch cable, to the left and right Audio Out channels. This balun is then plugged into the CAT-5e cable using a CAT-5e patch cable. At the other end of the network — down another leg of your home's CAT-5e that you've dedicated to audio — the process is reversed. The second balun plugs into the RJ-45 outlet on your wall (again using a patch cable), and then plugs into the left and right Audio In jacks of the remote amplifier or receiver that you're feeding the signal to.

We're talking about transporting line-level signals, not speaker-level signals. So you can't just plug the output of the remote balun into a pair of speakers and expect music. There is one exception to this: If you have powered loudspeakers (that is, with built-in amplifiers), you don't need an intermediate amp or receiver.

Audio baluns use one pair of the conductors in a CAT-5e cable for each of the left and right stereo audio channels. Remember that typical CAT-5e cables have eight conductors — so you have four left. Some balun manufacturers, such as MuxLab (www.muxlab.com) build baluns that use these four extra wires to carry composite or S-video signals (see Chapter 6 if you've missed what these are), so you can carry audio and video over the same CAT-5e. This is a great solution if you just need to share a source device such as a DVD player in one remote location — because DVD players also play CDs, you can carry video, audio, or both easily and cheaply using a couple of spare lengths of CAT-5e in your walls. (This is an example of why we've said — probably a million times — that it's a great idea to put plenty of CAT-5e in your walls, even in places where you don't think you'll use it for computers or phones. It will seem like a ridiculous amount of cable, but you'll use it.)

Single-zone CAT-5e audio-distribution systems

The next step up in the world of audio over CAT-5e moves beyond the point-to-point limitation of baluns and provides a single-zone audio-distribution network to multiple locations throughout the home. These systems, from vendors such as Russound (www.russound.com) and Leviton (www.leviton.com)

Keeping your music on the LAN

The CAT-5e audio-distribution systems discussed in this chapter are designed to use a different set of CAT-5e cables than those used by your computer LAN. This is due to plain old physics — these systems use overlapping frequencies on the CAT-5e cables and interfere with each other.

However, a few audio source devices can leverage your computer LAN to send music around the house — systems that use computers to store, download, stream, and otherwise deal with music. For example, you may have a huge hard drive with thousands of MP3 digital audio files, or you may subscribe to a computer-based online music service such as Listen.com. Most folks are stuck listening to these music sources with some headphones or tiny little speakers plugged into the back of the PC.

You do have an alternative. You can listen to computer-based music by sending it over your LAN to remote stereo components designed to play these signals over standard audio systems. For example, Philips — the big Dutch consumer electronics company — has a mini stereo system with a built-in Ethernet RJ-45 port. If you have a LAN outlet behind the stereo rack, you can plug an Ethernet patch cable into the Philips stereo and play back any MP3 or Windows Media audio file stored on your computer hard drive or listen to Internet radio stations on the *good* system.

typically use custom faceplates that replace standard RJ-45 faceplates in each room. These faceplates have a pair of female RCA audio jacks that can connect to any standard audio source device or amplifier/receiver.

In the room containing the source device you want to share throughout the home, you simply plug a stereo audio patch cable between the device and the faceplate. In remote rooms, you use an audio patch cable to connect the faceplate to the inputs of a local receiver or amplifier. Connecting these remote outlets is a special CAT-5e audio hub located in your wiring closet. This hub takes the source signal and distributes it to every other CAT-5e outlet connected to the hub.

Most of these systems are designed to connect to only one source device — they typically can't switch between different source devices. If you can afford it, and you have more than one audio source you want to share with the rest of your house, invest in a multizone, multisource system (which we'll discuss in a second). In most cases, the faceplates for single and multizone systems are identical, so — as long as you don't switch brands in midstream — you should be able to start with a single-zone system and upgrade to a multizone, multisource system when your budget permits (or as prices for these relatively new-to-market systems come down).

Like the baluns we discussed previously, these systems often don't use all eight conductors in a CAT-5e cable to carry audio. Many systems take advantage of this by carrying other signals. The Russound systems, for example, use the extra conductors to carry IR signals for your remote-control system, so you don't need to install a separate IR network. Leviton's system (the

Decora Media System, or DMS) uses the extra wires to carry video signals — so you can use this system for audio alone or with a DVD player to carry both audio and video around your home.

Multizone CAT-5e audio-distribution systems

If you want the utmost in flexibility and capability in a CAT-5e-based audio-distribution system, you need a system that can carry different audio programs to different parts of the house simultaneously — a multizone, multisource system. Like the multizone speaker-level systems discussed earlier in the chapter, multizone CAT-5e systems are the top-of-the-line, best-you-can-buy solution. Because audio over CAT-5e is still new, it's not cheap. You'll probably end up paying $1500 or more for the components alone, and that doesn't include the speakers and amplifiers or receivers in each room. And that's for the (relatively) cheap versions of these systems — some high-end systems can cost tens of thousands of dollars.

You do get what you pay for with some of these systems. For example, Crestron (www.crestron.com) sells some CAT-5e distribution systems that can basically do everything. They send line-level audio signals throughout the home (to dozens of zones, if your house is big enough); they carry video signals (not just composite video, but also S-video, and even the highest quality component video signals used by DVD players and HDTVs). The Crestron system can even carry the *digital* audio signals that come out of DVD players and multichannel audio systems such as SACD and DVD-Audio. With the proper decoder and amplifier system on the far end, you can have surround sound anywhere in the house, all fed from a central location.

In terms of network architecture, these systems are laid out in a fashion similar to the single-zone systems we talk about in the previous section. Custom wall outlets and faceplates connect to the CAT-5e in your walls and provide connections to and from audio (and in some cases, video) systems throughout the home. A hub system in your wiring closet ties everything together.

Wireless systems

The most popular way of getting audio around the house without a dedicated network is with an RF wireless system. These come in two main flavors:

- ✔ **Wireless speaker systems** connect to the line-level outputs of a source device or preamplifier and send the signal over a 900-MHz or 2.4-GHz channel to a pair of self-amplified stereo speakers.

- ✔ **Wireless line-level distribution systems** hook up to your source components in the same fashion but send their signal to a receiver that hooks into your own amplifier and speakers on the far end.

One major potential difficulty with this sort of wireless system is that it uses a line-level input — something that most source devices have only one of. So you may run into trouble hooking up a CD player, for example, to both a receiver (or amp) for local listening and to one of these devices for remote listening. Luckily, many of these units also accept the output of your receiver or amp's headphone jack, so you can avoid this problem if you have a head-phone jack available. Alternately, you can use one of the Y-splitter audio cables we mentioned earlier in the chapter. Prices for these wireless systems range from about $75 to $200. Major manufacturers include

- ✔ Recoton (www.recoton.com)
- ✔ Paradox (www.paradoxllc.com)
- ✔ RCA (www.rca.com)
- ✔ RF Link (www.rflinktech.com)

Another cool wireless product comes from the X10 Wireless Technologies folks. (You probably know them from their infamous Internet pop-up ads on many popular Web sites, or perhaps you read about their security camera systems in Chapter 17.) Their MP3 Anywhere! system works like the other systems we describe, but it's available with a feature that we think is pretty cool: X10's BOOM 2000 software. This software runs on your Windows PC and let's you remotely control and access the PC's MP3 music files, as well as CDs or DVDs played back in the PC's internal drive.

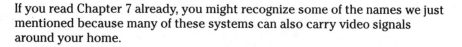

If you read Chapter 7 already, you might recognize some of the names we just mentioned because many of these systems can also carry video signals around your home.

Wi-Fi (the wireless computer networking technology — we tell you all about it in Chapter 16) is becoming wildly popular because it allows people to roam with laptop computers anywhere in the house, staying connected to the Internet without wires. For many people, computers are also becoming an essential source of music (using stored MP3 files or streaming audio coming over an Internet connection). Computer manufacturers have been paying attention to these two trends and are coming up with new products to bring them together. In particular, Intel has announced products that use Wi-Fi to send PC-based digital audio signals over a Wi-Fi wireless network to a small device that plugs into your audio system. These devices (called Digital Media Adapters) will contain the necessary computer hardware to convert digital signals into analog audio signals that can connect to an audio receiver or to the control amplifier of your whole-home audio system.

Part III
Now We're Communicating!

The 5th Wave — By Rich Tennant

"It was a compromise. I gave in on the home LAN connection, but I drew the line at the two-way video feed."

In this part . . .

The key to a great home-phone system is the flexibility to have many different types of endpoints hanging out of a good, solid base infrastructure. By the pool, you may want waterproof phones. In the office, a good conference capability. In the kitchen, a cordless option. You may also need to be able to transfer calls, intercom people, use Caller ID, and more, wherever you are in your smart home.

In this part, we tell you how to create a telephony backbone in your house. We discuss the major elements of a whole-home telephone network and describe the advantages of connecting all the telephone pieces and parts together. We also tell you about some cool wireless-phone systems that have all the functionality of wired phones but require only a limited amount of telephone wiring in the walls. Finally, we talk about all the different communications equipment and services available, as well as some tips and tricks for ensuring the success of your telephone system.

Chapter 10

Planning a Phone System

· ·

· ·

*M*ost people take their telephone service for granted. Plug your phone into the wall jack, pay your monthly bill to your area's telephone monopoly, and, as Donnie Brasco might say, fuggitaboudit. As life becomes increasingly wired, however, you may want to do things that require a more sophisticated phone system than the trusty AT&T model you bought back in the '70s when you switched over to Touch-Tone. For example, you may want to send faxes, transfer calls within your home, or use your phone system as an intercom.

Not only are our telephone needs more complicated than in the past, but we're also beginning to face a plethora of choices in how we get phone service delivered to our homes. Thanks to deregulation by Congress and the Federal Communications Commission, a whole host of companies — some familiar, some not — are ready to offer competitive local phone services to residential customers.

As if this were not enough, more and more people are using their cell phone as their home phone — finding that having both a local line and a cell-phone line is redundant.

Your phone network in your home is important not only because you can place your voice calls over these lines but also because you may need your phone network for your alarm system, your Internet access, to upgrade your music collection lists, and to do many other smart-home tasks. A phone line is a critical backbone element to your smart home.

In this chapter, we tell you about all the various pieces that make up a phone network and give you some advice in making choices for your phone networking needs.

Selecting Equipment for Your Phone Network

When you're considering any home-network system, one of the big questions you need to ask yourself is, what will plug into it? After all, why build a highway if it doesn't go anywhere?

You may be surprised at the number of choices you have about what you can plug into your home-phone network — much more than just phones. We don't even consider computer modems and network appliances here, just standard telephony equipment that lets you talk and otherwise communicate with the outside world.

Plug and play the old-fashioned way

The most common category of telephone equipment in a home network is analog, POTS-compatible (POTS is a telephone industry term meaning *Plain Old Telephone Service*) devices. Often called wireline phones because they are corded, all these devices plug into your network of wall jacks, using the standard modular phone plug (called an *RJ-11 connector,* which we describe in Chapter 11) or the four-prong plugs or hard-wired environments (meaning they're wired directly into the wall) in old homes.

Note: The RJ-11 connector family has several variations, based on the number of telephone lines wired to an individual jack. For simplicity's sake, we use the term *RJ-11* generically to describe the one-, two-, and three-line versions of these connectors.

The most basic and common analog telephone device is the standard corded telephone. This is the trusty old telephone that we've known and loved for decades and decades. Little has changed in corded phones for quite some time, although many features have been added to phones over the years — such as hold and speed-dialer buttons, speakers for hands-free talking, and liquid crystal display (LCD) screens.

Besides cool new features, the biggest difference among various corded telephones is their capacity to connect to multiple phone lines. Although most telephones are still single-line phones, a growing number can be simultaneously connected to two or, in some cases, three telephone lines at the same time. As more people install multiple phone lines for home offices, teen lines, and other uses, multiple-line telephones are becoming increasingly common — and necessary.

If your telephone needs run to several lines, you may want to consider a telephone system that gives you more control over your lines and enables you to

Features, features, and more features

The basic design and functionality of corded telephones hasn't really changed much over the years. With the exception of the transition from pulse to touch-tone dialing 15 or 20 years ago, the way corded telephones work has remained remarkably constant for generations.

What has changed is the number of additional features that the decreasing cost (and increasing power) of computer chips has enabled manufacturers to put into low-cost consumer telephones. For example, you can now buy — for not too much money — telephones that include:

✔ **Speed dialing:** This feature allows you do press one button to dial a preprogrammed number that you call often.

✔ **Voice-activated dialing:** This feature allows you to talk to your phone to have it dial. (For example, "Call Holly at work" would prompt the phone to dial her.) Some of the more advanced models allow you to interface between the phone and the PC so that you can access your PC contact databases, such as Microsoft Outlook, for the range of people and numbers.

✔ **LCD displays:** These displays tell you the number you called and how long you've been on the call.

✔ **Built-in phone directories:** These directories can store hundreds of names and numbers and display them on an LCD screen.

✔ **Speakerphones:** These phones, which let you talk hands-free, come in two types: *half duplex* models, which let you either talk or listen (but not both) at one time, and more sophisticated *full duplex* models that let you do both at once. Full duplex phones are immeasurably better, in our opinion, because you can carry on a hands-free conversation naturally, without choppiness or lost words. Few are half duplex today (only the cheapest models). Speakerphones are typically part of the base station of a phone, but can be found in more expensive cordless phone units as well.

✔ **Voice mail:** You hear a lot of different terms for the answering machine capability of a telephone, such as digital answering machine, tapeless answering machine, or voice mail. For the most part, that's semantics. Many phones offer an inherent function that allows you to have one or more voice-mail boxes in which you can store inbound messages. These can be checked remotely, as well as from your house.

✔ **Conference Calling:** Three-way, four-way, and even five-way calling is available on phones so that you can conference different parties. If you're doing this through your system, however, remember that you need to have a telephone line for each party you want to conference — if you want to conference two other people for a three-way conference, you need two telephone lines. Later in the chapter, we talk about conference services, which avoid this telephone line expense.

✔ **Caller ID displays:** This feature shows you the phone number and, in some cases, the name of the person who is calling you. Caller ID requires both the hardware on your end — either built into the phone or a stand-alone display unit — and a subscription to Caller ID service from your local telephone company. Some Caller ID services also include (for a bit more money every month) Call Waiting Caller ID, which tells you who is calling when you're already on the phone with a different person.

do things such as transfer calls between phones within your home. To take advantage of these features, you need something beyond a standard phone. Later in the chapter (in the "Key phones can be key" section), we go into more detail about the key telephone system unit (KSU) and sophisticated KSU-less multiline phone systems.

Cordless phones

Wireline phones are great, but sometimes you just don't want to get up from the couch to answer the phone. So it should be no surprise that cordless phones are now found in nearly 90 percent of all homes in the United States. These phones consist of two main components:

- ✓ **A base station**, consisting of a battery charger and a radio transceiver, which plugs into an RJ-11 phone jack just like a wireline phone
- ✓ **The cordless handset** that communicates with the base station and carries your phone conversation over radio waves

You can choose from six main types of cordless phones (which, like wireline phones, are available in both single- and multiple-line versions):

- ✓ **46- and 49-MHz phones:** These are the traditional cordless phones that have been widely available for many years. They send your phone signals over 46- and 49-MHz radio channels in an analog form. 46- and 49-MHz phones are the cheapest available and generally have the shortest range.
- ✓ **900-MHz analog phones:** These cordless phones are similar to 46- and 49-MHz phones, except they use a higher-frequency radio channel to carry your phone signals. These higher-frequency radio waves have a longer range and are also a little less susceptible to interference. Because these phones are analog, they're susceptible to being monitored by radio scanners.
- ✓ **900-MHz digital phones:** A step up in price from the analog models, these phones convert your phone signal into a digital format before sending it over the airwaves. These digital signals are less likely to suffer from interference and signal degradation, so you should end up with a clearer phone conversation with less static and noise.
- ✓ **900-MHz digital spread-spectrum phones:** The most sophisticated — and expensive — cordless phones, these models take the digital radio signal and send it over a large number of different radio frequencies in rapid succession. This *frequency hopping* decreases the likelihood that you pick up unwanted radio signals — such as your neighbor's cordless telephone — and also increases security (because it's much more difficult for someone with a radio scanner to tune into very much of your conversation as you switch frequencies).

✔ **2.4-GHz digital spread-spectrum phones:** The 2.4-GHz frequency is less crowded than the 900-MHz spectrum, so you're likely to get less interference, but it is used by many of the Wi-Fi wireless computer networks.

✔ **5.8-GHz digital spread-spectrum phones:** The newest product entries are in this spectrum, which up to now has been used largely for commercial wireless broadband applications.

You read all sorts of claims about distance comparisons between 900-MHz, 2.4-GHz, and 5.8-GHz phones. We'd love to give you a hard-and-fast rule about which is best, but it really depends on the phone and the implementation. Many factors — not just the frequency spectrum that the handset uses — go into your ability to hear well 150 feet from your base station.

You'll see reference in ads and on Web sites to *expandable* cordless phones. These systems are expandable because you can add more handsets to the system without buying extra base stations (traditional cordless phones have a limit of one handset per base station). You need to plug only the one base station into an RJ-11 or RJ-45 phone jack. The additional handsets require only a battery charger station — which plugs into your electrical power lines — so you don't need a separate phone jack for each additional phone. You can generally add up to twelve handsets on a given system, but some allow for as few as four, so check the feature listing.

Expandable cordless phone systems can dramatically change the way that you use phones in your house. Before, when you wanted a cordless phone in a particular spot, you needed a power outlet and a phone outlet. Now you're free to place these phones where there's just power. This means you have the freedom to locate your cordless phones anywhere in the kitchen, for instance. Of course, it's that many more phones to lose in the couch too! We like expandable wireless phone systems that have pager or intercom functions, so that we can "ping" the phones and find them.

Soon you'll start seeing multimode wireless phones. These handsets of these phones have both cordless phone and cellular (or PCS) phone circuitry built in. When you're within range of your home base station, phone calls are carried over your standard telephone lines. If you take the handset outside your home, the phone automatically switches to its cellular mode, and phone calls are carried over the cellular phone network. Some manufacturers are talking about having multimode 802.11b wireless and cellular phones, to allow you to make calls over your home's wireless data infrastructure.

A growing number of cordless phones have headset jacks on their handsets, so you can walk around without having to hold the phone to your ear. Most of these phones also have belt clips so you can clip the phone on and have both hands free. Cordless phones are designed to use headsets with 2.5mm plugs, and won't accept headsets with modular plugs, which are commonly used with office phones. Some of the more advanced headsets are phones unto themselves with clip-on dial pads and remote handset lifters that take your desktop phone off the hook so you can dial — from several rooms away.

Check out www.hellodirect.com and www.plantronics.com for more on headsets.

And for people who like the convenience of a wireless phone but the solid look and feel of a traditional handset station, some manufacturers offer wireless corded handsets. These look like a typical business phone, with an antenna to sync up with other wireless phones.

Although we love cordless phones and use them constantly, you need to be aware of a couple of drawbacks associated with them:

- **Quality:** No matter how expensive — and no matter what the ads may try to tell you — the quality of your phone signal on a cordless phone isn't as good as a wireline phone.

- **Security:** Your phone conversation is less secure and confidential on a cordless phone than it is on a wireline telephone. Although digital phones — especially spread-spectrum models — do offer increased security, any phone conversation that you have on a wireless system is susceptible to interception by unscrupulous folks with radio scanners. Some cordless phone manufacturers offer phones with a secure encrypted mode to lessen this hazard.

Fancy phone systems

We travel a lot internationally, and it's amazing the places we'll go to and see three or four phones on someone's desk, because the person needs three or four different phone lines. We saw seven in one office in Africa.

Lucky for us, we live in a country where technology has developed to meet the needs of the multiline user, and a broad range of options is available for someone who wants to be able to have more of a phone *system* in the house. Generally, you will find phones that can handle one, two, three, four or more lines today. A four-line phone system is great for many homes because you can allocate two lines to the business (you need two for conferencing, we suggest), one for personal use, and one vacant for your future (or present) teen phone line.

Much of the functionality for multiline phone systems was developed as part of key phone systems for corporate applications. A *key system* generally consists of a central unit, called the *key system unit,* or KSU, that handles the intelligence of the phone system and coordinates access to the outbound telephone lines connected to it.

With a key phone system, you can

- Make a call on a free line while other lines are in use

✔ Transfer calls from one extension to another

✔ Connect several lines for a conference call

✔ Use your phones as an intercom system, paging between rooms or using the phone's speaker systems for hands-free intercom use

✔ Dedicate a specific extension for all fax or modem calls and let the key system automatically route incoming calls

✔ Pipe in music for people who are on hold (we find that old Spike Jones hits are conversation starters)

If you wanted to install a telephone network in your house in the past, you had to install a KSU-based business phone system in the home, complete with 25-pair wiring and bulky handsets.

Well no more. Installing a telephone network in your home can be as simple as plugging in an AC adapter and plugging a telephone cord into a central unit. The rest can be wireless. Throughout most of the book, we pitch wired as the far preferred mode of networking. However, the benefits of wireless phone networking are so immense that it has distinct advantages that should be seriously considered. If it weren't for the problems inherent with signal fade as you go throughout the house, we'd say always do wireless. If you have a larger home, lots of concrete and brick walls, or just a lot of interference in the neighborhood, wireline options are still your best bet.

Key phone systems fall into two major categories:

✔ **Multiline key telephone system units (KSU):** These systems are based on a central control unit (the KSU), which performs all transferring, paging, and other functions. Each telephone extension is wired (or connected wirelessly) to the KSU.

✔ **Multiline KSU-less phone systems:** In a KSU-less system, the intelligence of the central control unit is built into the extension phone. There is no central unit — just independent, intelligent phones that communicate with each other rather than with a separate control device.

In practice, consumer applications — four telephone lines or less — have moved to a largely KSU-less environment. If there is a KSU, you probably don't notice it much because it's embedded in the master base station phone. If you need a more high-powered phone system at home — because you have many more rooms, or you need more inbound lines — you'll need a KSU-driven system.

KSU phone systems

A KSU telephone system consists of a central control unit (the KSU) and a series of extension phones that the KSU controls. Your incoming telephone-company phone lines connect to the KSU, which in turn connects to each individual extension phone by a single phone line or wireless connection.

Every phone connected to the KSU system has access to all the external phone lines — usually by simply pressing a line button on the phone, such as Line 1 or Line 2.

A KSU system has both advantages and disadvantages (like just about everything else). The advantages include the following:

- **The greatest capacity:** KSU systems that can handle four or more incoming phone lines are available.

- **More extensions:** KSU systems can often connect 16 or more extension phones — so if you have a large house with many rooms, you don't have to worry about limitations on the number of phones you install. You can see the benefit for businesses that grow from a few employees to hundreds.

- **More features:** Although KSU and KSU-less systems share many features (such as call transfer, paging, and intercom) typical KSU systems let you add additional features such as automatic routing of fax calls to the correct extension, sophisticated hold functions (like foisting your musical tastes on people you put on hold), and even high-capacity, multiple-mailbox, voice-mail systems.

The disadvantages to a KSU system include the following:

- **A higher price tag:** Base-model KSU systems start near $600, and the price can skyrocket as you add additional features.

- **More complicated installation:** Although KSU-less systems are more or less plug and play, a KSU system requires a more involved installation and setup procedure (but it's still pretty easy).

- **Special phone equipment:** Some KSU systems require you to buy a special key telephone for each extension, which can be an expensive proposition. A few systems even have specific requirements regarding the kind of telephone wiring you need to connect extensions to the central unit.

KSU-less phone systems

A KSU system requires a rather large upfront expenditure, but a KSU-less phone system provides many of the same features for less money. KSU-less systems, which are usually designed for three or four phone lines, connect to a standard RJ-11or RJ-45 phone jacks that you already use for your stand-alone phone systems and a nearby electrical outlet. Cordless KSU-less systems just plug into any nearby electrical outlet. They differ from standard phones in their internal intelligence. Built into each of these phones is an electronic brain that performs many of the same functions that are found in a central KSU system.

Choosing a KSU-less phone system over a KSU system offers some advantages, including the following:

- **The price tag is initially lower:** These systems usually range in cost from $200 to $300 per phone.

- ✔ **You can start off small:** All you need to get started are two KSU-less phones — you can add more as your needs or budget grows.

- ✔ **Installation is simpler:** Basically, all you need to do is plug the phone into one or more RJ-11 wall jacks, and you're up and running. Some systems require that you set some small switches to assign an extension number to each phone.

- ✔ **Wiring requirements are less stringent:** KSU-less phone systems work in just about any kind of telephone wiring architecture, unlike KSU systems, which can require a specific wiring *topology.* We explain all about topologies, architectures, and other important-sounding words dealing with phone systems in Chapter 11.

KSU-less systems have their share of disadvantages as well, including the following:

- ✔ **Less system capacity:** Most KSU-less systems don't handle more than four phone lines and more than twelve extensions. If your needs go beyond these limits, you should opt for a full-fledged KSU system.

- ✔ **Fewer features:** Compared to KSU systems, KSU-less systems typically have fewer features. Additionally, although most KSU systems are modular, meaning that you can add additional functionality to the system by plugging in components to the KSU, KSU-less systems have all the functionality in the handsets, so you have to replace all of them to upgrade.

As we mentioned at the beginning of this section, we think the multi-extension, multiline cordless and corded KSU-less (whew!) systems are exactly what most homes need and are the most flexible. Be prepared to go wired and KSU if your performance or feature requirements dictate.

Panasonic (www.panasonic.com), Siemens (www.siemens.com), and VTECH (www.vtech.com) offer a range of systems for single-line and multiline KSU and KSU-less systems.

Fax machines

Although traditionally an office device, fax (facsimile) machines are becoming increasingly common in the home. Fax machines scan printed material and transmit the scanned data over a standard phone line to a remote fax machine, which then prints the printed material on the far end. Fax machines fall into two main types:

- ✔ **Thermal paper fax:** Increasingly harder to find, these models use long rolls of thermal paper to print incoming faxes. Although inexpensive, these models have the distinct disadvantage of using thermal paper — the quality of the incoming fax is low, the paper tends to curl up and the image deteriorates over time. These machines are fine, however, for occasional use.

> ✔ **Plain paper fax:** Most fax machines these days print incoming faxes on plain paper, using a mechanism similar to that found in an inkjet or laser computer printer. These models offer significantly higher print quality and your faxes don't end up in a tightly wound scroll on your desk. We recommend that you splurge for the plain paper fax machine.

Many fax manufacturers — and computer printer makers, as well — combine fax machines, printers, telephones, and even copiers into a single, all-in-one home-office machine, sometimes referred to as a *multifunctional device* (MFD). These devices can be pretty handy and are usually less expensive than buying all the components separately (not to mention that they take up less desk space in your home office). The latest ones sport telephone base stations, so you can get a 900-MHz or 2.4-GHz cordless phone system as well. Whew, that's like a whole telephone closet in one package!

Multifunction devices usually provide lower-quality output than separately purchased components. Generally, getting a great deal of functionality into one box at a reasonable price dictates compromises in the quality of the components.

Color multifunction machines can be expensive for ordinary black-and-white faxing. Look for machines that have separate color and black ink cartridges, so that you don't have to replace your expensive color cartridges when you print only black-and-white faxes all the time.

If you operate a home office, you may want a dedicated number that rings to your fax machine. Should you get a fax machine if you don't receive many fax messages? For the most part, a fax machine is just a scanner and a printer — and your computer setup probably has both of those — you might try a free service such as eFax.com (`www.efax.com`), which gives you your own telephone number for receiving faxes — and forwards any inbound fax you receive to your e-mail. From your e-mail, you can print the fax on your printer. This saves you from having to dedicate a local phone line (which can be expensive) to your fax machine. For outbound faxes, you can use your scanner to scan the document into your computer, and then either send that as an e-mail attachment or sign up for the for-fee eFax Plus, which accepts your e-mail (with attachment) and sends that as a fax message anywhere in the world.

Answering machines

Remember *The Rockford Files*? The title sequence of that show featured the lead character's answering machine taking an incoming call — a rare event back then (in the 1970s) when answering machines were huge, ungainly, and expensive. The computer revolution has touched on these devices in the intervening decades, and now answering machines are compact, inexpensive, and — as you no doubt already know — everywhere.

The least expensive answering machines you can find are those based on the same technology found in that old Rockford machine. A cassette tape — or in most cases, a smaller microcassette tape — records your outgoing greeting message and incoming messages. A bit clunky, but these machines usually work pretty well, and they typically cost next to nothing.

Newer answering machines use digital technology to record your voice and that of incoming callers as digital data stored on a computer memory chip. These tapeless answering machines have a higher voice quality and — because they don't have a tape or moving parts to wear out — aren't as susceptible to catastrophic mechanical failures.

The most expensive digital answering machines often behave like voice-mail systems found in businesses, offering features such as multiple mailboxes (so incoming messages can be directed to specific individuals in the household), multiple-line capabilities, and remote operation (which allows you to check your messages when you're away from home).

Many answering machines are not stand-alone devices. Instead, they often include a corded or cordless phone as part of the same device or are part of multifunction printer/copier/scanner/fax devices.

Although answering machines have become increasingly sophisticated and capable, we've become proponents of the voice-mail services offered by most local telephone companies. These services offer you an answering machine in the telephone network, where that answering machine is really a giant computer that many subscribers share. You typically find out that you have a message when you pick up your phone and hear a stutter dial tone; small light attachments also blink when you have a message. These services have become inexpensive and convenient. Before you spend a bundle on a fancy digital answering machine, we recommend that you explore the voice-mail service available in your area and see how the features and price stack up. Note a difference between the telephone company voice-mail services and your own device — if your phone line is busy, the answering machine can't pick up. Because we blab a lot on the phone, we use the telephone company's service.

If you have multiple phone lines in your house, you need to think about how you work this with your voice mail. If you want to have one answering device for two lines, you'll need to get a two-line answering machine or tell the telephone company that "Line 1 rolls over to Line 2, on busy/no answer." (That is, if Line 1 is busy or there is no answer, send the call to Line 2, where the answering device will pick up if no one answers that line as well).

If you also have a cell phone that has voice mail, consider sending all calls from your home phone line on busy/no answer to your cell-phone voice-mail system. That way, you won't have to check multiple voice-mail boxes all the time.

External ringers/lights

If you've ever hung around an auto repair shop (Pat likes to do that — don't ask why, he couldn't possibly explain), you may have noticed that when the phone rings in the main office, bells and whistles seem to sound everywhere. Those are external ringers — stand-alone devices that alert you to incoming calls when you're not near the phone.

You don't need to be an automotive technician to appreciate one of these devices. You may just have a big, noisy house (if you read our bios, you know that Danny has four young children!) or spend time in the backyard far from the phone. Many hearing-impaired telephone users have attached to their telephone networks special visual indicators that light up when the phone rings. Such external indicators are cheap and easy to install — just plug them into an RJ-11 jack and — in some cases — AC power. You can find external ringers that let you choose what the ring sounds like, ringers that ring differently for different phone lines, and even ringers that give you a silent, visual indication of a telephone call.

TDD devices

A TDD, or Telecommunications Device for the Deaf, is a text device that enables hearing-impaired folks to communicate over telephone lines. Consisting of a display screen and a keyboard, it works like a computer chat system — without the computer.

Many telephone companies offer a service that lets non-TDD users connect with folks who are on a TDD. In these cases, an operator from the phone company gets in the middle of the conversation and types to the person with the TDD and speaks to the one without.

Choosing a Phone Service

In the old days, you had no choice when it came to ordering phone service for your home. If you wanted phone service, you had to go to the phone company, and you took the service that the company had to offer. In this section, we talk about the growing number of phone options to consider — both in terms of which company you buy service from and what kind of service you receive.

Changes in regulations in the United States are allowing other companies to go after your local phone business — everyone from cable television companies to wireless PCS (Personal Communications Systems) operators. Despite entry of these new competitors, however, the majority of homes in the United States receive phone service from the traditional local monopoly.

Regardless of who provides these services, however, you're basically offered the same options:

- ✔ **Analog telephone service:** Usually called *POTS* (for *Plain Old Telephone Service* — no, we didn't make that up). This is the service we all know and love.

- ✔ **Wireless services:** Cellular and Personal Communications Services (or PCS, if you're in the know), are increasingly available across the U.S. and are a viable alternative to traditional wired telephone services.

Although wireless service can be a replacement for the single phone line to your home for your voice calls, it's not going to be a replacement for your smart home's phone network backbone. You still need phone lines running in your house, and you are going to need to have access to a phone network for various things, such as your DirecTV dish calling in the movies you've purchased or your alarm system calling in to say "HEEEELLLLLLLLPPPPPP!" As with all technologies, cellular services have a role to play in a smart home, but it's not *the* role. Eventually, we believe that many of these services will run over your always-on broadband Internet connection, instead of over a standard phone line, but even in that case, it makes sense to have at least one regular phone line as a backup. Analog phone service is cheap, and although we may complain about the phone companies sometimes, they do an amazing job at making their phone lines reliable and available.

POTS

The common denominator in telephone services is the analog voice connection (provided over copper wires) known as POTS. When you call the telephone company and ask the service folks to install a telephone line to your home, you usually get a POTS line. In this section, we briefly describe how the telephone network connects to your home.

With POTS service, an analog, copper phone line connects your house to the telephone network. The local *telco* (telephone company) has a huge network of local central offices — each serving individual towns or even neighborhoods, as shown in Figure 10-1. These central offices contain digital switches (usually) that connect phone calls onto the public telephone network. A call travels through the PSTN (Public Switched Telephone Network, the telephone network we're all connected to) to another telephone somewhere.

The gauge and the number of wires running to your house varies from telco to telco and installation to installation (depending on when your phone service was first set up). Generally, you find what's called a *quad wire,* consisting of two separate pairs of copper wire in a single sheath. POTS telephone service requires only a single pair of wires, so most people find that they already have adequate wiring for two phone lines connected to their homes.

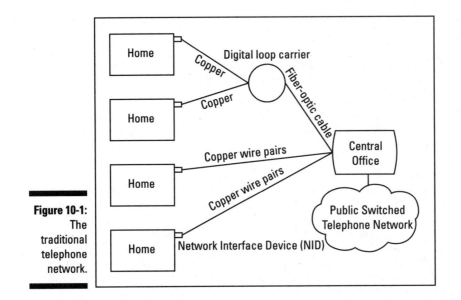

Figure 10-1:
The
traditional
telephone
network.

The telephone companies are working with manufacturers to find the right combination of technologies to make mass deployment of fiber-optic lines to the home economically viable. Many new subdivisions are being outfitted with fiber optics in a series of ongoing and expanding market trials. Fiber optics will carry voice traffic for sure, but the promise of being able to carry substantially more video and data traffic is attractive to the telcos.

Wireless

After television and radio broadcasts, cellular phones are probably the most common wireless communications systems found in people's homes (and cars, and purses, and shirt pockets).

In North America, all sorts of cellular systems are in use by the various cellular providers. Some of these are analog; others are digital. Analog wireless systems are susceptible to interference and distortion, and they make it easier for unscrupulous individuals to eavesdrop on your conversation. Their biggest flaw, however, is that they don't use the limited bandwidth allocated to cellular systems by the FCC very efficiently. This inefficiency limits the number of calls the systems can handle at any one time and makes providing services more expensive than digital systems (meaning you pay more).

The FCC has ruled that cellular providers can get rid of their analog signals by 2007, and because 85 percent of Americans used digital signals in 2002 and most carriers were changing plans to encourage analog-to-digital conversion by customers, it's doubtful you'd want an analog phone anyway. (Most analog phones are emergency phones sitting in people's glove compartments.)

Videoconferencing: I get the picture

The ability to see the person to whom you are speaking has been a topic of discussion since the phone was invented. AT&T tantalized and teased folks with its launch of its Picturephone at the 1964 World's Fair in New York, but the limited availability (three cities) and expense ($16 to $27 for the first three minutes) made sure that the service never went anywhere. AT&T tried again to launch a consumer videoconferencing product in 1992 with the ill-fated Videophone, which cost $1500 and offered only slow frame rates and jerky pictures.

Videoconferencing has been common in the business world for years and has required digital lines. Luckily, most people don't need business-class videoconferencing — their needs are much more restrained. Consumer-grade products are classified into a few areas:

✔ **Stand-alone analog devices:** These are phones with video capabilities that use your regular phone lines to deliver video signals in addition to the voice signals traveling over the same line. For example, Vialta (www.vialta.com) has a Beamer product line.

✔ **TV-connected devices:** These devices also use the regular telephone line to connect a camera mounted on top of a television to send pictures to someone else's television. For example, InfoView from Innomedia (www.Innomedia.com) uses a small set-top camera/conferencing unit to videoconference to another InfoView using regular phone lines.

✔ **PC-connected devices:** These devices enable you to use the power of your computer and its network connections to send video pictures to other similar devices elsewhere. We talk more about PC-based videoconferencing options in Chapter 12.

You generally find that only one kind can communicate with another of its kind. In other words, you won't find a TV-connected device that can communicate with a PC-connected device. They are usually paired offerings where you need the same capability on each end.

As the PC and entertainment center become more linked, and as displays for TV become more like computer displays, consumer videoconferencing over the Internet and your broadband connections will likely become commonplace.

The Cellular Telecommunications & Internet Association (CTIA) Web site (www.ctia.org) has a lot of great information for consumers who want to know more about how the cellular industry works. Here's what happens when a call is made: Your message is transmitted by low-energy radio signals to the nearest antenna site, which connects with the local phone network. From there, your call is delivered by the normal phone network to the office or home you dialed, or by radio signals to another wireless phone.

Wireless technology uses individual radio frequencies over and over again by dividing a service area into separate geographic zones called *cells* — hence the name *cellular.* Cells can be as small as an individual building (such as an airport or arena) or as big as 20 miles across, or any size in between. Each cell is equipped with its own radio transmitter/receiver antenna. (If you have poor service in your area, and you recall that a bunch of people in your

Wireless technologies are not all the same

Not all cell phones are alike, and understanding the technologies behind the offerings is a good start to choosing the right service. The CTIA (www.wow-com.com) represents a wide range of cell phone companies and equipment vendors in the U.S. They offer some good back-ground on the technologies and have a great consumer FAQ (frequently asked questions) document that explains the ins and outs of mobile phones better than we ever could. Check it out at www.wow-com.com/consumer/howitworks/.

neighborhood fought the construction of a new tower in your area, now you know why you can't complete a call. No tower, no signal.)

When a customer using a cellular phone approaches the boundary of one cell, the wireless network senses that the signal is becoming weak and auto-matically hands off the call to the antenna in the next cell into which the caller is traveling.

When subscribers travel beyond their home geographical area, they can still make wireless calls. The wireless carrier in the area where they are traveling provides the service. This is called *roaming*. The terms *home area* and *roaming area* designate these boundaries, which are important because different rates are usually assigned to calling in each area.

Each cellular antenna is linked to a wireless carrier's own mobile switching center (MSC) — the wireless industry's equivalent of the telco central office — which connects your wireless call to the local wired telephone network.

Too many cell plans, cell phones, and different approaches to the technologies particular to your specific operating area are available to adequately cover all your options here. And the topic is beyond the scope of this book, because these phones are mostly about your phone calling outside your smart home; they're not part of your core internal phone network, unless you use a cellular docking station. (See the "Stand by for docking" sidebar.)

That having been said, here are some thoughts about buying cell service:

- ✔ **Think about how you'll use the phone:** For the most part, you buy a cell phone that's compatible with your usage area. If you travel a lot locally, the carrier that has the best coverage area and best pricing for you locally is likely your best answer. If you travel a lot, check out roaming fees for where you travel or some of the national calling plans.

- ✔ **Think about hands-free use at home, not just in your car:** You can get desktop chargers for your cell phone that are also speakerphones, enabling you to have hands-free discussions in your home office, just like with a regular phone. Most manufacturers have some sort of charging station with this option.

✔ **Think about family plans:** If you have multiple phones in your household, call your provider and ask about family plans, where you can share a single bulk amount of minutes across the phones. This allows you to get some phones for your kids without having to worry about paying hefty fees every month to keep the phones active.

✔ **Think about getting your kids a prepaid phone account:** With a prepaid phone, you buy a certain amount of minutes and the phone stops making calls after that allotted amount (until you replenish the phone by buying more cell time). In this way, you can give your kids enough minutes to call home and ask for help but not enough to yak with friends.

Above all, accept the fact that your phone is something that is provider-specific. That is, with some notable exceptions, your phone is likely tuned and specifically featured by your provider; if you switch providers, you'll have to change your phone number and your phone (including all the expensive accessories you bought, which is a pain). So as the knight guarding the Grail in *Indiana Jones and the Last Crusade* says, "You must choose . . . but choose wisely."

Stand by for docking

Tired of carrying your cell phone from room to room? Are you missing calls because your cell phone was turned off? Wish you could use a more comfortable handset when using your wireless service? Wish you could use your cell phone as a second line in your home, for your office, or for your kids? Want to take advantage of the great free nights and weekends calling plans?

For those who want to use their cell phone as their primary connection to the world — and have their home network connected to that line, just as if it were the landline — a number of cellular docking stations are available that enable you to bridge the two domains. Some docking station look like chargers; others look like full-fledged phones. But the setup is the same: You plug your phone into the docking station, run a regular telephone cord from the docking unit to a telephone jack on the wall, and plug in the AC adapter. Any phone plugged into your telephone wiring can receive and make calls using the cell phone service, through the docking station. When a call comes in, the units ring your stationary analog phones with a special pattern so you know that the call's of cellular origin.

An upside of this approach is that many of the stations have an external antenna hookup, so if your signal reception is marginal at home, you can attach a Yagi antenna (a kind of super-sensitive antenna) and boost the signal.

A downside is that if your power goes out, you have what remains of your battery power until you lose your phone service. But the docking stations double as recharging units, so you'll probably have at least a full charge.

Vox2, Inc. (www.vox2.com) has a device that does all this neat docking stuff for a range of cell phones, including Motorola, Ericsson, and Nokia phones, for under $200.

Instant messaging: What's it all about?

If you don't know about instant messaging, you probably don't have kids, don't have a computer, and immediately throw away all those AOL advertising promotional packages you get in the mail.

Instant messaging has been around for a long time, but it took the mass commercialization power of AOL to get the general computing populace to adopt it. Basically, instant messaging is nothing more than typing a message in a window and getting a response back from the other person. It's real time (instant) and it's messaging.

You can expect that instant messaging will creep into all devices you have connected to the Internet, whether that device is a TV, computer, cell phone, pager, or PDA.

The good news is that most wireless providers will give you a month or so to try out the service on a money-back guarantee. If you don't like it, cancel the service.

Connecting in New Ways

Traditional telephone service and cellular phones are, for most of us, the only real options when it comes to getting telephone service. That's about to change — and soon — as companies that have had nothing to do with local telephone service take advantage of FCC deregulation and enter the local telephone marketplace.

Neighborhood watch

Offerings from long-distance companies change on a daily basis it seems, but sometimes an offering comes along that changes the rules of the game. MCI's 2002 launch of MCI Neighborhood was such as offering. For the first time, from one of the Big Three long-distance carriers, you could get unlimited local calls, local toll calls, and long-distance calls; free Call Waiting, Caller ID, Speed Dial, and Three-Way Calling; and a personal voice-mail box. With the voice mail, you can check your messages by phone or on the Web through the message center; a "Notify Me" feature alerts you to new messages via pager or e-mail. Other companies have offered bundled packaging before, but no national providers have been able to say you can have unlimited calls, and you can keep your local phone number on top of it all.

You can expect more long-distance carriers to get into the local business, and the local telcos to get into the long-distance carrier business. In general, bundled plans that combine local, long-distance and cellular service are getting popular, as are services that allow you to share minutes across your extended family.

The cable squawk box

Coming soon to a neighborhood near you is local telephone competition from your cable company — and you're going to like this. The cable industry calls it the triple play: voice, data, and video in one cost-effective package. You'll get local and long-distance phone service, cable-modem Internet service, and cable TV over the local cable plant.

When this service becomes available in your neighborhood, you won't have to worry about figuring out how to plug your telephones into the cable outlet. Instead, cable telephony systems will typically include a small device called a *splitter.* This small black box will be installed right at the point where your cable connection enters the home and will separate the telephone signals from the rest of the cable signals (television, audio, and cable modem). The telephone signals will then be connected to your home's standard telephone wiring (in place of the connection you now have with the local telephone company), and the rest of the cable signals will be carried over your home's cable network. Figure 10-2 shows such an arrangement.

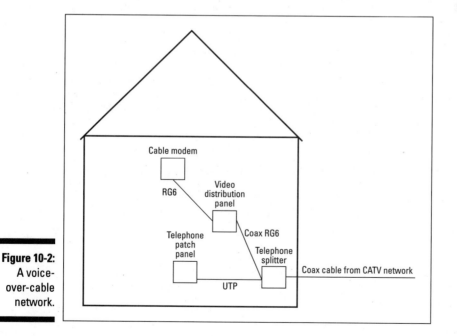

Figure 10-2:
A voice-over-cable network.

In 2002, there were more than 1 million customers of cable telephony in the U.S. This number is expected to grow tremendously in the future and drive prices down for local phone service. What's important to you is that the home-phone network you build today will still work if you shift your service to the cable company.

Voice over IP

People are getting excited about *voice-over IP* (as in *Internet Protocol,* the language of the Net). Your home's data network runs on IP. The Internet runs on IP. The traditional, voice telephone network does not. However, the telephone companies are in the process of migrating a lot of their traffic to IP, in the belief that it's a more efficient way to transport your calls.

As a result, a lot of focus is being placed on the IP-ization of telephone calls. And that's leading to voice-over IP (VoIP) services, which pick up your calls originating from IP devices and deliver them to either other IP devices or to regular phones anywhere in the world.

Voice-over IP services use your Internet connection to place and receive phone calls. This was the domain of hobbyists for a long time; they used a PC, special software, microphones, and headsets to make calls. Voice-over IP has become a little more mainstream as more user-friendly devices have come on the market, devices such as phones and videophones that can connect over IP.

In the voice-over-IP scenario, your Internet access provider (that is, your cable, DSL, or dial-up access provider) will carry your telephone calls as bits and bytes of IP data traffic through your Internet connection. That means you'll be able to make calls through your PC, home-phone network, or even through the set-top box on your TV. The VoIP providers will install a voice-over-IP gateway that will allow your calls to be carried from the Internet to regular phones on the POTS telephone network.

Over time, the devices and networks in your home will become friendlier to VoIP services. These services will help cut your telecommunications usage costs as well as provide for greater enjoyment and use of your IP networks — whether voice, data, or video.

Chapter 11

Making the Phone Connection

As we tell you in the Chapter 10, a ton of stuff fits into a home-phone network. A plethora of phone devices and a multiplicity of lines can add up to a big headache if you don't outfit your house properly for phone service. This chapter tells you how to avoid such headaches, as well as headaches that may come up if you have your house wired and connected wirelessly in ways that don't allow you to take advantage of tomorrow's technologies.

For example, although the cables that telephone companies run throughout your house are fine for most of today's uses, tomorrow you may be talking over a data networks such as the Internet. By running data-grade cabling to all your telephone and data outlets, you can futureproof your home.

With futureproofing your phone system firmly in mind, we tell you what kind of wiring to buy for your phone network and then discuss how to lay out your network. We concentrate primarily on how to create a phone network that relies on wires, which is the way that most people's phone systems work. But we talk also about some good whole-home wireless options that are widely available and not much more expensive than wired systems. We describe some of these options toward the end of the chapter.

What to Run Where

A good way to start planning a phone network is to make a list of places where you may need phone outlets. The phone network we describe here has the capacity to support up to four lines at each outlet station; you should be able to handle several devices at each outlet without any capacity problems.

There's a nuance we need to explain: the difference between the number of physical wires you run to each outlet box, and the number of jacks at the outlet box that you enable. For instance, you could run a single, four-pair line to an outlet that has four modular jacks, and one pair would go to each. This would give you four telephone lines. However, as we state in Chapter 2, those lines would not be well futureproofed for data and other applications because Ethernet computer networks require eight conductors to work fully. So our recommendation is that wherever you have a jack, you should run a full CAT-5e UTP telephone cable to that jack; a four-jack outlet would have four lines running to it. Sounds excessive? Well, in the four years since we wrote the first edition of this book, almost everyone in the industry has gone towards that recommendation. In this chapter, we'll tell you how you can use something less than one line per jack, because some of you will simply want to make do with what's in the walls already or need to keep budgets under control. But remember that we recommend one line per jack.

Now back to the planning. You need to determine each room's minimum phone communications requirements:

- ✔ **Living room:** Depending on your home layout and your plans regarding an entertainment center and home theater, your living room can be simple or complex. We recommend that you put a single telephone outlet next to your favorite seat and another multiline outlet where you plan to have your television entertainment area.

- ✔ **Dining room:** A single outlet should suffice in your dining room. However, if you work at home, your dining room may double as your conference room. In that case, think about adding both phone and data access to this room. If you intend to use the dining-room table as the place to put your gear, consider a floor mount in the middle of the room (but recognize that to do so you have to cut a hole in your floor covering, which can be rough on Oriental rugs).

- ✔ **Family room:** Again, your phone requirements here depend on where your main entertainment equipment resides. Because these rooms can be big, we usually recommend that you put one outlet on each of two facing walls. Otherwise, you may have to run 20-foot-long patch cables — which, trust us, kids and dogs have a knack for getting wrapped up in — to your telephone across the room.

- ✔ **Kitchen:** Most people spend a good deal of time in the kitchen, so at least one outlet is in order here. Many people base their answering machine or cordless phone in this room, so make sure that your phone outlet is also near a power outlet. Try to create a nook for your phone and related equipment — you don't want to spill honey on that stuff.

- ✔ **Bedrooms:** Plan for at least one multiline outlet in each bedroom. Your master bedroom may require an additional outlet on the wall opposite your bed, for your cable, DSL, or satellite set-top box access. Any bedrooms that you may eventually convert to a home office may also require a second outlet.

✔ **Home theater:** A phone jack behind your A/V component shelves gives your DSS receiver or PVR the capability to show you the movies you want to see (DSS receivers need a phone line to order Pay Per View movies, and PVRs need the phone to download programming information). You may also want to include a phone jack near the seating area if you plan to have a regular telephone in this room.

✔ **Home office:** Your home office is probably a communications hub, most likely using all your phone lines. We recommend that you install at least two multiline jacks on opposite walls to give you a bit of flexibility. If you have an assistant, you may need to add extra jacks in this room.

Don't just think about one home office per house; you might need two. They might be at separate ends of the house (which we recommend for marital reasons) or they might be in the same room, to share devices such as printers, fax machines, and photocopiers. The same is true of kids' computers. They need a space where they can concentrate to do their homework and to play. Consider a computer room, where they each have their own spot and you get the advantages of having a lot of gear in one place.

✔ **Other places:** Don't overlook other parts of your home when you're planning phone outlets. We recommend that you include phones in the garage, the bathroom, the basement, and the exercise room. Note: If you want your phone system to double as an intercom, you need to run outlets to the places you'd like to intercom as well.

Throughout this book, we show you home-network functionality in every room. Much of this functionality depends on the telephone. Don't shortchange yourself for a few dollars, counting on wireless options down the road. A wired infrastructure has many advantages. Almost any habitable room (closets excluded — for now) should have phone access.

Building the architecture

In Chapter 2, we mention that your phone network will include CAT-5e cabling, RJ-45 connectors, patch panels, patch cables, and more. Now it's time to discuss how it all fits together — the architecture of it all. Think Greek!

In the past, if you wanted two lines at an outlet, you took two pair from the same wire and created two two-conductor RJ-11 outlets. If you wanted three lines, you might have a three- or four-pair line, or two two-pair lines, and split them off that way. We're not recommending that. If you're building a house, we recommend one full CAT-5e line per jack. (If you have two jacks at a faceplate, two lines are running there.) This is so you can have a full RJ-45 CAT-5e data-capable line at each outlet. This gives you maximum flexibility in the future, and melds the phone network and the data network — at the physical level. If you have existing wiring, read on and we'll make do with what you have.

The *architecture* of a network refers to the logical model on which it's based. If you've ever seen one of those AT&T commercials where they show the company's switching network as red lines connecting big red dots and showing telephone calls boogying across those lines and dots, you've seen a model.

The not-so-good daisy chain

If you have an older home or are building a new one and let the electrician or telephone company wire your home for phones without any specific instructions, chances are that you have a daisy-chained telephone network.

In this type of network model, a telephone cable (typically a quad cable — four conductors, capable of supporting two telephone lines) is connected to the telephone company's NID (Network Interface Device). This cable runs throughout the home, from jack to jack, until it reaches the final, most-distant jack.

Phone companies and electricians often choose this method because it's easy and cheap. Unfortunately, many problems come with a daisy-chain system, such as the following:

✔ You lose your connection when more people pick up the line to take part in a conversation.

✔ You're limited to having the same outside line on each jack in the house — you won't be able to reconfigure a jack to connect to an extra phone line that you might purchase from the phone company.

Don't wire your telephone network in a daisy-chain configuration. The star architecture that we describe in the following section is much more flexible and capable than the daisy-chain architecture.

Reach for a star

In the *star architecture,* each jack runs to a wiring hub that acts as a central connection point. If you draw this system on paper, it looks like a star (or maybe a wagon wheel with the spokes connecting at the hub).

The star architecture provides many advantages over the daisy-chain architecture we describe in the preceding section. Here are a few advantages:

✔ **Reliability:** If you use a daisy-chain architecture, any physical or electrical problems in your phone cable affect all the phones farther along on that cabling system. In a star network, only the phones at the end of the individual affected cable are out of order.

✔ **Greater capacity:** Daisy-chained telephone networks are useful for only the number of lines that start out from the wiring hub, whereas a star network lets you handle as many lines as each home run carries.

✔ **Flexibility:** In a daisy-chained network, each telephone jack station is stuck with whatever phone lines its cable is connected to back at the

NID. In a star network, all the cables go back to a central point, which you can patch to different incoming lines with a minimum of fuss. If you decide to convert a spare bedroom into a home office, you simply reconfigure your connections — to connect those remote phone jacks to your incoming fax line, for example — at the network's hub.

Starting from the telephone company's incoming service feed, you build a typical star-wired telephone network as follows:

1. **The telephone company installs an incoming line or lines (called a** *feed***) from the local central office (or a remote unit such as a Digital Loop Carrier, or DLC).**

   Depending on a host of factors — when your telephone company's connection was installed, which company did it, how many lines you have — the telephone cable may consist of two, three, or four pairs of copper wire. The wire may or may not be twisted (most older installations aren't). For the most part, many recent telephone-company installations use four-pair, UTP cable. The telephone company connects the incoming feed to the Network Interface Device (NID) outside your home.

2. **Connect a UTP cable from the consumer side of the NID to the patch panel in your home's wiring center.**

   This line is the central feed between the outside world and your home-phone network. Attach each conductor wire within the line to the patch panel. (For information about choosing a location for your home's wiring center, beam yourself to Chapter 2.)

3. **Connect a UTP cable onto the terminal block.**

   This cable — commonly known as a *drop* — provides telephone service to an individual phone outlet.

   If you're planning to use RJ-11 jacks (not our recommended RJ-45, shame, shame) and four-pair UTP cabling, and your phone network is starting off with less than four lines used at a particular jack, no problem. You can leave some of the pairs of wires in your UTP cabling unterminated to start off. Just make sure that you label your cables so that you know which room each drop serves. Leave the unused cables coiled up out of the way at each end (in other words, behind your future wall outlet and near the patch panel). And in the future, if you add additional lines, you can simply connect additional feed and drop lines to the patch panel (and to your modular outlets at the endpoints of your network). Quick and easy reconfiguring is one of the biggest advantages of a star-wired phone network that uses four-pair cables.

4. **Run a UTP drop cable from your wiring center through the walls to a modular outlet in a room where you want to use a phone device.**

   Again, the entire cable should be allocated to its own RJ-45 jack. If you're going to use RJ-11 jacks, you have a fair amount of flexibility. You can connect your UTP cabling to two separate two-line outlets, four one-line outlets, or some combination thereof. The kind of phones and phone equipment you'll be connecting to the outlets drives your cable choice.

5. **Connect *end devices* — all the neat stuff we discuss in Chapter 10, such as phones, faxes, and modems — to the wall outlets by using simple telephone patch cables.**

6. **Repeat Steps 3 – 5 for each outlet in your phone network.**

Figure 11-1 shows the finished product — a star-wired telephone network.

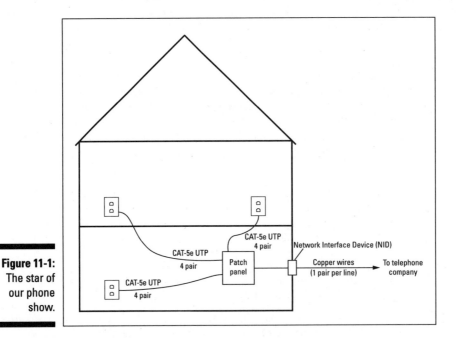

Figure 11-1:
The star of
our phone
show.

Hybrid networks

If you discover the need for an additional outlet someplace in your home that you didn't wire with a star run, you can use a modified version of the daisy-chained wiring scheme. Running a daisy chain from a new outlet from the nearest star outlet is easy and acceptable when necessary.

Ideally, you should avoid this kind of hybrid network, but adding an outlet or two to a star network by daisy chaining won't mess things up. Remember, however, that these new outlets lose the flexibility of runs back to a central point. They have to be connected to the same phone lines as the star-wired outlet they're connected to, so you can't use them for different phone lines. Some great alternatives using wireless and electrical technologies are available, as we discuss later in this chapter and in Chapter 16.

Low-cost home-phone systems

Some great, low-cost home-phone systems are available, such as Centrepoint Technologies' (www.talkswitch.com) $395 Concero Switchboard. This key telephone system allows you to do all the things big companies do — conference calling, call transferring, putting callers on hold, acting as an intercom, and using prioritized or selective ringing.

Concero integrates one or two phone lines with four extensions for your standard phones, fax machines, answering devices, modems, PCs, and cell phones. You can dial or answer either line from any phone. Any three outside phone numbers become remote extensions (cell/PCS phones, pagers, or satellite offices, for example). So when you leave the office, you can calls forwarded to where you are, giving you seamless one-number service.

If you answer a ringing telephone and you hear fax tones, you merely press the fax machine's extension number and hang up. If you enable the fax-tone detection feature, Switchboard automatically answers in fax mode. Switchboard also performs callbacks and call rerouting, which saves you money by letting you place long-distance calls through your home. (Ever make an international call on a cell phone? It's expensive.)

If you need more than two lines for your home-telephone system, Centrepoint's TalkSwitch 24 ($695) supports two lines, four internal extensions, and eight remote extensions, and its TalkSwitch 48-LS ($1395) supports four lines, eight internal extensions, and eight remote extensions. Panasonic (www.panasonic.com), Siemens (www.siemens.com), and others also offer good systems. Expect to spend $400 to $600 for a 3 x 8 KSU. Phones run $100 to $200 apiece, depending on whether you want a speakerphone, LCD, and so on. A 6 x 16 system is in the $600 to $800 range, with phones also in the $100 to $200 range.

Plugging into a KSU

The phone network described in the preceding section gets you up and running. It gives you multiline phone service available throughout the home, which is worth a good deal all on its own. However, you may decide that you want more. For example, you may want to transfer calls from one phone to another or use your phone as an intercom. You may even want to have some music available when you put that telemarketer on hold (ahhhh, sweet revenge). In that case, you need a KSU, or *key telephone system unit,* to control your phone lines.

The KSU serves as your phone system's intelligence. The phone lines plug into the KSU, which is usually located in the same place as your punchdown block. The in-home drops (the star-wired phone cables connected to each of your home's phone outlets) connect into the other side of the KSU, which allows the KSU to conference calls together, transfer calls, and ring any extension at any time.

The marketplace offers a huge variety of key systems, each with its own wiring and equipment requirements. Because the vast majority of these systems require exactly what you already have installed — a star-network architecture and UTP cabling — integrating a KSU into your phone network is simple. In shopping for key systems, you hear terms such as 6 x 16 (pronounced "six by sixteen"), which means that the system supports up to 6 lines and 16 extensions off those lines.

Here are a few things to keep in mind:

- ✓ **The central control unit — the KSU — installs in your wiring center between the incoming service feeds and the patch panel:** Incoming feeds use modular RJ-11 jacks to connect to the system's input side, and then additional patch cables connect the individual extension outputs to your service drops for each room.

- ✓ **Most KSU systems require just a single pair of UTP wiring to each extension, though a scant few require two or even three pairs:** Those requiring two or three pairs are either heavy-duty systems or are for providing extra services, such as ISDN capabilities, to the extensions. You can cover all your bases by installing four-pair UTP at the outset.

- ✓ **Many KSUs have additional inputs and outputs:** The additional inputs and outputs are designed for things such as door phones, music inputs, and even a printer interface for printing *call detail reports,* which itemize phone numbers and times that calls are made from each extension.

Using KSU-less phone systems

In Chapter 10, we discuss *KSU-less phone systems* — sophisticated, multiline telephones that have a degree of networking intelligence built into each phone (as opposed to putting all the control functionality into a central unit). KSU-less phone systems have a price advantage over KSUs. However, the handsets themselves can be expensive, and if you install several of them, dropping the money on a KSU system up front may be financially advantageous. You have to shop around.

KSU-less phone systems aren't nearly as picky about network architecture as a KSU system. Most KSU systems require the star-wiring configuration we describe earlier in this chapter, but many KSU-less systems work in either a star or a daisy-chained wiring architecture. So you can utilize your existing phone wiring and still get many of the intercom, call transfer, and conference call features that KSUs provide.

This approach does come with a couple of caveats, however:

- ✓ **The ultimate capacity of a KSU-less network is less than that of a full KSU:** If you need a big bunch of lines and extensions, you may be out of luck. You can, however, handle three or four incoming lines and up to a dozen extensions, depending on the system you buy.

✔ **If you want more than two active phone lines, utilizing this kind of system on your existing phone wiring assumes that your current wiring already provides three or four lines to each phone outlet:** If your house was wired recently, you very well may meet this requirement, but unless you are sure that you have three- or four-pair wiring connected to each outlet, you may have to run new wires after all.

Make sure that you figure out how many phone lines your current wiring will support before you decide on a KSU-less phone system. If you find that you need to run new wire anyway to get that third or fourth line installed, we highly recommend that you start at square one and build a star phone-line infrastructure. You can still use KSU-less phones if you like, but you have all the flexibility and expansion capacity of a modern phone network in place for future needs.

Connecting Alternatively

You also have non-wireline options for distributing phone service throughout your home. These methods don't give you the same ultimate capacity as a wireline phone network (they're limited to three or four lines at most), but you can get much of the same functionality with some of these alternatives.

For wireless phones to work, you have to have some kind of phone connection into your house, even if it's a 1937 Ma Bell wiring job.

Taking the wireless route

The simplest way to expand an existing phone network is to use wireless phones and phone systems. You most likely have a cordless phone of some sort, so you're already using this technology in a limited way.

Conventional cordless phones (typically available in one- and two-line models) expand your network by adding a degree of mobility to your telephone devices. What they don't do, however, is offer more sophisticated call-control features such as call transfer and an intercom (except between the handset and the base station). They also don't provide connectivity for other telephony devices such as fax machines and analog modems. All they do is give you another telephone handset, sans cord. Some new cordless phone systems, however, let you do much more.

VTECH Cordless Phone System

VTECH (www.vtechphones.com) has been showing up everywhere in recent years, and they have a knack for having feature-rich products at low price points. Their four-line multi-handset model 40-2421 is a wireless system that can handle up to twelve extensions. It operates as 2.4-GHz Digital Spread Spectrum. Each handset has a speakerphone and has a fifty name and number phonebook directory that you can use for calling and checking inbound caller ID. A host of other features includes hold, mute, intercom, do not disturb, conference calling, and a visual message-waiting indicator. What's amazing is the setup — you plug in the power cord, charge up the units, and you're all set to go. You can add numbers into the directory whenever you want. All this power — equal to many KSU-driven systems — for around $350 for the base station and around $200 per phone.

Panasonic Cordless Phone System

Panasonic (www.panasonic.com) makes great small office and home systems. We've been using them for years. Their KX-TG4000B 4-Line Multi-Handset Cordless Phone System uses 2.4-GHz Frequency Hopping Spread Spectrum (FHSS) transmission to offer four lines and up to eight extensions. The core of the system is a corded base station, and there's one handset and charger. Out of the box, you get private voice-mail boxes, intercom, auto attendant, conferencing, and most of the usual features such as hold, transfer, and caller ID. The Panasonic system is about $550 for the main unit and $200 per handset — a great price if you've ever shopped for a system as packed as this one is.

What's neat about many of these systems is that you can intermix corded and cordless units, including accessories such as door intercoms. You can buy regular phone sets, with an antenna on them, so you can carry them to the conference room for lunch (no more transferred calls). And wireless conferencing systems can fit into your network as well. Homeowners today are lucky to have such choices.

Adding a jack on the cheap, without wires

If you have only basic telephone needs and don't want to spend a pile of money, you may not want to go for an all-out phone system or expensive wireless solution. Suppose you need only a phone jack for your DSS receiver, and you don't have one anywhere near the TV location? Or perhaps you need a telephone in that unfinished attic that's now becoming a finished attic?

In that case, you may want to try one of the wireless phone jacks available from RCA (www.rca.com) or Radio Shack (www.radioshack.com). These devices use your home's power lines to carry phone signals — they're not really wireless; they leverage your existing wiring. The most basic configuration consists of a pair of small devices. The master unit plugs into an existing single-line phone jack and also into an AC outlet. The extension unit plugs into any of your home's AC outlets and has a standard RJ-11 receptacle for connecting a phone device. You can buy these remote units separately and add more extension units if you need extra outlets. A pair runs about $89.

These jacks aren't the end-all in sophistication — they handle only one line, and they won't work on modems faster than 14.4 Kbps — but they do allow you to plug in a DSS dish or add a phone or fax in some location that you never anticipated.

Part IV
Livin' Off the Fat of the LAN

In this part . . .

A home-data network used to be a rarity. Today, you may have a second, third, or fourth computer at home, and the fights over the printer, scanner, or more likely, the high-speed Internet access link may be causing you some grief. A home-data network is no longer a luxury; it's a necessity, if only to bring peace to the household.

Putting together a home network is getting easier and easier, particularly with the advent of new wireless networks and networks that use your existing electrical or telephone wiring. By planning, you can pretty much access your home-data network from anywhere in the house.

In this part, we show you how to create a data backbone in your home. We discuss all the major elements of a whole-home data network and how this data network interfaces with your home-telephone and -video networks — the three have a lot in common, especially if you have a broadband Internet connection. We also tell you about the different types of data-networking equipment and services available, as well as some advice for ensuring the success of your home-data network.

Chapter 12

A Cornucopia of Computers

More than 60 percent of homes in North America have a PC, and that number is going nowhere but up. Computers become cheaper and more powerful by the minute, and every year you find new ways of using your computer.

Home offices, Web surfing, e-mail, videoconferencing, computer banking — you name it, and people are doing it on their PCs right now. Even more importantly, they're doing it over a network, whether it be the Internet, America Online, a remote access connection to the office LAN, or even a home LAN between computers in the same house (an increasing number of computer owners now have more than one computer in the home).

In this chapter, we tell you about the equipment that fits into a home-computer network — everything from PCs to printers to peripherals. We also discuss some devices that aren't PCs but fit into a computer network and make use of your home's Internet connection — devices such as Web-enabled TVs and gaming consoles.

An important note upfront: You probably have a vision of a computer as a particular type of device — you know, that tan-colored box with a big monitor and keyboard and all those wires. You need to throw that constrained vision of a computer out the window. Although we do describe that form of computer, we also talk about how the computer is becoming distributed throughout the home and how many, many devices can (or will soon) connect to your computer network. So knowing the pieces is important, and that's where we'll start.

Another important note: You're putting together a computer network in your house for two reasons. The first is for the things you know you want to connect, such as connecting your PCs to each other. The second is for all the things you don't know you want to connect but which require a computer network to work. This includes all the home-entertainment devices and other home-automation devices that need to send messages all over the house and all over the Internet. If you're part of the 40 percent of people in the U.S. who don't yet have a PC at home, don't skip this section because you think you might never need a computer network. You will — we guarantee it — even if you never purchase a computer.

Considering Computers of All Kinds

If you have at least one PC in your home, it makes sense to think about your computer networking needs as part of your total home-networking needs. Your present network may consist of only a modem that connects your PC to the outside world or perhaps a simple A/B switch that lets two computers share a single printer. But the decreasing cost of PCs, combined with the increasing speed of Internet connection methods and greater use of the PC in a whole-home environment, makes it worthwhile to install a more sophisticated home-computer network.

In the environment of an office or school, computers are routinely networked to take full advantage of their capabilities — and we think the possibilities are numerous enough to justify your thinking that way at home.

Choosing traditional PCs

We use the term *traditional PC* to differentiate the types of PCs most families have from some of the emerging forms that computers are starting to take (such as Web-enabled TVs). We're definitely not disparaging your Pentium 4, 8-million-megahertz new PC with 3-D graphics as an obsolete clunker (even though by the time you read this it might be).

When we talk about PCs (whether they be desktop or laptop models), we're basically talking about one of two things:

- **Windows-based PCs:** These PCs have Intel CPUs (or similar CPUs from companies such as AMD) and use a Microsoft Windows operating system (OS). Some people call these *Wintel* machines — people like us, for example.

- **Macintoshes:** These are Apple computers that run the Mac OS.

More advanced readers may be using other types of computers — such as a Linux-based computer — but if you're advanced enough to survive in the Linux environment, you don't need us to explain what a PC is. (Hard-core Linux users think graphical user interfaces, such as the ones that come with Wintel

> ## Lease or buy?
>
> Just like cars and many other things in life, you can lease or buy computers. We're not financial experts, but we think the issues are largely the same with computers as with cars. If you want the latest features, you may want to consider the leasing option because you can turn over your computer every few years — about the same time that they tend to obsolesce. All major computer companies have leasing options. They also have on-site repair plans — we highly recommend you purchase that with any computer you buy.

machines and Macs, are for wimps. They prefer to do stuff at the command-line level — something you can do, by the way, starting with the 2002 and later UNIX-based versions of the Mac OS.)

For the most part, both Wintel and Macintosh computers fit into a home network the same way — other than a few minor differences in the connectors for peripherals. Which kind of PC you use is a matter of preference (we both have one or more of each in our homes).

Although both Windows and Macintosh computers work just fine in a home network, they can't easily talk to each other on the same network without special software. The networking software built into each operating system doesn't know how to talk to the other operating system's networking software — so Mac's AppleTalk and a Windows computer's Neighborhood Network software don't really communicate with each other. Check out MacLAN by Miramar Systems (www.miramar.com) or Dave by Thursby Software Systems (www.thursby.com) for a solution to this problem. If you have a Mac, you can probably avoid using this extra software if you have the latest version of Apple's OS X operating system. For more information on integrating different computers into the same home-PC network, check out *Networking Home PCs For Dummies* by Kathy Ivens (published by Wiley Publishing, Inc.).

Looking at laptops, desktops, and more

You need to consider the physical form of the computers you will be adding to your home network. For instance, you can choose between the following two types of computers:

- **Desktop computer:** Full-sized — and full-featured — computers that are portable only in the sense that a strong person can move them across the room without needing a quick dose of oxygen. Desktops are big and bulky, but dollar for dollar, they are also more powerful, have larger displays, and can be more easily expanded and upgraded than laptop computers.

✔ **Laptop computer:** As you may infer from the name, laptops can be taken with you from room to room or town to town. The first generations of laptop computers were inferior to desktops in just about every way — except, of course, in terms of portability — but current models have enough power and functionality to do just about everything the average user needs. However, they cost a bit more than an equivalent desktop computer. Most laptops have docking station options that allow you to plug your laptop into a system that has a large monitor and regular-sized keyboard attached to it. This makes it easy to have desktop style computing with the option of portability.

Which of these computers you choose for your home network is a personal decision based on your own computing needs, but it's important to make sure that the systems you choose have the capability to connect to your home network. In Chapters 15 and 16, we tell you about the various kinds of home LANs that you can install in your home, but regardless of which network type you choose, your PCs will require some sort of network interface card (or NIC). A *NIC* is the physical interface between your PC's internal systems and the outside network.

For desktop computers, the NIC — if it doesn't come preinstalled in the computer — generally fits into one of the internal *PCI* (personal computer interface) card slots in the PC. (The ones that look like they take a fat credit card.) Other slots in your computer can also accept NIC cards, but we prefer to use PCI NICs because they're a heck of a lot easier to set up. Laptop and palmtop computer NICs use an expansion device known as a *PC Card* (which looks rather like a thick credit card). Any PC built within the past three or four years has these expansion slots built right in — the only real concern is whether you have one free to install the NIC.

The tablet computer — don't wander your home without it

The increasing integration of computer parts, the greater availability of wireless connectivity, and the desire to roam the home have all conspired to create a new class of computers with a detachable screen that operates like a tablet when disconnected from its master unit. It's a laptop monitor that detaches. This class of device is called, not surprisingly, a tablet computer.

It's early in this product category's life cycle, so we can't tell you whether tablet computers will

be the next big thing that comes standard on so many PCs or the latest technology flop. However, we can tell you that the networking connections envisioned by these devices are compatible with the home networks we describe in this book. So if you like to cuddle with an e-book next to the fire, consult your e-recipe book in the kitchen, or work on your e-mail in bed, you might want to check out tablet computers.

What the heck is a home server?

In the computer networking world (and we're talking at a high conceptual level here — there are layers of nuance that we don't want to confuse ourselves or you with) computers can be broken down into two categories: servers and clients. For the most part, the computers you work with on a day-to-day basis are clients, at least in the networking sense. You use clients to connect to networks such as the Internet or a work network.

Servers are on the other end of that connection. When you get your e-mail, you connect to an e-mail server somewhere. When you read a Web page, you get the HTML files that make up that page from a Web server somewhere. Servers tend to be computers that share their data with many other computers. Until recently, most servers were outside the home, and you connected to them through an ISP.

As we discuss in Chapter 5, however, many vendors are beginning to launch servers for the home market. These servers store various kinds of computer data (such as movies, songs, pictures, and text documents) and are accessible to any computer or display device in the house. You probably won't even have a monitor, mouse, or keyboard directly connected to these servers, just a network connection. The goal is to provide a single repository for all this stuff — a data warehouse for the home that can be accessed by anyone in your family. When these become more widely available, you'll no longer have to try to remember which computer you downloaded the digital photos to or where that obscure MP3 file is — it will all be on the server!

PDAs, PDQ: Interfacing with Handheld Computers

PDAs (Personal Digital Assistants) are a step down in computing power from traditional PCs but a step up in portability. These portable devices range in functionality from simple electronic address books to powerful handheld computers that can send e-mail, browse the Web, and do basic word processing and spreadsheet tasks. You see business people in airports with these little devices, looking up phone numbers or checking calendars.

PDAs come in two broad categories:

- ✔ Handheld devices from companies such as Palm, Handspring, and Sony, which use the PalmOS operating system
- ✔ Handheld computers, called PocketPCs, which utilize a scaled-down version of the Microsoft Windows operating system (Windows CE)

Within each of these two groups, the functionality of PDAs differs greatly, but they are all capable of networking by connecting either directly to your PC to exchange data or through a modem connection to other data networks such as the Internet. Most have an infrared (IR) device that allows you to print to a printer (or update internal databases) by aiming the device at a printer (or computer) — nifty, huh? Figure 12-1 shows how a PDA can network with a PC using infrared networking.

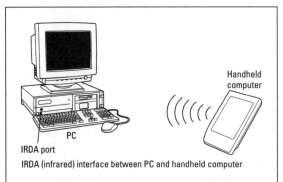

Figure 12-1:
Transferring
data with
light!

Most infrared equipment uses a common industry standard for networking called IRDA (which stands for Infrared Data Association, the group that created the standard).

The definition of PDA is becoming more flexible. Some PocketPCs are so powerful — with fast processors and the capability to run programs such as Word and Excel — that they're much closer to being small but full-fledged PCs than handheld organizers. Mobile phones are also becoming much more like PDAs. Companies such as Nokia, Sony, Ericsson, and Handspring make mobile phones with a ton of built-in PDA functionality, including address books, e-mail, and even the capability to view office documents. The lines are blurring with each new product announcement. One thing is for sure: Whatever you call a handheld device (phone, PDA, or Star Trek Tricorder), it's going to be more and more like a small PC.

The neat thing coming to the handheld world is wireless networking. Although IR connections are wireless too, we're talking about radio-based

Now that's handy — a PDA remote control

A PDA contains everything that's required — and more — to serve as a universal remote control for your house. You can load programs onto your PDA to control your home-entertainment center and your home-automation systems.

Some companies that build both PDAs and home-entertainment devices (such as Sony) market their PDAs as both organizers and universal remote controls. This is an area that will see a lot of development in upcoming years.

Knapsack . . . check; lunchbox . . . check; PDA . . . check

We find that many technologies are generational: Some generations don't buy into certain things while other age groups are fanatical about them. PDAs are one such group, and you can bet that your kids will want to take some sort of PDA to school — if for no other reason than to pass notes the twenty-first-century way.

In the past, PDAs were a localized device, slaved to a particular PC through a docking cradle and connection cable. With wireless networking included in many new PDAs, however, this connection is now more whole home, so PDAs can be updated anywhere in the home where they can log onto the network through its radio or infrared frequencies.

(not visual-light-based) networks — such as WiFi and Bluetooth. We describe these two networking standards in detail in Chapter 16, but for now we'll tell you why they're so cool compared to IR.

IR has a limited range (just a few feet at most) and must be within the direct line of sight of the target device you're beaming data to and from. RF signals, on the other hand, can pass through walls, doors, people, dogs, and everything, and they can go a lot farther too — so you can sit on the living room couch with your PDA and "talk" to your PC in the bedroom. In the case of WiFi (the more powerful of these two wireless systems), you can find public access points in schools, airports, hotels and coffee shops, so you can connect your PDA to the Internet even when you're far from home and a phone line.

Monitors

Computer monitors are constantly evolving. It's one area where people tend to want the latest and greatest because it's what they look at all the time.

We talk in Chapter 5 about the changes in TV displays, and it's not surprising that the same changes have been flowing through to computers as well. Soon, all computers will likely have flat-screen PC monitors like the flat-screen TVs. It's just a matter of increasing volumes driving production efficiencies, resulting in lower prices. And now the prices are low enough that you can have monitors in the seats of cars, under the cabinets in the kitchen, and hanging on the wall in your home office.

Some key terms that you'll hear discussed in the computer publications follow:

   ✔ **CRT:** Like the conventional direct view televisions described in Chapter 5, CRT monitors are based on *cathode ray tubes* — the traditional picture tube found in televisions since the 1940s. Although CRTs are bulky, they are cheap to make, can be very large (for a bit more money), and can have excellent picture quality.

✔ **Plasma:** Also discussed in Chapter 5, plasma screens are the most common technology used for big, flat-panel, hang-on-the-wall TVs. Plasma screens aren't used much as PC monitors, mainly because LCD screens are cheaper and tend to have a better picture in the sizes typically used for PC applications. But like every other new computer-related technology, plasma displays are experiencing improved quality and reduced price. We expect that they'll be used in larger PC monitor applications where LCDs are too expensive and CRTs are too bulky.

✔ **LCD:** We bet that you're already familiar with LCD screens — they're standard in every laptop or PDA on the market. LCDs used to be expensive to manufacture, but since the mid-1990s the technology has improved immensely, and dozens of LCD factories have been built in Japan, Taiwan, and Korea. As a result, LCD prices have dropped a ton, and most PC vendors now offer LCD screens as an option (or even standard) with their new PCs. The advantages of LCDs are many, but we think the biggest one is that they're much more space efficient than clunky old CRT monitors, so they can fit in a lot more places in your home. The biggest downside to LCD monitors is that the larger ones (about 22 inches, measured diagonally, and more) are expensive.

✔ **Touchscreens:** These monitors can be constructed based on CRT, plasma, or LCD displays. Electrical sensors are built into the face of a touchscreen monitor, enabling a user to simply point and touch with his or her finger to perform actions on the computer — instead of using a mouse or other pointing device. Touchscreens aren't as flexible as traditional pointing devices but can be useful in applications in which you want to use a more limited set of functions with your computer — such as controlling lights, TVs, or AC settings.

Keyboards

There have been a lot of funky attempts to reinvent the keyboard over the years, and nothing has caught the fancy of the mass market. (The only thing Danny has added to his keyboard is a big red panic button).

However, we did want to make three comments about keyboards. First, you can buy remote keyboards that have an infrared connection to a set-top box or other device. We think that RF, not infrared, is the way to go for these connections because infrared communications can be slow and unreliable if you type fast or move around a lot. To us, no better devices are available for keyboards and computer mice than those made by Logitech (www.logitech.com). As the Bluetooth technology that we mention earlier in this chapter (and discuss in more detail in Chapter 16) becomes more widespread, we believe it will become the most prevalent way of connecting wireless keyboards.

Second, if you have kids, you might be tempted to buy a kid's keyboard. All sorts are available with large buttons and color coding, designed for very young kids. We advise against these because kids learn really fast, and they should learn on a real keyboard. Danny tried a lot of these kiddie keyboards on his kids, and in a week junked them all for regular keyboards. (His four-year-olds were beating him at *Ages of Empire* in no time flat.)

And finally, keyboard functionality will be used more and more around the house, so the interfaces might change some from application to application. In some instances, you'll need a waterproof keyboard (so you can type in the hot tub, on the boat, while washing the dog, and so on.). In other instances, you might find that you're using a remote control as your keyboard interface. And in yet other examples, such as with refrigerators, touchscreen is the way to go. If you find that your keyboard just doesn't look right with a particular application or use, go hunting around for other options.

The coolest keyboard we've ever seen has been announced by Siemens (the big German technology company). Their virtual keyboard (`http://www.siemens.com/axx-picture/axx20020539`) is a small box that sits on a desk, table, or other flat surface. The virtual keyboard projects a keyboard-shaped (and labeled) light pattern on the desk, and can follow the motion of your fingers as you tap away on — well basically on nothing. The virtual keyboard hasn't made it out into the general marketplace yet, but it seems like a great way to add a keyboard to devices such as PDAs or mobile phones, because it gives you a way to type messages or e-mails but doesn't take up a lot of space.

Eeek! There's a Mouse on My Desk!

Mice share much of the same development attention as keyboards, with a range of options on the market. We think no one should have a wired mouse, having used Logitech wireless mice since they were invented. And there are different styles of wireless mice — for example, a simple, three-button, hand-held wireless mouse for office presentation applications is great in the exercise room of your house, where you might have a remote monitor for Web surfing while you walk or ride the fat away.

If you've never used an optical mouse — the kind that use a small light and sensor instead of a moving mouse ball — you haven't really lived. We think that the difference in functionality is amazing, and you never have to clean out the gunk that builds up inside your mouse. We've had some mice-cleaning gizmos over the years, and boy, were we glad to be able to finally throw those away (and usually we like gizmos). On the other hand, if your desk is as messy as ours, the old roller mouse is great because it works on top of the mess!

Plugging in Printers and Such

Although a computer, monitor, keyboard, and mouse are all that you need to get up and running, no computer fulfills its potential without being hooked up to all sorts of neat peripheral devices — and indeed to other computers. The number of things you can plug into a computer is almost limitless these days. Here are a few examples:

- ✔ **Printers** for getting your text and pictures on paper. New printers for your color photographs are surprisingly inexpensive — although beware the costs of ink refills!

- ✔ **Scanners** for getting text and pictures onto your hard drive and into e-mails. There are scanners for business cards and photographs as well as all-purposes scanners. We love the scanners from Visioneer (www.visioneer.com).

- ✔ **Modems**, including analog telephone, ISDN, xDSL, wireless, and cable modems — all of which we explain in Chapter 13.

- ✔ **Digital still cameras** that can capture still pictures and save them to your hard drive.

- ✔ **Digital video cameras** that let you videoconference or record movies to your hard drive.

    You can also use these PC digital Web cams for security and monitoring — something we discuss in Chapter 18.

- ✔ **Telephone management devices** that display, for example, Caller ID information on your screen or even open your contact management software and tell you exactly who is calling.

- ✔ **Docking stations** for a range of portable devices, including cell phones, cordless phones, PDAs, and wireless headsets.

You can connect peripherals to a computer in two ways:

- ✔ **Connect peripherals directly to a single computer using that computer's parallel, serial, SCSI, Universal Serial Bus (USB), FireWire, infrared, Bluetooth or other port.** These peripheral devices are called *locally connected.* If you want to know more about setting up your PC, check out *PCs For Dummies,* 8th Edition, by Dan Gookin (published by Wiley Publishing, Inc.).

- ✔ **Connect peripherals to a computer local area network (LAN) so that you can share the peripherals among several computers.** This type of peripheral is often called a *LAN-capable* or *networkable* peripheral. Many devices today sport a wireless connection to the network, making them LAN-capable.

Using a PC as a videophone

As we discuss in Chapter 10, the videophone has been almost the Holy Grail of the telephone industry — something they've been searching for a way to do for nearly 40 years. The two big issues with telephone-based videophones are that the phones themselves are expensive, and the analog telephone lines that the majority of phones are connected to are too slow to carry a decent video signal. But while stand-alone videophones remain rare, videoconferencing on the PC has become almost commonplace. The PC has a few big advantages over a telephone system when it comes to videoconferencing:

✔ The CPU and video card of the PC can be leveraged to do the video signal processing — in modern computers, these devices are so powerful that you don't need a lot of pricey add-ons to handle video. This functionality, by the way, is one of the things that makes video telephones so expensive.

✔ Fast peripheral connection methods, such as USB and FireWire, can handle the signals from video cameras at full speed, so there's no longer a need for a special card inside the computer to attach a camera.

✔ Video cameras for PCs have become inexpensive. USB Web cams can cost as little as $40 and are available just about anywhere you buy PC accessories.

✔ Most importantly, PCs tend to be connected to high-speed broadband networks such as DSL or cable modems. These broadband connections, unlike analog telephone lines, have enough bandwidth to carry color video at frame rates fast enough to make the video look like video, instead of just a slideshow of still images.

Videoconferencing programs for the PC aren't just cheap — oftentimes they're free. Many free Instant Messenger programs (such as Yahoo! Messenger) have videophone capabilities, and conferencing programs such as Microsoft NetMeeting are also free. So buy a cheap camera and get videoconferencing. If you have kids, one great use for these videophone programs is to use them to connect to the grandparents. Why wait until the next holiday for the kids to say "Hi!" face-to-face?

Many computer peripherals have either local connections or network connections (usually the LAN-capable type costs a bit more). Some peripherals, such as many laser printers, may come equipped with both types of connections. In an ideal world, you'd probably want to choose only peripherals that are networkable, but this standard isn't always practical.

Keep in mind that many devices that connect to a single computer may still be used remotely by other computers on that network. For example, an inkjet printer that isn't configured to plug directly into the LAN may be accessible to other computers on the network if the computer that it *is* plugged into is properly configured as a print server.

Now, this description is a little techie, and the purpose of this book is not to teach a lesson in computer hardware. Some great *For Dummies* books do that perfectly. But the message is this: In buying hardware or trying to make use of hand-me-downs, you need to consider whether the equipment itself is networkable. Your local hardware dealer can help you determine that. So can that neighbor kid who knows everything. In other chapters, we talk about many more issues that you need to know about, so don't try to decipher everything now.

Beyond the PC — Next-Generation Computers

The pieces and parts that make up a PC get smaller, faster, and cheaper every year. They also get used in more and more places — so you find computer hard drives, for example, in PVRs and MP3 players, and computer graphics chips and processors in video game machines. Dozens of items in your home have most of the functionality of a personal computer — but few tie all that functionality together in a way that allows you to move seamlessly among them to read e-mail or surf the Web.

We think this is probably okay — PCs are very good at what they do, and PC-like devices are good at what they do. So we probably wouldn't want to throw out our PC in favor of a TV set-top box that we can use to surf the Web. Having said that, sometimes we might want to do PC stuff on our TVs or elsewhere in the home. Following are some good example of times when PC on the TV makes sense to us:

- **PC-powered TV:** In Chapter 7, we talk about PVR functionality and how a PC with a video connection can drive your viewing habits. Indeed, with PC remote controls that work from your living room, your dumb TV can do a lot more.

- **Context-based TV Web browsing:** This mouthful of terms refers to the times when you see something on TV (in an advertisement or during one of those PBS documentaries that we're nerdy enough to watch) and think, "Wouldn't it be nice to click a button on my remote control to display a Web page related to whatever's on the screen of my TV show?"

- **Quick checks of your messages:** Eventually *unified messaging* will hit the market (it's been promised by telephone companies for years). UM (that's the insider's acronym) takes all your disparate voice-mail, e-mail, and fax accounts, and puts them together into one *uber* in-box that you can access from anywhere. The long-term vision is that you'll be able to read text conversions of your voice mail on a screen or listen to a computer read your e-mail to you on your phone. Why run back into the home office to check e-mail when you're sitting in front of the TV screen?

- **T-commerce:** The *T* stands for television. With the proper computer-like set-top box plugged into your TV, you can do online shopping or order a pizza from your comfy chair in front of the tube. Several telephone and cable companies in the U.S. and Canada let you do this today.

The common thread to these devices is that they take advantage of the computer power already built into set-top boxes and gaming machines, and eliminate the need for one of the most expensive parts of any computer — the display screen — by using your TV screen.

As technology makes small, LCD, flat-panel screens less expensive, we expect to see some next-generation computers that *do* have their own screens. A fridge with a computer screen is available today, but it costs about five times as much as a regular fridge.

The advent of digital television (discussed in Chapter 5) will have a big effect on the integration of TVs and PCs as well. Today's analog TVs aren't well suited for Web surfing or e-mail reading — the screens aren't sharp enough to display text clearly. As higher-resolution digital TVs become more common-place, the capability to do PC tasks on a TV increases. In fact, many HDTV-capable TVs are more like huge computer monitors than regular TVs, with the higher resolution and picture quality you expect from something that can display tiny letters on the screen in a readable form.

Game consoles on the Net!

The most popular alternative computing devices for the TV are gaming consoles — stand-alone gaming machines from Sony, Microsoft, and Nintendo. When you include both the hardware to play the games on and the software — the games themselves — the gaming industry is larger overall than the Hollywood movie industry! Gaming is not only big business; it's also big technology. Current generations of gaming consoles are basically high-end graphics computers, with lots of RAM, hard drives, fast CPUs, and killer graphics chips that may very well put your PC to shame.

The primary purpose of gaming consoles is — you guessed it — playing video games. But because these boxes are really high-powered, special-purpose com-puters, there's more to them than just gaming. Sony (with their PlayStation 2), Microsoft (with the X box), and Nintendo (with the GameCube), have all created gaming boxes that are capable of storing and playing music files, stor-ing files on their hard drives, and even surfing the Web. Sony has even shipped a Linux-based kit (designed more for software developers than regular people) that lets the programmatically inclined do all this stuff.

Despite these capabilities, actually having these functions on game consoles falls more into the realm of product plans and corporate visions. What is a reality today, however, is the concept of using video gaming consoles in a *net-worked environment* to allow owners to use them for multiplayer, online gaming. All the gaming manufacturers accept that the default connection required for a home network is an Ethernet LAN connection, and almost all have this on their machines today or will shortly. Using these Ethernet con-nections, you'll be able to connect your game consoles to your home network, so you can play multiplayer games with other consoles in the house or use your Internet connection to play against others around the world. Imagine having that car race against someone 5000 miles away! First one to Monte Carlo wins!

Web-enabled TV — is it for me?

Another far less popular alternative computing device is the Microsoft MSN TV Internet Receiver (the descendent of the WebTV box that made a big splash a few years ago) — a small, proprietary Net computer that attaches to your television screen. (America Online makes a TV computer too, called AOLTV.) Although it isn't designed to replace a full-fledged computer, Web-enabled TVs are useful tools that allow you to do some neat stuff, such as

- Surf the Web
- Send and receive e-mail
- Participate in USENET newsgroups online discussions
- Print e-mail or Web pages
- Simultaneously view Web pages and TV programs using a picture-in-picture (PIP) system
- Access TV program listings and automatically program your VCR

If you don't need to do traditional PC tasks such as word processing, Web-enabled TV is a great alternative to a PC. The low price of Web-enabled TVs (under $100 for the top-of-the-line model) makes it affordable enough for the living room even if you have a PC in the house (so the kids can stay online but off your PC while you're trying to work at home, for example).

The current state of the Web-enabled TV's art, however, has a few drawbacks:

- **MSN TV uses its own proprietary Internet service provider:** You can't add your Web-enabled TVs to the same account that you use for your PCs — instead, you have to pay for two ISPs.
- **You have to connect to the Net using the built-in analog modem:** You're limited to the speeds possible with a 56K modem, even if you have fast cable-modem, ISDN, or DSL access. (This will undoubtedly change.)
- **Web-enabled TV doesn't have the capability to be networked with other home-computing devices:** Bummer. We hope this will change too.

MSN TV is not the only option for using a TV as an Internet terminal. Other options include the following, although they aren't widely available:

- **Personal Video Recorders (PVRs),** with built-in Web functionality, such as Microsoft's UltimateTV. Microsoft has been developing a special version of XBox that will include Microsoft's UltimateTV.

> ✔ **Cable TV (and in a few regions, DSL) set-top boxes** that have enough computer power for surfing the Web and sending e-mail and can convert digital television signals to a format your TV can display.

Since 2001, the big set-top box vendors, such as Scientific Atlanta, have been shipping devices that already contain enough power to perform PC functions. They've seen that the future is in supporting a seamless marriage of PCs and TVs. Most service providers (who control the software and functionality of the set-top box) haven't launched services that take advantage of all this horsepower yet. They will . . . don't ask us when, but they will.

Chapter 13

All Roads Lead to the Net

. . . .

In This Chapter

▶ Marveling at the cool things the Internet can do

▶ Getting connected by wire, cable, wave, and even extension cord

. . . .

Most people think about the Internet in terms of the neat (and not-so-neat) things it allows them to do, such as send and receive e-mail, surf Web pages, and watch video clips of that annoying dancing baby. If you think of the Internet in this way, give yourself a gold star, because this way of thinking allows you to get the most out of your time on the Internet.

Before you do all this cool stuff on the Internet, however, you have to get connected to it. In this chapter, we tell you about the pros and cons of the many ways you can make that connection.

A World of IP Devices

Today, devices that communicate on the Internet — or on private networks using IP — are basically all the same thing: computers. Personal computers, microcomputers, handheld computers, network computers, mainframe computers, and any other type of computer that you can think of (except, of course, that old Radio Shack TRS-80 that you now use as a doorstop). In fact, hundreds of millions of computers in the world are somehow, sometimes connected to the Internet. And many more will be connected in the future.

Here are a few ways that the Internet may soon play a greater part in your daily life:

✔ Telephone companies and Internet service providers are realizing that using the Internet is a much more efficient (and inexpensive) way to carry voice telephone traffic than the old-fashioned circuit-switched method. So don't be surprised if your next phone call is routed over the Internet.

✔ Independent musicians and record labels are finding that using the Net is a great way to get music sent to people around the world. Yes, we know that Napster has already come and gone, but newly launched services such as Listen.com's Rhapsody service are a new, *legal,* way of distributing music over the Net, and they're really cool. (In fact, Pat is listening to Rhapsody while writing this chapter.)

✔ Hundreds of companies, big and small, are finding that *electronic commerce* — using the Net to buy and sell stuff — is much cheaper and more convenient than traditional methods. You've probably already used Amazon.com or checked your bank balance online, and in the future you'll be able to do a lot more than this online.

✔ Appliance and electronics manufacturers have decided that using the Internet is a great way to let future generations of smart products talk with each other and with service centers. Imagine a dishwasher that knows when it needs maintenance and can automatically notify the manufacturer — and even tell the technician which parts to bring for the service call.

Making the Internet Connection

All the wonders of the Internet and devices that speak its IP language aren't going to do you a darn bit of good if you're not connected. Getting connected to the Net is — in our opinion — as important as getting telephone service into your home and is probably a higher priority for most of us than stuff like television. (TV watching has never been the same since *Seinfeld* went off the air.)

Not everyone shares this priority, of course — only about 55 percent of homes in the United States are connected to the Net — but the number of connected homes has grown immensely in the past few years (as if we needed to tell *you* that) and will continue to grow until every house, apartment, condo, shack, tree house, houseboat, trailer, and slow-moving sport utility vehicle has its own Internet connection.

For the vast majority of residential users, access to the Net is provided the old-fashioned way — through an analog telephone modem. This arrangement won't last much longer, however, because a whole bunch of companies have decided that they can make a pretty fair chunk of change providing faster Internet access to people like us.

Analog modems

Maybe you're lucky enough to live in a city where high-speed Internet access devices such as cable modems and DSL are available. If not, the primary connection between your computer — or computer network — and other computers (like all those millions of computers on the Internet) is most likely an analog modem. On a personal note, we both have high-speed connections available — Pat has both a cable modem and a DSL modem in his house (he likes the belt-and-suspenders approach), and Danny has a cable modem in his house in Connecticut — so we tend to gloat and say "nyah, nyah" to our friends who are still using analog modems.

Okay, we'll cease and desist the gloating and get back to analog modems. These devices get their name from their function — which is to modulate and demodulate the digital data coming to and from your computer into analog signals that can be carried over the standard analog telephone system.

Figure 13-1 shows the route that information takes between an analog modem and the Internet. Your phone line goes to the telephone company's central office and then to your ISP, which has a group of modems that answer several phone lines. From there, you can use some of the bandwidth of your local ISP's connection.

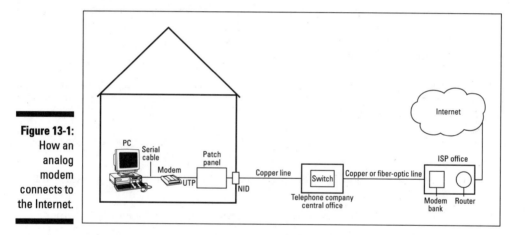

Figure 13-1:
How an
analog
modem
connects to
the Internet.

Analog modems come in many different speeds, but the following two are what you'll run into while modem shopping:

✔ **V.90 56-Kbps modems:** These modems are the most common and are standard equipment in just about any computer these days. The V.90, by the way, isn't some randomly chosen cool name. It's the name of the international standard that allows these modems to talk to each other, regardless of who sells them. The 56 Kbps name is a slight misnomer, because FCC regulations force manufacturers to make these modems operate at a slightly lower ultimate speed (about 53 Kbps). 56K modems reach this high speed only in one direction — the downstream flow from your Internet service provider (ISP) to you. The upstream speed — from your computer to the Internet — is limited to 33.6 Kbps, the same as standard 33.6-Kbps modems.

- ✔ **V.92 56-Kbps modems:** The latest and greatest technology, V.92 was, according to some statistics we've read, included in about 10 percent of the modems sold in the U.S. in 2002. V.92 modems have a few benefits that V.90 models lack:

    - • **Internet Call Waiting:** This feature works with your phone company's call waiting feature and lets you suspend your Internet connection when the phone rings. When you hang up, things pick up where they were, without you having to redial your ISP.

    - • **Quick Connect:** The way the modem connects to your ISP (called the handshake) is improved because the modem remembers how it worked the last time you dialed up — so you can connect up to 50 percent faster.

    - • **V.PCM:** Yet another super-secret industry code name, V.PCM gives you a faster upstream speed (up to 43 Kbps).

    V.92 modems are backwards-compatible with V.90. Therefore, if your ISP still uses V.90, things will work, but the special features are enabled only if the modem on the other end of your connection is also V.92. Unfortunately, few ISPs have adopted V.92.

Besides speed, modems can also be differentiated by their *form factor* — what they look like and how they connect to your PC. Analog modems come in three basic forms:

- ✔ **External modems:** These are freestanding devices that connect to your computer's modem serial port (often called the *COM* port).

- ✔ **Internal modems:** These devices plug into an internal slot inside your PC. Almost all PCs shipping today have an internal modem.

- ✔ **PC Card modems:** Roughly credit-card-sized, these modems (which adhere to the PC Card, or PCMCIA — Personal Computer Modular Card Interface Adapter — standard), slide into the corresponding PC Card slot found on most notebook computers and some handheld computer devices.

You may also encounter modems that expand upon the basic computer-to-computer data communications function and add extra features. For example, many modems also contain circuitry that enables them — with some corresponding software on your PC — to act as fax machines. With a fax modem, you can send just about any document on your PC's hard drive to remote fax machines, and you can receive incoming fax messages, which you can view on your screen or print.

Other additional features often found on analog modems include the following:

- ✔ **Speakerphone.** A few modems come with speakerphone software that lets you use your PC (with microphone and speakers) as a hands-free phone.

> ✔ **Voice mail.** Using your PC's hard drive to store messages, modems with voice-mail software can handle any calls that come in when you're away (or just don't feel like answering the phone).

As good as analog modems have become — we remember the days of 2400-baud modems, which were agonizingly slow — we think that today's broadband Internet access technologies are so much better that we'd never go back to dial-up. We won't try to sell you on the upgrade based on the Web surfing and file downloading benefits (as good as they are), but rather on this point: Broadband technologies are always on, not dialed-up. When you connect not just your computer but an entire house full of devices, all of which can potentially connect to the Internet, a constant and persistent connection makes all the difference. In fact, it's almost downright required.

DSL

Digital subscriber line, or DSL, is the phone company's broadband method of sending data over existing copper telephone lines. Several DSL technologies have been widely developed, which is why we sometimes refer to DSL technologies as *xDSL,* with the *x* representing a range of other letters, such as *A* for *asymmetrical.*

Digital subscriber lines — ADSL in particular — were developed as a way for telephone companies to compete with cable television providers — the high downstream speed is capable of carrying lots of digital television programming. In fact, in the mid-1990s, most major telephone companies had large divisions and joint ventures in place to jump into the cable TV market. This plan never worked out, though — the trials of such services weren't such great successes that cable TV seemed like a profitable direction for these companies to move in.

But then the Internet became popular, and there was finally a new need for providing this kind of bandwidth to the home.

DSL modems use the same single copper-wire pair that POTS (Plain Old Telephone Service — in other words, regular phone service) does, but their sophisticated Digital Signal Processors (DSPs) can make use of a lot more of the frequency spectrum, giving them greater bandwidth capabilities. The frequencies that DSL devices use are generally much higher than those used for carrying POTS phone calls, so there's no interference between the two. You can literally pick up the phone in the middle of a DSL connection and make a phone call without a problem.

When we wrote the first edition of this book, we spent a considerable amount of time discussing something called ISDN (or Integrated Services Digital Network). ISDN is a phone company technology that allows — among other things — phone lines and special ISDN modems to connect to the Internet at about 128 Kbps. ISDN is still out there in some places (especially outside the

U.S.), but for the most part it's been superceded by DSL and other forms of broadband connectivity. That's because ISDN isn't fast enough for future (or even current) Internet connection requirements.

Table 13-1 shows some of the many flavors of DSL. Note that *downstream speed* is the speed at which data is sent to you from your service provider, and *upstream speed* measures the data heading back the other way.

Table 13-1	Types of DSL Technology	
DSL Technology	*Downstream Speed*	*Upstream Speed*
ADSL	Up to 8 Mbps	Up to 1.5 Mbps
G.shdsl	2.3 Mbps	2.3 Mbps
VDSL	52 Mbps	8 Mbps
RADSL	Up to 8 Mbps	Up to 1.2 Mbps
IDSL	144 Kbps	144 Kbps

Different service providers offer DSL services using just about all of the technologies shown in Table 13-1, but for the residential market, ADSL is by far the most common technology. Keep in mind that the table lists the maximum speeds. When you get ADSL service, it will probably be a bit slower, but it's so far above analog modems that the difference doesn't matter.

Services driven by ADSL technology have the disadvantage of being *asymmetric,* which means that the upstream and downstream speeds are different. The problem with asymmetric bandwidth is that some symmetric applications that send large quantities of data both ways, such as videoconferencing (you want to see them as much as they see you!), can't take advantage of the maximum speeds available. If you have 1.5 Mbps downstream but only 64 Kbps upstream, symmetric applications run at 64 Kbps down and 64 Kbps up.

Fortunately, most applications for the Internet are asymmetric — your request to view a page is very small, typically just the address of the page on the Web, but the page downloaded is usually packed with data. Most home users are incredibly happy with even 256-Kbps upstream speeds (about six times faster than analog modems), and the majority of home users tend to utilize much more downstream bandwidth anyway (for things such as Web browsing and file downloading).

Regardless of which DSL variant your service provider offers, the interface is similar. The DSL service enters your home through a standard copper telephone line that carries your POTS traffic. To extract the high-speed DSL data, you need a DSL modem. Generally, you'll find two variants of these:

Going V-ery fast with VDSL

One of the DSL variants in Table 13-1 probably stood out to you as being the one you'd want in your smart home. VDSL, or Very High Speed DSL, is like a super tricked-out, twin-turbo V8 compared to ADSL's economical 4-cylinder speeds. VDSL is fast enough to let phone companies do all sorts of neat services, including multiple channels of TV, HDTV, voice, and high-speed Internet, all on the same phone line. The downside is that VDSL is very short range (about 6000 feet max) compared to ADSL (18,000 feet; some variants go even farther). So VDSL works well only if you put the VDSL equipment (called a DSLAM) right out in the neighborhood, near the houses. Putting all the equipment near the house is a great thing for performance, but not necessarily a great thing for phone companies trying to trim expenses. VDSL is also com-pletely different than ADSL, so phone companies who want to deploy it would need to abandon their investment in ADSL (and they've spent billions).

These factors add up to a limited availability for VDSL today. None of the big phone companies are offering it (except in a few limited trials). But if you live in a smaller town with an independent phone company, VDSL might be available to you. These smaller phone companies — faced with a huge competitive threat from cable companies that offer video services, cable modems, and now telephone services over cable — have been fighting back with their own mix of video, high-speed Internet, and TV using VDSL. If you can get it, you should consider it. You'll be on the cutting edge.

✔ **External DSL modem:** This device looks and acts just like a souped-up version of the analog modem that you're probably familiar with, but it doesn't plug into the modem serial port (the COM port) on the back of your computer. Those modem serial ports are just too darned slow to handle the kind of speed that xDSL gives you. Instead, a DSL modem typically has an Ethernet (10BaseT) connection running to your computer and an Ethernet Network Interface Card (NIC) inside your computer. Some modems also use a USB (Universal Serial Bus) connector to hook up to your computer or have both Ethernet and USB.

✔ **Internal DSL modem:** Just like an internal analog modem, this one plugs into a slot inside your PC — an ISA or PCI bus slot for desktop computers or a PC card for laptops. Because these internal buses are much faster than the serial port that connects standard modems, you don't need an Ethernet interface.

If your provider gives you a choice, choose a DSL modem with an Ethernet interface. The other kinds of DSL modems are great if you're looking to hook up a single computer but make it more difficult to connect to your home network (because almost all networking equipment connects using the Ethernet standard). You shouldn't have a hard time convincing your DSL provider to do this for you because Ethernet modems are the most common.

Filtering out noise

We mentioned that DSL — particularly the ADSL technology used in residential DSL — uses different frequencies on the phone lines than your voice telephone service does. Unfortunately, electronic systems don't always work so neatly in the real world, so even though your phone (on the lower frequencies) and your ADSL modem (on the higher frequencies) are not supposed to interfere with each other, a little bit of overlap can occur.

Early DSL modem installations used a device called a POTS splitter to keep your voice and the DSL modem on different segments of phone wiring in your house. This brute-force approach of keeping things separate solved the interference problem but came with a price: A phone technician had to come to your house to install this splitter, which took time and cost money, and only one phone outlet in the house could accept your DSL modem.

The current solution is more elegant. When a DSL modem is installed, you simply plug some small filters into your wall outlets — between the phone and the outlet. These filters (known as low-pass filters because they let only the lower frequencies pass through) fix any interference problems and let you plug the DSL modem into any phone outlet in the house. They also let you do the installation yourself, which saves you both time and money.

If you want to get DSL, you need to choose a provider. Unfortunately, the number of companies offering DSL has been greatly reduced over the past few years due to some prominent failures in the telecommunications market. Two types of companies can offer DSL: incumbent telephone companies (your local telco) and competitive telephone companies, who lease lines and facilities from the incumbent. During the Internet boom years of the late 1990s, dozens of companies entered the competitive telephone company market and began offering DSL services — too many, in fact. Because of the intense competition (among other factors), a lot of these companies ended up going out of business. Today, residential DSL service is offered primarily by the incumbent telco and one remaining large competitive provider:

- Verizon: Serves the northeastern U.S. and a few markets elsewhere in the U.S. — areas where GTE used to be the phone company (www.verizon.com)
- BellSouth: Serves the southeastern U.S. (www.bellsouth.com)
- SBC: Serves much of the central and southwestern U.S. (www.sbc.com)
- Qwest: Serves the northwestern and mountain region of the U.S. (www.qwest.com)
- Covad: The last remaining big competitive provider, serves nationwide (www.covad.com)

When you choose a DSL provider — such as Covad or your local telco — you usually have a choice of which ISP you want to use. The DSL provider gives you the connection, and the ISP provides Internet services such as e-mail,

Getting your IP fixed

When you connect to a broadband service provider, your computer or home networking router (if you're using one) is assigned an IP address. You can think of the IP address as the Internet equivalent to your home's street address — it's a universally understood address that lets other computers find yours, just as a street address lets other people find your house. Most broadband service providers (and all dial-up Internet providers) give you a *dynamic* IP address that changes on a regular basis. This is fine for regular Web browsing and e-mailing and the like, but just won't do for certain applications (such as videoconferencing or hosting a Web server on your own computer).

For these kinds of applications, you need an IP address that *never* changes — a *fixed* IP address. Most broadband providers will give you one for an extra $10 or $15 a month; a few, such as Speakeasy and DirecTV DSL, include a fixed IP address in the base price. Think you'll never videoconference or have your own Web site, so you don't need this? Think again — many applications require or would benefit from a fixed IP address, such as a home-automation system that has a built-in Web interface so you can adjust things remotely through a Web browser.

Web site hosting, and music services. Most DSL providers offer their own ISP service, but you can also choose from both local ISPs (in most cases) and big national ISPs. Some of the bigger ISPs who focus on DSL services include the following:

- ✔ EarthLink (www.earthlink.net)
- ✔ DirecTV DSL (www.directinternet.com)
- ✔ Speakeasy (www.speakeasy.net)
- ✔ AOL (www.aol.com)

Which to choose? We recommend that you look at the options and prices and find the ISP that offers the services that best fit your needs. This isn't earth-shattering advice, but each of these ISPs has their own specialties and services. We like to choose ISPs that explicitly support home networks. Many will often provide you with networking hardware, extra e-mail boxes (one for everyone in the house) and other neat Internet features such as fixed IP addresses (helpful if you want to use applications such as videoconferencing) and firewall services (to keep the bad guys out of your computer).

When it comes to planning your home network, DSL services will play a major role down the road for the telcos and therefore should have a major influence on your planning. DSL services will bring a lot of bandwidth into your home, bandwidth that is likely to be shared by a lot of applications. If your spouse is watching TV in the living room, you are working in your office in the basement, and the kids are playing online games in their rooms, you all may be using the same DSL link.

One of the neat things about DSL is that you're always connected to the net-work, 24 hours a day. If you leave your computer on the entire time, all sorts of things are made possible. For instance, you can receive automatic software downloads while you're asleep. Or you can receive phone calls on your PC through Internet telephony. Or you can have all the major newspapers down-loaded to your PC for when you wake up. A DSL line turns a historically reac-tive relationship with the telecommunications networks into an active one.

If you want to find out even more about DSL, check out TeleChoice, Inc.'s Web site at www.xdsl.com.

Cable modems

Cable television providers are in a frenzy to provide additional services beyond television. First among these services, for most cable companies, is cable-modem Internet access. A cable modem is basically a very fast modem that connects to the cable company. It can transmit at up to 30 Mbps and connect to your computer through an Ethernet connection. Like the DSL modems we talk about in the preceding section, cable modems are usually rented as part of the service. Monthly service is typically priced in the $50 or so range.

Although many independent cable television companies are going it alone and working to offer their own versions of cable-modem services, big nation-wide cable companies (often called MSOs, or multiservice operators) pre-dominate. The biggest ones include the following:

- AT&T Broadband and Comcast: These are two separate cable operators, but AT&T has spun off its cable division and the two are merging, result-ing in the largest cable company in the U.S. You can get information about their services at www.attbroadband.com and www.comcast.com.

- Cox Communications: www.cox.com.

- Charter Communications: www.chartercom.com.

- Road Runner: Time-Warner, one of the largest cable television providers, as well as one of the biggest content producers in the world (movies, television, music, magazines, books, you name it), merged with AOL (the world's biggest ISP) in the 1990s. The combined company, AOL Time-Warner, runs its cable modem operations under the Road Runner brand. Moving forward, many Time-Warner cable areas will also allow you to use AOL as your ISP, so you'll have a choice of Road Runner or AOL (and usually another, unaffiliated ISP such as Earthlink). You can find out whether Road Runner is available in your area at www.rr.com, or check for AOL broadband at www.aol.com.

If you live in Canada, cable-modem service is available from the following big providers:

Why are cable modems so hot?

Cable companies are well positioned to offer cable modems, the leading-edge Internet service, for several reasons:

✔ **They get it:** By this we mean that the cable industry, as a whole, has committed itself to broadband and has invested both money and brainpower (through an industry group called CableLabs, which helps develop standards for cable systems and which approves equipment to be interoperable within cable networks) to creating full-service broadband networks. Cable providers want to give you every data service you'd ever need (with the possible exception of mobile wireless services), and they've spent billions creating an infrastructure to do so.

✔ **They already have a high-speed network:** Most cable television networks consist of super-high-capacity fiber-optic cable running from the central offices to local distribution points and — even more importantly — coaxial cable running from these distribution points to your home. Coaxial cable can carry a lot of data — a heck of a lot more, in most cases, than the copper wiring that connects telephone companies to your home.

✔ **They have an important booster:** That booster is Microsoft, which has invested billions of dollars into the industry in an effort to move things along. In addition to Microsoft itself, Paul Allen, one of the co-founders of Microsoft, has spent a few billion dollars of his own nest egg to buy some cable companies and turn them into providers of Net access and other advanced services.

✔ Rogers: `www.rogers.com`.

✔ Shaw: `www.shaw.ca`.

✔ Videotron: `www.videotron.com/portail_en/index.htm`. This is the English version of the page, but they have a French one as well because they're based in Montreal.

Most of the time, the company that provides your cable television service and your cable modem is also the company that provides your ISP service. In other words, if Cox is your cable company, you'll get your cable modem from them, and your e-mail address will be something like `smarthomesfordummiesreader@cox.net`. As something called *open access* becomes more common, however, the cable world is becoming a bit more like the DSL world. With open access, other ISPs, such as Earthlink or AOL, are allowed to sell services to cable-modem customers. If you have open access, you'll still get your cable TV service from your MSO, and your cable modem will be connected to them as well, but you'll get all your Internet services from someone else. This is happening across the country, but it's most likely to be found wherever AOL Time-Warner owns the local cable company — that's because the FTC (Federal Trade Commission) required AOL Time-Warner to open up their cable systems to other ISPs as a condition of the merger.

Regardless of your service provider or ISP, cable modems fit into one of two categories:

- ✔ **Telco-return modems:** These modems are used in less sophisticated cable systems and are generally much less desirable. The one-way modem receives data at high speeds over your cable system's coaxial cable, but any upstream (outgoing) data uses a standard analog telephone modem — so you send data as slowly as you would with a conventional analog modem (plus you tie up your telephone line whenever you're online). These modems are okay for e-mail and surfing Web sites, but their asymmetric nature makes them less than perfect for all the neat new things you can do on the Net — such as videoconferencing, Internet telephony, and online gaming. Luckily, telco-return cable modems are gradually disappearing as cable providers complete the updates of their systems to full two-way networks.

- ✔ **Two-way modems:** These are the modems you hope your service provider uses (and the big ones, such as Cox, AT&T and Road Runner, typically do). Two-way modems both send and receive data over the coaxial cable and typically offer high speed both ways (although the reception is often still faster than the upstream data rate — the upstream is usually limited to about 200 Kbps, and the downstream is closer to 2 Mbps).

A few cable modems are internal devices (which plug into an ISA or PCI bus slot in your PC), but most that we've seen are external, stand-alone boxes. The cable system's coaxial cable connects to the modem, and the modem connects to your computer (or your computer LAN) through a standard Ethernet 10BaseT connection (which we talk about in more detail in Chapter 15). If you don't have an Ethernet card in your PC already, don't worry — the cards are cheap, and many cable-modem service providers give you one as part of the service package. In Figure 13-2, you can see how a cable modem connects to the Internet.

DirecWay dishes

We describe the DirecTV TV network in Chapter 5. Hughes Electronics, the company that built the DirecTV system, has also developed a satellite Internet access system called DirecWay (`www.direcway.com`). DirecWay uses a 21-inch dish, slightly larger than but similar to the one used by DSS, to receive high-speed Internet data from the satellite. You have two options for how data gets sent from your computer to the Internet:

- ✔ **You can buy** *one-way* **service:** In this scenario, a standard analog modem sends data back upstream (onto the Internet). This limits your upstream speed to the same 33 Kbps as a dialup ISP account.

✔ **You can buy *two-way* service:** With two-way service, which requires a different antenna and receiver (one with a built-in radio transmitter), you can use the satellite to send data in both directions. Because of FCC regulations, if you get two-way service, a professional must install and aim your dish.

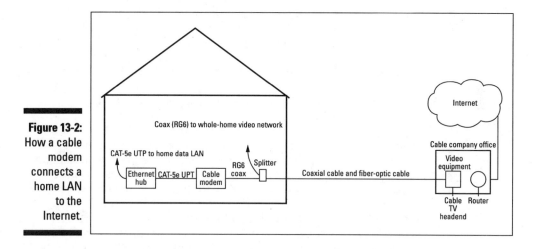

Figure 13-2: How a cable modem connects a home LAN to the Internet.

With DirecWay, you can receive Internet data at up to 400 Kbps — more than six times faster than the fastest analog modems. There are a few catches to DirecWay, however:

Whatever happened to . . .?

Like the DSL companies discussed in this chapter, cable companies have not been immune to the economic downturn that hit the entire telecommunications and broadband industry in the early 2000s.

A few big bankruptcies and shutdowns have occurred in the cable industry. For example, the original big cable modem company, @Home, built a huge nationwide network and acted as the ISP for a bunch of cable MSOs such as AT&T and Cox. Unfortu-nately, despite doing some great things to get the cable modem business off the ground, @Home ran into serious cash problems. By early 2002, the company's debt was just too much, and they shut their doors. AT&T, Cox, and other @Home-affiliated cable MSOs underwent a gigantic effort to quickly create their own cable modem ISPs, and did a great job of keeping almost all their customers online without a hitch.

Failures like this tend to make potential customers nervous, and we can't say we blame them. We also think that broadband is just too compelling to pass up if its available.

- ✔ **Relatively low upstream speeds:** The one-way system maxes out at a speed of only 33.6 Kbps; the two-way system goes as fast as 128 Kbps, which is roughly equivalent to the lower speed offerings of DSL and cable companies.

- ✔ **High latency:** Latency is the measure of delay in a signal — the time it takes to get, for example, from a Web server on the Internet to your computer. Because of the sheer distances involved in sending radio signals up to a satellite and back down (and some other factors as well), satellite systems have higher latency than DSL or cable. This isn't a big deal for Web pages or e-mail, but it can be a big deal if you're videoconferencing or audioconferencing over the Net or playing multiplayer online games.

The following temporary disadvantages will disappear over time:

- ✔ **You can't share your Internet connection (right now):** The satellite receiver for DirecWay connects through USB to a single computer. DirecWay *does* sell special receivers for connecting to a business computer network and promises a home version will be available in the future. Check with DirecWay to see whether this has happened yet.

- ✔ **You must have the right operating system:** You need to have a PC running Windows 98 Second Edition or later — Macintoshes and PCs using Windows 3.11, Windows XP, or alternative operating systems such as Linux need not apply.

Despite these disadvantages, DirecWay has one big advantage over most competing high-speed Internet access systems. You can use it just about anywhere in North America, something that can't be said about cable modems or DSL. DirecWay offers similar services in Europe and in Japan.

If you want to have both DirecWay and satellite TV from DirecTV, you can do so without having two dishes on your roof. The 21-inch DirecWay dish, which is slightly larger than the 18-inch TV-only DirecTV dish, can pick up the signals from both systems and feed them to your PC and televisions.

Figure 13-3 shows a one-way satellite connection that uses a regular modem to send data out to the Internet. The two-way connection looks pretty much the same, except that data returns to the Internet through the satellite link.

Wireless Internet connections

While the telephone and cable television companies slowly develop and build network connections to bring data into your home at high speeds, a host of companies are working on ways to do the same thing without wires.

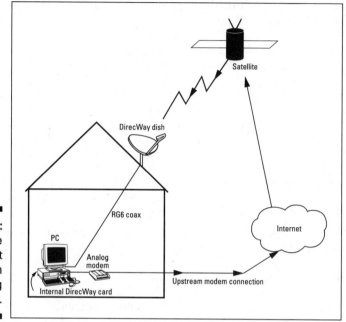

Figure 13-3:
A satellite
Internet
connection
using
DirecWay.

Traditionally, most of us equate wireless with portable — and indeed many wireless services companies are emphasizing this benefit of using wireless technologies. Increasingly, however, service providers are looking toward wireless technologies as a way to quickly and cheaply provide data and tele-phone services to a fixed location — such as your house. New advances in wireless technology are rapidly bringing down the costs of the network equip-ment such as transmitters and receivers, and setting up a wireless service is usually quick. Instead of digging trenches or putting up utility poles and run-ning wires, wireless providers need only put up an antenna and then provide one for each of their customers.

Only a few wireless Internet services are available to residential customers today — in the early 2000s, the first generation of wireless companies went into Chapter 11 and out of business in an industry-wide flameout about as spectacu-lar as any we've seen. That doesn't mean that wireless to the home is dead (and, by the way, we know you sharp readers picked up on the fact that the DirecWay satellite system is wireless, but we're using the term to refer to *terrestrial* wire-less systems, not space-based systems). Although a lot of wireless startups went broke during Generation One of wireless mania, the big guys (such as your local phone company or big nationwide telecommunications companies such as Sprint) are testing their next-generation wireless services and will be launching them in the future, so check their Web sites if your other options are limited.

These wireless service providers will be offering service to residential customers in a few ways:

- **Fixed and portable NLOS (non-line-of-sight):** These solutions (and we use the plural because there are many different ways to skin this particular cat) use a series of base-station radio/antenna towers that can transmit and receive data communications out to homes and businesses in their cell (like a cell for a mobile phone system). Fixed systems refer to those that require an antenna that is mounted (usually on the roof) and then aimed to get the best transmission possible. Portable systems are designed with antennas that aim themselves, so you can perform the installation, without the need of a professional radio engineer to align and aim antennas. As long as you're within the cell, you can take your system from work to home to a new house when you move across town, without needing a new professional installation.

- **Mesh networks:** Mesh networks are based on smaller, lower-powered antenna/radio systems that don't necessarily have to talk back to the master base station. In a mesh network, traffic is bounced from antenna to antenna within the network footprint. So your traffic might bounce off three other peoples' antennas before it gets to the base station and sent off to the Internet over a wired connection (such as a fiber-optic line). Similarly, your antenna might not only pick up and receive your Internet traffic but also relay someone else's traffic. The big advantage of mesh networks is that they tend to use more inexpensive components, so the service provider can build up the network gradually as new customers sign up, instead of investing a big chunk of money up front.

- **Wi-Fi networks:** These short-range networks make use of the 802.11, or Wi-Fi, wireless local networking technology that you might be familiar with in your own home or office network (we talk about this technology in Chapter 16). Although Wi-Fi was designed for short-range transmissions (300 feet or less), it can be modified to go greater distances. Most service providers offering Wi-Fi networks are *not* using it to send data to and from people's homes. Instead, they're using it to provide broadband services in hot spots such as hotel lobbies, airports, and cafes for people toting laptops or PDAs with Wi-Fi capabilities. However, a few service providers are examining Wi-Fi with an eye towards providing broadband to homes, particularly where homes are close to each other (and may therefore be within range). The biggest disadvantage of Wi-Fi in this scenario is the extremely short range we mentioned. The biggest advantage is the fact that Wi-Fi gear is extremely inexpensive, and millions of people already have it in their homes and computers.

- **3G mobile services:** Mobile phone providers have launched data services across the world. Most current services are 2.5 G. (The *G* stands for *generation,* and these services are an interim step after 2G — 2G is the transition to digital voice services for cell phones.) 2.5G services offer speeds up to about 40 Kbps, roughly equivalent to analog modem speeds, but forthcoming 3G systems will eventually be as fast a 1 to 2 Mbps. For the most part, 3G systems will remain the province of mobile users — mainly business users — because they'll probably cost significantly more than other broadband solutions.

The bottom line on wireless Internet connections to the home is that the technology is here, the service providers are testing it, and we'll probably see it soon. The biggest roadblock is whether wired solutions such as cable modems and DSL will reach enough homes to alleviate the need for wireless solutions. We don't think that will happen because too many people in rural areas of the U.S. and Canada are out of cost-effective reach of wired networks. So we expect to see wireless offerings hit the market in a real way in the near future.

Power companies

We know what you're thinking right now. "Power companies? What the heck do they have to do with the Internet, besides maybe having a Web site that tells me what to do when I have a gas leak?" (Incidentally, when you have a gas leak, run like heck.) Well, believe it or not, utility companies are trying to figure out how to jump on the Internet bandwagon themselves.

Just like telephone companies with DSL technologies, cable television companies with cable modems, and wireless companies with some of the new services they're planning to offer, utility companies want to offer you high-speed Internet access to go along with their traditional services.

Why are power companies a good candidate to jump into a business they don't have any experience in? They have a few things in their favor:

- ✔ **An existing communications backbone:** You'd probably be surprised at the complex and sophisticated communications network these companies already have — hundreds of miles of fiber-optic cable, copper wire, and wireless systems are already in place and online for these companies' internal use. The smarter ones thought ahead and laid down extra capacity while building out their own networks, so they have much of the infrastructure in place and ready to go.

- ✔ **Rights of way:** If you were to try to build your own communications network, one of the biggest problems you'd run into is getting the so-called *rights of way* to lay your fibers and cable across literally hundreds of miles of private and public property. Even wireless providers run into this problem when they try to put up antennas (seems the neighbors like having the phones, but they hate seeing all those working parts). The power companies already have these rights of way for their electrical lines.

- ✔ **Ubiquity:** Think it's rare to find a home without a cable television connection or at least a telephone line? It is, but it's even rarer to find one that's not connected to electrical power. You'd have to go far into the backwoods to find one, and even then, chances are good that those households don't have power because they don't want it — back-to-nature types, you know.

Power companies can provide high-bandwidth communications services to you in two ways:

✔ They can use their rights of way to run new wiring to your home from their network. This option isn't necessarily cheap, depending on how far their network access points are from their customers' homes.

✔ They can devise ways to use the existing electrical power line to also carry broadband data and communications signals into the home. If they can do this — and some big power companies and communications equipment vendors say they can — all they have to do is install some sort of box in your home that splits the data out from the power. The data is then sent off to your telephones, computers, and whatever else needs it in your home network. This is a neat idea, and something that you may be seeing in the not-so-distant future.

Note: The first deployments of this technology are happening outside the U.S. because of differences in how the electrical-power distribution networks are designed. Basically, the first systems being tested use a converter box at each transformer in the power network to connect the fiber-optic backbone to the power line. Compared to Europe and Asia, the U.S. has fewer customers served by each individual transformer in the network, which means that many more of these (expensive) converters would be needed. At the present pricing levels, this state-of-the-art, experimental equipment is too expensive to install here. We do think, however, that the almost inevitable increases in computer chip power and corresponding decreases in prices will soon make this idea an economically viable solution in the U.S. as well. If you live in Germany, you can buy broadband over power lines today!

We want to point out a recurring theme here. Many different companies have sophisticated, high-speed communications networks (cable, telephone, and power utilities) in place right now but none have a widespread, high-speed, two-way means of connecting your home to these networks. Although it would be nice if they would all get out their backhoes and work crews to upgrade this last-mile connection, the procedure is expensive. So most of the companies are looking at ways to reuse their existing connections in new and bandwidth-rich ways.

Chapter 14

Designing a Data LAN

*I*n a simple form, a home-computer network can consist of a single computer connected by modem to the Internet or to another external network (such as your office's network). A network can also be two stand-alone PCs that share a printer with a simple A/B switchbox. We strongly encourage you to think beyond these examples, though.

As the number (and type) of computers in the home increases and the price continues to decrease, consider installing (or at least preparing your home's wiring for) a full-fledged computer *local area network (LAN)* to allow your computers to quickly share access to the same resources. A home LAN provides a high-speed data connection among all the computers in your home, allowing them to do things such as share files, share networked peripherals (such as printers), and even play networked games. Multiple computers can more easily share high-speed Internet access devices, such as DSL or cable modems, over a home-computer LAN. Media Servers, which we discuss in Chapter 5, also fit into your computer LAN because they provide content not only to TVs and audio systems but also to computers throughout your house.

In this chapter, we discuss the basics of computer LANs and some of the ways to set up a LAN in your home. We also talk about some of the difficulties you may encounter when you try to connect several networked computers to your Internet account at the same time.

Flipping the Wired or Wireless Coin

The first step in choosing a LAN technology for your home is to decide whether you should go with a wired or wireless solution. If you've perused other sections of this book, you know that we spend most of our time talking about wired solutions. Data networks, however, have experienced an explosion of no-new-wires networking systems.

Here's our take on the issue: If you're building a new home or undertaking a major remodeling of an older home, and if the walls are open, by all means choose the wired alternative.

Although we think that putting the right kinds of wires and cables into the right part of your home is the best solution to creating flexible and future-proofed home-networking solutions, we do live in the real world. And in the real world, you may not be able to get the necessary cabling systems installed in your home for a number of reasons, including the following:

- ✔ You rent your home.
- ✔ You live in a condominium and can't easily access shared spaces in walls, attics, and basements.
- ✔ You live in a historic home and have to run any changes past the planning commission.
- ✔ Your home has design problems that keep you from easily running cables, such as no crawl space, basement, or attic in which to hide wires.

Whatever the reason, you may not be able to squeeze those fat CAT-5 and coaxial lines through the walls in your home. Luckily, you have some options: You can use wireless systems to do the job, or you can use the phone and electric power wires already in your walls (often called no-new-wires solutions). We discuss these alternatives in Chapter 16.

Wireless and no-new-wires systems are great, but they do have some disadvantages when compared to a wired infrastructure:

- ✔ **Lower speeds:** Although wired LANs can run at 100 or even 1000 Mbps, the fastest wireless alternatives max out at well below 50 Mbps. This isn't a big deal if you're talking about sharing a 1- or 2-Mbps Internet connection, but it is when you start thinking about sending large video or other media files between computers in your home.
- ✔ **You'll probably pay a bit more:** Prices of wireless-LAN equipment for the home have dropped like dot.com stock prices over the past few years, but they're still higher than those of wired LAN equipment.

✔ **You'll have to contemplate which industry standard to use:** Although the early competition between standards in wireless LANs is over, at least three new standards are on their way to market to make things even more confusing, and most are not compatible. So you'll have to choose carefully to make sure everything in your network works together.

✔ **You may not like the way the wireless options work:** In optimal conditions, wireless systems work great, but things such as long distances (if you have a big house), thick walls, and metal objects can cause problems. Danny, for instance, has a house that was built in the late 1800s, with 18-inch stone walls. He loves his wireless LAN, but unfortunately it doesn't work very well upstairs.

We hope we don't sound down on wireless LANs — because we're not. We think they're just about the greatest thing since sliced bread. Being able to take your laptop to the bed, or the sofa, or the back patio without any tethers is an almost life-changing experience. You'd be in for a big fight if you tried to take our wireless LANs away from us. But we've seen many situations where a wired LAN connection can be better. In practice, if you have the opportunity to wire your house, we think you'll probably want both a wired and a wireless LAN — they coexist nicely.

The effect that choosing all wireless options — phone, data, audio, video, and so on — has on your home is unclear. We can tell you that many wireless technologies compete for the same spectrum in your home, though. For example, many cordless phone systems use the same 2.4-GHz frequency band that most wireless LANs use, and they can cause interference. Because these are *unlicensed* frequencies, there's not really any authority controlling all the devices in them — so there's no one out there ensuring that phones and wireless LANs and wireless video transmitters don't run into each other on the airwaves. And even if you are in control of your airwave use, there's nothing saying that your neighbor is as well.

Running Cables Here, There, and Everywhere

In Chapter 15, we spend a bit of time discussing the various methods that you can use to create LAN connections throughout your house. In this section, we want you to think about where you may want to place these network connections in your home.

Bedrooms

You may not consider bedrooms as prime locations for computer LAN outlets, but you probably should. With a bedroom outlet, you can work from your bed by plugging a laptop into the network, for example. You may also want a network outlet near the bedroom TV that allows you to connect future generations of Web-enabled TVs or similar products to your LAN for some TV-based Web surfing.

Current generations of Web on the TV products aren't particularly networkable, but you can bet the mortgage that future versions will be.

Also, the latest versions of PVRs are able to synchronize over high-speed Internet connections, so you'll want to have a data connection nearby.

The master bedroom isn't the only place to consider providing LAN connection points. Your kids are probably hogging time on your PC, but with PC prices plummeting, getting the kids their own computers and connecting them to a home network is beginning to make sense.

You should also think long term here: Today's nursery is tomorrow's teenage room, and someday maybe a home office. Or your guest room may be hosting one of your computer-geek relatives, who just can't leave home without his or her laptop. Having those rooms LAN-ready just makes sense.

Living room

Computers in the living room? Probably not in most homes, especially if you limit your concept of computers to PCs (although Pat is trying hard to convince his wife that they need a new 17-inch flat-screen iMac next to the living-room sofa). New devices are coming to market, however, that require LAN connections *and* fit into the living room. Leading the way are today's networkable gaming consoles and PVRs (discussed in Chapter 5). But also think about screen phones or set-top boxes that let you read e-mail or shop on e-commerce Web sites. Eventually, you'll probably want to access this stuff from your recliner.

Home office

You obviously want to have a LAN connection in your home office. However, we suggest that you think of your home office not in terms of whether or not to include LAN connection points but in terms of how many and where. Consider providing at least two or three network outlets in your home office — enough to support two computers and a networkable printer.

More and more devices are being network-enabled, and the concept of a monitor, printer, computer, and keyboard all in the same place is rapidly going by the wayside. Danny has extended an extra keyboard, wireless mouse, and extra monitor to his treadmill and can now read the *New York Times* every morning and clear his e-mail before work — using the same computer that's on his desk in the home office down the hallway — while losing weight. (Pat needs to do the same.)

What's great about Ethernet hubs is that you can cascade them throughout your house if you run out of ports on your central hub. Suppose that you're using all your ports to run to different rooms, but your kids want four Ethernet ports in their room instead of the two you provided. No problem: Connect your Ethernet's uplink port to the wall outlet, and the other ports are available for that room's networking — and everyone can still communicate with everyone else on the home LAN.

Home theater or media center

You should consider including your home theater in your LAN plans for a couple of reasons. First, you'll probably have a ReplayTV or TiVo or some other Internet-enabled media server in your home theater, or you may want to have some sort of Web-enabled TV set-top box mentioned in the preceding section, so you can take a break from movies and surf the Web on your widescreen tube. You may even want to install a regular PC in your home theater to surf the Web, keep track of your movie inventory, or even to feed streaming media (such as RealAudio broadcasts) from the Web to your audio or video systems.

Right now, broadband Internet service from DSL or cable TV companies reaches your house through a modem (and you'll probably install that modem in your home office or wiring closet). Some providers, particularly cable companies (but also some DSL providers who are looking to offer television services over DSL) are bringing to market set-top boxes that incorporate the broadband modem. If this is the case, you'll definitely want to have a network connection behind the TV so that you can share this Internet connection with the rest of your network.

Kitchen

We think that having some sort of Net-connected computer device, whether a full-fledged PC or something scaled down (such as the Internet refrigerator or Internet microwave), is going to be a great way to do a whole host of kitchen tasks. Imagine accessing your network's recipe database CD-ROM from an inexpensive PC on your kitchen counter, placing your grocery order online while standing next to your empty fridge, or quickly ordering your favorite pizza when you don't feel like cooking. (While some of the online grocery startups such as WebVan have shut their doors, many brick-and-mortar grocery chains such as Safeway, www.safeway.com, still do online grocery ordering and delivery in limited areas).

Some day, your kitchen appliances will use IP to send information about themselves to repair facilities and possibly to your home-automation system. (Warning! The freezer is malfunctioning!) In fact, if you want to spend about $6000 for a refrigerator, a few companies will sell you one with a PC and flat-panel display built in. Right now, most of these appliances use an Ethernet connection, but we think that they'll ultimately use the power line to communicate — there's just not enough kitchens with extra Ethernet jacks behind the fridge these days, and no matter how many people read this book, that isn't going to change any time soon. We still think it's a good idea to get at least one Ethernet outlet in the kitchen, just to be on the safe side.

Other places

Where else in the home should you extend your data network? Well, personally speaking, we're proponents of including data cabling in just about every room in the house.

We're not going to give you any specific recommendations for network connections in other places in your home. Instead, we challenge you to spend a bit of time thinking about the long-term uses of each part of your home. For example, do you hope to one day finish your attic or basement? If so, you may as well get the wire there ahead of time.

Toiletly serious business

In Japan — where people evidently take certain elements of the bathroom a bit more seriously than Americans do — high-tech toilets are all the rage. Besides heated seats and other luxury items, these toilets have ... er ... facilities that perform medical evaluations of the ... umm ... contents of the toilet.

Look at Jasmin by TOTO USA, Inc. (www.toto usa.com), which has an optional warm seat feature and built-in catalyzed-disk fan that freshens the air (activated by sitting down). Also, by pressing a button on the LCD remote control, which looks like a Nintendo control pad, you are "bathed in a gentler, aerated, warm water stream with massaging action." Ohhhh-kay.

We wouldn't be surprised to see this kind of thing become more common. The next step is a Net-connected toilet that can give reports to your healthcare provider (yes — really). Frankly, if these catch on in the U.S., we have no clue how you'd network. We'll leave that to the third edition of this book.

Some of the wireless or no-new-wires (telephone or electrical) networking solutions that we discuss in Chapter 16 can also be good ways of extending a network to unexpected places. Most of these products allow you to interface with an existing wired network and get the connection to places that you just never anticipated during your planning process (places such as the garage, where soon-to-arrive cars will dock into a home port to update their files and do their diagnostic workout).

Migrating Your Computer Flock to the Net

Coming up with a general design of your home-computer LAN is the first step, admittedly a big step, forward on this long march. A home LAN helps you get all your computers onto the Internet and certainly makes your computing life easier and more fun.

Unfortunately, most consumer Internet accounts allow a single computer to attach to the Net. In other words, when you log on to your analog modem, DSL, cable modem, or other high-speed network Internet account, your computer and modem communicate with your ISP's server and are assigned a single IP address. (The *IP address* is how the Internet knows what information you've asked for and received — kinda' like your mailing address for data.) A single IP address works fine when the modem is connected to a single computer — you don't need or want more than one IP address in this case. When you're trying to serve several computers at the same time with that Internet connection, however, you need some way to separate those different requests so that the data doesn't get jumbled. To solve this problem, you can choose a router, which is a hardware solution, or a proxy server, which is a software solution.

Many DSL and cable modem accounts give you only a single IP address for the base price but will provide your other computers with their own IP addresses for a monthly fee (usually about $3 to $5 per month per additional computer). If you choose this option, you need just a regular Ethernet hub — not one of the home-networking routers or proxy servers we're about to discuss. Each approach has pros and cons — the primary benefit of paying your service provider to do this for you is that you don't have to lift a finger to make it work, but the costs can add up if you have lots of computers and computer-like devices on your network. In the end, however, we think you'll want to add a router to the network.

Understanding home-network routers

If you were to go into the dark recesses of your office's telecommunications and data center, you'd probably find several weird-looking devices mounted on racks and shelves. One of these devices is most likely a router.

A *router* is the piece of equipment that consolidates all Internet traffic coming in and out of your office's LAN and sends it to the appropriate computers in the public network. The router performs this bit of Net magic by creating its own *subnet* (or private IP network) within the office and assigning private IP addresses to each computer connected to the router. The router is assigned a public IP address (one that other computers on the Internet can send data to and from) when it connects to the Internet, and then it figures out which packets of data go to which computer in the subnet.

Setting up a router for a large network is a complicated procedure — another one of those reasons why IT workers in your office make such good salaries. Luckily, routers designed for small home networks are relatively easy to configure.

These *home-network routers* or *residential gateways* act as the interface between your modem or broadband connection to your ISP and the rest of your home LAN, receiving all incoming Internet data and sending it to the correct machine on your network without your intervention. The first time you set up your router (or when you change the configuration of your network by adding or removing computers), you'll have to use some network management software to get things organized, but most of these routers have easy-to-understand, wizard-style programs to lead you through this process. Figure 14-1 shows how you would set up a home-network router.

The technology that makes your home router work is called NAT (Network Address Translation). The name is descriptive; NAT *translates* between the private IP addresses of the computers on your network and the public IP address that they all share, and is smart enough to make sure everything ends up in the right place.

Many home-network routers use your Internet browser as the software to configure the system. The configuration software is written as *HyperText Markup Language* (HTML) files — the language of Web pages. To set things up, you simply open your Web browser software, type the Web address of your router (it's usually a number, something like 192.168.1.1), and open these files. Fill in a few blanks, answer a few questions, and click a few buttons, and your router is ready to go.

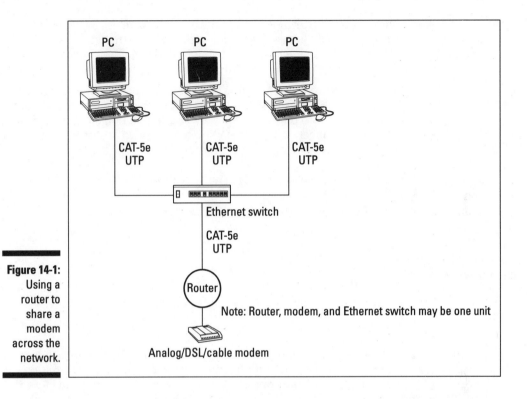

PC   PC   PC

CAT-5e   CAT-5e   CAT-5e
UTP   UTP   UTP

Ethernet switch

CAT-5e
UTP

Figure 14-1:
Using a
router to
share a
modem
across the
network.

Router

Note: Router, modem, and Ethernet switch may be one unit

Analog/DSL/cable modem

Home-network routers range in price depending on what kind of modem is
included (if one is included at all) and how many computers they can work
with. The majority of home-network routers on the market today work with
only cable or DSL broadband connections — they have an Ethernet interface
to hook into the DSL or cable modem, and no way to connect to an analog
modem. So, if you're still stuck on dial-up, you'll have to shop around a bit to
find a model that works for you. (A few models are available with a built-in
analog modem, but they're getting scarce.) Other features that influence the
price of a home-network router include the following:

✔ **Firewalls:** Although NAT itself provides some network security functions,
   many home-network routers also contain sophisticated firewalls, which
   keep hackers out of your computer.

✔ **Wireless LAN support:** The wireless networks we talk about in Chapter
   16 are often supported by home-network routers — many have built-in
   wireless access point functionality, so you can support both your wired
   and unwired computers from a single device.

✔ **Other home-networking support:** Besides the wireless systems just mentioned, many home-networking gateways also include support for connecting PCs to your network using existing telephone lines or even electrical power lines. We talk about these systems in Chapter 16 as well.

✔ **Support for VPN:** Many business use VPNs (Virtual Private Networks) to allow their employees to securely connect their computers from remote locations back into the corporate network. Not all home-network routers will let you connect in this way. (VPNs have special protocols that not all routers will pass through to the Internet.)

The cheapest home-network routers start at about $100 (these boxes were at least $500 just three years ago). The major vendors of home-network routers and router/modem combos include the following:

✔ Linksys (www.linksys.com)

✔ NetGear (www.netgear.com)

✔ D-Link (www.dlink.com)

✔ Siemens SpeedStream (www.speedstream.com)

✔ 2Wire (www.2wire.com)

Although you can buy your own home-network router directly from the manufacturer or from online and other retailers, you may also have the option of getting one directly from your Internet service provider. DSL providers such as BellSouth, SBC, EarthLink, and DirecTV DSL will provide you with a home-network router — usually for a monthly fee. Although you might end up paying more for such a solution over time than just buying the router yourself, you do have the advantage of having someone to support you if you run into any problems.

Some broadband companies don't like the idea of a customer being able to hook up multiple computers to your broadband connection without paying more to do so — so they frown upon customer-owned home-network routers. We haven't heard of any providers prohibiting their customers from doing so (it would be hard for them to even know that you're using a router, technically speaking), but some folks in these companies are looking into ways to keep you from doing it yourself.

Using your PC to route packets

Routers are the hardware-based way of sharing an Internet connection. Given their low prices, we think they're also the best way. But they're not the only way. The software-based alternative is to install a *proxy server* program on one of your networked PCs. This program performs pretty much the same function as a router — that is, it distributes Internet data packets from a single connection to multiple PCs on a network.

In this scenario, you designate one of the PCs in your network (the one with the modem connected to it, generally) as the proxy server for the rest of the network. This proxy-server PC collects all incoming and outgoing Internet traffic; the proxy-server software then determines which networked computer the data is intended for and sends it on its way. Figure 14-2 shows a typical proxy server setup for an Internet connection other than through an analog modem. (This configuration requires two NICs in the proxy server.)

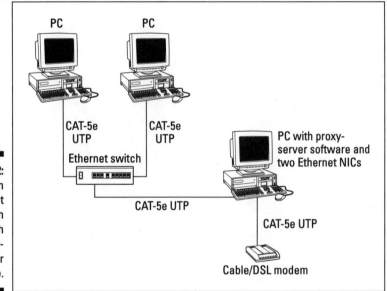

Figure 14-2:
Sharing an Internet connection through proxy-server software.

Proxy-server software is usually easy to set up, and the programs themselves are inexpensive. The most popular software for home-LAN users is made by a company called WinGate (www.wingate.com). For Mac users, a program called IPNetRouter is probably the most popular choice (www.sustworks.com).

If you have a Windows computer with Windows 98, Second Edition, or newer operating system, you can do this without additional software, using the Internet Connection Sharing (ICS) control panel built into the OS. Mac users with OS X also have this functionality built in to the OS, but you'll need to use either UNIX commands (ouch!) or a shareware program such as Brian Hill's BrickHouse (www.securemac.com/brickhouse.php) to configure it.

If your modem connects to your computer with an Ethernet interface, as do most DSL and cable modems, and you have a Windows computer, you need to install two Ethernet Network Interface Cards in your proxy server — one for the broadband modem connection and one to connect the proxy server to the rest of your network.

Routing and bridging with data networks is a complicated topic, and we've just touched on it here. As you get into your data networking plans, check out *Networking Home PCs For Dummies* by Kathy Ivens (published by Wiley Publishing, Inc.) — it'll help you figure out the next level of detail on this topic.

Chapter 15

Choosing the Parts for a Wired Data LAN

*A*s prices plummet and more members of your household find uses for a computer (or computer-like devices), chances are good that you'll use several networked devices. What most people don't have but need to take full advantage of the Internet, file sharing, and other computer technologies is a home-computer network — a local area network, or LAN.

In this chapter, we tell you about the equipment and wires in a wired LAN and how to have it installed in your house.

Building CAT-5e LANs

The backbone of a computer network — regardless of what types of computers are connected to it or what kinds of network software are used to make it work — is the physical wiring and components that connect everything. The most common type of wired computer LAN uses a special type of copper cabling, CAT-5e UTP (unshielded twisted pair), which we discuss extensively in Chapter 2.

Nearly all LAN technologies share a few basic building blocks:

✔ **Cables:** Cables usually provide the connection between networked devices. But in some cases, the physical connection doesn't take place via wires — many emerging LAN technologies make use of wireless communications techniques to get data around your home (discussed in Chapter 16).

✔ **Network interface cards (NICs):** You must install NICs (pronounced like the New York basketball team) — in each device that connects to the network. The NIC bridges the gap between the cables (or wireless devices) and the individual computers or other networked devices. NICs generally work with only one kind of network, such as an Ethernet NIC for Ethernet-based networks. Many computers today are shipped with Ethernet NICs already installed.

✔ **A network protocol — such as Ethernet:** *Ethernet* is a hardware specification that controls access to the network, allows individual devices on the network to find and identify each other, and determines when each device can transmit and receive data. The key thing about Ethernet is that each Ethernet system adheres to a set of protocol standards that enable various devices from different manufacturers to communicate.

Ethernet is the most common LAN for the home or small office (or in big business for that matter). The total bandwidth and the type of cable the network uses define different variations of Ethernet. For example, 10BaseT — the most common variation — transmits data at speeds up to 10 Mbps and uses UTP copper wires as its physical media.

We discussed UTP twisted pair cables in detail in Chapter 2.

Scores of Ethernet variations are available, but you need to consider only the following:

✔ **10Base2:** 10 Mbps over coaxial cable

✔ **10BaseT:** 10 Mbps over twisted-pair cable

✔ **100BaseT:** 100 Mbps over twisted-pair cable — often called Fast Ethernet

✔ **1000BaseT:** 1000 Mbps over twisted-pair cable — often called Gigabit Ethernet, or Gig-E

The first number in each of these names stands for the bandwidth of the system in megabits per second, so 10Base2 is a 10-Mbps connection. The last number or letter tells you the kind of cable that it goes over; for example, *T* means twisted pair.

Like the other networks we describe in this book, local area networks support different architectures. LANs are particularly flexible, however, in allowing you to mix and match architectures as you grow.

The shortest Ethernet primer in computerdom

Ethernet in its traditional form is a shared network. All computers and other connected, networked devices share the 10 (or 100 or 1000) Mbps of bandwidth available on the network. Ethernet uses a protocol called *CSMA/CD (Carrier-Sense Multiple Access with Collision Detection)* to divide access to the network. Basically, CSMA/CD means that all devices on the network listen for a free moment on the network before sending data. When the coast is clear, the data goes out. If two devices happen to pick the same moment to send data, a collision occurs. The devices then each wait a random amount of time before resending their data.

Newer versions of Ethernet hardware systems are *switched.* These Ethernet networks use a sophisticated device — the switch, of course — to direct data throughout the network. Instead of sharing 10 or 100 Mbps, each device has that amount of bandwidth dedicated to it at all times. The switch basically keeps each segment of the Ethernet network separate from the others — directing data between the devices that are talking and keeping data off the wires running to other devices, instead of sending the data to every device. This process can reduce the number of collisions and make the overall network faster as more and more devices are connected to it.

The two basic choices for how you model your LAN are the bus architecture and the star (or home run) architecture. If you've read other chapters in this book, you already know that we prefer the star architecture, hands down. In fact, we don't believe the bus architecture is really worth talking about, so we just concentrate on the star.

Twisted-pair Ethernet LANs (such as 10BaseT or 100BaseT) use a network architecture called a star. In a *star configuration,* all hardware connects to a central device called a *hub* or a *switch.* The hub transmits the data from each incoming cable to every other cable that attaches to the hub — and, therefore, to each device that attaches to the far end of those cables.

Hubs and switches do basically the same thing. They are the central point to which each run of CAT-5e UTP cabling connects back to, and they allow data to flow down different legs of the network to get from device to device. The difference is that a switch uses internal intelligence to figure out which legs of the network the data needs to flow over, but a hub just sends the data (usually called *packets*) down every leg of the network simultaneously. If only two computers are talking to each other, the difference between these approaches isn't significant. But as more devices start to talk to each other, a switch can make things much faster. Because switch prices have dropped immensely, we recommend that you install a switch rather than a hub in the center of your network.

We show a network built using a star architecture in Figure 15-1.

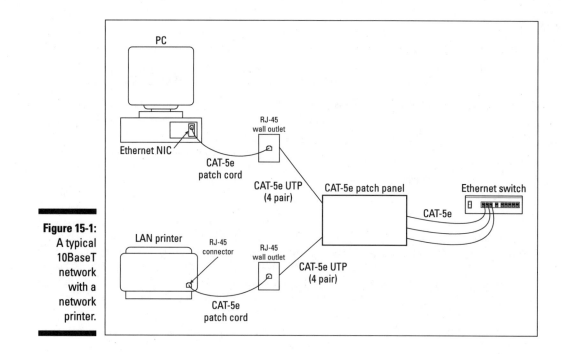

Figure 15-1:
A typical
10BaseT
network
with a
network
printer.

Need to add another device to the network? Just run another length of network cabling and connect it to the hub. Someone drive a nail through one of your network cables? Your whole network doesn't go down — just the affected segment.

Star architecture is a key concept in home networking because you can use it for all sorts of networks, such as a telephone system or a video-distribution system. In these systems, as in Ethernet and other LANs, the star topology greatly increases the flexibility, reliability, and expandability of a network.

Your star network can be easily expanded by hooking up a hub at one of the endpoints you've wired into your network. So if you have a single Ethernet outlet in a bedroom and need to connect two or three devices to it, you can just plug a hub into the outlet, and then connect those devices to the hub. All computers connected to this remote hub will be able to "see" the rest of your network — just as if they were connected to one of your Ethernet jacks.

Cables and Connectors

If you're getting ready to create a new data network (or telephone network, for that matter) in your home, you'll have to make sure that your baseline cabling for this is CAT-5e wiring, as we discussed in Chapter 2. For data, you need CAT-5e, period.

Of course, cables don't do you much good when they're just a bunch of bare wires hanging out of the wall — you need something to connect them to your networked equipment. Luckily, this problem has an easy solution. Like telephone networks, computer LANs utilize a common connector, the RJ-45. The standard jack and plug for all UTP computer LANs, RJ-45 connectors look exactly like the familiar (old-fashioned) telephone jacks called RJ-11s, which we discuss in Chapter 2, only bigger (wider). RJ-45 connectors are designed to terminate all four pairs of wire found in typical CAT-5e UTP cables.

CAT-5e cabling is designed for high-speed, high-performance networks. Therefore, if you use CAT-5e, the entire system — the plugs, jacks, patch panels, and connectors, in addition to the cable — must be CAT-5e rated. A LAN is only as good at its weakest link, so if any one piece of the puzzle is rated less than CAT-5e, the entire LAN will be as well.

The network components

Besides the cables and connectors, a few other pieces are necessary to install a smart-home LAN. This equipment is pretty universal, whether you're installing an inexpensive 10-Mbps Ethernet network or a sophisticated ATM system. The key is to use CAT-5e components throughout the network. That way, even if you start off with just a 10BaseT Ethernet system, your wiring is in place to upgrade by simply replacing a few components — no ripping down walls and starting over from scratch for you!

The 1000BaseT, or Gigabit Ethernet, system is being deployed in corporate office networks. It's still expensive, relative to 10BaseT and 100BaseT networks, and there's no need for it in the home today. Some day, however, we may see Gigabit Ethernet in the home — mainly because it's fast enough to let you use your computer LAN to carry things such as HDTV signals. As long as you have a star-wired CAT-5e network, you'll be ready for Gigabit Ethernet when you need it. Just upgrade your NICs and your switch or router, and you'll be there!

Punch it down!

Your home LAN's *central node* — the place from which all your cabling runs start — begins with a device called a *patch panel* or *punchdown block* mounted in your central wiring closet. If you read Chapter 2, where we discuss wiring, and Chapter 10 on telephone networks, you're already familiar with this device. A data network uses a punchdown block or patch panel that is just about identical to the one your telephone uses. The one major exception is that the punchdown block needs to be CAT-5e rated to allow high-speed data transmissions. You don't need this level of cable and component quality for telephone service — but it's a good idea to use this for all your UTP wiring infrastructure because it lets you easily repurpose cables (for example, turn a phone jack into an Ethernet jack by just reconnecting it in the wiring closet).

Switches and hubs and routers for everyone

The key component in an Ethernet network is an *Ethernet hub or switch,* the device that ensures that data gets from point A to point B in the network. A hub or switch (we'll just talk about switches from here on out, because they're the superior way to go and don't cost much more) is a small electronic box with a number of RJ-45 connectors (called *ports*) across the front. Inside the switch is a circuit board that electrically connects all these RJ-45 connectors to each other in the proper way — *the proper way* means that the wire carrying outgoing data from one computer connects to the wires that carry incoming data to all other computers that are part of the switch. We know all this information can be confusing, but don't let it stress you out. Honestly, you don't need to spend much time thinking about how hubs and switches work. They're simply one of those magical boxes that allow your computers to talk to each other.

The *uplink port* (also sometimes called a *WAN port*), which is a special RJ-45 port, is another feature of a typical switch. Unlike the other ports, the uplink port doesn't cross the incoming and outgoing data signals. Instead, it sends them straight through (incoming to incoming, outgoing to outgoing). This capability becomes useful if, for example, you want to connect two hubs or if you have an Internet connection device, such as a cable modem, that you want to connect to all computers in the network. In these cases, you use the uplink port instead of a standard port.

It's just about impossible to find a hub, switch, or router without an uplink port, but if you ever do run into one, you can use a special kind of CAT-5e patch cable, called a *crossover* cable, to connect your network to your broadband connection. A crossover cable *crosses over* the transmit and receive conductors in the CAT-5e cable so that data flows the right way between your modem and your LAN. By the way, the regular cables used to connect computers in the LAN are sometimes referred to as *straight through cables.*

Some Ethernet switches and hubs don't have a dedicated uplink port. Instead, they have a switch (a button, in other words) next to one of the regular ports that lets you configure the port to act as an uplink port.

You might be thinking, "Well, where do home-network routers fit in?" Great question. Most home routers have built-in Ethernet switches. So you don't need to buy a router *and* a switch. Just go shopping for a home-network router (from companies such as NetGear, Linksys, and D-link), and you'll be set. (For more on home routers, see Chapter 14.)

Like ice cream, switches (and routers and hubs for that matter) come in many flavors — the one you purchase is a matter of taste. Be sure to look for the following, though:

✔ **Number of ports:** Be sure to buy a hub that has enough ports to connect all the computers and networkable devices (such as printers and cable modems) that you plan on installing in your home LAN.

✔ **Speed:** 10 Mbps (10BaseT) is still the standard Ethernet installation for most residential applications, but you may want to move up to the faster 100BaseT.

Both 10BaseT and 100BaseT use the same wiring infrastructure, so you can start off with one and upgrade to the other just by changing the switch and putting new Network Interface Cards (NICs) in your PCs. Even better, most modern home-network routers and newer computers are compatible with both 10BaseT or 100BaseT networks. (These devices automatically connect at the fastest speed available to them.)

✔ **Price:** Take a quick trip to any computer superstore or browse through any computer equipment catalog, and you'll find an amazing range of prices for switches that are equivalent in speed and number of ports. The last time we went shopping for a small, 4-port, 10/100BaseT router, we discovered that some relatively unknown companies offered them for about $50, while more well-known data networking companies charged around $100. Doing a little online detective work at a site such as `shopper.cnet.com` can help in these cases.

NICs galore

All the cables in the world won't do your computer a bit of good if it doesn't have the right hardware that lets it "talk" on your LAN. The Network Interface Card, or NIC performs that job.

NICs come in different forms to fit the varying kinds of internal buses in today's (and yesterday's) PCs and Macs. The most common internal buses found in new computers are the PCI (or Peripheral Component Interconnect) bus and the ISA (Industry Standard Architecture) bus. These are the card slots visible at the back of your computer. You insert these cards by popping the cover off your computer and sliding a card into an empty PCI slot inside, leaving the RJ-45 jack part sticking out of the back of the computer. Although the PCI bus theoretically offers faster data throughput, for the NIC cards used in a home LAN there's really no difference. We recommend that you utilize whichever slot you have available — just be sure to check what's free inside your computer before you buy one (or go to your local computer superstore, have one installed, and ask a lot of questions).

NICs offer different interfaces to the LAN — in other words, they have different connectors on the back for different kinds of LAN cabling. If you're following our advice, and we hope that you do, you should choose a NIC with an RJ-45 jack.

Finally, NICs are designed to connect computers to different kinds of networks. For example, some connect to 10BaseT Ethernet networks, some to 100BaseT Ethernet, and some to ATM networks. We recommend that you install NICs that have dual capabilities — that will work on both 10BaseT and 100BaseT networks. These NICs, which cost about $30, automatically sense what kind of network hub you have installed, and set their own speed accordingly. They also allow you to upgrade your network in the future without having to buy a bunch of new NICs.

Many PCs are now being sold with NICs preinstalled from the factory — a great thing, in our opinion. All Macintosh computers, for example, come standard with 10/100BaseT autosensing NICs. If you're in the market for a new computer, get one with a NIC and avoid the hassle of installation.

With cables and connectors, patch panels, NICs, and hubs, you're 90 percent of the way towards putting together a home LAN. The final key to the puzzle is another set of CAT-5e cables called *patch cables*. Patch cables fill the gap between wall outlets and computers; they also connect the patch panel to your Ethernet switch or home-network router.

Just like all the other components in your network, your patch cables should be rated CAT-5e. Most are, but some of the cheaper ones are rated CAT-3 or even unrated. You don't want these — they're a false economy that may keep your network from reaching its maximum speed or working reliably.

Software to put it all together

The one additional component to making a LAN work — probably the most difficult one for many people — is configuring all the network protocols and software on each of your home's PCs. This used to be the domain of hard-core networking experts, but it has become less onerous with each successive release of Windows and Mac OS software.

Our focus in this book is to get you the infrastructure you need to have a home LAN — we simply don't have the room to talk about binding protocols and configuring networking software. If you're not comfortable with doing this on your own, check out *Networking For Dummies,* 6th Edition by Doug Lowe or *Networking Home PCs For Dummies* by Kathy Ivens (both published by Wiley Publishing, Inc.).

Visualizing How a Data LAN Works

In the star architecture, each *LAN station* — the outlet into which you can connect a computer to the LAN — is served by its own length of UTP cable radiating out from a central node, like the spokes on a wagon wheel.

Probably the best way to visualize this kind of LAN network is to follow your data from a PC back to the central node of the LAN and back over the network to its final destination:

1. The computer uses its networking software to send a chunk of data from a program to your NIC.

2. The NIC converts the data into the proper format for the network (Ethernet, for example) and sends it as an electrical signal over the patch cable.

3. The patch cable carries this data signal between the NIC and the nearest RJ-45 connector installed in a wall outlet.

4. The RJ-45 connector attaches to one end of a length of CAT-5e UTP cabling, which carries the data signal back through your walls to the central node of your LAN (in the basement, garage, or utility room — wherever you choose to house it).

5. The UTP cable terminates where it's punched down into the patch panel, which carries your data signal across its internal wiring to another RJ-45 connector.

6. Another patch cable carries the data signal from the back of the patch panel to the Ethernet switch or home-network router.

7. The hub takes your outgoing data signal and sends it on a U-turn trip back through the patch panel and over a different CAT-5e to its final destination on your network (another computer, a printer, or elsewhere).

The devices that communicate over your Ethernet LAN don't have to be computers. Many peripheral devices such as printers have Ethernet ports, as do things that might have nothing to do with your PC — such as a video gaming console. If you want to use your X Box with Microsoft's online gaming service, you need to use Ethernet to connect it to your broadband Internet connection.

Working with your Internet connection

The scenario we just went through describes how data is shared between computers across your LAN. But that leaves out what is, for many folks, the most important thing: getting data to and from the Internet. That's where the home-network router that we've talked about so much fits in. A router's main purpose (besides switching local LAN traffic) is to send data between your Internet connection and the computers and devices on your LAN.

A switch is a device that connects multiple PCs on a LAN. A router connects the computers on a LAN to a wide area network (such as the Internet). Most home routers that we discuss have a built-in switch, but not all switches are also routers.

Conceptually, this is really just like Steps 1 through 7 in the preceding section. The difference is this: In the scenario in that section, the "local" LAN traffic gets U-turned around and sent back to another computer in your home. When you're using your network for Internet access, the Internet traffic goes through the router and gets sent to your cable or DSL modem and off to the Internet (and vice versa for the data that you receive from your Internet connection).

This leads to a key question: Where should you put the broadband modem? In pre-networking days, you just stuck it on your desk, right next to the computer. After all, that computer was the only thing using it, why put it far away? But now that we're all networking our computers, there's no obvious place to put the broadband modem. Most people narrow it down to two options:

✔ Put the broadband modem in the wiring closet, next to the router and the CAT-5e patch panel. This is a nice, neat, easy solution, with everything in one place. Your cable or DSL lines come into the home here, so you'll have something to hook the broadband modem to.

✔ Put the broadband modem in your home office (or wherever you keep your primary computer). In this scenario, you need two CAT-5e cables — one to connect the output of the broadband modem back down to the router or switch in the wiring closet and another that connects the output of the router or switch to the computer in the room.

We like to use the second solution. Running that second CAT-5e cable up to the home office is simple (we recommend extra CAT-5e cables to the home office anyway), and it gives you a chance to keep an eye on your broadband modem. These modems are notoriously unpredictable, and sometimes you just need to pull the plug and restart them to get them working properly. You'll also be able to quickly check the status lights on the modem to make sure everything is hunky dory.

Integrating with no-new-wires networks

In Chapter 16, we describe several networking technologies that don't use CAT-5e UTP cabling. Instead, they use wireless, powerline, and phoneline technologies to hook computers together. Even if you have a *wired* CAT-5e network in place, you still might find these networks useful — particularly wireless LANs that let you roam around the house with your laptop or handheld computer without plugging into anything.

Combining these networks with your wired LAN is simple. Wireless LANs are the easiest of all — wireless LAN access points (the hubs of a wireless network) in almost all cases have an RJ-45 Ethernet connection, which is designed to be connected to a wired LAN. So just find a good place to put your access point (we give you some tips in Chapter 16), and plug it into the nearest wired LAN outlet (and into the wall power outlet too) and you're set.

You'll need to do a little bit of software setup, of course. This varies from access point to access point, but there's one tip we want to give you. Most access points can act as DHCP servers as well — assigning IP addresses to computers. If you're using a router on your wired LAN, the router is already set up to do this, and letting the access point do it again will mess up your network. Instead, you should set up your access point in what's usually called *bridging mode*. This lets the router do its job — the access point just transparently connects, or bridges, between the wired and wireless sections of the network.

Some vendors of wireless networking gear have realized that people with wired home networks and routers need access points only to act as bridges, so they now offer cheaper access points without all the DHCP and router functionality. These lower-end access points make sense for many folks — you want to be able to control all your networked computers from your home-networking router, which is located in your wiring closet, but you might want to put a cheap access point elsewhere in the house so that you can get better wireless reception.

For networks that run over power lines or phone lines, there typically isn't a central network hub such as the access point of a wireless LAN. What you will find, however, are Ethernet-to-power-line or Ethernet-to-phone-line *bridges* (there's that term again!). You'll use two (or more) of these bridges in your network. One bridge connects to an Ethernet outlet somewhere in the house (or directly to the switch or router in the wiring closet), and then plugs into a phone or power outlet. On the far end (where your remote devices are located), you use another bridge in the reverse fashion — the bridge plugs into a phone or power outlet (to pick up the data sent by the first bridge), and then connects to the Ethernet port of the device that you want to connect to the network.

Phone and powerline bridges are a great way to extend your Ethernet network to places where you just didn't think to put CAT-5e cables. For example, if you don't have CAT-5e next to your gaming console, but you want to connect that console to your LAN and to the Internet, use a pair of bridges and you're all set. We've been using some of these bridges from NetGear in our homes, and they work great.

Infrared — using light instead of wires

Infrared networking — using light waves instead of radio waves — is already a part of many computer networks. A relatively mature standard known as IRDA (Infrared Device Association) is in place. IRDA devices are commonly found in three main sets of equipment:

✔ **Printers:** Using an IRDA interface, you can beam print jobs from one or several computers to your printer without cables. You find IRDA interfaces mainly on high-end laser printers — the inkjet models that most people have in their homes don't have this capability yet. Remember, though, that a printer with an IRDA interface doesn't do you any good unless your PC has one as well.

✔ **Notebook computers:** Many laptops have a built-in IRDA interface to facilitate printing and to make for easy data synchronization with your desktop PC.

✔ **Handheld computer devices:** You also find IRDA interfaces on many handheld, PDA (Personal Digital Assistant) computers, mainly for synchronizing data with your desktop computer.

Depending on its implementation, infrared networking can be efficient and speedy — with data throughput rates reaching several megabits per second in some cases.

Infrared does have a major downfall, however, that makes it unsuitable for a whole-home network: Infrared signals are line-of-sight only. In other words, an infrared signal won't penetrate some of those pesky things you often find in the home — such as doors, walls, and giant-screen televisions. So although infrared is useful in a single room, it won't get you very far beyond that. In Chapter 16, we talk about a bunch of solutions that can give you whole-home networking without using CAT-5e wires; IRDA is more of an adjunct to a home network for connecting peripheral devices and syncing things — not a replacement.

One more thing: IRDA is a computer protocol used for computer communications. IRDA is not typically used for noncomputer purposes, such as remote controls for stereos and TVs. Although these remote controls also use infrared signals, they're an entirely different critter.

Chapter 16

Alternatives to a Wired Data LAN

. . . .

. . . .

*W*e think that a wired computer network — using CAT-5e cabling in the walls — is the best way to set up a home-computer network. Wired networks are faster, more reliable, and more secure. Having said that, we absolutely LOVE our wireless networks. Just try to take them away from us — just try. . . .

We think that the no-new-wires computer LAN technologies have come a long way in the past few years. They can fit into your smart home in one of two ways. First, if you can't get into the walls to run CAT-5e cabling, and your house isn't huge, you can build a satisfactory data network with no-new-wires technologies. Second, even if you have a wired LAN infrastructure in your walls, you'll probably find a reason to use one of these no-new-wires networks. You might want to add a wireless network so that you can use your laptop untethered, or you may find a spot where you don't have CAT-5e but need network connectivity (such as behind your new Internet fridge).

In this chapter, we tell you about the three leading technologies for no-new-wires computer networks: wireless, phoneline (using your existing telephone wiring), and powerline (using your existing electrical wiring). You'll probably use all three in your home.

Cut the Cord!

Probably the most exciting development that we've seen in the home-networking field over the past few years has been the emergence of wireless computer networks. Wireless networks have such a high coolness factor that many other networking technologies have taken the back seat in people's minds — despite some limitations to the technology. We can understand this because we too have been caught up in the wireless LAN mania.

Wireless networks have relatively limited bandwidth, are subject to interference from other electrical devices in the home (such as cordless phones and microwave ovens), and have some security issues (wireless signals will go right through your walls and into your driveway, street, or neighbor's living room). We think the best way to use wireless is to incorporate it into your wired network — using your wired LAN for things that don't move (such as the desktop PC) and adding a wireless LAN for portable devices such as laptops and PDAs.

As is the case for many new and emerging technologies, various companies, industry groups, and international standards bodies are involved in the wireless LAN industry. If you shop for a wireless LAN, you'll run into competing standards.

Standards are vitally important to networking. For example, the various standards for wired Ethernet networks allow equipment from different vendors to work together right out of the box, with no special tweaking or esoteric settings to configure. The same is true in wireless LANs — equipment conforming to a specific standard should work seamlessly with other equipment that also conforms to the standard, regardless of the manufacturer. In fact, many standards bodies sponsor interoperability bake-offs on a quarterly basis to ensure that this is the case.

The problem with wireless networks is that five or more standards are available. For the most part, interoperability between different devices within a standard can be taken for granted, but deciding on a particular standard can be difficult, especially if you haven't spent a lot of time researching wireless networking technologies. That's where we can help: We spend a fair amount of time at our day jobs researching just that issue!

First, let's discuss what is available (or soon to be available) in your favorite online store:

- **802.11b:** Also called Wi-Fi, 802.11b (the number refers to an international standard for wireless networks), is *by far* the most common wireless LAN technology on the market. Millions of 802.11b devices are sold every month around the world, giving this standard a ton of momentum. We spend most of our time talking about it (though much of what we have to say will apply to other wireless LAN systems as well). And here's the technical detail we know you're waiting for: 802.11b uses the 2.4-GHz radio spectrum (we discuss the radio spectrum in Chapter 11) and can deliver a maximum of 11 Mbps of shared bandwidth to the devices in your home that are connected to the wireless network.

✔ **802.11a:** In a textbook example of the weirdness of standards naming, 802.11a is a newer technology than 802.11b. Because it uses a higher-frequency chunk of the radio spectrum than 802.11b (5 GHz instead of 2.4 GHz), 802.11a is also known as Wi-Fi5. With a maximum speed of 54 Mbps, Wi-Fi5 is potentially much faster than Wi-Fi, but because it uses a different frequency (and has other differences in the way the signal is encoded and sent out over the radio) it is *not* compatible with Wi-Fi. That means if you want to move to 802.11a, you have to junk your 802.11b gear (or use it elsewhere in your network).

✔ **802.11g:** 802.11g is an emerging standard that uses the same 2.4-GHz frequency spectrum as Wi-Fi. It will be backwardly compatible with Wi-Fi, meaning that it will work with any 802.11b system on the market, dropping to the lower 802.11b speeds when interworking with those devices. They won't work with Wi-Fi5 (802.11a) systems. So what's the big deal? When 802.11g systems work with each other, instead of with an 802.11b system, they'll be twice as fast, with a maximum bandwidth of 22 Mbps.

802.11e: Another wireless technology that's not quite here, 802.11e is designed to work with any of the three systems mentioned (Wi-Fi, Wi-Fi5, and 802.11g) and will provide quality of service functionality. This means that an 802.11e-enabled system will be able to give priority over the shared wireless network to certain devices or applications.

✔ **HomeRF:** Before Wi-Fi (and it's sister 802.11 technologies) hit the big time, many makers of home-wireless network products were pushing an entirely different standard — HomeRF. Like Wi-Fi, HomeRF uses the 2.4-GHz chunk of the radio airwaves. In its latest iteration, HomeRF gives about 10 Mbps of potential data throughput and can support mobile phone handsets as well. However, HomeRF is not compatible with any of the other systems we mentioned — you need to use all HomeRF equipment. Although it had an early lead in the market, most people (including us) now think that HomeRF has lost the battle with Wi-Fi, and fewer and fewer companies sell HomeRF equipment these days.

Got all that straight? Ready for your wireless LAN pop quiz? Don't worry. We won't do that to you. But what we will do is give you the handy little Table 16-1 to summarize what we just talked about.

Table 16-1		Wireless LAN Technologies		
Technology	*Frequency*	*Speed*	*Compatibility*	*Availability*
802.11b (Wi-Fi)	2.4 GHz	11 Mbps	802.11g	Now
802.11a (Wi-Fi5)	5 GHz	54 Mbps	none	Now
802.11g	2.4 GHz	22 Mbps	802.11b (at 11 Mbps)	Emerging
HomeRF	2.4 GHz	11 Mbps	none	Now

Note: We didn't include 802.11e in the table because it can work with any of the other 802.11s (802.11a, b, or g). 802.11e works with another 802.11 standard, not separately. The key thing to remember is that the special Quality of Service features of 802.11e will work only if you have 802.11e devices on *both* ends of your wireless connection.

Right now, Wi-Fi is by far the most available and widely used wireless LAN standard. It's also the cheapest (about $50 per computer as an add-on but will increasingly be built into the computer). Many offices have Wi-Fi networks, and thousands of hotels, airports, cafes, and other public spaces have Wi-Fi networks in place where you can get online wirelessly. Because of this ubiquity, we think 802.11b is the best way to go, despite its relatively low speed.

Products certified as compatible with the Wi-Fi or Wi-Fi5 standard have a logo on the box saying as much. This testing and certification process means that these devices not only meet certain technical requirements but also can connect to Wi-Fi or Wi-Fi5 products from other vendors. If the logo is not on the box, don't be surprised if the product doesn't work in a mixed-vendor network. You can find a list of certified products on the Wi-Fi Web page at `http://www.wirelessethernet.org/certified_products.asp`.

Although we think that 802.11b is the best way to go right now, we're intrigued by the added speed of 802.11a systems. If you decide to try 802.11a, protect your investment by buying a dual-mode wireless LAN system, which has both a *and* b functionality. Then you can take advantage of the higher speed of Wi-Fi5 in your home and fall back on Wi-Fi when you take your laptop or PDA on the road. You'll also spend more because this type of system basically uses two radios and two of a bunch of other components to give you both systems in one device.

Back to base (ics)

Regardless of the underlying wireless protocol or technology, wireless LANs share a few common elements, the most important of which is the base station or *access point*. If you think of your wireless network in the same way that you think of the wired LANs we discuss in Chapter 15 — in terms of having a hub and spokes — the access point is the hub of your wireless network. A wireless access point is usually a stand-alone, purpose-built device, but there are several ways to implement a wireless hub for your network:

✓ **Buy a wireless-only base station:** These devices, which you can buy from a host of vendors (NetGear, Linksys, Apple, and D-Link are just a few), connect through a wired Ethernet connection to your home LAN or directly into your broadband DSL or cable modem. The base station distributes Internet or local network traffic among all the wireless endpoints on the network (PCs, laptops, PDAs, and more).

✔ **Buy a base station and home router combo device:** Many of the home routers we discuss in Chapters 13 and 15 are available with built-in wireless base stations. Because they have both wireless and wired outputs (usually a multiport Ethernet switch), you can connect these devices directly to your broadband modem and use them as the central hub for your entire LAN, connecting both wired and wireless computers.

✔ **Buy a home-wiring system with wireless on-board:** Some of the structured home-wiring systems have wireless modules that plug into the central wiring hub or into the jacks at the endpoints of the system. SerCoNet's Smart Outlets (`www.serconet.co.il`) have 802.11b access-point modules that you can put in several places around your home to make sure that the devices don't suffer from signal fade.

✔ **Use a computer as a base station:** With some operating systems, you can replace the hardware base station with a dedicated PC. In this scenario, a broadband modem is connected to an Ethernet port on the base station computer, and then the computer is set up to share the Internet connection over an installed wireless network card. (This is really just a wireless version of the Internet-sharing proxy server concept we discuss in Chapter 13.)

Out of these four options, we think that the hardware-based approaches (first, second, and third options) make the most sense, unless you have a dedicated home server with wireless-LAN functionality bundled in. You'd have to try really hard to spend more than $200 for a wireless base station, and we've seen them advertised for well below $100. Using a computer as the base station means that you'll need to have that computer running all the time — and you'll probably take a performance hit if you use that PC for other things.

In the NIC of time

Just as computers need Network Interface Cards (NICs) to connect to a wired LAN, they need wireless NICs to connect to a wireless LAN. Wireless NICs, or wireless LAN cards (as they're often called), either plug into a slot in your computer or sit next to it on the desktop and plug into a USB connector on your computer. Four main types of NICs are on the market:

✔ **PC Card NICs:** These are probably the most common — because they're designed for mobile computers, and mobile computers are the most likely candidates for a wireless network. The PC Card is about the size of a thick credit card, with a small antenna module on the end, and fits into the PC Card slot of a laptop or handheld computer.

- ✔ **PCI Card NICs:** For desktop computers that don't have a PC Card, there are wireless LAN cards that fit into an internal PCI slot (the same slots used for many wired Ethernet NICs or for video cards). If you use a PCI Card NIC, you still need to have an external antenna (which will come in the package), so everything won't be all neat and hidden inside your PC.

- ✔ **USB external NIC:** A better alternative for desktop computers is an external NIC that connects through a USB port. Virtually every computer made since 1999 has USB ports, and the external NIC requires no real installation — just plug it in and load the software driver.

- ✔ **Built-in wireless NIC:** In the laptop and PDA world, built-in Wi-Fi NICs are increasingly common. There's nothing for you to do here — just turn on the computer and connect to the network. Because the NIC is built-in, you can keep your PC Card slots free for other peripherals.

Battening down the hatches

The biggest advantage of wireless networks — the fact that you can connect to the network just about anywhere in range of the base station (up to 300 feet) — is also the biggest disadvantage. Because the signal is carried over the air, on radio waves, anyone else within range can pick up your network's signals too. It's sort of like putting an extra RJ45 jack for your wired LAN out on the side-walk in front of your house — you're no longer in control of who can access it. So securing a wireless network takes a bit more work. To make matters worse, if you've spent any time reading computer industry publications, you may have heard about the weaknesses in wireless network security systems. The bottom line is this: If someone is dedicated and motivated enough, they can get onto your wireless LAN. The flip side of this coin, however, is that the chances of someone targeting your LAN and breaking in are slim. They need to be within a reasonable distance to be able to receive the radio signal, and then they need to have the skills, equipment, and interest to break in. Not too likely, we think.

That doesn't mean that you should leave your wireless LAN wide open for any and all comers — unless you want to (we talk about some reasons why people do this in the "Opening up to your neighbors" sidebar). You can take the following steps to secure a wireless LAN. Note that these steps vary from system to system, so we give only general instructions:

- ✔ **Turn on WEP:** WEP (Wired Equivalent Privacy) is the security system built into all Wi-Fi systems (other wireless LANs have similar systems). It *encrypts* all data flowing between the access points and computers on the network. This encryption basically uses a mathematical function to make the data flowing across the network look like a bunch of random numbers to someone who doesn't have authenticated access to the net-work. WEP also includes an encrypted password, which is required for users to log onto your network.

✔ **Hide your SSID:** All wireless access points broadcast a network name or Service Set Identifier — basically the name that you give your network when you set it up. When someone with a wireless-equipped computer comes in range of your network, the SSID identifies your network as being available. With many access points, however, you can set things up so that the SSID is not broadcast, and only people who know the name of the network will be able to find it.

✔ **Use a decent password:** This is probably the number one complaint we hear from IT folks running corporate networks. People use easy-to-remember passwords, because it's a pain remembering some obscure one. But if it's easy for you to remember, it's easy for someone else to guess. Use alphanumeric combinations (numbers and letters together).

✔ **Create a closed network:** Like wired Ethernet NICs, every wireless NIC has an alphanumeric ID called a MAC address. Most wireless LAN access points let you set up your network so that only MAC addresses to which you're granted permission (your own MAC addresses) can get on the network.

None of these security measures is perfect — WEP encryption can be decoded, SSIDs can be sniffed even when they're hidden, passwords can be guessed, and MAC addresses can be spoofed. But taken together, and in light of the relatively low threat to residential networks, they should do the job.

Opening up to your neighbors

We're not talking about group therapy or wild hot tub parties. Wireless networks can carry through walls, across yards, and potentially around the neighborhood. Although wireless LANs were designed from the start for in-building use, the technology can be used in outdoors settings. For example, most college campuses are now wired with dozens or hundreds of wireless access points so that students, staff, and professors can access the Internet from just about anywhere on campus. At UC San Diego, where Pat's wife works, freshmen are outfitted with wireless PDAs and can schedule classes, send e-mails and instant messages, and even find their friends at the student center (using a locator program written by a student). Many folks are adapting this concept and setting up community wireless LANs.

Some creators of these community LANs have taken the openness of the Internet to heart and have opened up their access points to any and all takers. There's even an Internet subculture with Web sites and chalk markings on sidewalks identifying these open access points. In other areas, where broadband access is scarce, neighbors pool money to buy a T1 or other business-class high-speed Internet line, and then share it wirelessly.

We think that both of these concepts make a lot of sense, but we do have a warning. Many ISPs don't like the idea of people sharing an Internet connection without paying (you may, for example, have to pay for a more expensive commercial ISP line). Before you do this, check your ISP's Terms of Service, or look at the listing of wireless-friendly ISPs on the Electronic Frontier Foundation's Web page (www.eff.org).

Many wireless access points ship with all these security settings turned off by default. If you want to be secure, turn them on.

Putting together a wireless LAN

Putting together a wireless LAN is simple, because you don't have to spend any time running new wires or punching down UTP cables. If your house isn't too big, just plug the access point into your broadband modem or into an Ethernet jack fed by your home router, and turn it on! You'll need to go through a few additional steps, such as naming your network (the SSID) and assigning passwords. Keep the following in mind:

✔ **Assigning IP addresses:** Every computer (or handheld or whatever) connected to your wireless network needs to have an IP address to talk on the Internet. The overall architecture of your network (all wireless, mixed wired and wireless, and so on) plays a big part in how you do this, as does the kind of access point you're using.

• If you have a broadband connection connected to a home router and LAN (as discussed in Chapter 15), you need to set up your access point to be a *bridge* connection. In this case, the router assigns an IP address to your wireless computers, and the access point just provides a connection between the wired and wireless networks (a bridge — get it?). You can plug your access point into any outlet in your wired network, set it to bridge mode, and start computing.

• If you're using a wireless access point incorporated into a router, the access point *is* your router. In this case, you will most likely set up the DHCP functionality of the router (we talk about this in Chapter 15), and use it to assign IP addresses to your wireless computers (as well as those attached to your wired LAN).

✔ **Finding a good spot:** Wireless LAN signals can travel through walls, doors and the like, but some things are not nice to wireless signals. Huge chunks of metal (think full-sized filing cabinets) or really dense walls (such as the 18-inch-thick brick walls in Danny's house in Maine) can kill the strength of a wireless signal — which either keeps you from connecting or lowers your speed if you do get connected. Most access points include software that displays how much signal strength you're getting and provides tips for placement of the base station. Access points vary a bit model to model, because they have different antenna systems and the like. We recommend that you place your access point somewhere in the middle of the main floor of the house (or the floor on which you'll be most often using the wireless network), in a high location (Pat has placed his high up on top of a pair of speakers in his home office, after much trial and error). Keep the access point away from potentially inter-fering devices (such as microwaves, power outlets, TVs and stereos — Pat's speakers are shielded, and don't interfere).

After trying different locations, you might find that you just can't get by with a single access point. For example, Danny couldn't get a signal upstairs. This situation can be easily resolved if you have a wired net-work infrastructure; just get a second (inexpensive) access point and plug it in on a different floor or on the other side of the house. If you don't have a wired infrastructure, you may want to try connecting a remote access point using a phoneline or powerline technology (dis-cussed later). This works great if you want an access point outside on the porch or covered patio.

✔ **Securing the network:** We recommend that you plug in the network and find a spot for your access point *before* you turn on all the security fea-tures. This is exactly why most access points ship with security turned off by default — what you might think is a defective access point or an impenetrable wall is just a mistyped password. So begin with security features turned off, get the network working and the computers talking to each other and to the Internet, and then go back and turn on WEP and do the rest of the security stuff we mentioned.

We put together two diagrams of a wireless network. Figure 16-1 shows a wireless network added to a wired LAN infrastructure, and Figure 16-2 shows a wireless-only network.

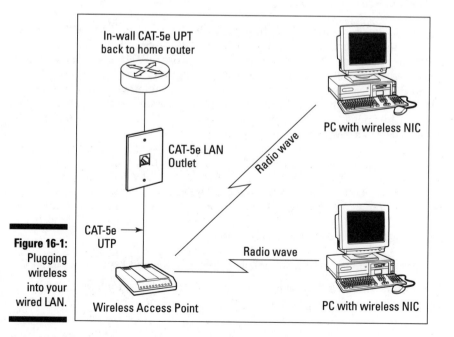

In-wall CAT-5e UPT back to home router

CAT-5e LAN Outlet

Radio wave

PC with wireless NIC

CAT-5e → UTP

Radio wave

PC with wireless NIC

Wireless Access Point

Figure 16-1: Plugging wireless into your wired LAN.

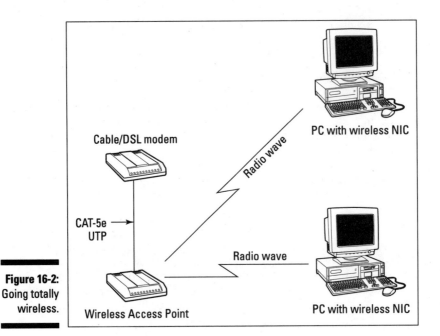

Cable/DSL modem

Radio wave

PC with wireless NIC

CAT-5e →
UTP

Radio wave

Figure 16-2:
Going totally
wireless.

Wireless Access Point

PC with wireless NIC

But wait — there's more to wireless networks

The technologies we've talked about so far in this chapter have been wireless LAN technologies. There are some complementary wireless technologies known as wireless PANs, or Personal Area Networks. PANs, the most prominent of which is called Bluetooth, are shorter in range and typically lower in speed than LANs (which, in turn, have a shorter range than WANs, or Wide Area Networks, such as the Internet). A LAN is designed to cover an entire home or business (or at least most of one), but a PAN is designed to connect devices within a few feet or yards of each other.

Most PANs are covered under the 802.15 standard. The initial version, 802.15.1, was adapted from the Bluetooth specification and is fully compatible with Bluetooth 1.1. Other short-range, in-home wireless standards that focus on very short-range mesh networks to interconnect home devices are on the way.

Following are some uses for PAN technologies:

✔ Connecting peripherals (such as printers, mice and keyboards) to a PC
✔ Connecting handheld computers and PDAs to a desktop computer for syncing and file transfer

✔ Connecting PDAs and mobile phones together, to share Internet connections or contact lists

✔ Connecting voice-enabled PDAs or mobile phones to wireless headsets or to hands-free systems in cars

The bottom-line distinction between LANs and PANs (which tends to get blurry) is this: If something connects to a computer by a network cable today, its wireless connection is a LAN; if it connects by a local cable (such as USB), its wireless connection is a PAN.

As mentioned, by far the most common PAN technology is Bluetooth. This isn't what you get when you eat too many blueberries or blue-dyed Popsicles. Instead, Bluetooth is a wireless PAN technology developed by big mobile communications companies (including Nokia and Ericsson) to expand what their mobile devices could do and to make their devices easier to use. Today, Bluetooth is controlled by an industry consortium called the Bluetooth SIG (Special Interests Group) at `www.bluetooth.com`, which also includes companies such as Microsoft and Intel.

You're going to ask, so we'll tell you: Bluetooth is named after Harald Blåtand ("Bluetooth"), King of Denmark from 940 to 981, who was responsible for uniting Denmark and Norway.

Bluetooth uses the same 2.4-GHz radio spectrum that Wi-Fi LANs use (though most tests have shown that they don't interfere with each other too much) and is designed to be a low-power (good for battery-powered devices) and low-cost (good for everyone) alternative to a LAN. Bluetooth radios are embedded in cell phones, PDAs, and laptop computers, as well as a range of peripheral devices such as headsets and keyboards. Bluetooth has been around since the late 1990s and has taken off a lot more slowly than everyone (including us) anticipated, but it finally seems to be gaining some mass-market adoption.

Making the Most of Your Phone Lines

Another alternative to using CAT-5e Ethernet cabling or wireless LANs is to leverage your home's existing telephone wiring to carry Ethernet data. *Phoneline networking* (the term for this networking technique) is a relatively mature technology — the first systems were shipped in the mid-1990s. An industry group called HomePNA or sometimes HPNA (Home Phoneline Networking Association — `www.homepna.org`) provides standards and product certification. As of 2002, there were two variants of HomePNA networking systems:

✔ **HPNA 1.0:** This is a slower speed protocol (1.3 Mbps), and is used in few products today.

✔ **HPNA 2.0:** This is a faster protocol (advertised as 10 Mbps, though the maximum speed is actually 16 Mbps), which is used in just about every HomePNA product on the market. HPNA 2.0 is backwards compatible with HPNA 1.0, so newer products can talk to older ones. The bad news about this backwards compatibility is that having even one HPNA 1.0 device connected to your phone lines slows *all* the HPNA 2.0 devices down to 1.3 Mbps.

As we write, the HomePNA group has announced a forthcoming 3.0 version of the standard that will allow much higher speeds. They're still working out the details, but the goal is to reach speeds of up to 128 Mbps initially, with later versions reaching 240 Mbps — enough speed to carry even high-definition video signals. This new version will also have improved backwards compatibility, so that HPNA 3.0 devices (when they show up) will not be slowed down just because older HPNA endpoints are connected to the phone lines.

HomePNA products are available in several different variants, including the following:

✔ **HomePNA chipsets:** Installed in peripheral or entertainment devices (such as Internet-enabled stereos) right from the factory. These chipsets can be installed also in home routers or even broadband modems. It was once not uncommon to find HomePNA chipsets built into laptop and desktop PCs, but these have largely been phased out in favor of Wi-Fi or Ethernet connectors.

✔ **HomePNA Network Interface Cards (NICs):** Internal NICs are available in both PC Card and PCI Card forms, to fit into laptop and desktop computers, respectively.

✔ **HomePNA Ethernet and USB adapters:** HomePNA NICs are available also in external devices that connect to a computer's Ethernet or USB ports using a cable.

The HomePNA system operates on different frequencies than analog or DSL telephone services, so you can simultaneously use a single phone line for your computer LAN and for all the other things you currently use it for — such as making phone calls, sending and receiving faxes, or connecting to the Internet.

To connect your HomePNA endpoints (the computers or audio systems or other devices using HomePNA in your home) back onto your Internet connection, you need to connect the HomePNA network through your router to your Internet connection. The good news here is that HomePNA is built in to many home routers (such as those from NetGear, Linksys, and 2Wire), so if you think you might want to use HomePNA, choose your router accordingly.

Like wireless LANs and the powerline networking systems we are about to discuss, we think that HomePNA systems fit best as an adjunct to wired Ethernet LANs. You can always go faster for cheaper with a wired network if you put the cables in the walls when you're building the house.

HomePNA is the biggest game in town when it comes to phoneline network-ing, but it's not the only one. A company based in Israel called SerCoNet (www.serconet.co.il) has developed its own phoneline networking tech-nology that can reach speeds of up to 100 Mbps over standard phone wiring. The really neat thing about SerCoNet's solution (besides the speed, which always makes us happy) is that the technology is built right into replacement faceplates for your existing phone jacks. A technician replaces all your phone jacks with SerCoNet jacks, and your phone wiring is converted to a 100-Mbps data backbone.

This solution is especially cool because it crosses into the wireless world — SerCoNet has a faceplate with an integral Wi-Fi access point, so you can use your laptops and PDAs untethered. In a bigger house, where a single access point might not cover everything, this is a great solution for adding an access point any place that's hard to reach from a central location.

Powering Your Network

Using electrical power lines for something more than sending juice to your appliances is not a new concept. If you read Chapter 19, for example, you know all about X10 — a home-automation protocol that uses electrical wires to send control signals to lights, appliances, and more. For decades, people have been using X10 and other low-speed powerline networking systems, but attempts to use power lines for high-speed networking have largely failed. In 2002, a bunch of networking companies (including Linksys, NetGear, and D-Link) began releasing high-speed powerline networking products based on a system known as HomePlug.

To set up a LAN in your home under the HomePlug specification, you use a HomePlug-supporting device that runs an Ethernet cable to your computer and an electrical cord to the electrical outlet. That electrical cord *is* your LAN connection — along with all the rest of the electrical cabling in your house. Cool, huh?

Like the HomePNA group, HomePlug is an industry consortium designed to develop standards and promote products using HomePlug technology. Development of the HomePlug standard took several years, mainly because networking on power lines is a technically challenging task. Power lines are noisy, electrically speaking, with surges in voltage level and electrical inter-ferences introduced by all sorts of devices both within and external to the home. The state of the electrical network in a home is constantly changing as well, as devices are plugged in and turned on. Because of this, the HomePlug standard adopts a sophisticated and adaptive *signal processing algorithm* — the technique used to convert data into electrical signals on the power wiring. Because HomePlug uses higher frequency signals than low-speed powerline communications systems such as X10, the technology can avoid some of the most common sources of noise on the power line.

The result is a system that can provide up to 14-Mbps networking over the power line — faster than Wi-Fi or HomePNA, but slower than Wi-Fi5 and some of the Ethernet variants discussed in Chapter 15. Besides the speed, there are a few other neat things to consider about HomePlug-based networking systems:

✔ Power outlets are the most common and ubiquitous jacks in the home. Even if you heavily wire your home with CAT-5e cabling for an Ethernet network, chances are you won't have more than two LAN jacks in the majority of rooms in your house. With HomePlug, every one of the dozens or even hundreds of power outlets in the house becomes a data-networking jack.

✔ HomePlug can be built right into many networked appliances. The almost legendary Internet refrigerator that we've discussed in several places in this book is a cool concept, but even we don't have a CAT-5e outlet in the dark nook behind our fridges. We do have a power jack, and so do you.

✔ HomePlug automatically crosses phases in your electrical system (the majority of homes have two-phase electrical power). As we discuss in Chapter 21, systems such as X10 may require a bridge device installed in the main electrical panel so that different parts of your electrical system can see each other, and so that signals can reach all parts of your home. Because of the higher frequencies that HomePlug uses, it can cross these phases without a bridging device.

✔ HomePlug can reach beyond the limits of your home (and at lower signal levels) right into your neighbor's house. Although the signal levels are attenuated at longer distances, you could use HomePlug to create a community network with your neighbors, like the ones we describe in the "Opening up to your neighbors" sidebar. This works as long as you share the same power transformer with your neighbors as well as your encryption key, so it might not be the best thing to do.

✔ HomePlug has a built-in encryption system. Because it can reach beyond your house, and because you may not want to share your LAN with your neighbors, you can turn on HomePlug's encryption. In that way, only devices that have your password can be on the network.

Like the wireless systems we described previously, most HomePlug systems come with encryption turned off by default. We recommend that you get your network up and running first, and turn on encryption after you've proven to yourself that your network is working.

✔ HomePlug is compatible with other powerline communications systems. Because it operates on such high frequencies, HomePlug doesn't interfere with X10 and other low-speed powerline systems, so you can use your LAN and your home-automation system at the same time.

HomePlug products are available in a variety of devices — you can buy HomePlug routers and switches (which often include wired Ethernet ports as well). As we write this, there aren't any HomePlug NICs. Instead, the most common application for HomePlug is Ethernet or USB bridges. These devices look and act a lot like the external USB Wi-Fi NICs we discussed earlier. You'll need two of them, one to connect to an Ethernet port on your router (or any LAN jack in your home), and another to plug into the wall outlet where you need LAN access.

The bridge typically has a power cord on one side of the box and an Ethernet or USB connector on the other. Plug the power cord into any wall outlet, and plug the Ethernet or USB into the computer or other networked devices, and you have a connection. Pat has been using a NetGear Powerline Ethernet bridge like this for a spot in his house that has neither Ethernet nor good wireless coverage — and he loves it. Danny has a NetGear bridge connecting his office (where the cable modem is) to the kids computing area (where all the screaming is). Figure 16-3 shows a typical use of HomePlug bridges.

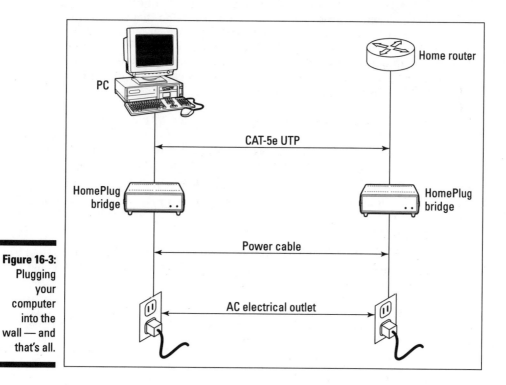

Figure 16-3:
Plugging your computer into the wall — and that's all.

We think powerline networking through HomePlug is great, but we probably would never use it to replace our wired networks or even our wireless LANs. But HomePlug is quick, cheap (bridges cost about $120 a piece, with prices dropping rapidly), and perfect for those spots that you never thought you'd need to wire.

We hinted at this already, but let's just come right out and say it. We think HomePlug will have a huge effect in the non-computer market — stereos, TVs, gaming machines, Internet fridges, and other pieces of electronic equipment that might benefit from an Internet connection. And as HomePlug becomes incorporated into new generations of appliances, you'll need just the power cord to make it work.

Mixing and Matching

Although many vendors will try to push you into one solution ("You need Wi-Fi," "No, you need HomePlug"), you might find that these various no-new-wires networks can complement each other. You know that we think a wired CAT-5e network should be the basis of your computer-LAN infrastructure (and phone network, and maybe even your audio and video network), but we think also that all four of these technologies can be used in concert when you build a whole-home network.

Just for fun, here are a few examples:

- Build a wired Ethernet LAN, but plug a Wi-Fi access point in your living room for cordless sofa-based Web surfing.
- Use Wi-Fi as the basis for your home-computer LAN, but use HomePlug or HomePNA (or SerCoNet) to extend your network to access points in distant locations out of reach of your primary base station (such as by the pool).
- Use wired Ethernet for your computers, but use a HomePlug system to connect your Xbox to the broadband Internet connection for online gaming.

We could keep this list going and going, but we think you get the picture. Think creatively, and use wired and unwired technologies together to get your LAN wherever you need it to go.

Part V
Keeping the Bad Guys at Bay

The 5th Wave By Rich Tennant

"This is amazing. You can stop looking for Derek. According to an MSN search I did, he's hiding behind the dryer in the basement."

In this part . . .

Most people are familiar with some of the core concepts of home security and safety. Smoke detectors,
fire extinguishers, and shrieking alarms tend to come to
mind, but a smart-home security system is much, much
more. In this part, we talk about how to protect and prevent. We introduce you to a home-security infrastructure
that goes beyond just setting off an alarm when someone
opens a door. We tell you about sensors galore that not
only run your home-security subsystem but also lay a
foundation for later use in your home-automation environment. We also tell you about how some security services
can utilize a broadband Internet service to make your
home-monitoring system more interactive.

Chapter 17

Home Security Boot Camp

In This Chapter

▶ Determining whether or not you need a security system

▶ Finding out about the basic components of a security system

▶ Watching the world from a camera lens

▶ Putting the security system in place

*E*ven though you have to plan for all sorts of scary disasters — robbery, fire, carbon-dioxide poisoning, floods, and so on — you don't need to be afraid of your alarm system. You may find that your alarm system is one of the more fun systems to plan because you can do so much with sensors and control panels. For example, you can configure an alarm system to detect when someone is standing on your front door mat and have it turn on a light or even call you at work and let you know you have a visitor.

An alarm system should fit your style and tastes. The system design should work around your daily schedule, your kids and pets (if you have any), and the overall way you live your life. For instance, the design should take into consideration whether you have valuable possessions in your home — a stash of jewelry, mattress money, gold, silver, baseball cards, or a wine cellar. The system can also contain a medical alert capability if you're elderly or a pool alarm if young people live in the house. A smart-home alarm system simply reflects you.

Security systems entail a great deal of planning to make sure that you literally cover every angle. Just one glaring hole in your system makes you vulnerable. Still, the security component of your home network is probably one of the easiest to understand and plan because it's familiar and intuitive. And, because you'll likely have someone else wire your security system, you have to only think about where all those sensors need to be.

In this chapter, we show you how to batten down the hatches on security. Specifically, we describe what security systems can do for you and how they work. We also talk about the components that make up a security system and how they sense conditions that might be cause for alarm.

Deciding That You Need a Security System

People install security systems for three main reasons:

- ✔ To protect their home when they aren't around
- ✔ To protect their home when they are around
- ✔ A combination of the two — in other words, to protect both their home and its occupants (different sensors and sensor arrangements are necessary to protect your home and to protect occupants, and many people want both)

Protecting your house when you're not home typically serves as a baseline goal. If this goal is your only concern, you can take the minimalist approach — apply contact sensors on the doors, install a few passive infrared scanners on the interior of the house, and throw in a siren and control panel.

To protect your house when you are at home requires a more intense approach. Beyond what we just described, you have more to cover, especially the windows on the basement and first-floor levels. Security experts have determined that nearly 90 percent of break-ins involve a door. That is to say, 90 percent of the time, the burglar either enters or leaves the house using a door. When all you want to do is determine that a break-in has occurred, a simple perimeter defense like we just described is considered adequate. If you want a more thorough system that can detect the presence of an intruder and immediately sound an alarm, you need additional sensors.

Cut your insurance rates

With fire and burglar alarms in your home, you're much less likely to be robbed or to lose a significant amount to fire damage. Consequently, insurance companies will give you a break on your payments if you have alarms in your home. If you pay a third party to centrally monitor these alarms, your rates are even lower. Call your insurance company — you may find that you can finance your security subsystem on your insurance premium savings. And check for additional protection from your security company in case of a loss. For instance, BellSouth's Safety Program, with Protection One (www.bellsouth.com/security/), will reimburse up to $1000 of your paid homeowner's insurance deductible.

You may want to consider glass-breakage detectors along with contacts (the contacts only detect if a window has been opened, while the glass-breakage detectors can tell if someone smashes a window). If you don't want to see the devices for cosmetic reasons, you can install *stress detectors* — which are mounted to support beams under the floor and can register an individual's weight and activate the alarm — which you often find in historic homes. You can also add other sensors as we discuss in the "You fill up my sensors" section.

Security Basics

Before you head out shopping for a security system, you should know what these systems are designed to do. A smart home's security system has at least three goals:

- ✔ **Detection:** Your system should be capable of sounding an alarm when something triggers a sensor (though you may choose *not* to sound an alarm for certain types of events).

- ✔ **Emergency response:** Your system should be able to call for appropriate help, depending on the circumstances.

- ✔ **Prevention:** Your system should help prevent problems — such as scaring away potential intruders by automatically turning on outside lights at night. Well-built doors, windows, and quality locks help determine whether a criminal attempts to break into a home — alarm or not. Bringing prevention into the equation means connecting your security system with your home-automation system (see Part VI).

Your alarm system accomplishes its goals in three steps:

- ✔ **Input:** The system can't act if it isn't aware of a problem. The sensors in your system alert your security subsystem when something deserves attention.

- ✔ **Processing:** Something has to interpret these inputs to determine whether the system needs to do something. Your security system is constantly analyzing real-time inputs from all its tethered sensors, monitoring the status of your home's health.

- ✔ **Output:** After your subsystem decides what to do, it reaches out and runs through its preprogrammed checklist of to-do items. Sirens, flashing lights, silent alarms, and more are possible with a smart system.

Although every manufacturer has variations on the pieces and parts that make up a security system, your system should include at least the following basics:

- A control panel
- A keypad and corresponding key
- Basic sensors, such as an inside motion detector, door and window contact sensors, glass-breakage detectors, and a smoke alarm
- A siren or flashing strobe light

You should also link the system to a central monitoring station (a security company, in other words) for around-the-clock coverage.

Getting control of your security panel

You usually find the control panel — your security system's brain — in your home's wiring closet. This room also houses your telephone and home-automation subsystems. The control panel is basically an electronic box that serves as the core interconnection point for all the wiring (and wirelessing) in your subsystem. A sophisticated control panel has outputs that allow you to interface with X10 home-automation systems (which we talk about in more detail in Chapters 19 and 20) to control lights, for instance, and with RS-232 serial ports for more proprietary and custom-programmed automation systems. The control panel also has ports for interfacing with telephone systems. In addition, the control panel has an internal battery for battery backup in case of a power failure.

Control pads range in size — some are the size of a telephone keypad, and others utilize several separate boxes mounted out of sight. In small systems that require only one keypad (perhaps for a small apartment), the keypad and control panel are often integrated into one unit.

Don't panic — use your keypad!

You can use different systems to activate and deactivate your security system. The most common interfaces for residential applications are *keypads,* which resemble telephone keypads, and *key switches,* which take a physical key. The majority of new installations use keypads because they offer a lot of flexibility.

Most people use a four- to five-digit code to activate and deactivate their alarm system and to gain entry for maintenance. Different systems record this activity in different ways. Higher-end systems track which codes are entered at which times; lower-end ones merely record that the system was activated or deactivated on a particular date and time.

Are you the keymaster?

Security arming and disarming is getting more sophisticated. ADT's Safewatch EZ system (www.adt.com) dispenses with the need to remember passcodes by arming and disarming with the turn of a deadbolt lock. You unlock the door, the alarm goes off — as simple as that. ADT has even bundled a motion detector and sounder (which beeps inside the house to alert you of alarm conditions) into the keypad, making this package an ideal entry-level system that still allows multiple-zone coverage for people who have difficulty remembering numeric codes. Just don't lose your keys!

You can also program your system directly from the keypad. A quick glance at the keypad's status display immediately tells you whether your system is armed, ready-to-arm, and so on (for example, if you've disabled sensors in a certain zone). You can change your system pass codes at any time, giving additional users temporary entrance. For instance, you can give out-of-town guests temporary codes that automatically erase when you return.

If something triggers one of the sensors, the system has many options, including sounding the alarm, notifying remote monitoring services, paging you, or calling you on the phone and alerting you to the problem. The most common quickly activate an audible panic alarm, fire alarm, or medical emergency alarm.

Some alarm systems have a module that turns any Touch-Tone phone into a fully functional keypad. This saves you money because you don't have to distribute wired keypads all over the house. And if you're on vacation, you can check the status of your system for greater peace of mind. You can also dial in and activate the system if you forgot to turn it on when you left.

You fill up my sensors

You can use all sorts of sensors and detectors to drive your security system. And although some security-system purists try to make a strong technical differentiation between sensors and detectors, everyone that we know uses the terms interchangeably.

Sensors are the central part of your security architecture because your security subsystem operates solely on the inputs of the sensors — it can't act on something that it can't sense. You can surmise what most detectors do, so we won't take up your time detailing how each one works. Later in this section, however, we cover the main sensors you're likely to encounter in a base system — contact sensors, passive infrared sensors, and smoke detectors.

You can use the following sensors in your smart home:

- **Break sensors:** Mounted near windows to detect the specific high-frequency sounds of glass being shattered

- **Carbon monoxide detectors:** Used inside a home to detect hazardous levels of CO gas

- **Contact sensors:** Mounted in doors and windows to detect when doors and windows are opened or closed

- **Flood sensors:** Mounted in basements or other flood-prone spaces, often used to trigger sump pumps

- **Freeze sensors:** Mounted outside to detect freezing temperatures for plant protection

- **Gas detectors:** Detects the presence of gas fumes

- **Heat detectors:** Part of a smoke- and fire-alarm system, detects high temperatures

- **Ionization detectors:** The actual smoke detector in a smoke detector

- **Magnetic sensors:** A kind of contact sensor, determines when a door or window is opened

- **Moisture sensors:** Mounted indoors to determine humidity, often used to trigger air-conditioning or dehumidifier systems

- **Motion sensors:** Mounted in halls and stairways to detect the movement of unwanted intruders

- **Photoelectric sensors:** Shines a beam of light across a hall or doorway to detect motion (activates when a person walking by interrupts the beam)

- **Plunger switches:** Another kind of contact sensor that uses a small plunger (that looks like a refrigerator or car-door light switch) to determine when a door or window is opened

- **Power status sensors:** Detects power outages and then possibly starts a generator

- **Pressure sensors:** Often mounted in doormats or under driveways to detect weight

- **Rain sensors:** Mounted out of doors to trigger or cancel sprinkler systems

- **Smoke detectors:** Used for fire protection, but *smoke detector* is a bit of a misnomer because most include heat detectors

- **Snow sensors:** Mounted outside to detect snow and then activate, for example, a heated driveway

- **Tamper switches:** Mounted in vulnerable areas of alarm systems to sound in case of tampering

- **Temperature sensors:** Unsurprisingly, used to detect temperature

- ✔ **Vibration sensors:** Mounted under floors or elsewhere in a home's structure, to detect people walking above

- ✔ **Water disturbance sensors:** Used in a swimming pool or hot tub to determine when someone or something has entered the water

- ✔ **Weather sensors:** Mounted outside to detect a number of weather conditions

Not only do these sensors drive your security system, but many can drive your home-automation capabilities as well. For instance, you can use the magnetic detector along your driveway to note that a car has pulled in and use an infrared motion detector to note when someone walks to the door.

DesignTech International Inc.'s (www.designtech-intl.com) Wireless Garage Sentry will tell you whether you left your garage door open or closed. (We call this the "Nothing is worth more when you just climbed into bed" device.) A mercury switch inside the sensor determines whether the garage door is up or down. When the door changes state, the sensor sends a radio signal to the receiver to update the position change. A green light glows on the receiver when the door is closed. When open, a red light on the receiver flashes. For added assurance, the receiver audibly beeps each time the garage door is opened or closed. One receiver can monitor up to four doors. Stick that puppy by your bed and just say, "Yes dear." Pat wishes that he'd had this installed a few months ago, when one of San Diego's finest banged on his door at midnight to tell him that he'd left his garage door open. (Thanks officer!)

Contact sensors

Some 90 percent of all break-ins involve outside doors — whether going in or going out. So only 10 percent of the time will someone come in and leave through windows. Clearly, protection for your doors is probably the single most important element of security-system planning.

Magnetic switches are one of the most popular ways to protect doors. You put a magnet on the edge of the door itself and then, with the door closed, place a switch across from it in the doorjamb. When you open the door, the magnet loses contact with the switch, causing it to change electric states. The control panel recognizes this change and triggers an alarm or other course of action.

Passive infrared receivers

Passive infrared receivers (PIRs) are another popular security-system item. These devices see heat in the infrared spectrum. A series of lenses on the receiver's cover guide a PIR's vision (which is fixed in one direction). PIR technology has been refined to the extent that false alarms are minimal.

You can get different coverage areas by using different lenses on the front of the PIR. A good security team can further aim or restrict this vision by placing opaque tape over portions of the lens to reduce the opportunity for false alarms from roving dogs and other unintended motion.

Prepare to repel boarders!

Security systems work great on burglars — but did you know that they can protect your tomatoes too? A smart security system can help you with unwanted animals in your yard day or night. How about a motion-detector-based animal repeller that keeps wildlife and neighbors' pets out of your garden by spraying them with water? One model, the Scarecrow Water Spraying Animal Repeller by Contech Electronics Inc. (http://www.scatmat.com/), has a range of up to 35 feet with a spray head adjustable from 10 to 360 degrees.

PIRs are relatively cheap and small (about the size of a light switch), can mount on a wall or ceiling inconspicuously, and go a long way toward protecting your home. The idea with PIRs is to guard your most sensitive areas, while attempting to catch a criminal early in an intrusion. A PIR covering the stairway to the second floor is always a great plan — you don't want the bad guys to get upstairs. Hallways leading to family rooms where electronics and saleable items are kept make sense, too.

Many PIRs offer different zones in the sensor's vision so that you can create events based on the sequence in which the sensor's zones are tripped. One of the neat things about sensors is that you can team them together for unique applications. Because software drives and enables sensors, you can attach additional detectors, such as active IR beams or magnetic contacts, to trip only in special combination circumstances.

For instance, with certain manufacturers' sensors, such as Optex America's VX-40A (www.optexamerica.com), you can wire two PIR detectors together and use different software modes to do different things:

- Set a mode that lets the two PIRs work together to double the size of your detection area
- Set your PIRs to activate alarms directionally — so they trip an alarm if they detect a person walking in a certain direction in your home
- Select a sequential mode to generate an alarm only if two detectors activate sequentially and separately

You can combine the VX-40A is with a voice warning feature. When the system is armed, the voice-warning feature (a weatherproof speaker lives inside the sensor) delivers one of two types of voice messages to anyone entering the protected area. This warning is designed to deter a would-be intruder from continuing toward the protected area.

One security idea that many homeowners can use for security and notification is a wireless enunciator system. The wireless Voice Alert system from Cross

Point Industries (www.voicealert.com) alerts you with a custom voice message based on PIRs. You record your own alert messages. And it has extensive reach — up to 1000 feet in open space and up to 300 feet through walls. For high traffic areas, it has a sleep mode that will wait three minutes before waking up and triggering again, so all your guests arriving at a party don't hear, "Hey, thanks for coming!" over and over. The sensor/transmitters can be used indoors and outside and can notify you of just about anything. "Alert, Pat's in the cookie jar!"

We talk a fair amount about X10 Wireless Technology, Inc. (www.X10.com) products in this section for one reason — they make a lot of reasonably priced, practical products that we would use in our own homes. Danny's favorite is the FloodCam (www.X10.com), which combines the best of wireless surveillance and motion-activation technology in one easy-to-install dual floodlight. The video camera is a weather-resistant, wireless, color video camera with built-in 2.4-GHz transmitter. The floodlight has a motion detector mounted between the floodlights. The camera turns on when motion is detected, and the floodlights turn on when it's dark and motion is detected. When combined with X10's VCR Commander II, which connects to your VCR, you can automatically turn your VCR on and off based on motion detection — thereby recording what your camera views.

Smoke detectors

Battery-powered smoke detectors (you know, the little jobbies that you stick to the wall or ceiling) help you get clear in an emergency, but they don't do much to protect your home when you're not around. Neither a control panel nor a central station can monitor these detectors. If no one is around when the alarm goes off, the alarm beeps, buzzes, and whirs until, well, it melts. You need to ensure that your security system monitors for fire and automatically calls for help when necessary.

These smoke detectors are hardwired back to the alarm control panel and typically offer several levels of protection — a temperature sensor that sounds the alarm at a preset temperature, a temperature sensor that measures the rate of rise of a room's temperature and sounds the alarm when it meets its preset minimum, and an ionization detector that "smells" smoke and sounds the alarm.

In some parts of the country, these detectors may not meet your local fire regulations for hardwired smoke detectors because the security control panel itself (which powers the detector) may not be hardwired, but may instead be attached to a transformer.

Tying in to home automation

One of the great things about these security devices is that they're multi-use. A sensor just senses something — how the system acts on a trigger event is a different issue. If you tie these sensors into a home controller, you can set different states for these sensors. For instance, if someone trips an infrared beam across your lawn while you're working at home, you may see a display video on a monitor in your office. If the same trigger occurs when you're away on vacation, the system may instead phone your alarm-monitoring station.

As you think about automating your home, be careful when replacing non-automated devices with automated ones, because the results will not always be to your liking. If you don't like the effect of an X10 adapter, for example, because you can simply unplug it. Other devices, however, might require that you have to climb a ladder or call the electrician or plumber. For example, people often leave floodlights on when guests are arriving. If you replace these with motion-sensitive floodlights, you might need to make other adjustments, such as adding sensors to your driveway to turn lights on when people arrive. Think twice about why your device works that way at the start, and how it would work differently after being adjusted.

Sirens

You should complement your alarm system with visible and audible outputs, such as external sirens and flashing strobe lights. Your alarm system will probably allow different tones for different situations, such as an intermittent tone for fire but a steady tone for burglary.

Position your visible alarms in as high and as obvious a place as possible so that people coming to your aid can easily locate the beacon. Firefighters, police, and so on all look for these visible alarms first as they speed to your rescue. Remember, their siren is likely going off, too, so being an obvious target can work to your advantage.

Monitoring

You have to make the key decision of whether or not to have a central monitoring station monitor your alarm. Because this option offers the bonus of professional security response, we highly recommend that you choose it. For a minor cost of $20 to $25 or so per month, you can give yourself peace of mind — and possibly save your life.

Most of the 12,000 plus alarm companies in the U.S. don't have their own central monitoring station. Rather, they bundle someone else's monitoring service — businesses that do nothing else but monitor systems for alarm companies — with their own installation and maintenance service. Your control system calls out to this monitoring station when an emergency or other problem situation arises; the central station interprets the information coming from your alarm system and calls the appropriate parties.

Gathering Your 007 Security Equipment

Your security system can get quite extensive, depending on what you choose to place under the master control panel's domain. You can program your system to respond automatically or manually to almost any type of sensor or input device. One popular application for security systems — in fact, an area of considerable growth within the industry itself — is in video surveillance.

In Chapters 6 and 7, we talk about distributing video throughout the home by using modulators to send video from one room to every TV in the house. You are effectively doing the same thing here. You can buy security and safety products that transmit video signals so that you can see front, side, and back doors, garages, driveways, pool areas, play areas, valuables, babysitters, cleaners, and other people helping in sensitive areas of your home.

In fact, you can record video signals to VHS tape to review at your leisure. Have you hired a new nanny? Want to see if your cleaning person is really cleaning all day long, or just eating your food? This technology lets you see what's happening at home — whether you're inside your home or 500 miles away.

Video surveillance

Many alarm, intercom, and telephone systems have an extension capability that includes video distribution for monitoring applications, such as checking out who's at the front door or how the baby is doing in the nursery. This area is one where the lines between security, telephones, and intercom subsystems blur because any of them can provide video distribution throughout your smart home. It's also an area where you can find solutions ranging from really cheap to really expensive — those guys in Las Vegas don't use X10 to monitor the craps tables, you know.

It's important to note the difference between surveillance and security. *Surveillance* products tend to require some sort of active involvement on your part. You have to watch something or take part in something for it to have a full effect. *Security* tends to be more passive — it does the watching for you. However, not all vendors adhere to this distinction.

You'll want to consider two forms of video surveillance: still image and live picture. Although you may love to have live, detailed, color pictures as part of your video surveillance system, you have to determine whether the feature is worth the cost. A number of inexpensive systems that are either black and white or still image may do the trick, and they're easier on your budget. As you go up to color and faster frame refresh rates, the cost of the product increases substantially.

Video surveillance products have seen a lot of development in recent years. Prices have dropped for off-the-shelf consumer solutions, and more robust professional grade cameras (for consumer applications) have likewise become much cheaper. Most consumer-oriented imaging products for surveillance are stand-alone, closed-circuit style cameras, or they're tethered to a local PC. Some of the newer products have networked cameras, which means they connect directly to a network without a host PC. This is the way to go if you can afford it because you can place these cameras just about anywhere, and you don't need to have a PC running for them to work.

The size of today's cameras and how secretive their locations can be is amazing. Securityandmore.com carries a line of hidden cameras that look like thermostats, tissue boxes, radios, books, PIRs, and even fake plants. These devices pick up video as well as audio signals from their field of view. And at a few hundred dollars per camera, they're not that expensive an add-on to your system.

CCTV options

You used to see closed-circuit television (CCTV) only in movies and convenience stores. This technology is ideal for surveillance — you can monitor and record CCTV to stop theft, limit liability exposure, maximize productivity, and protect yourself from safety incidents. You can get CCTV products at a range of prices and functionality. They start out at the low-end, black-and-white, low-frame rate models and move up to color, multi-camera, high-frame rate models.

X10 Wireless Technology, Inc. (www.x10.com) has a huge range of cameras that offer a great entry point for someone wanting to put almost any type of camera in their home, with the capability to link these cameras to a VCR, TV, or PC. Its Ninja Robotic Pan 'n Tilt mount can hold any X10 wireless camera; you can use the controller to easily move your XCam2 Camera from left to right 180 degrees and up and down 70 degrees. With its Ultra Sweep & Scan feature, you can put your camera on autopilot to sweep between four preset locations automatically. And with the PanTilt PRO Software, you can log on from the Internet and scan, pan, and switch your various cameras around the house — all visible through your browser. With the XRay Vision software and a USB converter, you can view live color video from your XCam2 cameras on your PC. And you can use a remote PC, such as your office PC, to check on your home through the Internet. XRay Vision can e-mail fresh images to you (or update a Web site) at timely intervals (10 seconds to 2 hours) — so you don't need the software loaded on your office (remote) PC. X10 offers free storage of images on its servers for X10 customers, so you don't have to have your own Web server. Note that XRay Vision works with X10's wired and wireless cameras, so unlike PC-based Webcams, you can monitor any room within 100 feet of your computer! Typical Webcams require a cable connected to your PC, so you can monitor only the room with the PC! (More below on PC Webcams.) CCTV systems can get quite sophisticated. Continental Instruments, a division of Napco Security (www.napcosecurity.com), has SmartVideo product, a complete turnkey PC digital surveillance and recording system that supports up to 16 cameras and can store thousands of quality pictures on an 80-GB hard drive — great for reviewing images from the past weeks or even months.

If running a coaxial cable for your video-camera signal distribution is out of the question, you can use a *video balun* (basically a cable converter) to convert the signals for transmission over CAT-5e cabling. You use two of the eight conductors in the telephone/data cabling for each signal. Surprisingly, line noise, cross talk, and attenuation are low, approaching the performance of shielded coaxial cable. You need one balun for each of the receiving and the sending devices.

PC options

Another option for viewing and storing video in a home-video surveillance network is to leverage your PC investment. You can do so in two ways:

- ✔ **Use special-purpose, PC video cameras that connect to the video capture card installed in your PC:** Most of these cameras are designed for other uses, such as videoconferencing, and can't get too far away from your PC (the average cord doesn't get much beyond 12 feet), but a few companies have wireless systems that will let you connect several cameras spread throughout your house. (See Chapter 12 for more info on these cameras.)

- ✔ **Install a TV card inside your PC and then connect your video surveillance cameras to your home's video network:** Using devices called modulators (see Chapter 7), you can put these cameras on unused television channels and watch them on your PC or any TV.

Network options

By far the best option — and one of the most expensive — is a network camera, which is a camera with the internal parts of the computer to give it a presence on a LAN or on the Internet. In other words, you don't need the camera enslaved to a PC for it to work. All you need is a regular Web browser to access the cameras to set up the parameters; all other required software, including control software and e-mail software (for automatic e-mailing of images) is inside the camera.

Like the other cameras, wireless and wired options are available. Panasonic has both in its Network Cameras product line (www.panasonic.com/consumer_electronics/gate/cameras.asp). Panasonic's cameras have built-in software to record data to a Web site using the FTP protocol (which you may be familiar with if you download or upload software on the Internet). You can use its subscription-based service at www.myeyecam.com to view your images from anywhere in the world. The myeyecam.com service basically creates a personal Web address for you. Or you can use the same FTP interface to record to the hard drive of a local computer. The cameras can be mounted on walls, tripods, a desk stand, or even the ceiling.

The Panasonic software allows you to view images from up to four cameras at once, and each image is a link to the control Web page for that camera. These cameras transmit up to 15 frames per second of live motion video with resolution of up to 640 x 480 pixels. The Panasonic wireless models are compatible with standard 802.11b wireless devices, allowing the flexibility to install and operate the camera without running network wires. These products can range up to $1000 for each camera, but pricing will come down over time.

Audio surveillance

Audio surveillance hasn't taken off in most home-security installations, but it's pretty neat nonetheless. By adding a device called a *two-way audio module* into your alarm's central panel, you can send and receive audio to and from your alarm company's central monitoring station. Most two-way audio systems communicate through a microphone and speaker installed in the alarm keypad. After an alarm is triggered, the alarm system notifies the central station, and the two-way audio system automatically kicks in.

Using the same telephone line that connects you to the monitors, you can have hands-free conversations with the monitors, which could be very handy in the event of a medical emergency. (See the "I've fallen and I can't get up!" section in Chapter 3.) If you're not home, the monitoring station can record all the sounds that your uninvited visitors make while they're in your home — not that you'd probably want to listen to their take on your home-decorating skills.

Finding and Installing the Right Security System

Security systems are easily expandable, provided that you have the right foundation. To choose a security system, look at both hardwired and wireless systems and determine how these systems will interface with your other smart-home subsystems, such as home automation.

Hardwired systems

We've heard one company compare wiring a wireline security system with wiring a train set. If you can do one, you can do the other. (If you don't have a train set, buy one, install it, see if it's hard, and then come back to reading this book.)

Wireline systems are

✓ **Reliable:** There are no batteries to worry about; wires are hidden reliably in the walls. Control panels routinely have battery backup in case the power fails.

✔ **Sophisticated:** Because the alarm industry has its roots in wireline instal- lations, wireline systems are by far the more sophisticated systems. Most of the innovations have taken place with the wireline as a foundation.

✔ **Supervised:** Wireline systems are constantly in touch with their end- point devices, querying them to check their health and availability. Doing so ensures that your system is at peak efficiency at all times.

On the other hand, wireline systems are much more complicated to install and are permanent after you install them.

Wireless systems

Wireless systems are easier to install than the wireline systems, particularly if you're doing the work yourself after your house has been built.

Wireless systems are

✔ **Portable:** If you move, simply unplug the wireless system and take it with you to your next home. You can get monitoring services from anywhere in the U.S. All you need is electricity and a phone line.

✔ **Easy to use and install:** The only tool you need is a screwdriver. Some systems come in a nice tidy do-it-yourself package, such as Magnavox's Wireless Security System (www.securealert.com) or X10's Monitor Plus Wireless Security System (www.x10.com). These systems are shipped to you with simple instructions and 24-hour customer support (for all of those 2 a.m. installations!). Magnavox's system is around $300, and the X10 systems are around $100 — great deals!

✔ **Private:** No strangers come into your house, drill holes in your walls, or know your home's layout or system password.

Wireless systems require you to change batteries, so if you're the type who hates to change the batteries in your smoke detectors, you may want to opt for a wireline system.

You may hear people say that wireless systems are less reliable and more prone to false alarms. Years ago, wireless systems were inferior to wireline sys- tems (and lower-end wireless systems are still inferior to wireline systems), but manufacturers of wireline systems are feverishly bringing high-quality, reliable wireless interfaces to market today.

Wireless systems used to be totally unsupervised — meaning that the central control panel did not know whether the sensor batteries were running low or whether the sensors had some problem. Now, however, some of the more pro- fessional wireless systems have been outfitted with a supervision capability that makes them increasingly accepted as part of a wireline implementation.

More than 25 percent of all alarm systems installed professionally are hybrid wireline/wireless now. We give you more information on supervision issues in Chapter 18.

Getting someone to do the job

You have two options when installing a home-security system — do it yourself or hire a professional contractor to do it for you. Most do-it-yourself projects are wireless in nature. You can buy a range of sensors and control panels from home-improvement stores or electronics stores.

You can also choose a kit that offers everything in one box. Most of these kits come with a control box, an alarm siren, and various combinations of wireless contact and keychain remote controls. One such vendor is X10 (www.X10.com), which sells several systems over the Internet. They also sell all sorts of add-ons devices for surveillance, appliance control, and more.

Few homeowners install wireline systems themselves (although they could do so rather easily); the wireless options are just too attractive from an ease-of-install point-of-view. Rather, most homeowners hire professionals to install wireline security systems that are designed explicitly for their homes. Professional security installers provide a proposal and make recommendations on the type and location of each sensor. They may have promotional deals that provide you with a starter system.

The choice between putting in a security system yourself and hiring a professional is a matter of budget and preference. We recommend that you seriously consider hiring a professional to install this system. Messing up the cabling of your stereo system is one thing, but messing up your security system could be life threatening. Don't scrimp on your security system.

Some companies install a basic system in your home for free if you sign a long-term (usually five-year) agreement with them for monitoring services. The upside of these deals is a low initial cost. The downside is inadequate coverage and higher fees as you go along. Most of these secure-now, pay-later packages include coverage for only four doors or windows and a single motion sensor. If you want to expand your coverage, you have to pay high additional costs. Moreover, you lease the system rather than own it. Monitoring fees are higher, and you have to agree to a long-term contract with a hefty early-termination fee. Be sure to check out comparable deals with non-free systems and figure the costs over time; you're generally better off just paying for a system up front.

The National Burglar & Fire Alarm Association (301-585-1855, www.alarm.org) offers advice on how to shop for a security system as well as the names of contractors who have qualified for their Installation Quality certificate.

Chapter 18

Wiring a Security System

· ·

· ·

*H*ome-security systems are better suited for installation by professional specialists than by do-it-yourselfers. Too much is at stake, whether you think in terms of your family's safety or the potential troubles that an improperly installed system can cause (such as false alarms, which drive the police and fire departments crazy and can result in fines to the homeowner). If you're using a wireless system, do-it-yourself is feasible, but for a full-up wired security network, hire a professional.

That said, we think it's important to have an idea what kinds of wiring and equipment make up a home-security system so that you can have an intelligent conversation with potential installers. This chapter discusses these wiring and architecture issues and explains how security systems work.

How to Prewire

The best place to start thinking about a home-security system is to look at how you can prewire your home to meet your short- and long-term security needs. In this section, we discuss the layout, or architecture, of a security system and the types of wire (or wireless systems) that connect the components of a security system.

Running a security loop

Your home-security system is based on the star architecture, in which every cable meets at a central wiring control panel (see Figure 18-1). Locating your wiring control panel in the central wiring closet that we describe in Chapter 2 makes sense; your control panel should be near the point where your telephone service comes into the house so that you can configure the system to call for help in an emergency. We cover this connection in the "Super supervision" section later in this chapter.

The cables that connect to the sensors and other elements of your security subsystem extend from the control panel. Although you can daisy-chain sensors — adding an extra sensor sometime after the initial installation to the line that runs to a nearby sensor — the control panel can't differentiate between devices that share a line to the control panel.

The cable that connects security devices generally contains two or four smaller wires called *conductors*. Half the wires cover the circuit that delivers information to the sensor; the other half delivers information back to the security control panel. The signals form a loop between the control panel and each sensor. These loops enable the control panel to tell whether the sensor is functioning correctly.

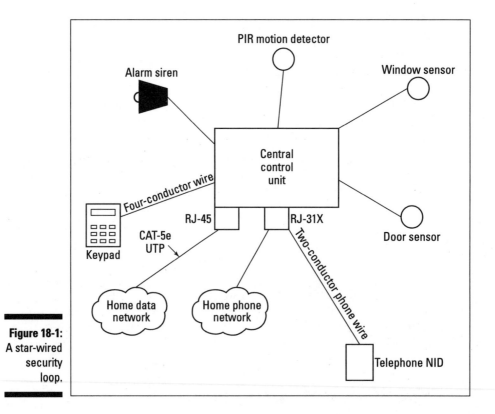

Figure 18-1:
A star-wired
security
loop.

Wiring choices

You use the following main types of wire in typical alarm installations:

- ✔ **Normal telephone wire:** This is 22-gauge, four-conductor telephone wire.

- ✔ **Fire-alarm cable:** You must connect fire alarms with special fire-alarm cable that rates to 105 degrees centigrade so that it doesn't burn. You see this wiring strung as bright red cabling in your basement.

- ✔ **Intercom cable:** Some intercom systems allow you to add intercom monitoring stations to the security system. If you decide on such a system, make sure that your installer uses special 22-gauge stranded and shielded wiring and grounds on every run. Failure to do so exposes the intercom system to electrical interference, which generates an annoying hum.

Wiring for wireless

Prewiring for wireless systems may sound weird, but it makes sense. Few professional installations are totally wireless; you usually install some sort of hybrid system. Wireless systems don't require prewiring at each point where you install the wireless endpoints, but you need to be careful about where you install your phone-line interfaces (as we discuss later in the chapter in the "Phone-line interfaces" section) and how you tie your central system into your other wireline assets.

If you trip a wireless sensor, it sends a high-frequency coded signal to the central station, which interprets and acts on the signal as necessary. Wireless systems basically act just like wired ones, sending electrical signals to and from sensors, keypads, and central stations, but the wireless systems use radio signals instead of cabling to send and receive the signals.

Good news for basement dwellers

Unlike other subsystem wiring schemes, security systems are expandable because so much of the wiring runs through the basement ceiling and then up short distances to the first-floor terminations. (In most cases, you don't need many sensors on upper floors.) So, unless you use sheetrock or otherwise close off your ceiling in the basement, running an extra cable shouldn't be an issue if you decide to add another sensor or end device. As long as you have an unfinished basement or drop ceiling, you don't need to overbuild your system. You merely install what you need today and add on to the system as you want to expand.

Beware of all-in-one wireless security solutions. These systems are wireless designs for apartments and other smaller applications that combine a *passive infrared receiver,* or *PIR,* with a siren. (We explain how these passive units monitor the infrared spectrum in Chapter 17.) When the PIR detects a burglar, the siren sounds to alert the family or frighten the burglar away. In practice, however, these systems are questionable because many issue a beeping tone if you trip them, which enables you to disarm the unit with a user-entered code. This time delay gives a burglar a chance to locate the alarm device on entry and smash it before the siren goes off.

All Zoned Out

The central security control panel tracks each circuit as a separate *zone,* and ideally, each circuit connects to only one sensor or device. So if you have a room with three window contacts and a passive infrared receiver, you have four zones here, not one. Typical security control panels for home applications can monitor 6 to 48 zones.

Zones enable the control panel to query the status of each device and interpret the inputs from each device. By tracking triggers sequentially from three related zones, for example, you can interpret that someone is walking a specific direction down a hallway.

Still, in some cases, you may need to run multiple sensors on the same circuit, known as dividing a zone into *subzones.* The drawback to the subzone approach is that all the sensors that connect to the same circuit appear as a single sensor to the control panel. If you connect a door, a window sensor, and a PIR to the same circuit, you can't tell which is causing the alarm.

Wireless systems work by zones, too. Each wireless device that's part of a professional installation has its own port on the control panel, just like on the wireline devices. The wireless devices typically communicate in the 300- to 900-MHz frequencies, which are highly reliable — unless a lot of radio activity is nearby.

Super supervision

A key element of your security subsystem is the concept of *supervision,* which is the capability of an alarm system to sense the status of any attached device.

The control panel continuously monitors its attached devices — how often and which things it monitors vary from panel to panel. Among the things that most systems monitor for are power failure, telephone-line trouble, loss of internal clock, trouble in any part of the system, low-battery conditions, attempts to tamper with systems, and other internal faults.

Alarm systems send in periodic test signals to central monitoring stations — typically, once a week. You'd be amazed at the number of customers whose systems aren't functional. People install computers on telephone lines, and the telephone installer may reroute or cause problems with the same phone line that your subsystem is on. People put additions on their houses and mess up wiring. Lots of simple things can conspire to throw part of your security system into chaos, which is why supervision is so important.

Wireless supervision

Wireless systems need supervision to be successful, too. Control panels that support wireless systems should also enable you to supervise these devices. Unsupervised wireless systems can detect whether a sensor circuit opens. This sort of system can tell you whether someone opens the front door, for example, but can't tell you the state of the remote sensors at any particular time. It can't, for example, tell you that its batteries are low.

Phone lines — the weak link

The most vulnerable part of your security system is your phone-line interface. Your phone line isn't monitored. The alarm system relies on that phone line to call the monitoring station and implicitly assumes that it's always there. And the monitoring service, which may be located hundreds of miles away, also assumes that the line is there and working.

As a result, many phone-line-based alarm systems are vulnerable if someone cuts the phone line before entering the house and tripping the alarm. As you're building your house, think about hardening the access to your telephone lines. If you're in a new home division, the builders usually bury many of these lines, which is great. Many other homes, however, have exposed NIDs (Network Interface Devices) on

the outside of the house, and the telephone line is in plain view. If you telephone company requires an outside interface, work with them to protect it as much as possible with a lock box and hardened conduit.

You can also buy a special alarm line called a *derived channel* from your local telephone company. The phone company puts a little black box in the central telephone office serving you and another where the line from your house ends. This box creates a subaudible two-way communication that provides a channel for your alarm's supervision. If the signal trips open, the central station gets a signal signifying that the phone line is down. Because of its cost, which is about $45 per month, the derived-channel approach has never taken off.

Supervised wireless systems mimic wireline systems. Typically, the system sends each wireless zone a supervisory round every so often. If the receiver hears from the wireless device at least once during that query, it doesn't report a trouble. If it doesn't receive a response, it treats the situation just as it does any other fault and reports a problem with the system to the monitoring station.

Within the supervisory transmission, the system usually queries the device about the status of the battery. If the battery is low, the system reports a fault.

Connecting to Other Systems

The power of your security system is measured not only by its inherent capabilities, but also by what subsystems you can add to it.

Phone-line interfaces

If you can afford it, a monitoring service should remotely monitor your security system. Your control panel then dials the alarm-monitoring service if any event that you programmed into your system occurs.

To dial out, your system needs access to an outside phone line. In most cases, it accesses the phone line that you use as your home-telephone number, unless you opt for derived-channel service. (See the "Phone lines — the weak link" sidebar in this chapter.)

The alarm system must be *inline* with your service, meaning that the telephone line physically runs through the panel on its way to your in-home telephone network. If something trips a sensor, the system seizes the telephone line to make an outbound call. The alarm system uses a piggybacked jack with a shorting bridge that disconnects the rest of the home-phone network. In doing so, the system effectively disconnects all the phones in the house while it makes that outbound call for help.

Stand-alone wireless systems, such as those you find at the do-it-yourself outlets, enable you to merely plug them into the nearest phone outlet in the house. But if someone leaves a phone off the hook or if the phone is in use as the alarm trips, the wireless system can't seize the line and make the emergency call for help. For this reason, we recommend that you don't install a wireless system from a normal telephone extension in the house. Instead, run a phone line to the inline jack at the control box where your phone line enters the house.

Don't connect the alarm-panel communicator to telephone lines that you use with a fax machine. Fax-machine lines may incorporate a voice filter, which disconnects the line if it detects anything other than fax signals. This filter can result in partial transmissions to the monitoring center.

Your central security control panel connects with your home-phone lines with an *RJ-31X connection.* This interface — called the digital communicator — transmits the signal from the control panel to the central monitoring station. The connection is straightforward; the conductors from the local telephone line connect to the panel and then route back out of the panel to connect with the in-home telephones. One of the big advantages of the RJ-31X interface is that it enables you to dial into your system from a phone to do stuff such as turn the system on and off or turn up the temperature inside the house.

You can add enhanced phone functionality to your house through your alarm system. Sounds backwards, doesn't it? But because the alarm system is in-line with your phone connections, it can act as a gatekeeper to all the phones in the house. ADEMCO (www.ademco.com) has a TeleSmart module for its VISTA security systems, for instance, that adds a digital answering machine to your alarm system. With TeleSmart, homeowners can arm or disarm their security system, check messages, screen calls, block calls, and more. Additional features include caller ID, memory and repeat dial, customized mailboxes for up to four family members, and a family message center that lets users record, play back, and retrieve voice memos.

Alternative phone-line interfaces

Having the control panel send alarm signals to a remote monitoring station is not the only way to accomplish your goal of getting help if an emergency arises. Other possibilities are the focus of this section.

One alternative to having a phone-line connection to the central security control panel is to use wireless communications — cellular-phone technologies, for example — to dial into the remote monitoring station. You can use wireless technologies as an alternative to a phone-line connection or as a supplement (in case someone cuts the phone line). At least two national networks are vying to get your wireless monitoring business: Uplink (at www.uplink.com) and Alarmnet (at www.alarmnet.com), both of which use cellular and wireless data networks to carry signals between your local control panel and the monitoring station. These networks enable two-way wireless alarm communications to any monitoring station.

The radio transmitter typically costs around $300, with an $18 or so monthly charge. ADT (www.adt.com) offers cellular backup systems that retain dialup communications with a monitoring center for as little as $199 installed and a monthly charge of $8.

Another way to get emergency help — one that's popular among the do-it-yourself products — is to use a *voice dialer*. This feature is an electronic tape-recording application that automatically dials out on the telephone lines to a police station, fire department, or ambulance emergency service. The upside is that you save the monthly monitoring charge by using such a system. The downside is that you have no way to ensure that the party the dialer calls actually receives the call. An automatic recording can't answer questions or give interpretation. Some localities have banned these items, so check your local ordinances.

If you're planning to control your security system by telephone from remote locations, you need to plan how this system will work with your other telephone services. You can, for example, set many security systems to answer your phone after a certain number of rings so that you can then send commands to the system. But if you have an answering machine, voice mail provided by the telephone company, or even call forwarding on the line, you must design a way to ensure that the right device answers the phone. If controlling your system remotely is important to you, you may need to dedicate a phone line for your security system.

Home-control interfaces

Various control panels sport X10 home-control modules that, through the addition of programming and timers, can also turn your lights on and off. By using such modules, you can program your security system so that if the fire alarm goes off, for example, you can turn on specific lights to guide you out of the house.

You can program more sophisticated systems, such as those that we discuss in Chapter 20, to utilize the inputs from your sensors to perform all sorts of tasks. You can use a driveway sensor that you connect to your security panel to issue home-automation commands that turn on the garage and porch lights, for example, or sound a chime in the home office.

X10.com (www.x10.com) has keychain-fob interfaces for its that work from up to 40 feet away. You can arm and disarm the system with the press of a single button as you pull into the driveway! Modes on the remote include arm (instant mode), disarm, control of lights, and a panic feature to trip the system immediately. Each remote effectively has a unique code that is identified to the alarm panel so that only the remotes that the user has set up can be used to control the system. Napco (www.napcosecurity.com) has a fob unit with eight intuitive icons for system status (that show up on an LCD display. Additionally, corresponding beep sequences on the minisounder confirm commands. BellSouth (www.bellsouth.com/security/) issues these as standard on its security services. So much for having to remember a code or special siren sequences.

Audio interfaces

Some alarm systems enable you to connect a number of standard interior and exterior intercom stations or sensors to your alarm system. You can use these for listening in on the baby, playing background music, seeing who's at the door, answering incoming phone calls, and paging people around the house. A neat feature of such systems is that the central station can also access these intercoms, so monitoring agents can listen and talk through these systems.

Broadband interfaces

The Internet interface is a natural extension of the security subsystem, and some of the more progressive firms are making use of it. With a constant broadband connection to the Internet, you could have constant connections to your monitoring center and not have to rely on grabbing a dialup phone line to communicate your status. You could also set up Web-based interfaces to control various aspects of your security system, including real-time video.

Two things about this connection are critical: the speed of the connection (how much information can be crammed up and down your access line) and the fact that the connection is always on, meaning that your home is always connected to the Internet. These systems use two-way communications that confirm your system is online and working, and the sheer size of the bandwidth available means you can do all sorts of neat things to provide service.

Serial port connections via RS-232?

A few home-security systems, such as those made by Napco (at www.napcosecurity.com), provide an electronic interface known as *RS-232*. This connection is basically the same kind that the serial port on most PCs uses. If you install a security panel with an RS-232 interface and you also have a home-automation controller with its own RS-232 input, you can connect them to get even more sophisticated sensor-to-automation relationships.

Why doesn't everyone use RS-232? Well, that involves a big problem. Although the RS-232 interface itself is standardized and common, the programming code that works the alarms and home-automation controllers is proprietary. So a security panel from manufacturer X may not be capable of talking to a home-automation controller from company Y. This lack of compatibility can be a major pain in the neck, although some companies are beginning to open up their programming to ensure interoperability.

Right now, however, security and automation interfacing is iffy. Unless you're a serial-programming expert, you need to leave this kind of system integration to a professional installer who's trained on both alarm and automation systems.

SafeVillage (www.safevillage.com) is a great example of security of the future. Check out their Web site, where several film clips show how your interface with the alarm company would change. First, they have embraced the concept of remote control of your system, enabling you to arm and disarm the system or specific zones, change contact information, check your bill, and more over the Internet with a browser. You can also set up guest codes to let in people who might be staying with you temporarily. Second, they make audio and video monitoring a basic part of the offering, not an expensive add-on service. If an alarm goes off in your house while you're at work, you can go to the Web site, check out the zone, and see what's up. In the traditional mode, you have to hop in your car and go home. Third, they still use standard telephone access as a backup. If your cable modem is down, they can use the dial-up voice phone.

In addition to companies specializing in broadband access, many alarm systems and individual devices allow for access and control through the Web. The X10 cameras mentioned in Chapter 17, for instance, can be controlled and recorded through the Internet; you can even view four cameras at once with X10's WebView program. And certainly a lot of home-automation programs also have Web interfaces to enable you to access those programs to drive your security needs.

Many broadband cable and DSL connections use a system called DHCP, which assigns your network an IP address (the phone number of the Internet) dynamically. That means your IP address will change over time (often on a scheduled basis that you don't even know about). Try to find a broadband service provider who will give you a *fixed* IP address — one that never changes. This makes it easier for alarm monitoring companies to find your home (out of the billions of devices connected to the Internet worldwide). Most services also use software tricks to deal with a dynamic IP address (basically, they put software on your computer that sends the current IP address to a directory somewhere). However, if you don't have a fixed IP address, make sure you tell them you have a dynamic IP address before you sign up for service.

Part VI

Putting It All Together — Home Automation and Control

The 5th Wave By Rich Tennant

"The kids are getting up right now. When we wired the house we added vibrating pager technology to their bunkbeds."

In this part . . .

In a sense, we're reaching the climax of the book! This part is where it all comes together, where your home networks really hum (but your wiring doesn't). This is where your house reaches the status of a smart home.

We describe two closely related topics: home-control and automation systems and remote-control systems for your home's entertainment networks. Both topics help you interconnect and take advantage of all the other subsystems — audio, video, telephony, computer LAN, security, and so on.

Chapter 19

Home Automation Extravaganza

*I*n other chapters, we describe how to create a backbone that enables you to distribute various kinds of signals around your smart home. The next step — one that can make things more useful and more fun — is to install home-control and -automation networks that can help you take charge of your smart home's subsystems.

You can get an amazingly wide range of home-control and -automation systems — everything from simple X10 powerline controls that cost in the tens of dollars to custom-built proprietary networks that cost in the tens of thousands of dollars. In this chapter, we give you a taste of what's on the market and what these devices can do. We also talk a bit about some emerging standards that can make home automation and control easier, cheaper, and better than what's available today.

Where an Automated Home Begins — and Ends

An automated home can be a simple grouping of controls, such as a few lamps that turn themselves on and off, or it can be an extravaganza, where just about everything electrically powered is remotely controlled. The great thing is that you can start small and grow over time.

Any home-automation and -control system includes the following basic parts:

✔ **Protocol:** The common language that all the devices in the home-automation network understand. X10 is the predominant protocol in home automation today.

✔ **Wiring infrastructure:** The wires that carry signals to each automation or control device in the network. Many home-automation systems (including X10) use the existing electrical wiring to transmit signals, but a few require special wiring. A few systems use wireless technologies to control things such as lights, so you need no wires at all.

✔ **Controller device:** A device that sends signals over the infrastructure in a way that conforms to the protocol. The signals tell specific pieces of equipment what to do.

✔ **Device controllers:** Because most appliances and electronic devices aren't designed from the factory to be automated or remotely controlled, you need individual controllers that can respond to signals from the main controller device and make individual components do what you want them to do — such as turn on or off.

The big difference among the various implementations of home networking comes in the realm of controllers. You can start off with a small, stand-alone controller that costs about $40, or you can go with a high-end PC-type controller that runs into the thousands of dollars (you can find much cheaper PC controllers, however). These PC-type controllers can be software and hardware interfaces for a general-purpose PC in your home, or they can be stand-alone PC-like hardware devices purpose-built for home-automation control.

X10 Is the Reigning Champ

X10 actually refers to two things: a protocol and a company name (we lied — it refers to *three* companies' names). X10 is the dominant protocol for controlling (turning on and off) electrical devices such as lights and appliances through your home's electrical lines. Three X10–named companies are involved in the X10 automation industry: X10, Limited bought the original patent for X10 technology back in the 1980s and held the patent until it expired in 1997; X10Pro is a subsidiary of X10 Limited and builds X10 equipment for the professional installer market; and X10 Wireless Technologies is a manufacturing and marketing partner of X10 Limited that sells X10 equipment directly to consumers.

Confused yet? Most people type www.X10.com in their Web browser and find the third one, X10 Wireless Technologies. If you want to find X10Pro on the Web, type www.X10pro.com. X10 Limited doesn't sell anything to consumers under that name, so don't bother trying to find that one.

X10 is now an open standard, sold by the two X10 companies mentioned, as well as by other companies, such as Leviton and Stanley.

We use the term *X10* to refer to the protocol or to mean a device that's compatible with the X10 protocol because thinking of X10 in this way reminds you that you don't need to buy from one of the X10 companies to get X10. All compatible products display an X10-compatible logo on their packaging or on the product itself; when you see this logo, you know that the product works with other X10 products regardless of manufacturer.

X10 basics

To work in a home, X10 doesn't require specific network architecture other than your existing electrical system. X10 sends its control signals from the controller over your power lines to every outlet in the house. You plug into these outlets specialized X10 *modules* — devices that receive and translate X10 signals to turn individual lights, appliances, or other electrical devices on and off. Figure 19-1 shows a limited X10 network.

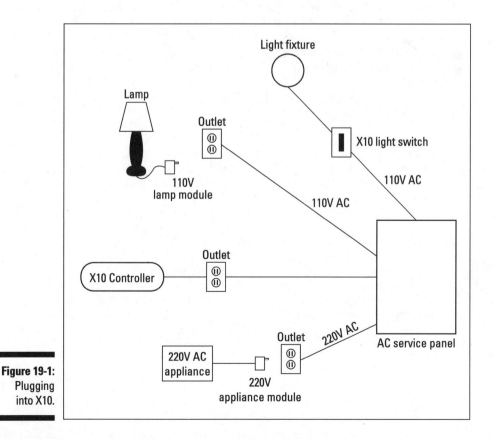

Figure 19-1:
Plugging
into X10.

The electrical wiring infrastructures of some homes isolate the circuits of some outlets — so a controller in the living room may not be capable of sending a signal to a module in the guest bathroom. By using a device known as a *signal coupler* (which we discuss in more detail in Chapter 20), you can overcome this problem.

Your X10 module is a small, box-shaped device that's no bigger than the "wall-wart" AC plug-in transformers that power many home appliances, such as telephones and answering machines. The module has a standard electrical plug on the back and a place to plug in your lamp or other device on the front or bottom. You place the device that you want to control in the on mode (for example, turn the light switch on), and then the X10 module turns the device off and on.

Most modules have a *local-control* feature that enables you to manually turn devices on and off without involving your X10 system. To activate this feature, you typically use the device's own on/off switch (not the module's) and turn it off and then back on.

Because every module in the house can "see" the control signals coming from an X10 controller, the system needs some way of identifying which module is which. Otherwise, you'd end up with a chaotic situation with the wrong things turning on and off. The solution to this problem is an addressing scheme that uses 16 *house codes* (using the letters *A* through *P*) and 16 *unit codes* (using numbers 1 through 16). Every module in an X10 network is assigned one of each of these codes. The house code is also used by controllers to perform multiple control actions at once. For example, you can put all downstairs lights on a single house code (code A, for example), and then have your controller send a signal that says, "Turn on all lights in house code A."

The person installing each module programs it to a unique combination of these codes (usually by turning a small wheel with a screwdriver) so that the module answers only to signals sent to that code. This method of identifying modules on the network enables up to 256 (16 x 16) unique, controllable pieces of equipment in your home-automation network.

Although 256 is the maximum number of modules that an X10 network can control, it can control a larger number of end devices. You can, for example, plug two lights into the same module with multiple outlets (as long as the total wattage of the two lamps isn't higher than the module can handle). These two lamps aren't *individually* controllable, but both respond to the on/off commands sent to that module. You can modify this technique for lights in different parts of the house by using two modules set to the same address.

Modules

If you look in a home-automation catalog or go to a place that carries home-automation gear, such as Radio Shack or Home Depot, you'll find X10 modules ranging from generic lamp modules to specialized devices that control specific pieces of equipment. The main distinctions among modules are as follows:

- **The kind of device they control:** Modules that control devices such as lamps are cheaper (and handle less electrical current) than those that turn on and off such high-powered devices as electrical dryers.

- **The control signals they can understand:** The simplest X10 modules know how to turn things on and off in response to a control signal. More sophisticated modules can perform additional functions, such as lamp dimming or brightening or ceiling-fan speed adjustments.

- **Their capability to deal with noise on the power line:** Fancier modules use sophisticated *Automatic Gain Control (AGC)* systems, which can adjust the sensitivity of the X10 module's signal receiver. What this means is that the module has enough intelligence to discern between real X10 signals and random noise on the power line (such as the electrical noise produced by fluorescent lights).

We like the modules and equipment made by Leviton (www.leviton. com) for their capability to deal with noisy environments. Leviton's DHC (Decora Home Control) gear uses the company's Intellisense technology to do some neat AGC stuff — we find it makes our X10 network very reliable.

- **Whether they're one-way or two-way.** Most X10 modules are one-way — that is, they receive control signals but don't respond back to the central controller to tell it that the module has performed an action. The least expensive modules don't offer a confirmation signal back to the controller, but a new breed of two-way modules provides this status confirmation.

Sometimes electrical noise and interference on a home's power lines can prevent an X10 module from understanding or receiving the X10 signals. The new two-way modules tell you (or your controller) whether a command worked, which is a handy feature for such important commands as starting the coffee pot in the morning. Most of the modules that we discuss in this chapter are available in both one-way and two-way configurations. You can use them interchangeably in your X10 network, but only two-way modules send confirmation signals back to a two-way compatible controller.

Some newer modules can receive something known as *extended X10 codes* to perform additional functions, but in general, a module can perform only six actions (if told to do so by a controller). Table 19-1 describes these six actions and their results.

Table 19-1	X10 Actions
Action	*What It Does*
On	Turns on the module corresponding to a house/unit code combo
Off	Turns off the module corresponding to a house/unit code combo
All on	Turns on all X10 modules within a house code range
All off	Turns off all X10 modules within a house code range
Dim	Dims the module corresponding to a house/unit code combo (can dim lights or slow down a fan)
Brighten	Brightens the module corresponding to a house/unit code combo

The following sections describe some of the modules available for your use.

Lamp modules

The simplest and most common X10 modules are *lamp modules.* These modules simply plug into any standard 110-volt AC outlet, between the lamp cord and the outlet. You can use these modules only with incandescent bulbs, usually up to 300 watts. (Check the labeling as you're choosing a module to make sure that it can handle the type of bulb involved.) Fluorescent and halogen bulbs don't work with these kinds of modules — you need an appliance module for such devices.

Lamp modules respond to on and off commands for the particular house and unit codes that you assign to the module. They respond also to all-on/all-off commands from your controller — commands that turn on or off (you guessed it) all the lights in the house that X10 modules control. In addition, many lamp modules respond to dim/brighten commands that an X10 controller issues, so you can set the mood for dinner or a movie — or whatever you have in mind.

Appliance modules

For all the stuff in your house that uses a bit more juice (electrically speaking), you want X10 *appliance modules.* These modules can handle the higher draws of electric current required by devices such as coffeemakers, portable heaters, and other household appliances, and they also enable you to connect fluorescent lamps (something that you can't do with an ordinary lamp module).

You don't find dim/bright commands on most appliance modules, which makes sense, because you can't really dim a coffee pot. You also don't find an all-on function on these modules, which is for safety reasons — some devices that connect to appliance modules are things that you *don't* want to turn on if you're just trying to light the house. You do usually find an all-off command — if you want everything off, you generally want *everything* off.

You can find appliance modules in both 110-volt AC and 220-volt AC versions. Heavy-duty stuff, such as hot tubs, window air conditioners, and clothes dryers, may require the 220-volt versions.

Universal modules

Universal modules are special-purpose appliance modules that control the electrical and electronic devices in a home that a *relay* (or remote switch) turns on and off. These devices include garage-door openers, electric drapery controls, sprinkler systems, and low-voltage lighting systems (such as yard lights and some track lighting).

You can set the universal module to provide a *momentary* or *continuous* relay closure. You might use the momentary mode for the garage-door opener (which creates the equivalent of pressing the open/close button) and the continuous mode for sprinklers and other devices that you want to remain on until you turn them off.

Universal modules don't receive all-on or dim/brighten signals (for the same reason that appliance modules don't) but do receive all-off commands.

X10 receptacles

Most X10 modules are small and discrete, but for a truly invisible appearance, you can have your electrician install in-wall X10 receptacles. These outlets are the same size and shape as conventional power receptacles but function the same as X10 appliance modules. The main consideration in installing X10 receptacles is whether you want the X10 to control one or both outlets in the receptacle. Some models have an X10 outlet on top and an always-live regular outlet on the bottom.

Duplex X10 wall receptacles offer control over both outlets. We often see companies marketing these kinds of receptacles to parents who want to ensure that their kids aren't watching TV beyond certain time limits. After TV time is over, the controller can turn off the outlet and disable the TV set in the children's room. Boy, will *that* make them mad!

Switches

Another way to make X10 connections less visible in your home is to have your electrician install X10 *wall switches* to control hardwired lights, fans, and other devices. These switches enable both local and X10 control of the devices that the electrician wires to them — so you can have your controller turn a light on or off, or you can just walk over to the switch and do it yourself.

If you use two-way X10 switches, they can inform your intelligent controller that you manually changed the state of the switch (from on to off or vice versa). If you don't have two-way switches, you can end up getting your control system out of whack by manually controlling a switch. This system confusion arises when the switch is manually set to a different position (on or off) than the controller thinks it is set to.

You need to consider the following points when purchasing X10 wall switches:

- Special switches (known as three-way *master* and *slave* switches) are necessary for applications in which more than one switch controls a particular light. Regular switches can't handle this job, because they can't keep track of the light's status when another switch turns the light on or off. Three-way switches can communicate with each other to keep track of this status.

- Switches with dimmer functions work only with incandescent light fixtures — not with fluorescent lighting systems.

- Ceiling fans and low-voltage lighting sources (such as halogen track lighting) require a specific *inductive* switch — which by design specifically controls fan speeds or dims and brightens low-voltage lights.

- Certain 220-volt devices, such as pool pumps, hot-tub heaters, and some air conditioners, require special heavy-duty switches because of the large amount of electrical current they draw.

Some X10 wall switches have extra features that you might appreciate when you're building a smart-home system. For example, many of Leviton's DHC switches have a soft on/fade off feature that makes your lights turn on gradually, starting from dim to whatever brightness you have set them to, and turn off like the lights going down at a theater rather than just switching off. This is supposed to increase the lifespan of your light bulbs, but we like it because of its cool factor.

Controllers

All the X10 modules, receptacles, and switches in the world aren't very useful without some means of controlling them remotely. Luckily, you have at least as many options for controlling X10 systems as you have module options.

Standard X10 controllers range from $10 minicontrollers, which provide remote control (but not automation) of a number of modules, to $500 touch-screen controllers that provide a more sophisticated means of controlling your network. Throw into the mix wireless controllers, specialized lighting controllers, telephone-activated controllers, timers, controllers that activate by light (or darkness), controllers that your security system triggers, voice controllers, and even controllers that use your PC to run your home network, and you have quite a selection to peruse. And that's not even considering some of the high-end, proprietary systems that control X10 systems, HVAC systems, alarms, and other controllers.

The sheer number of choices in the controller world can be a bit bewildering, but we have some good news: You don't need to limit yourself to just one controller. You can start small, if you want, and as you expand your X10 network, you can supplement your controller inventory with more sophisticated models — while keeping the original controllers active in the network.

You could begin with just a simple minicontroller, for example, and then as your expand your network, use a PC-based controller system to automate your entire house. You don't need to throw the minicontroller out; transfer it to the master bedroom and use it to control certain lights or appliances that you want to turn on and off from the comfort of your bed.

As we discuss controllers, whenever we use *module*, we're also including X10 receptacles and switches. We just figured that you didn't want to read *module or receptacle or switch* a whole bunch of times.

The following sections describe some of the various controllers available to you.

Stand-alone controllers

The simplest and most inexpensive X10 controllers are *stand-alone* X10 controllers. These devices don't need a PC — or anything else — to operate. Just plug them into a wall outlet, program them to match the house and unit codes, and you're ready to go.

Minicontrollers and tabletop controllers

Among stand-alone controllers, the cheapest and easiest to install and set up are *minicontrollers*. These small boxes simply send on/off, all-on/all-off, and dim/brighten commands to a small number of X10 devices (usually eight). The minicontroller doesn't do any automation — that is, it requires input from a person to perform a task — but it does provide you with remote control from anywhere in the house.

Tabletop controllers do basically the same thing as minicontrollers — the only real difference is that they can control a larger number of modules (and they're bigger).

Programmable controllers and timers

The next step up in controllers — *programmable,* or *timer,* controllers — begins to offer a degree of home automation to complement the home-control functions of minicontrollers. These devices, which you mount on a wall or place on a desk or table, enable you to control a number of X10 modules (usually eight or sixteen) manually or automatically.

To make the controller work automatically, you simply need to program the controller to perform an X10 command or sequence of commands at a particular time. So you can, for example, tell your controller to turn on modules A1 (the kitchen lights) and A2 (the coffee pot) at 6:30 a.m. every Monday through Friday. This kind of automation isn't the end-all in sophistication, but it's a good way to get started down the road to an automated home.

Telephone interfaces

You don't need to be in the house to control your X10 modules. By installing a *telephone interface,* you can dial into your network from any Touch-Tone phone and turn on the lights or get the hot tub warming up before you get home from the office.

Telephone interfaces plug into a phone line (using a telephone cord with a standard RJ-11 jack) and into any power receptacle in the house, and use Touch-Tone keypad tones to perform various X10 actions in your home. Prices for these devices range from about $70 for a simple unit that controls ten modules up to about $300 for units that can control one hundred or more modules.

When choosing a phone interface for your X10 network, look for the following features:

- **Local control:** Some phone interfaces enable you not only to dial in remotely, but also to pick up any phone (on the same line) in your home and enter commands.

- **Voice enunciator:** More expensive models have built-in *voice enunciators,* which confirm your commands (a handy feature if you're not sure whether you just turned on the porch light or the hot tub).

- **Answering-machine mode:** Some models enable you to put an *answering machine* on the same phone line as the controller, an important feature if you have only one phone line in the house. To use the controller, you just ignore the beep on your answering machine and punch in your commands. This feature doesn't work with telephone-company-provided voice-mail services, however, and may not work with every answering machine.

Sensor controllers and interfaces

Although programmable and timer X10 controllers add some degree of automation to your home network, they're basically dumb devices. A certain time passes, and they initiate X10 commands that you previously programmed into them. That's handy, but what happens if you want an X10 command to activate under circumstances that don't adhere to a predictable schedule? What if, for example, you want the lights in your hallway to come on whenever your children walk to the bathroom in the middle of the night? (And believe Danny when he tells you that no predictable schedule exists for that.)

For these kinds of scenarios, you may want to use sensor-initiated X10 controllers, such as those described in the following list:

- ✔ **PIR controllers:** These controllers send out an X10 signal whenever a passive infrared (PIR) motion detector picks up someone walking into a room (or past your back door in the middle of the night).

- ✔ **Photo sensors:** These controllers send out X10 signals as it gets dark outside (or, alternatively, as the sun rises).

- ✔ **Alarm interfaces:** These controllers use an input from your X10-compatible security system and sensors from the alarm system to trigger X10 commands.

Wireless controllers

After you start getting an automated home up and running, you're likely to find that you have less and less inclination even to get up and walk over to the controller sitting on the table across the living room from your comfy couch. X10 systems have exactly the answer you need if you face this problem: wireless controllers.

Wireless controllers consist of two parts — an *RF (radio frequency) receiver,* which plugs into the wall (and sends X10 commands), and the handheld or tabletop *RF transmitter.* Overall, wireless controllers function basically the same as minicontrollers and tabletop controllers but from a distance. Some of these handheld remotes also serve double duty as IR remote controls, so you can use a single remote to control the TV and audio systems as well as the lights.

You can find wireless controllers in all sizes and shapes, ranging from sixteen-device controllers for the living-room table to small three- or four-module controllers that can hang on your keychain. (These smaller devices are great for controlling the modules that open your garage door or turn on your porch lights.)

You can also get wireless X10 wall switches that stick on any wall in your house and communicate with corresponding light modules by sending an RF signal to the wireless controller, which then sends an X10 signal to turn the light on or off. These devices are great for adding light switches.

Touch panels

The fanciest X10 controllers are the programmable *touch-screen panels* made by companies such as SmartHome Manufacturing (at www.smartlinc.com). For about $500, these controllers enable you to control and automate hundreds of X10 modules by using a touch-sensitive LCD screen.

You can use these systems also to create *macros,* or sequences of X10 actions that you want to trigger through a single touchpad command or a timed, programmed command. Most touch-panel controllers are also compatible with two-way X10 modules, so you can see an on-screen confirmation that your action has been performed.

The combination of two-way modules and macro capability also enables these controllers to set devices to certain levels of brightness. If you want to set a light to a medium level of brightness, for example, this type of controller can turn on the light, send a dim signal a certain number of times (to reach your desired level of brightness), and then confirm remotely that the light is set where you want it.

If you're going to shell out a significant amount of money for a touch panel or other high-end X10 controller, make sure that you get one that is two-way compatible and buy modules that can do two-way communications. These systems will make sure that your control signals get to modules in your home and are carried out.

PC interfaces

If you want to get fancy with an X10 network, you can supplement or replace your stand-alone controllers with a *PC-based control system*. These controllers use the horsepower of your PC and the familiar graphical interface of Windows (or the Macintosh) to enable you to set up and control all X10 modules in your home.

The majority of PC-based controllers are two-way capable, so they control and monitor the status of two-way modules. Many also provide inputs from external sensors such as temperature monitors and photo sensors and use these inputs to trigger X10 commands.

Following are the two key components of a PC-based controller:

- ✔ **Control software:** Lets you program and control your X10 network using a graphical interface on your PC.
- ✔ **Interface unit:** Connects your computer to the home's powerline network.

Most interface units connect to one of your PC's serial ports (the ones labeled *Com* on most PCs), but you can find other interfaces, such as internal ISA cards. You may think that you can just use your computer's own powerline connection to the wall to do your controlling, but the internal design of a PC doesn't allow you to do so. That's why you need this interface unit to create and send X10 signals over your home's power lines.

Most PC interface units download and save your preferred settings in their internal memory, so you don't need to keep your PC running for your automation system to work. Some systems, however, require a PC that's always on (and always has the home-automation software running). Unless you have an extra PC that you can dedicate to your home-automation network, think long and hard about this requirement. On the other hand, if you have an old computer sitting around, this sort of setup may be a great use for it.

You can interface with your PC home-automation software in the following ways:

- ✔ **Keyboard:** The simplest and most common way to set up and control PC-based automation software is to use your keyboard and mouse. Using a graphical interface, you can sit in front of your computer and program timed and macro events for your controller to perform, or you can manually control modules.

- ✔ **Telephone:** By using your computer's modem, you can dial into your home controller or PC from remote locations and trigger X10 commands using Touch-Tone key commands.

- ✔ **Internet:** With a broadband, always-on Internet connection (such as DSL or a cable modem) and the right software, you can access your automation software from anywhere in the world using a Web browser. Your PC turns into a Web server, creating remotely accessible Web pages displaying the status and controls for your house.

- ✔ **Voice:** The neatest way to utilize PC control of your X10 network is by voice command. Systems such as the HAL2000 (check out www. automatedliving.com for information) and HomeVoice (at www. appliedfuture.com) enable you to use a telephone connection or a microphone connected to your PC to speak commands into your computer to trigger X10 commands. These systems not only listen to (and obey) you, but they also answer back to provide confirmation of your spoken commands.

If you want to check out computer control of your X10 network on the cheap, try one of the kits sold by X10 Wireless Technologies. They have two kits for under $50: the Firecracker kit ($39) provides a PC interface, software, and three other pieces of X10 gear, and the ActiveHome kit ($49) offers a PC interface, more comprehensive software, and five other pieces of X10 gear (including a universal remote control that can run your stereo, TV, and DVD and control X10 modules).

Lights, AC (Powerline), Action

One of the most important areas of home automation is control over your lighting systems. When we say *control*, we mean more than just turning lights on and off (though that can be useful). With a true lighting control system, you can move beyond on and off and into the world of *scenes*, which allow you to control groups of lights in a room or throughout the house to set the mood for various occasions.

For example, you might have a scene programmed into your lighting controller to dim the lights in your home theater when you want to watch a movie, and another to dim all but your reading lamp when the TV is off and you just want to catch up on your current favorite novel. Many people like to create special scenes for the sleeping parts of their homes, so that the hall light can remain on at a very dim setting, for example, and the bathroom lights can be turned on to a nonblinding brightness when needed at night.

Although many general-purpose programmable X10 controllers can be programmed with macros to create scenes to control lighting (and a scene is basically a special-purpose lighting macro), we like to use a purpose-built lighting system to create and control our scenes.

Traditionally, lighting control systems have been the province of the very rich, and have used extra wiring, switches, and control panels. Big lighting and wiring manufacturers, however, have brought high-end scene lighting to the mass market using X10 powerline controls or wireless RF systems.

Internet-controlled electric usage

Energy companies are launching a range of variable-rate pricing plans for consumer electricity, such that the rates during peak demand times are higher than those during off-peak times. Because no consumer wants to have to memorize energy rate tables, Internet-connected thermostats, such as those from market leader Lightstat, Inc. (www.lightstat.com), provide consumers with a user-friendly way to program their thermostats to do certain things during specific rate periods. You log onto a Web site that enables you to set your temperature preferences for sleeping at night, when you're away at work during the day, and so on. And you set your preferences for what to do when the prices hit certain thresholds, such as turning off one of your two water-heater elements to save energy.

Some of the smarter thermostats go beyond just the heating and cooling in the house. These have a discrete output (like a relay) built into the thermostat to control the water heater, for instance. There has to be a relay on the water heater, and the signal gets to the water heater from the thermostat either by a low-voltage cable or a wireless transmit/receive signal (Bluetooth or similar). In the same way, the thermostat could also turn off an electrical load such as a pool pump (until the rates are cheap again). In one implementation, Lightstat turns on a natural-gas-fired emergency generator with the thermostat and takes the whole house off the utility grid when the price is high enough! Houses that have alternate power-storage capability, such as solar cells, can tap this power in peak periods.

Leading home-automation programs, such as HAL2000, are starting to link to the utility energy databases to do the same thing for other devices around the home, including appliances such as dishwashers. Suppose a dishwasher uses around 58 kilowatt-hours per month. In one real-life example, the electricity rates range from 4.2 cents a kilowatt-hour on nights and weekends to 10 cents on weekday afternoons — more than double the cost. Add in air conditioning, the washer, the dryer, and other devices, and you can save a lot of money.

A good example of the X10 approach to scene control is the Toscana Deluxe controller from Leviton. This system uses Leviton's Intellisense enhanced X10 protocol and can control up to 256 devices (the maximum allowed by any X10 system) and be programmed for up to 64 scenes. The Toscana controller can be controlled and programmed by a Windows PC and a standard RS-232 serial port, and can be controlled also using an IR remote control (we'll talk about these more later in the chapter). The Toscana system is mounted in a standard wall outlet — but it's wider than a regular wall switch so it uses a four-gang outlet box. The system is two-way X10 compatible, so we recommend that you use two-way modules with it. And if you want to get the benefits of the Leviton Intellisense AGC, you'll need to use Leviton modules (though any X10 modules will work with the system).

On the wireless side of the coin, Lutron (`www.lutron.com`) offers a system called the RadioRA. The system consists of wireless-enabled dimmers and switches, wireless controller keypads (called master controllers), and an RF repeater system. Control signals are sent from the master controllers (mounted on the wall or in tabletop form) to the appropriate remote dimmer switch. If necessary, the RF repeater picks up and resends any signals it detects to ensure that faraway modules receive their signals. Lutron offers other wireless receiver devices (basically like X10 modules) to control other electrical devices, and also offers an RS-232 serial port interface that lets you use a home-automation program on a PC to control or program the system. You can control up to 32 dimmers and switches with the RadioRA system. You can even buy a remote controller for your car that lets you control the lighting system from up to 100 feet away.

We think that both the powerline (X10) approach and the wireless (RF) approach are valid ways of controlling lighting in the home. Both work well and the cost is about the same. As with the rest of your home, you'll likely use some of both approaches, albeit probably within one manufacturer's product line. We do recommend that you buy a good quality product (like the two we mention), because the higher-end products tend to have more robust capabilities to deal with interference from other devices in the home.

A Next-Generation Solution

X10 is the most common protocol for controlling devices in the home, but it's not the height of technology. The basic powerline protocols for X10 are pushing 35 years old. The good thing about X10 is that it's cheap, it works relatively well (especially with higher-quality modules and controllers), and it's become ubiquitous (so you can buy X10 devices from different manufacturers and they work together seamlessly). That's the good stuff. On the flip side is the fact that X10 remains a low-speed communications protocol that is best for simple commands (on, off, dim, bright, and so on).

Various industry groups and technology companies have tried (and mainly failed) to come up with next-generation protocols to help automate a home. For example, in the 1990s, a bunch of companies grouped together with a standard called CEBus (or Consumer Electronics Bus), which was designed to be a replacement of X10 and other in-home communications protocols. There was a lot of fanfare, but at the end of the day, we never saw any products hit the market that used the CEBus Home Plug & Play standard.

CEBus wasn't the only potential replacement for X10 to come and eventually go — just the most recent. However, a new industry group called the Universal Plug and Play (UPnP) is likely to be successful. If you check out the UPnP Web site (`www.upnp.org`) and look at the member companies, you might be able to guess why we give this effort a better-than-even chance to succeed: It's a Who's Who list of the computer, networking, software, and consumer electronics companies, including Microsoft, Intel, Linksys, Philips, and Sony. A lot of home-automation leaders, such as Lutron and Leviton, are members of this group as well — so it's not just outside companies trying to push something on the existing home-networking business.

UPnP won't necessarily be a direct replacement for X10. Instead, it will be a set of protocols that lets PCs, consumer electronics devices, appliances, and home-control systems talk to each other over a variety of network types. You can think of UPnP as a common language that allows every device that's UPnP compatible and certified to talk with other such devices.

In a UPnP network, devices identify themselves and their functionality on the network and use a common set of protocols to set themselves up and do their thing. The first generation of UPnP equipment has been directly related to the PC and to home-entertainment systems. For example, you can combine Philip's UPnP-certified Streamium Internet stereo system with a Linksys UPnP home router and a PC using MUSICMATCH's UPnP-certified Jukebox software (`www.musicmatch.com`) to create an audio system that plays MP3 files and streaming music from the Internet. Now you could probably set up such a system on your own, without UPnP, but because UPnP products can *talk* with each other, setting up a system like this becomes a fairly automatic thing. We might even buy into the name and say, "It's plug and play!"

Moving forward, UPnP will be moved into more and more devices in the home. Smart appliances, for example, or smart thermostats, may eventually be UPnP compatible and combine with a PC and a home-control system without special programming or configuration.

We're not going to promise you that UPnP will be a huge success — we've seen similar initiatives go by the wayside — but we do know that a lot of equipment vendors throughout the electronics industry are beginning to put UPnP functionality in the next generation of their products. That's the key to any solution like this taking off: It has to be widely available in products that people will buy anyway. As the number of UPnP devices in the home grows, so does the usefulness of the protocol.

Getting fancy with home automation

For home automation and control that goes beyond even the functionality of most PC-based X10 control systems, you may want to consider a high-end, proprietary home-automation system. These are stand-alone systems that you usually mount in a panel in your home's wiring closet. They have their own central-controller unit (usually a PC-based computer), X10 controllers, and interfaces to a large number of other systems, such as security systems, audio and video networks, telephone and intercom systems, and external sensors.

The most sophisticated PC-based controller systems, such as HAL2000 and HomeVoice, perform many of the same functions as these stand-alone systems but use your PC in the place of the central controller. The HAL2000 system includes a voice-to-PC interface, and the HomeVoice System offers one as an extra.

If you walk into a really high-end A/V dealership (the kind of place with $50,000 speaker systems and the like), chances are you'll see Crestron's

systems on display next to the megabuck A/V gear. Crestron is *the* choice for expensive smart homes, and it's not for the shallow of pocketbook: A typical Crestron installation in a residential setting costs about $50,000.

If you can afford it, Crestron is a cool way to go. The keys to Crestron's system are a series of touchpad controllers and a centralized computer-based controller. With these pieces in place (along with a wiring infrastructure of CAT-5e and Crestron's own powered CrestNet cable), you can use the system to control just about everything in your home — HVAC systems, lighting, security, audio and video systems, and more. Crestron is more than just a control network. The combination of CAT-5e and CrestNet cable is used also as a distribution backbone for audio, video, and even computer LAN networks throughout the home. If you're looking for the ultimate in smart homes, check out Crestron's systems at www.crestron.com.

Control Networks for Entertainment Systems

Home-audio and -video systems present a special case for home automation and control because you probably want to do a lot more with a VCR or CD player than just turn it on and off. In fact, you need a whole host of commands such as start and stop, pause, and fast forward that X10 doesn't even begin to address.

In a single room, you can take care of these functions using an infrared (IR) remote control — either the control that came with your equipment or one of the programmable universal remotes. Unfortunately, IR remote controls are line-of-sight and can't carry signals between rooms. So unless you can somehow suspend the laws of physics, pressing repeatedly on the pause button of your VCR's remote doesn't do you a bit of good if you're in the bedroom and the VCR is downstairs in the living room.

You have the following three common ways of getting around this problem:

- ✔ Use a *radio frequency (RF) remote system,* if your equipment supports it.
- ✔ Use an *RF repeater* system to expand the reach of your IR remote.
- ✔ Use a *wired IR repeater system* to send the remote-control signals from one room to another.

You can use X10 to control audio and video systems by buying an *X10-to-IR converter,* such as the one that SmartLinc makes, which learns the IR commands that your system uses and maps them to certain house and unit-code combinations. Any X10 controller in your home can then send IR signals to your audio and video equipment — the controller sends X10 signals to the X10-to-IR converter, which translates the X10 into IR and sends the signals to your equipment.

We prefer to use a dedicated IR network such as the ones we describe in the following sections, but using X10 is a perfectly legitimate solution to your remote-control needs if you're an X10 diehard.

Using RF remotes

Radio waves have one big advantage over light waves (including those of the infrared variety): They can get through and around obstacles such as walls, furniture, and large house pets. This particular trait makes radio waves ideal for whole-home remote-control systems. Unfortunately, because they cost more, RF remote controls are rarely part of the consumer-electronics package. If your entertainment-network needs are simple (for example, you just want to watch the output of your DBS satellite dish from a different TV), you may be able to find components fitted with an RF remote. Sony, for example, sells a DSS receiver system with an RF remote for just this purpose.

If your network becomes a bit more complicated, or if you already have the components and are stuck with IR remotes, you do have a solution. Several manufacturers offer wireless, RF-repeater systems for IR remotes.

Setting one of these systems up is a piece of cake. Most consist of just two parts: a *transmitter* that converts IR signals from your remote control to radio waves and beams them out throughout your home, and a corresponding *receiver* that reverses the process and sends the reconverted IR signals to your audio and video equipment. All you need to do is plug the receiver into a wall near the equipment that you want to control and do the same with the transmitter in your remote location. Some transmitters even come in a small, battery-powered package — simply slip such a transmitter over the end of your IR remote control and carry it to wherever you want listen or watch.

We've seen another variation on this theme as well. Consisting of the same transmitter/receiver duo, some systems plug into a wall outlet and carry your remote-control signals over your home's AC power lines instead of using RF signals.

Both these systems should work reasonably well, but they do have the following downsides:

- ✔ RF signals are better than IR at getting through and around obstacles, but as anyone with a cordless phone can tell you, they're not foolproof. Long distances, thick walls, and interference by other RF sources can cause problems.

- ✔ Powerline solutions can also suffer from interference and electrical noise in your electrical wiring.

- ✔ RF and powerline repeater systems aren't sophisticated enough for use in elaborate, multizoned audio-and video-distribution systems — they can't distinguish between zones or discriminate between multiple pieces of audio or video source equipment.

Using a wired IR repeater system

The best way to distribute audio and video control signals throughout your home is to install a hardwired, IR-signal-distribution network. In this kind of system, the IR signals from a standard handheld remote or wall-mounted keypad convert to electrical signals. These signals then travel to your entertainment center over in-wall wiring that runs to your audio or video equipment room and, by using devices known as *emitters,* are converted back into IR signals that can control your systems.

You can wire an IR network in one of the following three ways:

- ✔ You can run dedicated IR cables along with your audio and video signal-distribution wiring.

- ✔ You can use an IR repeater system that uses CAT-5e UTP cabling to carry the signals. Many of the CAT-5e video and audio systems that we discuss in Chapters 7 and 9 carry IR control signals along with your audio and video source signals, so you can carry everything on a single CAT-5e.

- ✔ You can piggyback the IR signals on the RG6 coaxial cabling that you use for video distribution (as we mention in Chapter 7).

The third option, using existing coaxial video-distribution cables, requires you to have audio and video network outlets in the same locations. If you have some audio outlets (or wall speakers) in places where no video outlet is present, you can't control the system in that location.

The following components are common to any IR network:

- **Infrared sensors:** These devices convert the IR signal from a handheld remote into a DC electrical signal that you can distribute over your IR wiring. IR sensors come in a variety of shapes and sizes, including wall-mounted units, tabletop units, and even minisized sensors that you can hide in a small hole in the wall.

- **Infrared emitters:** At the other end of an IR network (next to your audio and video equipment), you install devices known as emitters. An *emitter* converts the DC electrical signal back into an IR signal and beams this signal to your equipment. Some companies call these devices *IR blasters*.

- **Emitter-connecting blocks:** These devices enable you to connect IR sensors in different rooms to single or multiple emitters. If you have a multizone audio system, an emitter-connecting block is an essential component of the IR control network because it enables you to separate IR signals by zone — so the signals from a particular zone go only to equipment that serves the same zone. For a system that uses CAT-5e cabling instead of IR cabling, you can use a standard CAT-5e patch panel to connect cables and route IR signals to and from your media room.

- **IR keypad controllers:** You can use a keypad controller in place of a handheld remote and IR sensor. Keypads are not required and cost more than simple sensors, but they're really cool. Mounted on the wall, like a light switch, the keypad controller can learn the IR commands that your system uses and send them back to your emitters at the push of a button.

Chapter 20

Making Home Automation
a Reality

In Chapter 19, we talk about all the things that make up your automated home. In this chapter, we talk about wiring and design strategies for putting it all together. Specifically, we talk about home-automation networks and IR-control networks. Neither of these networks requires much in the way of special wiring — especially X10-based powerline networks for home automation, but certain IR networks do require the installation of control wiring.

Installation is only half the battle in these kinds of systems, however. The real trick is to configure all the sensors, modules, emitters, keypads, and so on to make sure that they work together correctly. For simple networks — such as X10 lighting controls or IR controllers for single-zone audio networks — this configuration job isn't too difficult a task, but more complicated systems can test your patience, diligence, and skill at reading manuals. We can't simply tell you how to get your Xantech IR controller keypad, for example, to turn your Toshiba VCR and Harmon Kardon amplifier on and off — just too many variables exist for us to cover everything.

What we can do, however, is give you a good jumping-off point for getting a home-automation and control infrastructure in place and provide you with some useful tips for getting started.

X10 Marks the Spot

The wonderful thing about X10 (and other home-automation standards that use powerline communications) is that the installation's effects on your home's wiring infrastructure are minimal. However, you should consider having an electrician do a few things to optimize your home's wiring for X10 control (and we describe such changes in the following sections), but these optimizations aren't complicated or expensive.

After your power lines are ready for X10, setting up the X10 components is the epitome of plug and play. Plug a module into a power receptacle, plug the light or appliance into it, and that part of your network is complete. This simplicity, combined with the low cost of components are the main reasons why X10 continues to be the default recommendation for home-automation systems.

You can take a few additional steps and precautions to ensure that everything works together in happiness and harmony: install bridges, noise blocks, signal amplifiers, and X10-compatible surge protectors, as well as make sure that all your receptacles have three wires rather than two.

Building bridges

Depending on the state of the electrical wiring in your house, your electrician may need to install a device known as an *X10 signal coupler* in your electrical service panel. This handy-dandy little unit — which costs about $50 — enables the X10 signals to get around the house even if the electrical system is split into two circuits (not an uncommon situation).

The power line that comes into your home from the utility company usually consists of a two-phase, 220-volt power line (two 110-volt phases). After this line connects to your service panel or breaker box, the two phases split from each other to provide 110-volt power lines to all standard outlets, switches, and hardwired fixtures. (A few outlets in your home, such as those for electric clothes dryers, use both phases for 220-volt circuits.) Because of this separation, X10 signals in some homes have a hard time getting across from one phase to the other. So a controller connecting to an electrical circuit in one room may not "see" a module in another room that runs on the other phase of the circuit. The signal coupler forms a bridge that enables the X10 commands to jump across to the other phase.

A good way to tell whether an X10 problem is caused by this phase issue is to turn on an electric oven or dryer (these devices typically use 220-volt AC and effectively create a temporary bridge between the two legs when they're on). If your problem goes away when the oven's on, you need a coupler to correct the problem permanently.

Keep those nosy (or noisy) neighbors off your X10

X10 signals aren't very powerful — you don't need to worry about one traveling back up your power lines and sending your local nuclear reactor into meltdown. X10 signals could, however, go from house to house in the small local area served by the local transformer for your house (that round thing on the telephone pole), disrupting your carefully planned X10 system.

Other X10 signals aren't the only thing that can make X10 signals act a bit funky. Electrical interference of all kinds finds its way into power lines, giving you a noisy power supply, which can disrupt X10 signals.

If your X10 network is behaving weirdly or if you're just the cautious type, you may want to have an electrician install a *noise block* inline to your electrical power feed, just before the circuit-breaker box. This device should stop any incoming interference and keep the neighbors' controllers from triggering your modules.

Most of the noise blocks we've seen (ranging from $70 cheap ones to fancy $500 models) include signal-coupling functionality as well. So the electrician can make only one trip to kill these two birds (the noise block and the coupler).

Dozens of items in a typical home can interfere with X10 signals by creating noise on the electrical power lines — for example, fluorescent lights, air conditioners, fax machines, and even computers or audio equipment. In some cases, the circuits and chips within these devices send unintended electrical energy back into the power infrastructure that is similar enough (electrically) to block X10. In these cases, you can install an in-line noise filter (that plugs in between the noisy device and the wall) or a hardwired filter (for devices that are hardwired into the electrical system — such as air conditioners).

Noise-blocking filters are easy to install (especially the plug-in inline filters). The hard part is figuring out which of the dozens or hundreds of electrical devices in your house are causing the problem. You can buy an X10 signal-testing device, which may help you track down problems, but for most people, the best approach is good, old-fashioned trial and error. When you have issues with a certain X10 module not receiving signals, start turning off electrical devices until your module works again. Nope, it's not rocket science, but it does work! When you find the offender, simply install a noise filter and get back to your X10 lifestyle.

Boost that signal

In an average-sized home, X10 signals coming from controllers (or back over the network from two-way modules) are usually strong enough to reach any spot in the house — as long as there's a signal coupler in place. Like many other things (cars, packs of toilet paper, and supersized fries, to name a few) houses are getting bigger. After a house hits about 3000 square feet, X10 signals start having a hard time reaching distant nooks and crannies. The solution here is to install an X10-signal amplifier/repeater in the main electrical panel.

There's no big mystery about what a signal amplifier/repeater does (this is definitely a case where the name fits). X10 signals entering the electrical panel pass through the signal amplifier/repeater, and the signal is boosted (amplified) and repeated to ensure that it reaches remote modules with sufficient strength to be understood by the module.

Even in smaller homes, a signal amplifier/repeater can come in handy as a way of getting around noisy electrical lines, because the stronger signal is easier for modules to pick out from background noise. In fact, Leviton recommends that you always install their signal amplifier/repeater whenever you install their DHC X10 systems.

Signal amplifier/repeaters almost always have a built-in signal coupler, so you won't need a separate coupler.

Surge protectors kill X10

Surge protectors, devices that protect your sensitive electronic equipment from transient voltages (such as lightning strikes on utility poles), can be real lifesavers. Ask people who have had a power surge zap a computer or television, and they'll tell you how much they wish they'd invested $30 or $40 on a decent surge protector.

Unfortunately, many surge protectors not only filter out bad stuff such as lightning but also remove or disable X10 signals. So you're left with an unpleasant choice: Protect your equipment from surges or automate it with X10?

Luckily, you have the following two ways of getting around this problem:

- ✔ Install X10-compatible surge protector strips (which don't cost any more than good-quality conventional ones) and plug your appliance modules into the strips.

- ✔ Take a whole-home approach to surge protection and have an electrician install a whole-home surge suppressor at your breaker box. These suppressors cost about $200 (the same as five or six good-quality strips), and they protect every circuit in your home.

When lightning strikes, no one can predict where it will hit. Your power line (safely protected behind a surge protector) may not be the thing that gets struck. There are plenty of other electrical paths to your home's other sensitive electronics — antenna and cable TV cables, phone lines, or even satellite dishes and their cables. It makes good sense to install surge protectors on all these systems, just in case.

Wire those switches right

As your electrician is installing junction boxes and wiring for light switches in your home, tell him or her to do the following (and you'll *really* sound like you know what you're doing!):

> *Run the neutral wire to the light switch's junction box instead of bypassing it.*

Having all the wires run to the switch rather than some to the switch and some directly to the light gives you more freedom to install X10 switches in the future.

Each of the 110-volt electrical circuits in a house consists of three separate wires: a *hot* wire (usually black), which supplies the current to the circuit, a *neutral* wire (usually white), which provides a return path for the current, and a *ground* wire (usually green), which grounds the circuit for safety. The conventional way to install light switches is to connect the hot wire to one side of the switch and run another wire, called the *load* (usually blue), from the switch to the light (or other device) itself. The neutral and ground wires often bypass the switch and run directly to the light. So the switch just interrupts the flow of the hot wire's current to the light: The light itself completes and grounds the circuit.

In an X10 environment, the wiring scheme for switches limits what you can control with an X10 light switch. X10 switches can control only incandescent light fixtures if you wire the switches this way — because the light bulb filament itself provides a path for the X10 signals, something that fluorescent and low-voltage lights can't do. If you want to use a switch to control fluorescent lights, low-voltage track lighting, or appliances, you need to use a special inductive dimmer or appliance switch that connects all the wires: the hot wire, the load wire, and the neutral wire. So all these wires must be available at the junction box.

For more information on how to wire electrical switches and how not to fry yourself while working with them, please check out *Home Improvement For Dummies,* by Gene and Katie Hamilton and the editors of HouseNet (published by Wiley Publishing, Inc.).

Some of the fancy X10-controllable mood-lighting switches also require this neutral wire connection, even for incandescent lights.

Controlling Your Home-Automation Systems

You can use X10 and other home-automation protocols and equipment in one of the following two ways:

✔ As a simple home-control system that enables you to perform actions in one part of the house while you're in another part of the house

✔ As part of a true automated system that performs actions on its own, based on a schedule or on events that it detects

The modularity of X10 and the fact that it's based on a common standard that ensures that each manufacturer's equipment works with another's make starting off with a simple home-control network and gradually building your way up to a fully automated system easy. You just add new components to the network as you go. So if you're not convinced that an automated home is for you, you can start with a few components and — if the X10 bug bites — go crazy with it later.

Keeping it simple

If you just want to get your feet wet in the home-automation world, we recommend that you start with a simple X10 home-control network. You probably don't need to worry about electrical-wiring considerations or how to connect your computer to the network. All you really need to do is to plug a few lamp or appliance modules and a minicontroller into your AC power line.

We can't promise that you aren't going to experience some electrical-wiring difficulties, even in a simple X10 network, but most people don't.

For a total investment of less than about $75 (about $11 for the controller and $8 for each lamp or appliance module), you can set up a simple network that controls eight lights or small appliances from a central location.

Expanding this network is as simple as adding more modules and controllers as your needs expand. You may want a controller in the living room to set the right lighting levels for movie watching and another in the master bedroom to turn on a bunch of lights if you hear something go bump in the night.

Linking your car and home with HomeLink

More than 140 new car models are now available with a remote-control system called *HomeLink*. For most folks, the main selling point for this system is its capability to operate most garage-door openers; you don't need to search under the seat for the door-opener remote. HomeLink is integrated into your car's interior — usually in the headliner above the rearview mirror — and usually consists of two or three pushbuttons (each of which controls a single device). Some cars include HomeLink controller buttons on the car's remote entry key fob.

In a smart-home environment, however, you can also use one or more of the HomeLink's RF

channels (most versions have three) to trigger wireless X10 controllers to send commands to such devices as lights and even X10-compatible security systems — from the warmth and comfort of your car. HomeLink doesn't sell as an after-market add-in — instead, it sells as a built-in, integral part of the car (although some automakers sell HomeLink as a dealer-installed accessory that you can have installed in certain car models after the fact). To find out more about HomeLink, look on the Web at `http://www.homelink.com`.

You can also expand your control network by installing X10 wireless controllers that enable you to trigger controls without leaving the comfort of your couch or the front porch with a key-ring wireless controller.

You can also train some universal "learning" remotes for home-entertainment systems to send X10 commands. That way, you don't need both an audio/video and an X10 remote in your home theater.

If you want to add a degree of automation to this X10 control network, simply plug a programmable controller into an AC receptacle. Doing so enables you to create simple timed programs to activate or turn off various modules.

Adding a computer for more control

Adding a personal computer to the mix enables you to bring a new level of sophistication to a home-control and home-automation network. The addition of an X10 interface and graphical-interface software on your PC enables you to create complicated on/off schedules quickly and easily. The ease of using a computer interface for this purpose — instead of trying to fiddle with a small, somewhat unintuitive programmable controller — is worth the price of admission.

But wait — there's more! (We loved those old Ginsu knife commercials.) By using the computer software, you can program your PC's X10 interface box to perform *macros* — sets of consecutive commands, such as turn on the

Put your network on the Net

Suppose that you control your home's X10 network with a PC. You also have an always-on cable-modem or DSL connection to the Internet. Why not put the two together and use the Internet connection to control your PC from work or even from your laptop's wireless Net connection wherever you are? Well, you can do just that with HAI's Omni controller system and WebLink II software (check out www.home auto.com).

The total package (the high-end hardware controller and the Web-based software) typically costs about $1500, which includes the professional installation of a system that controls not only lights but also the thermostat and a security system. HAI can also integrate touchpad controllers for remote control of your audio/video network.

WebLink II uses a standard Windows PC as a Web server. The WebLink II software creates a series of interactive Web pages which can give you a current status of your home and control of any devices in your home that are connected to the Omni controller. You can turn lights and appliances on and off (individually or by using lighting scenes as discussed in Chapter 19), adjust the thermostat, and arm or disarm the security system. You can even use the software to remotely view video surveillance cameras that you've connected to the PC. The WebLink II software can also be set up to send you e-mail alerts or messages when certain conditions have occurred (such as an alarm condition or the kids returning home from school).

kitchen light, start the coffee pot, and open the curtains. After you create a macro, you can save it and use it again. For example, you could create a lighting macro for TV watching, and then schedule it for whenever your favorite shows are on. You can even download macros from the Internet and apply them to your system.

To see some neat downloadable macros, check out the X10 ActiveHome site at www.x10.com/products/macros.htm.

Making your home interactive

Remotely controlling and scripting your home-automation systems are pretty cool ways of automating your home, but you can bring an automated home to a higher level by making it interactive and intelligent. By combining sensors with your X10 control systems, you can program your home to react to certain events by turning on lights, alerting you with a chime, or even muting your TV.

You can integrate sensors into a home-automation system in the following three ways:

 ✔ You can keep things in the X10 realm, utilizing sensors with built-in X10 controllers to trigger events.

✔ You can integrate an alarm system with your home-automation network and use the alarm's sensors to trigger home-automation events.

✔ If you have a sophisticated PC-based or stand-alone home-automation controller, you can directly connect sensors to the controller.

The following sections elaborate on these three methods.

X10 sensors

The simplest way to integrate sensors into a home-automation network is to install X10 sensors in your home. These sensors combine the sensor itself (a photocell or passive infrared detector, for example) and a controller that can send X10 commands to several addresses. You don't need to go through a central controller for these devices — just assign some X10 actions to them (such as turning on certain lights) and plug them into a power line receptacle. It's that simple.

Among the X10 sensors that we've seen are the following:

✔ **X10 photocells:** Unless you live way up North, you can plan on the sun coming up and going down every day. By using an X10 photocell, your home can distinguish the light from the dark and automatically turn lights on at dusk and off at dawn.

✔ **X10 motion detectors:** By using a PIR, these wall-mounted sensors can send several X10 commands if they detect motion. You might want to install one in the upstairs hallway, for example, and set it to automatically turn on the hall lights if someone walks by.

Many X10 motion detectors also have a built-in photocell so that you can set them to turn on lights only as darkness falls.

✔ **X10 motion-detector floodlights:** These outdoor lights function just like the standard motion-detector lights that guide your path down the front walk after your dog forces you into yet another late-night walk. By using a PIR, these lights turn themselves on if someone (or something — such as that pesky dog from next door) walks into their detection field. After they turn on, the floodlights also send out a number of X10 signals (usually up to eight) and trigger other X10 devices such as inside lights or chime modules.

Some of the motion-detector floodlights that we've seen (such as the X10 Wireless Technologies FloodCam mentioned in Chapter 17) include photocell sensors so that you can use them to turn on other lights at dusk. Many also have X10 functionality so that you can use any X10 controller to turn them on manually.

✔ **The X10 PowerFlash module:** This module accepts the output of almost any stand-alone sensor — such as a magnetic door-closure sensor, a doorbell, a driveway sensor, or even a non-X10 burglar alarm — and sends an X10 command if something activates the sensor.

Using an X10 alarm

As we discuss in Chapter 11, a typical home-security system is chock full of sensors — door-contact sensors, window-contact sensors, glass-breakage detectors, PIRs, pressure-sensitive doormats, and many more. The primary function of these sensors is, of course, to monitor your house for bad guys and trigger the alarm if necessary. By using an X10-compatible alarm system (or by adding an X10 controller expansion module to certain brands of existing alarm systems), you can make these sensors serve double duty.

The simplest of these X10-compatible alarm systems simply activates an X10 command (such as All On) in an alarm condition — in other words, they turn on your lights if the alarm siren sounds. This setup isn't really the kind of home automation we're talking about, but it does add a nice security feature. (Being able to see where you're going sure would be nice after you peel yourself off the ceiling during a middle-of-the-night alarm.)

More sophisticated systems take a more subtle approach in that they offer levels of reaction to various sensor inputs. In other words, these security systems are smart enough to know that certain sensor inputs don't necessarily spell doom. A pressure-sensitive doormat or a driveway sensor, for example, tells the system that someone is there, whether a burglar or the UPS delivery person. Obviously, the system's reaction to these sensor inputs should be something less than a full alarm. (No need to call out the cavalry if it's just the pizza guy.)

These security systems can interface with your X10 network in the following ways:

- A sensor input can trigger a random X10 output to create a "lived-in" look. An outdoor PIR motion detector, for example, may cause your alarm control panel to send X10 signals to lights in several different rooms, turning them on and off at seemingly random intervals.
- In the most advanced of these systems, you can program specific sensor inputs to trigger specific X10 outputs. So the motion detector in the backyard can turn on the rear porch lights, or the driveway sensor can turn on the carriage lights running from the driveway to the front door.

Combining sensors with a central controller

The biggest drawback to having an alarm trigger X10 events is that X10 alarm systems are somewhat limited in their capabilities. Specifically, X10 alarm systems allow you to respond to a sensor input with only a limited number of X10 commands — usually four to eight for an X10 sensor and up to about sixteen with an X10-compatible alarm system.

If you want to create a sophisticated, interactive home-automation system — one that combines a large number of sensors with a whole bunch of potential corresponding commands — consider using a high-end PC-based or stand-alone home-control system. These systems directly accept the inputs of a

Voice control, the ultimate in interactivity

A few home-automation control software packages include voice activation as the primary means of controlling your home's systems. Using recent developments in speech recognition, these systems (most notably the HomeVoice system by Applied Future Technologies and the HAL2000 from Home Automated Living) enable you to speak in plain English to initiate X10 or IR commands. So you can boss your house around, *Star Trek* style, turning on lights or opening drapes without lifting a finger.

A discreet, omnidirectional microphone (or a telephone, for remote access) picks up the sound of your voice and feeds it into the microphone input of your PC's sound card. The speech-recognition software then translates your commands and correlates them with stored X10 or IR commands and sends the appropriate control signals out over your home's powerline or IR network. These products can also use speech synthesis to talk back to you — giving you a confirmation that your command was heard and carried out. Neat stuff.

Connecting a microphone to the sound card of your PC and getting the system up and running in the same room that contains your computer and computer-to-X10 interface are simple tasks. The job becomes a bit trickier, however, if you want to use voice control throughout the house. To do so, you need to install microphones in each room and run microphone cable back to the controller location. Because most sound cards have only one microphone input, you need to combine all incoming microphone leads into a microphone mixer, which sends a single signal into the PC. (On the horizon is a method that uses distributed microphones built into light switches or other distributed devices that can process the sound at the origin and send over X10 only the actual command inputs.)

Both systems are software-based and run on most Pentium-class PCs. They're compatible with most computer-to-X10 interfaces, so you can add voice control into an existing system easily. Microphones cost about $90 each, but the mixers we've seen are expensive. (The HomeVoice mixer kit, which also includes a limiter/gate device to help filter out background noise, costs nearly $700.) The software itself isn't too expensive — $239 for HomeVoice and $169 for HAL2000.

We think that voice control is a logical next step for home-automation and home-control networks and something you're going to see more of in the future.

number of sensors and can control hundreds of X10 modules and non-X10 hardwired systems (such as heating, ventilation, and air conditioning systems and sprinkler controls), based on the settings you enter into the system's control interface.

These intelligent home controllers can accept the following two types of sensor inputs:

- **Analog inputs:** These sensors can detect a range of measurements, such as temperature sensors or moisture/humidity detectors.

- **Digital inputs:** These sensors either detect a condition or don't detect one, such as motion/no motion sensors.

The wiring for these sensors varies — depending on the individual sensor type and manufacturer — but most use wiring similar to what you use for wiring alarm sensors (two- or four-conductor wiring, although some temperature sensors use three-conductor wiring). The key to integrating sensors into such a system is to anticipate as much of your sensor needs as you can upfront so that you can have your installer run the right wires ahead of time.

After you connect the sensors to your controller, you can program them (using a computer or a television and the system's graphical-interface software) and even create event-driven macros that map sensor inputs to specific control outputs. The sky's the limit here — if a system is controllable, you can match it to a sensor input. We'd like to find a way to turn on the lawn sprinklers if a salesperson comes to our door, but we haven't yet been able to find a sensor that can differentiate between the Fuller Brush man and the next-door neighbor.

Getting IR Around the House

As we mention in Chapter 19, X10 is a great system for controlling all sorts of devices in a home, but it's not ideal for taking care of the complicated commands that you need to control audio and video systems. You can rig up an X10/IR converter system to perform this task, but doing so is complicated and a case of reinventing the wheel.

We make that last statement because you already have a great way of controlling audio and video systems — by using IR remotes. The only problem with

Yet another use for CAT-5e

We've mentioned — oh boy, we're not sure we can even count it, but a lot — of ways to use Cat-5e cabling in your house. Phone networks and data networks use Cat-5e; audio and video networks can use it. There's really not much you can't do with Cat-5e cabling. It's useful stuff.

So it probably won't surprise you to learn that you can use Cat-5e cabling in place of 3-conductor IR cabling in your home. There are two ways this can work for you:

✔ You can use 3 of the 8 conductors in Cat-5e cabling as a direct replacement for the 3 conductors in IR cabling. This is a pretty

simple process, just use the same three conductors on each end of the connection, and leave the others unterminated.

✔ You can use IR receivers and keypads, which have been designed to work with Cat-5e wiring. Many of these keypad-based systems, for example, Leviton's Chopin Volume control, or Kustom's Nuvo E6M keypad system need more than two conductors to do their job, and are built from the start to accept only Cat-5e cabling to send control signals back to the media room.

IR remotes is that IR signals don't pass through walls and floors. You can solve this problem by using a radio frequency IR-extender system — this is the cheap and easy solution. Unfortunately, the RF method isn't quite up to the job of controlling multiple systems in multizone networks. To do that, you need a wired IR-repeater network.

If you're sending audio and video signals around your house using one of the next-generation CAT-5e systems — such as Leviton's Decora Media System or ChannelPlus's SVC-10 system — you probably don't need an extra network to handle your IR networking needs. Most of these systems (including the two mentioned) use spare conductors on the CAT-5e cable that carries the audio and video signals around the house to also carry IR signals. This is a neat, integrated way of creating an A/V network — you don't need separate audio, video, and IR control infrastructures. Remote control of these network systems is usually accomplished with a touchpad or an IR sensor built into the remote CAT-5e faceplate (or sometimes both — a touchpad with a built-in IR receiver).

Making your coaxial cable work overtime

If you have a coaxial cable network to distribute video signals throughout the home *and* if the endpoints of this network correspond with the endpoints of your audio network (or you don't have a whole-home audio network), you can avoid running extra wires throughout the home by running IR signals over that coaxial cable.

To do so, you need to install devices known as *IR signal injector/splitters,* which perform two tasks. In remote locations, the signal injector/splitter combines the electrical signal that an IR sensor sends with the video signals running over your coaxial network. In your media equipment room, another signal injector/splitter splits the same signal out from the coaxial cable and feeds it to an IR emitter to control your equipment. Figure 20-1 shows how these devices fit into a coaxial network.

Many newer audio/video devices, such as receivers and DVD players, are built with the home networker in mind and come with a jack on the back for connecting to remote IR systems. In these cases, you don't need to use an IR emitter. Instead, you connect the IR cable directly into this jack, usually using a stereo miniplug like the one used for headphones on iPods and portable CD players. Makes for a neater appearance and usually works better — we like this trend a lot.

The signal injector/splitter needs electrical power to do its thing, because it's creating an electrical signal from an IR sensor output. You have the following two ways of providing this power to the devices:

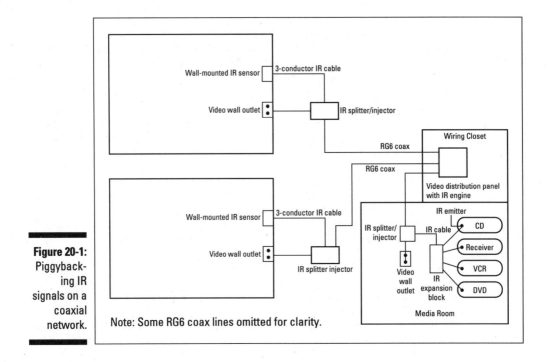

Figure 20-1:
Piggyback-
ing IR
signals on a
coaxial
network.

Note: Some RG6 coax lines omitted for clarity.

✔ You can install a device known as a *remote power injector* near your coaxial distribution panel. One of these devices provides power for the entire network.

✔ You can use a video-distribution panel (discussed in detail in Chapter 7), which has a built-in power injector. *Note:* Some coaxial panel makers call this feature an *IR engine* (and no, it doesn't burn high-octane fuel) because it powers all remote IR sensors.

You can configure the guts of this IR network — where the IR signal splits off the coaxial network and goes to IR emitters — in one of the following ways:

✔ If you're controlling only one or two devices (such as a single VCR or an audio receiver and CD player), simply connect the IR output of the signal injector (it has both an RF output and an IR output) to a single or dual IR emitter. The emitters themselves usually stick right onto the IR sensor of the equipment they control, so you need one per piece of equipment.

✔ If you're trying to control more than two pieces of A/V equipment in one location, you can connect your signal injector/splitter to an IR expansion block, which enables you to connect multiple emitters to a single injector/splitter.

You can find IR-over-coax gear from most vendors of coaxial video network equipment. We like the stuff from ChannelPlus (www.channelplus.com).

TECHNICAL STUFF

Multizone IR considerations

If the roster of devices that an IR network controls includes a multizone audio system, you need to use a connecting block specifically designed for multiple-zone systems. This requirement stems from the fact that some of the components in this system are zone-specific, and others are common to the entire system.

The amplifier that powers the speakers in a particular zone, for example, is used (and controlled) only in that zone, while all zones share the CD or DVD player.

A multizone connecting block separates the common and shared IR signals by providing separate sets of emitter connections: common emitter signals and zone-specific emitter signals. This separation is especially important if, for example, you use the same type of amplifier in several different zones. By using the zone-specific emitter signal, you can direct *which* amplifier you actually want to turn up (or turn off).

Getting a multizone system up and running can prove a difficult and frustrating process — and one best left to a professional. Trust us on this one.

Being dedicated

Using coaxial cable is a perfectly adequate method of IR distribution, but the optimal way of carrying IR signals throughout a house is to build a separate IR control network using its own wiring. This setup provides the most flexibility and reliability and makes controlling several components in a multizone audio system easier.

The majority of hardwired IR-distribution networks use simple three-conductor shielded cable (sold as IR cable in most catalogs and stores) to connect remote locations back to your audio and video network equipment. You wire this cable in a simple star architecture, with an individual run coming from each control point back to the audio/video equipment room, as shown in Figure 20-2. You can also run your IR cabling in a daisy-chain fashion, with a single cable running from room to room, connecting all your sensors and keypads. This type of wiring works only with a single-zone audio network, and we recommend that you don't try to save money on IR cable (which costs only about ten cents a foot) by running your cabling this way.

Even if you start off with a single-zone speaker-wire audio system, you may want to upgrade to a multizone system some day. A star-architecture speaker-wire system used for a single-zone audio network can easily be upgraded to multizone with some additional equipment in the network. Don't get caught with an IR system that has to be completely reworked — wire your IR network the same way, with individual cabling runs to each remote location.

Plugging in the PC

As the PC becomes more integrated into your home's audio and video networks, you'll find that having a way to control audio equipment while sitting in front of the computer (or having your computer do this automatically) can come in handy. For example, if you're using your PC as a PVR and recording TV shows on the PC's hard drive, it's necessary to give the PC (and your PVR software on the PC — such as Snap Stream's Personal Video Station) the capability to tune your TV, cable set-top box, or DSS receiver to the channel you want to record.

Most of these solutions use an IR emitter with a USB interface to the PC. The PVR software on the PC then sends an IR signal out through this USB interface, which can control the channel changing. If your PC isn't in the same room as the video source equipment (and it probably won't be), you can aim the IR emitter from this USB interface at an IR receiver installed in the room where the computer is located, and use your wired IR infrastructure to carry the commands back to your media room.

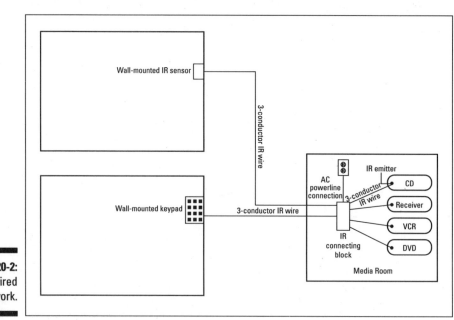

Figure 20-2:
A hardwired
IR network.

The MonsterCable company (at www.monstercable.com on the Web) sells some neat in-wall speaker cabling that includes IR cable in the same cable jacket. If you run this cable to speaker locations, you automatically prewire these locations for IR control as well.

IR control isn't like an Ethernet or telephone network. You don't have a fixed standard that all emitters, IR receivers, or remote keypads must adhere to for their cabling. You may find equipment that needs some different type of cable than the three-conductor version we're discussing. Some keypads, for example, use CAT-5e cabling or special IR cabling that uses a fourth conductor. Although the majority of equipment uses three-conductor cable, you need to determine the requirements of your equipment *before* you prewire your house.

Connecting the endpoints of this network — the IR sensors and keypads and IR emitters — to the IR cabling infrastructure is easy. Sensors and keypads connect directly to the end of the IR cable in remote locations — nothing complicated about that. On the equipment end of the network, all your IR cable "home runs" terminate on a connecting block, which then provides a number of outputs for IR emitters. The IR emitters simply plug into these outputs and physically sit right in front of the IR receivers on your audio/video equipment.

Like the IR-over-coaxial network that we discuss in the "Making your coaxial cable work overtime" section, the hardwired IR network needs a power supply to make the sensors sense, the emitters emit, and the keypads . . . er . . . key. Providing this power is a secondary job of the connecting block.

Using emitters, sensors, keypads, and connecting blocks from a single manufacturer ensures that everything works together smoothly. Major manufacturers of these systems, such as Niles Audio (at www.nilesaudio.com), Nuvo (at www.nuvotechnologies.com), and Xantech (at www.xantech.com) make all these parts in matched sets.

Part VII
The Part of Tens

In this part . . .

Top ten lists! You love 'em — we love 'em. We won't claim to top David Letterman's daily list in terms of humor, but we do try to be useful.

In this section, we give you some tips on things to avoid as you network and automate your home. These are big "uh-ohs" that we did ourselves (back in the early days) or that we've seen others do. We want to spare you the pain.

When it comes to smart-ifying your home, it's all about the toys, right? We discuss ten of the coolest new toys on the block — things that make your smart home a fun home. Some of these you can buy today, and others are well along in their development. All are very cool.

Chapter 21

Ten Common Pitfalls When Building Your Smart Home

● ●

In This Chapter

▶ Missing the basics of automation

▶ Not reading the manual

▶ Thinking that AC and low voltage are friends

▶ Using the weakest link

▶ That PPPPPP thing

▶ Thinking that wiring is a dirty word

▶ Falling into the proprietary pitfall

▶ Falling into the all-in-one trap

▶ Forgetting to add conduit

▶ Not bothering to use labels

● ●

*T*hroughout this book, we try to point out potential gotchas that we've run into when building a smart home — things we've seen other people do, horror stories our friends in the smart-home industry have told us, and even a few dumb things we did when we were first getting started.

Building a smart home isn't rocket science or brain surgery. It's a common-sense approach to home building and wiring that makes your house more valuable to you now and more useful in the future. But we all know that common sense ain't all that common, so here are ten things we think are important to remember not to do as you get going.

Missing the Basics of Automation

X10 automation is simple. Plug a module in one outlet and a controller in another, and you're ready to go. But (as we mention in Chapters 19 and 20), X10 relies on communications over your home's electrical power lines, which were never designed to be a communications network. So your electrician, the power company, and companies that make electrical lights, appliances, and devices that connect to your AC power spent little time making sure you'd have a nice, noise-free power network over which you could automate and control your house.

You need to keep the following in mind:

- ✔ In the U.S., the electrical main line coming into your house consists of two 110-volt phases, which are split off at the main distribution panel. Some outlets in your house are connected to one of these phases, and the other outlets to the other phase. To get X10 signals to cross over to different phases, you need to install a signal coupler in your main distribution panel. This is serious, high-voltage, zap-yourself-and-don't-live-to-tell-about-it stuff, so hire a qualified electrician to do it for you.

- ✔ Low-powered electrical signals such as X10 get weaker as they travel over long distances. If you have a big house, consider installing a signal coupler that also includes a signal amplifier/repeater to boost your signal strength.

- ✔ The surge protectors that you should (and probably already do) have connected to electronic gear in your home will not let X10 signals through. Instead of buying a bunch of individual surge protectors, have your electrician install a whole-home protector at the main electrical panel. This will keep the noisy stuff out, and let your X10 signals work inside your home.

Not Reading the Manual

There are hundreds of different kinds of X10 automation modules on the market. Some are designed to turn regular incandescent lights on and off, some are designed for dimming, some can control fluorescent lights. Pay attention when you buy and install modules (or X10 switches).

Our friends at companies who make X10-type products tell us that the number one reason for returned products and calls to their tech support lines isn't defective modules or noisy electrical systems, but rather people trying to do things that the equipment they bought just won't do such as trying to dim a light with an X10 module that handles only on and off signals, or trying to use a dimming switch on a fluorescent light. No matter how many times you hit that switch on your controller, you're not going to get a module to do something it simply can't, by design, do.

Thinking That AC and Low Voltage Are Friends

With the exception of X10 signals and the HomePlug data-networking systems we discuss in Chapter 16, everything we talk about is a low-voltage system. AC power is high voltage; CAT-5e, RG6 coax, IR cable, and the rest are low voltage. High-voltage systems, because they carry so much power, emit stray electromagnetic fields. Low-voltage systems, because they use very little power, are easily interfered with by these stray fields. It's not a marriage made in heaven.

If you install low-voltage lines too close to the high-voltage ones, the interference can cause major havoc with the networks in your home running over the low-voltage wiring. Have your installers keep low-voltage lines at least 18 inches from high-voltage lines. Try to not run these lines parallel to each other whenever possible. And when crossing high- and low-voltage wiring, do it at a right angle to minimize the length of cables that are near each other.

Using the Weakest Link

We hope that we've convinced you that it's worth the small amount of extra money to use CAT-5e cabling wherever you run cable for telephones, computer networks, and the like. Even if you don't plan on having a phone or a LAN outlet in a room, the sheer usefulness and flexibility of CAT-5e makes running a length or two to every room worthwhile. Every day, we see new systems that let you run audio, video, surveillance cameras, IR controllers, and more over CAT-5e.

The problem many folks run into doesn't have anything to do with the cable — most people accept the need for CAT-5e cable. But what they don't realize is that all the pieces and parts of the CAT-5e network are just as important as the cabling in the walls. The outlets, the jacks and plugs, the patch panel in the wiring closet, even the patch cords used to connect a device to an outlet all have to be rated CAT-5e as well. Having even a single $1 piece of equipment that's not CAT-5e-rated connected to the network lowers the rating of the overall network.

It's not hard to hard to find CAT-5e equipment; most connectors, cords, and cables qualify for the rating. But there's still plenty of stuff on the market that looks exactly like CAT-5e–rated equipment, but isn't.

Now, to be honest, this really isn't going to matter much for some things you do on CAT-5e networks. Phones, for example, don't require CAT-5e (or even lower-rated CAT-3 cable) — heck, they'd probably work over a string and two tin cans. But as you start looking towards the future and doing things such as installing gigabit Ethernet LANs and S-video or component video networks over your UTP cables, you absolutely need CAT-5e.

That PPPPPP Thing

Nope, we're not coming up with a new networking acronym for you. PPPPPP, or *proper planning prevents pretty poor performance*, means you get out of your home network what you put into it. In Part 1, we emphasize the planning aspect of building a smart home. Thinking through what you want to accomplish, what you can afford, and what kind of help you need to make your smart home happen. These are vital steps. Skip them at your own peril.

Don't think you need cable in the nursery? Well you might not, if the kids stay toddlers in perpetuity. But when they're in school and need a computer, wouldn't you like to have an Ethernet LAN port next to the desk? We would.

You can do a pretty good job of prewiring your home by following the basic formula of two CAT-5e and two RG6 coax cables to every room in the house (four and four in your home office and media rooms). There's not much you can't do with this setup. Plan well, and remember: You can't prewire too much.

Thinking That Wiring Is a Dirty Word

We absolutely LOVE wireless technologies. Love as in can't live without. Wireless LANs for our laptops, wireless phones, Bluetooth mobile phones. But despite all the hype, wireless networking technologies don't take away from the basic usefulness and necessity of wired connections in your walls.

Compared to wireless networks, purpose-built, wired networks using CAT-5e and RG6 are cheaper and more capable. For example, wireless LANs today top out at about 50 Mbps; wired LANs that cost no more can reach speeds of 1000 Mbps. That's an astronomically high difference.

Now, if you live in an apartment or historic house or for some other reason you can't run new wires, by all means take advantage of wireless and no-new-wire technologies. And in any case, use them where appropriate as an adjunct, companion network to your wired networks. Just don't think they're somehow better or more capable than a wired network.

Falling into the Proprietary Pitfall

Some cool home-networking and home-automation and -control systems are built on a specific vendor's proprietary protocols. These proprietary systems often have tangible benefits. For example, they may offer tighter integration between different subsegments of the network than systems built on industry standards, or they may have a special feature (such as the capability to distribute component video) that standards-based systems don't yet have.

The downside of these proprietary systems is that you'll often find yourself locked into them — if you want to expand, upgrade, or otherwise modify your system, you need to go back to the same vendor who provided the rest of the system. Worse, if the vendor suddenly goes out of business, you may find yourself without any future support.

Sometimes you just can't avoid a proprietary system. For example, if you want to send audio and video over CAT-5e, you need to use some particular vendor's own equipment on all endpoints in the network. (This is the main reason we still recommend that you consider using speaker wire and RG6 coax for these networks.)

You may find that the benefits and features of a particular proprietary system are too compelling for you *not* to use it. That's a perfectly valid decision. Just make sure that you go into such an installation fully aware of the consequences.

Oh yeah — even if you do use one of these proprietary wiring systems, we still recommend you put in some CAT-5e and RG6 cabling. It will probably come in useful someday.

Tumbling into the All-in-One Trap

A close relative to the proprietary systems mentioned previously are all-in-one packaged solutions that some vendors sell. A single vendor offers all your cabling, all the wiring-closet hardware, all the outlets and receptacles, as well as active electronic equipment such as audio amplifiers, Ethernet switches and routers, and speakers.

We differentiate these approaches from the proprietary approach because typically you don't get locked in — these systems just use standards-based equipment from a single vendor. We're not really opposed to people using them. There's nothing wrong with going this route.

But (you knew there'd be a *but,* didn't you?) we prefer the best-of-breed approach. That's the beauty of standards: You can choose the equipment that best meets your price and performance requirements from a host of vendors and be assured that it will fit in with the rest of your network. So if you think that XYZ Company's amplifier or router or whatever is the best one for you — buy it! The same goes for the rest of your smart home — use standard infrastructures and choose the endpoints you like best.

Forgetting to Add Conduit

In Chapter 2, we mention adding conduits — PVC piping with pull wires — in your walls so that you can easily run new cables in the future. Someday there may be home-networking technologies and related wiring requirements that no on has even dreamed of yet. For example, networks running over fiber-optic cables hold much promise, but so far no one has figured out how they would be configured in a residential setting.

Having conduits in your walls makes it much, much, much easier to run new cables later. Ripping open walls is dirty, destructive, and expensive — accessing a conduit and pulling a wire through it isn't.

Not Bothering to Use Labels

Having a wiring closet is really handy. When you need to reconfigure your network, you just go in the closet, change the connections of cables on the patch and distribution panels, and you're finished. If you've ever peeked into a wiring closet, however, you'll notice one thing about wires. They all look the same. As in identical. As in "uh, I wonder where this one goes?"

So take a little time when you're doing your initial wiring (or have your installer take a little time) and label every single cable. Label both ends: in the wiring closet and at the outlet or receptacle in the remote location. Do this for your electrical panel too. Be obsessive about it (you might even want to print labels on your PC printer if, like Pat, you can't read your own writing). Secure the labels to the cables well.

Chapter 22

Top Ten Toys of the Future

Smart homes never want for innovation. People are constantly inventing things. Things that seem niche-oriented and expensive today may be high-volume consumer products tomorrow. In this chapter, we introduce you to some neat things that are available, from robots to Jacuzzis. If you're like us, you'll want to mortgage something to get at least one of these toys!

We have more to say about these gadgets and ones like them, but we ran out of room. Check out smarthomesbook.com for more information as well as reviews of smart-home gear.

Robotic Servants

On TV, it all started with robots like Klaatu in *The Day The Earth Stood Still*, Rosie on *The Jetsons*, and Robot on *Lost In Space*. It's progressed to Data on *Star Trek*, Max Headroom, and Simone. Whether on a screen or in person, robotic personalities offer the opportunity to create a life of leisure for us, while plotting to take over the world, apparently.

Although there are academic trials of various types of android-style robots, the marketable robots that will be available commercially are focused on specific tasks, so we call them *taskmasters*. Something as simple as a breadmaker (which takes ingredients, mixes them, kneads the bread, and then bakes it automatically) can be considered a robotic kitchen aid, says Colin Angle, CEO and Co-Founder of iRobot, Inc. From cooking meals to cleaning windows, robots are on the way.

A dishwasher washes our dishes, a washing machine washes our clothes and answering machines answer our phones. Here are some of the neater toys either on the market today or in refinement, that could be inexpensive enough soon for you to buy.

- **Robotic lawnmowers:** Cutting the grass is a repetitive and basic task, so it's a logical jumping-off point for robotics in the home. Products such as Friendly Robotics' Robomower (www.friendlyrobotics.com) and Toro's iMow (www.toro.com) have hit the streets. These are reasonably priced at around $500 and work great.

- **Robotic vacuum cleaners:** Okay, we admit it, we're lazy when it comes to cleaning the house. (And we're constantly reminded of it by our spouses.) So when a product such as a robotic vacuum cleaner comes along for only $199, we get excited. iRobot (www.irobot.com) was first to market with a mass-production model that uses intelligent navigation technology to automatically clean all household floor surfaces. This machine, dubbed Roomba, looks like a squat little space saucers that can roam around the house sensing obstructions and switching floor modes automatically. Other vendors are following suit with their own approaches: Maytag's Hoover (teaming up with Friendly Robotics, www.hoover.com) has the RV400, AB Electrolux has its Trilobite (www.electrolux.com), its subsidiary Eureka has Robo Vac (www.eureka.com), and European appliance maker Dyson (www.dyson.co.uk) has its DC06. Pricing can top $3000 for some of these units, so shop around.

Here are some product ideas that manufacturers are working on now:

- **Robotic garbage disposers:** Robotic firms are designing units that will take the trash out for you, on schedule, no matter what the weather.

- **Robotic snow blowers:** Manufacturers are working on devices that will continually clear your driveway and sidewalks, as the snow is falling. Danny says he'll believe this when he sees it, given all the various forms of snow and how heavy it can be.

- **Robotic golf ball retrievers:** These are initially being designed for driving range use and are being modified for your back yard.

- **Robotic guard dogs:** If you think about it, all the elements are there for a robotic sentry. You have wireless connectivity, video sensors, audio sensors, programming to navigate the lawn. So robotic guard dogs are not too far away, we think.

✔ **Robotic cooks:** We've seen it with breadmakers, why not other kitchen devices? Put the ingredients in, select a mode, and wait for your dinner to be cooked.

✔ **Robotic pooper-scoopers:** If you have a dog, this is a no-brainer. We haven't found any market-ready products yet, but prototypes are out there. There's almost no price too high for this item, as far as we're concerned.

Networking the Family Sedan

You may not realize this, but your car contains a massive computer network that touches many of its most critical parts, such as brakes, airbags, and monitoring systems. You don't see most of that stuff, so it's more useful than fun.

The focus on enhancing a car's internal smarts is driven mostly by the convergence of a number of add-ons, such as mounted cell phones, in-car video systems, and laptop wireless access devices. These previously unrelated items are starting to be linked to similar devices and services outside the car. For instance, the music you want to play in your car is probably much the same that you play at home.

Much of the focus has centered on a few key areas, such as network connectivity (being able to communicate with things outside the car) and the inherent computing capability of the car (being able to load new software to enable new functionality). If it sounds like we're talking about a computer and a network, we are: a network for your car, linking various endpoint devices to a central computer with the smarts to do a lot of things.

One of the most noticeable technologies you'll see soon is Bluetooth connectivity, which we talk about in Chapter 16. Bluetooth will reach out to laptops, cellphones, PDAs, watches, and other such devices to interact with the car.

Mow your lawn from the couch!

Danny is allergic to anything green — except money. Now he can mow the lawn from the luxury of his living room using Robomower from Friendly Robotics (www.friendly robotics.com). In most instances, Robomower guides itself using a sophisticated navigation system and by sensing the presence of a small electrified wire that you fasten to the ground surrounding the edge of your lawn. (Don't worry about the perimeter cable electrocuting you; the voltage in the perimeter line is only 4.5 volts.) This wire serves as the virtual fence for Robomower. Sensors sense trees, shrubs, and other obstacles and automatically guide the unit around them. For around $500, you can sit back and let the robot do the work for you.

AM, FM, XM . . . XM?

Welcome to the newest thing in the radio world: satellite radio. Two companies, XM and Sirius, offer a hundred (plus!) channels of music, news, and entertainment over a satellite link that has nationwide U.S. coverage. You can turn on a station you like and drive clear across the country without changing the channel or losing the signal. To get satellite radio, you need two things: a satellite radio receiver and a subscription to one of these two services.

Some of the coolest satellite radios we've seen come from Sony, which has a portable unit. If you're digging a particular show, you can just pop the unit out of the car when you get home, plug it into your home-audio system (with regular RCA audio jacks), and keep listening. You'll need an in-home antenna to plug into the receiver as well, and it helps to have that antenna in a window that faces south (that's where the satellites are).

Some day soon, Bluetooth and cellphones may interact to function as a car's modem, updating onboard data such as CD players or video storage systems, while you drive. When docked at home in the garage, Bluetooth can interface with the home's Internet connection. When the car's at the mechanic, Bluetooth can talk to the shop's computers to diagnose problems.

BMW is showing off several early models of future standard items, such as access to the Internet. A wireless connection in the car enables you to talk to your car through the Internet. Wouldn't it be great to sit at your desk and check whether you left the headlights on, instead of heading all the way down forty floors to the parking garage? You could allow the dealer to check your car's service status through the Internet. Or you could switch on the auxiliary heating, call up numbers in the car's telephone or addresses in the navigation system, or unlock and lock the car — even from the comfort of your smart boat.

Mercedes-Benz USA is working with 802.11a wireless technology (which we discuss in Chapter 16). The manufacturer is showing prototypes of cars that can access Web and media content services from roadside units to a sedan's onboard computer. The driver can purchase music and other digital media that they hear about on the radio and have them transparently download to vehicle's onboard computer as they pass by DriveBy InfoFueling stations.

In future systems, automobiles could access up-to-date map data, traffic and road conditions, and information on local points of interest as the vehicle drives by roadside beacons. In addition, rich audio, video, and gaming content could be downloaded from a person's home computer, entertainment center, or residential gateway. Commercial vehicles could exchange detailed cargo status and other information as they pass truck stops and gas stations.

Losing Weight on the Internet

There's something about riding an exercise bike to nowhere. It just doesn't work for us. Danny has a computer monitor, keyboard, and wireless mouse mounted just above the front of his treadmill to take in the best of the Web each morning.

But the folks at Icon Fitness (www.ifit.com) have taken it a step further by linking your exercise equipment, the Internet, live personal coaches, and library of audio and video slide tours that will make each day exercising a new adventure.

You can hike up the hills of San Francisco or explore Hawaii's Volcanoes, take in the Canadian Rockies or climb in Yosemite National Park. You can be berated by a drill-sergeant-like trainer or soothed with a firm voice. You can choose background music, your level, your pace, and more. What's neat about Icon Fitness is that they not only provide you with something to watch, but they can remotely control more than 100 models of treadmills, elliptical trainers, stationary bikes, and incline trainers — from Icon's NordicTrack, ProForm, Reebok, HealthRider, and Image divisions (www.iconfitness.com). Pricing is less than you'd pay for a fancy gym workout — $9.95 per month. Not bad!

You can also get a live trainer, courtesy of Internet videoconferencing. For 45 minutes and $30, you see and hear the trainer — and the trainer sees and hears you. A great use of the Webcams we talk about in Chapter 12.

Getting Personal Television Service

If you travel a lot, you probably have trouble keeping current on your favorite TV shows. You could tape the shows on your VCR — if you remember to program the machine properly. But if you're tired of battling the VCR gremlins,

A computer in every car

Some specialty devices seem very functional for those who want a little more from their car. G-Net Canada's (www.gnetcanada.com) Revolution Auto PC, for instance, is a $1300 add-on (not including the LCD screen) that gives you just about all you'd want to drive your smart car. It includes an MP3 audio player, a DVD player, GPS navigation support, vehicle diagnostics, a digital dash software interface, as well as a full Windows PC that can run any application you want. Slap a simple USB-to-802.11b or Bluetooth dongle on it, and you can network it with your home network. They call this "the future of in-vehicle computing" — we tend to believe that!

you may want to investigate a new capability called PVR — personal video recorder. PVR functionality can reside in many places — in your cable or satellite set-top box, in your computer, in your TV, and in a stand-alone box. The three major players in this market are SonicBlue/ReplayTV (www.replaytv.com), TiVo (www.tivo.com), and Microsoft's UltimateTV (www.ultimatetv.com).

PVR players combine your telephone, broadband connection, and video programming service (satellite, cable, or broadcast TV) to let you pause, rewind, fast-forward, instantly replay, and play back in slow motion. With ReplayTV, you can even transfer recorded live television to other ReplayTVs.

A PVR is essentially a VCR with a huge hard disk inside that can store to hundreds of hours of your favorite programs. PVRs give you full control of live programs as well. A friendly and highly visual interface — similar to what you experience with digital cable or DSS systems — guides you through the available programming options (seven days worth) of more than 12,000 DSS, cable, and over-the-air broadcast systems in the U.S.

You can also create a personalized lineup of your favorite shows ready for anytime viewing. For example, ReplayTV's technology queries your TV preferences and puts them into a personalized channel, so you can watch your favorite shows at your convenience. Using sophisticated search software, the PVR software intelligently searches this database of programming information to locate the shows you ask it to identify. In a smart home, ReplayTV can interface with your broadband connection or dial into a secure server to download the latest channel-guide information, every night. And you can log onto MyReplayTV.com to program recordings while you're away from home.

We think the cost is reasonable, starting at $299 for a 40-hour storage unit. There is a monthly $9.95 fee for accessing the scheduling information — but you can get a lifetime subscription for $250.

TiVo has a PVR-only product line that has some features that ReplayTV does not — such as being able to distinguish reruns from new episodes. UltimateTV has Web access and interactive TV functions. And with UltimateTV and the DirecTV/TiVo combo, you can record two TV shows at once.

Going forward, the majority of PVR capabilities will be incorporated into cable boxes and satellite receivers themselves.

Depending on which unit you buy and which cable, satellite, or broadcast area you're are in, some of these PVR on-screen program guides will not totally map to the actual channel listings in your area or may not fully describe the channels (such as saying Pay-Per-View in each PPV listing, instead of the movie being shown). Be sure to ask about support for your specific content provider. Try these sites for more info too: AV Science Forum (http://www.avsforum.com), Planet Replay (www.planetreplay.com), and the TiVo Community

PVR on your PC — flexibility to the max

A few companies have great products for the PC that provide PVR functionality without having to add another box to your entertainment system. SnapStream Media's Personal Video Station (www.snapstream.com) is a great example of what you can do with a spare PCI slot in your PC, some RG59 cable, and an IR blaster. For a mere $50 ($80 if you don't have a video capture card for your PC), you can add a PVR to your household. What's more, if your PC is on the network, you can watch video from just about anywhere.

With SnapStream, you can watch, record, and transfer video programs from your viewing sources. With one click on a viewing guide, you can record your favorite TV shows. What's cool about the SnapStream product is that you can also move your favorite TV shows to your PocketPC handheld (using a PocketPC module, $30) or your laptop — forget about renting DVDs for that flight! For those who are more comfortable with a PC interface for everything, the SnapStream solution is about as simple and flexible as it gets.

If you want to add some more power to your system at the same time, ATI's (www.ati.com, $160) All-In-Wonder card adds 64MB of DDR memory to your system, not only allowing great TV and DVD features on your PC, but also awesome 3-D gaming and graphics.

No DVD on your PC? Pinnacle's Bungee DVD (www.pinnaclesys.com, $199) upgrades your Windows XP-based PC to a TV recording solution, complete with a DVD player! With Pinnacle Bungee DVD, you can record television shows, movies, or video from almost any source and burn it to a CD or DVD disc that plays in your set-top DVD player. As with to SnapStream and ATI, you can watch TV on your PC, store all your favorite shows on the hard drive, pause live television, and more. Another cool addition to a smart home.

These PC-based options can be as powerful as the PVR boxes you buy in the store because all the smarts are already in your PC. Hooking your PC up to display video on a TV is easy using a modulator and the RG6 coaxial network we discuss in Chapter 7 — or you can use a wireless system such as the Entertainment Anywhere box from X10 Wireless Technologies (www.x10.com). A range of new wireless devices are coming on the market to make it easier for information to flow from your PC to your entertainment centers, so the ability to access recorded programs on any TV in the house — even TVs not on a LAN — is getting easier.

Forum (http://www.tivocommunity.com). Over time, this problem will disappear, but for now, the situation favors companies who have their PVR functionality bundled with the cable or satellite receiver.

Figuring Out Which CD to Play

Do you have a few hundred CDs? CD jukeboxes that will allow you to store up to 200 or more CDs in a device, but that's hardly scalable as you add CDs for your kids as well. What you need is a CD server! And here's the one you want: Request, Inc.'s AudioReQuest system (www.request.com). Capable of storing as many CDs as you have (you can add additional storage by their swappable hard drives or getting higher capacity units), this is the ultimate in CD listening pleasure.

You can use your TV screen as the interface to your music collection. You create playlists from albums and artists stored in the system. Loading (ripping) a CD into the system is as easy as opening the tray and closing it. The system determines whether the CD is already in your system and then looks up the name of the album and artist in its internal database of 650,000 albums; if the system can't find the CD, it checks a master database on the Internet.

You can also add other units to the system and network them. Danny has one unit in his house in Maine and another in his house in Connecticut, and they stay synchronized. What's more, multiple units enable you to have a back up of your collection in case your hard disk crashes.

Higher-end units also support WAV and FLAK (lossless compression) protocols, for those who want audio fidelity. (These protocols take up more space on the hard drive, but preserve the nuances of the music.)

It's truly the future of music in the entertainment center. An entry-level Nitro system costs about $2500 and scales up from there depending on storage capacity and extra features. This is the box you put in your home if you're serious about music!

Remotes for Control Freaks

Let's face it — whoever owns the remote control rules the household. Remote capabilities are embedded into all sorts of devices, from cell phones to PDAs. We discussed voice control of your whole-home system in Chapter 20, and told you about neat panels in the home to control your home-entertainment center, like those from Crestron.

But the concept of a universal remote control to consolidate all the remotes on the top of the TV is now several generations into development. We're well beyond the simple $19.99 Universal Remote Control you buy at Radio Shack. Now products not only control different devices but also help you control different actions. The Harmony Remote Control (www.harmonyremote.com, $199) has an LCD screen and links to your PC through a USB connection to program the remote.

Suppose that you want to listen to a CD on your AudioRequest CD server. You have to turn on the TV, set it to video mode, turn on receiver one, set it to CD, turn on receiver two, set it to CD, scroll down to your desired playlist, and press play. Harmony reduces this to a one-click task. Harmony helps you perform other activities such as watch TV or play a DVD. That's what we call click and play!

Remote control for your car?

Well it sounds very 007, but remote controls for your car can be quite ordinary and useful. Remotes for cars now have the capability to automatically open minivan doors or turn on the lights. And a remote car starter is like having a personal butler who will start your car, turn on its heater/defroster or air conditioner, unlock power doors and trunk, and turn off the alarm system. Fancier ones, such as the Auto Command Deluxe Remote Starter w/ Keyless Entry & Alarm from DesignTech International (www.designtech-intl.com) have a built-in car finder capability as well as a remote headlight control. AutoCommand can be programmed to automatically start your vehicle at the same time the next day, at low temperature, or at low battery voltage. Its Quick Stop option lets you remove the ignition key and temporarily leave the car running with the doors locked while you quickly run into a store. All that for $200. What a deal!

The latest version of Harmony's remote has added number buttons, a docking and recharging station, and a bidirectional RF-to-PC home server or set-top box for automatic updates. Trés cool. For the price and simplicity, every smart homeowner should check out these Harmony remotes.

For more money, you can find a range of special remotes for controlling entertainment centers, including the popular Philips Pronto line of remotes (pronto.philips.com). Philips and Intel codeveloped iPronto ($1700), which combines home-theater system control and 802.11b wireless broadband Internet access, allowing you to control your AV system components, view program guides, and surf the Web from a PC tablet.

There are remote controls for your PC too. Your PC can run MP3s, CDs, DVDs, PowerPoint presentations, and more, but without a PC remote control, you're tied to the keyboard and mouse. That's why you need a StreamZap PC Remote (www.streamzap.com). Better yet — train your Harmony Remote with your StreamZap PC Remote, and use one remote that can control your entertainment and computing devices. Wow!

Want to use your PDA as a remote control? Philips has ProntoLITE ($19.95), which turns a Palm-based PDA into a universal remote control. Universal Electronic's Nevo (www.mynevo.com), initially built into Compaq's iPAQ Pocket PCs, is a remote-control operating system that uses the infrared port of the PDA to control devices. Nevo removes a lot of the hardware design from the remote vendor and allows them to focus more on software and usability.

And if you really want to get sexy — try out Midas from UEI (www.uei.com). Midas is a contemporary looking watch with coverage of most remote control functions for TVs and cable boxes. Hey, solves the problem of finding your remote!

A great site to check out remote control options is Remote Central (www.remotecentral.com). They have great reviews and track the newest remotes.

Giving a Concert

Entertaining tonight? Why not treat your guests to a stylish in-home concert of Mozart's Piano Sonatas K. 310, K. 333, and K. 533? Don't play the piano? No problem, try Baldwin Piano's (www.baldwinpiano.com) ConcertMaster.

Your smart home can plug into your Baldwin, Chickering, or Wurlitzer piano and play almost any musical piece you can imagine. ConcertMaster works in several ways: as a standard piano, as a player piano that utilizes special digital data instead of the rolls used by old-fashioned ones, as a playback system (with built-in amplified speakers) for your own CDs, and as a karaoke system. You can even plug it into your home network's VCR and watch the pianist creating the music your piano plays back for you. If you play the piano a bit yourself, you can use ConcertMaster to record your own performances.

You can use your smart home's Internet connection to download the latest operating system software from Baldwin's servers, too. Encore!

Gazing on a Starry, Starry Night

You want your child to see the space shuttle zooming across the sky, so you grab your trusty telescope and wait for it to appear across the horizon, right? Lots of luck. The space shuttle is moving at more than 17,500 miles per hour, and keeping an object moving that fast in focus is nearly impossible — unless you have a smart home. Imagine sitting on your couch and watching the night sky through your home-network-fed telescope.

Start with one of the finer telescopes, such as a Meade ETX or LX200GPS series (www.meade.com). With its super high-tech, motorized system for rotating the lens across the sky, the LX200GPS is a wonderful platform for satellite observing and tracking. As you use a handheld control to select specific planets or galaxies, the telescope slides over to that area of the sky. (The Meade telescopes start at about $500 and go up to $5000.)

If you want to get star-crossed, you can add an electronic eyepiece, a CCD camera, Meade's AstroFinder or Epoch 2000 software and a connector cable set to connect to your PC. Point and click to any celestial object on the PC display and watch as the telescope moves to the object and places it in the field of view. Of particular interest are the Iridium Telecommunication satellites, which are so bright that some outshine Jupiter and Venus. Great fun for the kids and you!

Singing in the Shower and Much, Much More

Okay, some people like to sing in the shower, some like to hang out in the Jacuzzi, and some like to watch the news in the morning. Now, you can do all these things at the same time!

We can't go to the Jacuzzi Whirlpool Bath (`www.jacuzzi.com`) Web site without crying. This is the ultimate for a smart-home enthusiast — far more important that a great home theater. We're talking about our bathroom time here.

J-Allure (`http://www.jacuzzi.com/products/showers/designer/lux_jallure.html`) combines a full-size whirlpool bath — which has a luxury shower system and soothing steam bath — with a built-in stereo/CD system and an optional television/VCR monitor. Cable ready, this feature allows you to enjoy the morning news or your favorite movie. The multichannel, 9-inch unit is waterproof and includes a remote control. You can adapt the monitor for DVD or WebTV. All these features for a mere $12,500. Talk about wired.

If that's not enough for you, try Vizion (`http://www.jacuzzi.com/products/baths/private/vizion.htm`), a whirlpool bath that sports an entertainment center, complete with a high-definition, 10-inch flat-screen TV, DVD/CD player, AM/FM stereo, and surround-sound speakers. A floating remote control offers fingertip access to the jet system, television, and underwater lighting. All this for only $18,000 (without installation). And you thought we were crazy for wiring the bathroom.

Playing with LEGO, the 21st-Century Way

Even toys can be made smart by your smart home. Driven by your PCs, LEGO's MINDSTORMS and Spybotics kits are the traditional LEGO building bricks on robotic steroids.

The LEGO MINDSTORMS kit ($200), targeted at kids 12+, lets you design, build, and program real robots using the standard LEGO brick system, a microcomputer core, and special bricks with light and touch sensors. You can create light-sensitive intruder alarms, line-tracking rovers, robotic soda-can retrievers, or even robots with collision and edge detection.

The brain is the RCX brick, an autonomous microcomputer that looks like a big LEGO brick with an LCD screen in it. The RCX uses sensors to take input from its environment, process data, and signal output motors to turn on and off. You can also download the system's upgradeable firmware to your PC over your smart home's Internet connection, and then send it by infrared to the RCX.

You build your robot by using the RCX and LEGO elements. Then you create a program for your invention by using RCX Code (a simple programming language). Your creation can now interact with the environment, fully autonomous from the PC. Want to get other programs? The LEGO MINDSTORMS Web site http://mindstorms.lego.com/ has scads of advice and downloadable software.

For the younger crowd (9+), the LEGO Spybotics kit ($60) offers challenging robotics experiences in a format more structured and theme-based than the LEGO MINDSTORMS RIS and with a lower price tag. With Spybotics, children role-play as secret agents by customizing and downloading action and strategy games to their Spybots in the form of missions. They then complete single or multi-player missions with their high-tech partners — any one or more of the four unique Spybots. The objective: successfully complete the mission to earn status and rise up the secret agent ranks! Players use infrared remote control to maneuver the interactive Spybots.

Index

Antenna/CATV input, distribution
  panel, 104
AOL. *See* America Online
AOLTV, 194
AOnQ Technologies (all-in-one systems
  vendor), 38
Apple OS X, 183
appliance module, X10 protocol, 290–291
applications, home infrastructure, 22
architect, hiring, 60
aspect ratio, digital television, 70, 73
AstroFinder (Meade), 340
asymmetrical DSL (ADSL), 202–203
ATI (All-in-Wonder card), 337
AT&T
  Broadband cable service provider, 206
  videoconferencing, 161
audio cloning device, 133
audio connector, 126–128
Audio In RCA jack, receiver, 140
Audio Out RCA jack, receiver, 132
audio source, connection options, 28
audio system. *See also* multizone audio
    network; single-zone audio network
  amplifier, 124–126
  audio connector, 126–128
  CAT-5e UTP cabling, 120
  digital-to-analog converter, 120–121
  home-theater standards, 118
  impedance rating, 124–125
  impedance-matching device, 125–126
  integrated amplifier, 82
  in-wall speaker, 128–130
  line-level interconnect, 121
  line-level signal, 119
  loudspeakers, 82
  multizone control system, 123–124
  networking, 15
  power amplifier, 82
  preamplifier, 81
  RCA cable, 121
  source component, 81
  speaker cable, 126
  speaker connections, 121–122
  speaker outlet, 128
  speaker-level signal, 119
  stereo standards, 118
audio transmission, wireless video, 115
AudioRequest (Request), 120, 129

audio/video consultant, hiring, 61
Auto Command Deluxe Remote Starter
  (DesignTech International), 339
automatic gain control (AGC), 289
automatic pool covers, 51
A/V interconnect, 86, 114
A/V loop through, 96
AV Science Forum, 336
AWG (American Wire Gauge), 126

● *B* ●

baby monitor, networking, 15
babycam, 113
balanced cable system, 140
balanced line-level cable, 132
Baldwin Piano (ConcertMaster), 340
banana plug, audio connector, 127
banana-plug receptacle, audio
  connector, 128
bare wire, audio connector, 127
base station, cordless telephone, 150
baseband distribution, 86–88
basement, using as wiring closet, 26
Beamer videoconferencing capability
  (Vialta), 161
Bell Canada, 80
Bell Telephone standard, 34
BellSouth
  DSL service provider, 204
  security system, 280
benefits of networking, 16–17
black-and-white ink cartridge, color
  multifunction machine, 156
blank cover, outlet box, 134
Bluetooth personal area network, 187,
  190, 248
BOOM 2000 (X10 Wireless
  Technologies), 143
BrickHouse software (Brian Hill), 225
bridge, X10 protocol, 306
bridging, patch panel, 32
broadband distribution, 88–89
budget
  all-in-one kit, 58–59
  data network cost, 60
  determining goals, 58
  home theater cost, 59
  home-automation system cost, 60

• U •

• V •

FOR

DUMMIES®

The easy way to get more done and have more fun

PERSONAL FINANCE & BUSINESS

0-7645-2431-3

0-7645-5331-3

0-7645-5307-0

Also available:

Accounting For Dummies
(0-7645-5314-3)

Business Plans Kit For Dummies
(0-7645-5365-8)

Managing For Dummies
(1-5688-4858-7)

Mutual Funds For Dummies
(0-7645-5329-1)

QuickBooks All-in-One Desk Reference For Dummies
(0-7645-1963-8)

Resumes For Dummies
(0-7645-5471-9)

Small Business Kit For Dummies
(0-7645-5093-4)

Starting an eBay Business For Dummies
(0-7645-1547-0)

Taxes For Dummies 2003
(0-7645-5475-1)

HOME, GARDEN, FOOD & WINE

0-7645-5295-3

0-7645-5130-2

0-7645-5250-3

Also available:

Bartending For Dummies
(0-7645-5051-9)

Christmas Cooking For Dummies
(0-7645-5407-7)

Cookies For Dummies
(0-7645-5390-9)

Diabetes Cookbook For Dummies
(0-7645-5230-9)

Grilling For Dummies
(0-7645-5076-4)

Home Maintenance For Dummies
(0-7645-5215-5)

Slow Cookers For Dummies
(0-7645-5240-6)

Wine For Dummies
(0-7645-5114-0)

FITNESS, SPORTS, HOBBIES & PETS

0-7645-5167-1

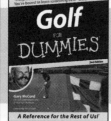

0-7645-5146-9

0-7645-5106-X

Also available:

Cats For Dummies
(0-7645-5275-9)

Chess For Dummies
(0-7645-5003-9)

Dog Training For Dummies
(0-7645-5286-4)

Labrador Retrievers For Dummies
(0-7645-5281-3)

Martial Arts For Dummies
(0-7645-5358-5)

Piano For Dummies
(0-7645-5105-1)

Pilates For Dummies
(0-7645-5397-6)

Power Yoga For Dummies
(0-7645-5342-9)

Puppies For Dummies
(0-7645-5255-4)

Quilting For Dummies
(0-7645-5118-3)

Rock Guitar For Dummies
(0-7645-5356-9)

Weight Training For Dummies
(0-7645-5168-X)

Available wherever books are sold.
Go to www.dummies.com or call 1-877-762-2974 to order direct

FOR DUMMIES®

A world of resources to help you grow

TRAVEL

0-7645-5453-0

0-7645-5438-7

0-7645-5444-1

Also available:

America's National Parks For Dummies
(0-7645-6204-5)

Caribbean For Dummies
(0-7645-5445-X)

Cruise Vacations For Dummies 2003
(0-7645-5459-X)

Europe For Dummies
(0-7645-5456-5)

Ireland For Dummies
(0-7645-6199-5)

France For Dummies
(0-7645-6292-4)

Las Vegas For Dummies
(0-7645-5448-4)

London For Dummies
(0-7645-5416-6)

Mexico's Beach Resorts For Dummies
(0-7645-6262-2)

Paris For Dummies
(0-7645-5494-8)

RV Vacations For Dummies
(0-7645-5443-3)

EDUCATION & TEST PREPARATION

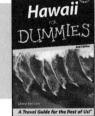

0-7645-5194-9

0-7645-5325-9

0-7645-5249-X

Also available:

The ACT For Dummies
(0-7645-5210-4)

Chemistry For Dummies
(0-7645-5430-1)

English Grammar For Dummies
(0-7645-5322-4)

French For Dummies
(0-7645-5193-0)

GMAT For Dummies
(0-7645-5251-1)

Inglés Para Dummies
(0-7645-5427-1)

Italian For Dummies
(0-7645-5196-5)

Research Papers For Dummies
(0-7645-5426-3)

SAT I For Dummies
(0-7645-5472-7)

U.S. History For Dummies
(0-7645-5249-X)

World History For Dummies
(0-7645-5242-2)

HEALTH, SELF-HELP & SPIRITUALITY

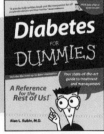

0-7645-5154-X

0-7645-5302-X

0-7645-5418-2

Also available:

The Bible For Dummies
(0-7645-5296-1)

Controlling Cholesterol For Dummies
(0-7645-5440-9)

Dating For Dummies
(0-7645-5072-1)

Dieting For Dummies
(0 7645-5126-4)

High Blood Pressure For Dummies
(0-7645-5424-7)

Judaism For Dummies
(0-7645-5299-6)

Menopause For Dummies
(0-7645-5458-1)

Nutrition For Dummies
(0-7645-5180-9)

Potty Training For Dummies
(0-7645-5417-4)

Pregnancy For Dummies
(0-7645-5074-8)

Rekindling Romance For Dummies
(0-7645-5303-8)

Religion For Dummies
(0-7645-5264-3)

FOR DUMMIES®

Plain-English solutions for everyday challenges

HOME & BUSINESS COMPUTER BASICS

0-7645-0838-5

0-7645-1663-9

0-7645-1548-9

Also available:

Excel 2002 All-in-One Desk Reference For Dummies (0-7645-1794-5)

Office XP 9-in-1 Desk Reference For Dummies (0-7645-0819-9)

PCs All-in-One Desk Reference For Dummies (0-7645-0791-5)

Troubleshooting Your PC For Dummies (0-7645-1669-8)

Upgrading & Fixing PCs For Dummies (0-7645-1665-5)

Windows XP For Dummies (0-7645-0893-8)

Windows XP For Dummies Quick Reference (0-7645-0897-0)

Word 2002 For Dummies (0-7645-0839-3)

INTERNET & DIGITAL MEDIA

0-7645-0894-6

0-7645-1642-6

0-7645-1664-7

Also available:

CD and DVD Recording For Dummies (0-7645-1627-2)

Digital Photography All-in-One Desk Reference For Dummies (0-7645-1800-3)

eBay For Dummies (0-7645-1642-6)

Genealogy Online For Dummies (0-7645-0807-5)

Internet All-in-One Desk Reference For Dummies (0-7645-1659-0)

Internet For Dummies Quick Reference (0-7645-1645-0)

Internet Privacy For Dummies (0-7645-0846-6)

Paint Shop Pro For Dummies (0-7645-2440-2)

Photo Retouching & Restoration For Dummies (0-7645-1662-0)

Photoshop Elements For Dummies (0-7645-1675-2)

Scanners For Dummies (0-7645-0783-4)

Get smart! Visit www.dummies.com

- **Find listings of even more Dummies titles**

- **Browse online articles, excerpts, and how-to's**

- **Sign up for daily or weekly e-mail tips**

- **Check out Dummies fitness videos and other products**

- **Order from our online bookstore**

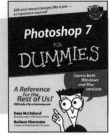

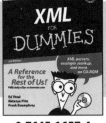